COLLECTED WORKS OF JOHN STUART MILL

VOLUME XIII

The Earlier Letters

of

John Stuart Mill

1812-1848

Edited by

FRANCIS E. MINEKA

The Class of 1916 Professor of English
Cornell University

With an Introduction by

F. A. HAYEK, F.B.A.

University of Freiburg i.B.

UNIVERSITY OF TORONTO PRESS
ROUTLEDGE & KEGAN PAUL

Contents

THE EARLIER LETTERS OF JOHN STUART MILL

1838–1848

India House
12th Oct 1863

My dear Sir

I have been a good deal surprised & even pained by some passages relating to my father, in the article on Bentham just published in the Edinburgh Review. Several of the statements made on the authority of Bowring are incorrect in point of fact, but what I chiefly complain of is the insertion of some things reported to have been said by Bentham, calculated to give a most unfavorable, & as every one who really knew my father must be aware, an utterly false impression of the character & temper of his mind. Mr Bentham's best friends well knew — I have heard some of those who were most attached to him lament — his entire incapacity to estimate the characters even of those with whom he associated intimately. The opinions he expressed of people depended very much

Letter 405, to Macvey Napier, from MS in the British Museum

1838

229. TO JOHN ROBERTSON[1]

Saturday
[Jan. (?), 1838]

DEAR ROBERTSON

I am going to have to fight a duel on your account. I have had a half hostile, half expostulatory letter from Hayward[2] on the subject of that passage, in the Martineau article,[3] in reply to which I have owned the proprietorship, disowned authorship & editorship, admitted having seen the article before it was printed off, & said that I did not consider the terms "blackguardising" & "lying" as applied to any one individually but to a *class* to which it was made matter of complaint against certain superior men that they allowed themselves to be assimilated. I of course did not tell him either who wrote the article or who edited it, and I told him that I had ordered any letter he might send to be forwarded to me. I have not yet received his answer & perhaps shall not till I leave town which will be today, so hold yourself prepared in case he should write a letter to you.

N.B. I told him that the writer had no malice against him, & I believed had never seen him.

ever yours

J. S. MILL

If you have anything to write, direct Post Office Southampton.[4]

1. MS at King's.
2. Abraham Hayward.
3. A review of Miss Martineau's *Retrospect of Western Travel, LWR,* XXVIII (Jan., 1838), 470–502. The offending passage (pp. 477–78) excoriated not only Hayward but also, among others, Lockhart, Wilson, Barnes, D'Israeli, and Theodore Hook for deserting their class to do "the base work of the aristocracy, fighting for them, writing for them, joking for them, blackguardizing for them, and . . . lying for them. . . ." The review was signed H.W.

A note was subsequently appended to Vol. XXIX of the *LWR* with reference to Hayward, stating "that neither against him nor against any of the other persons named was any distinct and personal charge made, because we were not in possession of proofs on which our charges could have been made distinct and personal."

4. This postscript is written at the top of the first page.

230. TO JOHN HILL BURTON[1]

India House
23[d] January
1837 [*sic, recte* 1838]

MY DEAR SIR,

Pray excuse my not having sooner answered your letter, as my whole spare time and thoughts were occupied with poor Canada, about which what I have to say will be published in the L. & W. review on Saturday next.

With regard to the note or rather the passage which I propose should be appended to my preface,[2] on reperusal I should wish that after the words "accordant with the spirit of the work itself" you would be so kind as to add "and, in Mr. Bentham, admissible" and then proceed "than what would be decorous" &c. as before. Otherwise I shall have the appearance of censuring the tone of the work, which I am very far indeed from intending. I still wish to suppress any direct mention of my name, not to prevent it from being known to the reader if he chuses to enquire about it which I know cannot be done, but because its suppression is as it were, an act of disavowal as to any appropriateness in the notes and additions to my present frame of mind, and because I do not like to perk in the face of the world in general that the person known by my name has written things which he is ashamed of, when my name has never in any instance been put to writings I am not ashamed of.

I should think Sir John Campbell's Law Reform Acts, the orders of the 15 Judges promulgated a few years ago reforming the system of Pleading, and the Reports of the various Law Commissions, were the best authorities for the recent alterations in the law. Not being acquainted with many law books I cannot direct you to any other sources.

My notions of Mr. Bentham's intentions with respect to the "Introduction to the Rationale" (though I confess it is but an indistinct notion) has always been that he intended to put it forth as a kind of feeler, at a time when he did not contemplate finishing the work itself for publication at an early period. My opinion is entirely adverse to publishing the Introduction at all; & if that is decided upon, the later in the collection it comes the better. I would much rather it followed, than preceded, the Rationale.

---

1. *Addressed*: J. H. Burton Esq. / 9 Warriston Crescent / Edinburgh. *Postmarks*: LS / 23JA23 / 1838, and JAN / C 25+ / 1838. Original in possession of Professor John Burton Cleland, of Adelaide, South Australia; copy supplied by Professor J. A. La Nauze, Dept. of History, University of Melbourne.
2. See Letter 226, n. 2.

Mr. Smith's[3] proposal appears to me prepos[terous][4] & from all you mention I should not suppose him to be a man to whose judgment any more deference should be paid in constructing the Edition than is indispensable. I know nothing of Mr Smith whatever except that I think I remember hearing that a gentleman of that name had been the editor of the Rationale of Reward.

Believe me Dear Sir
Yours truly
J. S. MILL

231. TO ALBANY FONBLANQUE[1]

India House
30th Jan[y] 1838

MY DEAR FONBLANQUE—I have not said or written one word to you in complaint of the extraordinary unfairness which you appear to me to have practised for some time against those radicals who oppose the present ministry—I know you never intend to be unfair, but you remember I always thought unfairness towards opponents to be one of your qualities even when you & I were on the same side in politics. It is especially in these late Canada discussions that I have thought your unfairness went beyond the bounds which in some degree confined it before. However I do not quarrel with you for this nor for your putting the last seal to your ministerialism by espousing the enmities of the ministry, & displaying personal hostility to old friends whom your new friends wish to hunt down. Perhaps if we chose to retaliate, we are not altogether without the power, but I at least never will, under whatever provocation, speak of you to the public in terms of disrespect, or even, if I can help it, of complaint. I will only, when the things you say touch me personally, point out to yourself the injustice of them, & my object in writing to you now is to do so in regard to what you say in your last number on the London Review.[2] You have entirely misstated facts. The London Review never bestowed the name

3. Richard Smith, identified only as "of the Stamps and Taxes Office." He had translated from the French and edited *The Rationale of Reward* (1825) and *The Rationale of Punishment* (1830). For a list of his contributions to the collected edition of Bentham's *Works*, see vol. X, p. 548.

4. MS torn.

* * * *

1. *Addressed*: Albany Fonblanque Esq. / 5 Pine Apple Place / Kilburn Road; *readdressed in another hand*: N 4 Up. Seymor St. West. *Postmarks*: 4 EB 4 / JA 30 / 1838, and 12 NN 12 / JA 31 / 1838. MS at LSE. Excerpt published in *Life and Labours of Albany Fonblanque*, ed. E. B. de Fonblanque (London, 1874), p. 32.

2. "Mr E. Bulwer and Mr Grote," *Examiner*, Jan. 28, 1838, p. 50: "The name of 'philosophical Radicals' was bestowed by themselves by the gentlemen whose opinions

philosophical radicals upon its own writers or upon the people whom Bulwer called so in his speech.[3] You knew at the time perfectly that it gave that name to the thinking radicals generally, to distinguish them from the demagogic radicals, such as Wakley,[4] & from the historical radicals of the Cartwright[5] school, & from the division of property radicals if there be any. You knew that if the London Review wished to be the review of this large body, we always considered the Examiner as the newspaper of it. You also knew that because this designation too often repeated gave a *coterie* air which it was felt to be objectionable, the phrase was varied, & phrases adopted to express merely those Reformers who were not professedly, Reformers only within the limits of the existing Constitution—such were the phrases thorough reformers, & so on—& yet for this very change of designation you blame the review & its writers just as the Chronicle yesterday[6] after founding a long attack solely upon identifying me with Roebuck or with Grote, concluded by reproaching me for differing from them.

I expected no better from the Chronicle but what is the meaning of *your* insisting upon identifying me with Grote or Roebuck or the rest? Do you in your conscience think that my opinions are at all like theirs? Have you forgotten, what I am sure you once knew, that my opinion of their philosophy is & has for years been *more* unfavourable by far than your own? & that my radicalism is of a school the most remote from theirs, at all points, which exists? *They* knew this as long ago as 1829, since which time the variance has been growing wider & wider. I never consented to have anything to do with the London Review but for the sake of getting together a body of writers who would represent radicalism more worthily than they did: you never could be induced to help me in this & until I could

are represented by the London Review. . . . To us it appeared better . . . that the world should find out that they were philosophical, than that they should proclaim it of themselves. But this is a matter of taste, and they are fond of calling themselves by good names, and, like ladies, seem glad to change them; so they have been 'philosophical Reformers,' and 'thorough Reformers,' and 'earnest Reformers,' and better still, 'entire Reformers.' "

3. In the House of Commons on Jan. 23, 1838.

4. Thomas Wakley.

5. Major John Cartwright (1740–1824), "the father of Parliamentary Reform."

6. An attack on JSM's article "Lord Durham and the Canadians" (*LWR*, XXVIII [Jan., 1838], 502–33): "It is by the writer of the political manifesto of the preceding number ["Parties and the Ministry," VI (Oct., 1837), 1–26] and is characterized by the same ability, the same absence of shrewd discernment in the adaptation of means to ends, and in the estimate taken of individuals, and the same tone of infallibility which were displayed in that production. The writer being thoroughly persuaded of the impossibility of himself and his friends being ever in the wrong, might take for his device '*nul n'a raison que nous et nos amis*', and possesses not a few of those qualities which in the days of the Inquisition would have made a good member of that tribunal." (*Morning Chronicle*, Jan. 29, 1838, p. 3.)

find persons who would, I could do little—but in proportion as I did find
such persons I have been divesting the review of its sectarian character &
have even gone this length that when Molesworth ceased to feel that the
review represented his opinions I took it off his hands & am now myself
the proprietor of it. In the face of this it is rather hard to be accused of
ascribing all wisdom & infallibility to a set from whose opinions I differ
more than from the Tories. But I cannot, because I differ from them, join
like you in crying them down for sacrificing their own popularity in maintaining *my* opinions about Canada, & while I myself seek the radical party
where it *is*, not where it is *not*, & endeavour to rest upon the general body
of radical opinion in the country, I will not throw overboard the most honest
men in public life for standing nobly in the breach on a great occasion.
I will rather risk myself there with them even at the hazard of being accused
by you of being exactly what it is my special object, my principle & also
my interest to shew that I am *not*. And I should think much higher of your
magnanimity if you did the same. Of your intentions & talents I have the
same high opinion which I always had.

ever yours

J. S. MILL

232. TO JOHN ROBERTSON[1]

I.H. Tuesday
[Jan. 30 or early Feb., 1838]

DEAR ROBERTSON,

It seems to me that in any future communication we have with Bulwer,
the points which it is our interest to make him feel, with the least possible
appearance of intending to do so, are these: *First*, that we have the power,
from our next number inclusive, either to begin preparing the radicals to
support & even to call for their ministry, or to begin impressing them with
the uselessness of their looking to any ministry for a long time to come:
that we shall certainly take one line or the other; & it will depend upon the
opinion we form of them, which: and *Secondly*, that our support of them
will depend not only upon their embracing the policy which we think
suitable to rally the body of moderate radicals round them, who are to be
our party whoever is minister—but also upon our confidence in their
personnel. That Ellice[2] & Stanley[3] (& we need not add, himself, but he will

1. Published by Towers, pp. 68–69. MS at LSE. Dated by Mrs. Towers as of "1837
during the Canada coercion and rebellion"; the last paragraph, however, apparently
refers to the preceding letter, to Fonblanque.
2. Edward Ellice (1781–1863), Whig leader.
3. Edward John Stanley (1802–1869), then chief government whip and Secretary
of the Treasury, who had been a disciple of Lord Durham.

see that *we* see through him, which always vastly increases such a man's respect for one) will make it their object to render the ministry a ministry of *intrigans*. That we need only call it that, and treat it as that, to damage it exceedingly, and that we *will* treat it as that if it *is* that. That we have no earthly objection to act *with* intrigans, but that we do not chuse to act *under* intrigans: that therefore if their ministry is *made up* of loose fish, & does not contain a due proportion of men who have a high character for private integrity and political earnestness, we will, even if we support their measures, attack & ridicule their persons, & then beware Messrs. Bulwer, Ellice, & even Lord Durham himself. The ways and times proper for insinuating such of these things as are to be insinuated & for stating such of them as are to be stated will present themselves to you as occasion arises.

I have written to Fonblanque[4] as I wrote to Black,[5] informing him of the same facts, telling him I think him excessively unfair towards us, but that no provocation shall induce me to attack him, & appealing to his love of truth not to mix us up with Roebuck, etc.

Ever yours,

J.S.M.

233. TO ALBANY FONBLANQUE[1]

India House
3ᵈ Feb. 1838

MY DEAR FONBLANQUE—If my letter[2] gave you concern you have returned good for evil, since yours has given me great pleasure. The kind feelings you express to me personally are & have always been & I am as certain as I am about any such thing, always will be, completely reciprocated on my part. With regard to imputations which you say I have cast upon you in the eagerness of advocacy, I give you my word that I never intended to cast any: one single sentence in my political article of October last,[3] though it conveyed no imputation upon anybody, & did not allude to you in particular (while in that very article the Examiner was twice mentioned in an approving tone) was I admit, written under the provocation of an article of yours, one of those you wrote against the Spectator,[4] & which as it appeared to me

---

4. The preceding letter.
5. No such letter to John Black, editor of the *Morning Chronicle*, appears to be extant.

* * * *

1. *Addressed*: Albany Fonblanque Esq. / 48 Connaught Square. MS at LSE.
2. Letter 231.
3. See Letter 217, n. 7.
4. See especially "Tory Radical Consistency," *Examiner*, Sept. 3, 1837, p. 563, and "The *Spectator* and Ourselves," *ibid.*, Sept. 17, 1837, p. 595.

at the time *did* attempt to fasten imputations on an article in that paper on evidence which I thought altogether insufficient. I remember thinking at the time that if I had been personally unacquainted with you, I should have thought that article (what I am in general much slower to think of any one than people generally are) intentionally uncandid. As it was, the effect on me was to make me think that your alienation from those whom I will call the extreme radicals, had now reached the point, at which with the most complete intention on your part to be fair towards them, they could no longer expect justice from you. And this impression has been made upon me often since. If it has been made upon me, who have fought your battles so long & to say nothing of our long friendship, had to vindicate the correctness of my own judgment in thinking so highly of you as I do, it cannot be but that the same impression must have been made much more strongly upon all those, holding the opinions you attack, who are differently situated from me. This is a result which you cannot yourself wish for, & I have seen it with great pain.

In my article in the present number of the review[5] there is only one passage in which you might perhaps suppose you were pointed to, that in which "radical writers" are spoken of—but in this instance I not only did not refer to you, but if I had mentioned you, it would have been to *except* you from the imputations conveyed—& if anybody should suppose that you were among the persons meant, I shall owe you a reparation which I shall not be slow to make.

I did not complain of you for calling me *philosophical* in a spirit of sarcasm, but for imputing to Grote, Warburton &c the assumption of a name which as far as I know, *they* never used, though I did; & after fixing the name on them, then applying it to the London Review as being identified with them. I am so far from being that, that I am most anxious to distinguish myself from them—but I do not think the radical cause so strong as to sustain no injury from lowering the character of such men as those I have named—& I thought this time peculiarly one at which they had entitled themselves to be upheld. I felt much disappointed at your not taking this view along with me—but I hope I need not repeat that I am quite convinced that in this as in all other parts of your conduct you act with the most perfect persuasion of your being in the right.

The difference between us is, I suspect, as you suppose, partly in our estimation of men—& I should like very much to know better in what instances you think I err in my estimation of them. I should like this because I have been accustomed to the same charge from various people & from nobody so much as from those whom you probably think that I overestimate, & I have generally thought that the ground of this judgment

5. "Lord Durham and the Canadians," *LWR*, XXVIII (Jan., 1838), 502-33.

of me from most of those who formed it, was, that I saw much to be valued & admired in persons whom they disliked. If I err egregiously in my judgment of men I am not at present in a way to correct my error, for hitherto my experience has generally confirmed the judgments of men, which I had formed for myself, while it has often weakened those I had formed wholly or partially on the authority of others. But I should like to compare notes with you on men, & to see who are those respecting whom we differ.

As the state of opinion in the electoral body, I do not think you would find me so unacquainted with it as you suppose. I do not think the electoral body are favourable to my views on the points on which we differ; but rather the reverse. But I think they would by this time have been so, if the principal radicals & especially yourself had taken the tone which I think ought to have been taken. There is a great deal of passive radicalism in the electoral body, but very little active, & the grounds of my present practical views, whether right or wrong, are, that if this passive radicalism is not very soon transmitted into active, it will become impossible to do so, & that if the present ministry continue, with their present line of conduct, until the Tories turn them out without aid from their own supporters, Peel & [Well]ington[6] will come in without the Orangemen & *will be supported by O'Connell & 150 of the 200 ballot men in the House.* The only alternative is in my opinion, a Durham ministry within a year (or thereabouts)—or else the strongest Conservative Ministry we have had since Lord Liverpool's,[7] and the longer we wait for this last, the less chance there will be of making a strong Opposition. We are letting the cards slip out of our hands. This is the view by which I am guided, & I am driving for a Durham ministry. I may be wrong, but my object is to rest upon the whole body of radical opinion in the country & I grieve to find one part of it eating up another.

ever yours faithfully

J. S. MILL

234. TO ALBANY FONBLANQUE[1]

India House
6th Feby 1838

MY DEAR FONBLANQUE—I was a little inclined to reproach myself for having written to you (as I have since thought) rather unkindly—but you

6. Part covered by seal.   7. From 1812 to 1827.

* * * *

1. *Addressed*: Albany Fonblanque Esq. / 48 Connaught Square. *Postmark*: 2 AN 2 / FE 6 / 1838. MS at LSE.

are more than quits with me by your article last Sunday.[2] Of that article I do not very well know what to say, because it is a new position to me, to find any assertion which I make about myself & my concerns, treated exactly as if it had never been made. Could I expect after what I said in my letter to you, or even before it, that I should have been treated through three long columns, by one who has the friendly feelings to me that you profess, as being in the most complete manner identified with some half dozen men whom I have nothing to do with, & to whose opinions you are far more nearly allied than I am. You take me moreover at a very ungenerous disadvantage, because you know that I cannot chuse the time when people whom I respect are under a cloud, to proclaim to the world anything disparaging that I may happen to think of them: I cannot cry out on the housetops, like a mean truckling coward, "do not confound me with these men, I am not of them": nor is it my way at any time to do so: it *is* my *conduct* which must shew wherein I differ from them. You are moreover quite as unjust in making *them* accountable for the review as the review for them, since they do not recognise it as in any way their organ, & about that particular article not one of them was consulted, & I have no reason to believe that any one of them would approve of the course recommended in it. I shall remonstrate no further with you on the subject: if you continue henceforth to identify the review with them, you do it with your eyes open: but when I have made you, as I shall do, ashamed to go on any longer doing so, do not say *you are glad to see I am changed*: I shall not have changed; I shall only have spoken somewhat more of my mind than that very small portion of it which can be spoken on so small a subject as Lord John Russell, or so special a one as Canada.

You may believe me when I say that I do not in the least complain of your expressing yourself so strongly as you do on the subject of my article: that is all fair; & as, from considerations which you are not bound to share, I do not chuse to answer you publicly, I do privately. I only want however to mark two things, especially as I have not your article by me at present. One is, to shew you what I mean by saying that you are habitually unfair to opponents. You exemplify this in the very first sentence, when you describe me as proposing to turn out ministry after ministry till I get one *satisfactory* to some five or six members of parliament & to myself—& in this strain you continue always speaking of us as wanting to bring *ourselves*

2. The leading article in the *Examiner* for Feb. 4, 1838, p. 65, "Look Before You Leap," was a slashing attack on JSM's *LWR* article for Jan., "Lord Durham and the Canadians," in which, said Fonblanque, "is propounded the Bobadil [*sic*] plan for overthrowing Ministry after Ministry till a Government can be formed satisfactory to the extreme section of Reformers commonly called the Ultras, but whom we . . . should rather designate as the Detrimentals or Wrongheads. . . ." [The "Bobadil" plan for carrying a fortress—"twenty more, kill them too; twenty more, kill them too." See Ben Jonson, *Every Man in his Humour*, Act IV, sc. 5.]

in. Now would not any one suppose from this, that what I was dreaming of attaining was an extreme radical ministry? would any one suppose that I could have said that the mere exclusion from the present ministry of all who were pledged against the ballot, was all that should be aimed at? You must think me very easily satisfied if you describe the present ministry *minus* Lord John Russell as a ministry satisfactory to me. You may think this a small thing; but it amounts to no less than fastening on an opponent what *he* thinks would be presumptuous & ridiculous instead of what only *you* think so: & it appears to me that all the ridiculousness you attribute to my suggestion, entirely arises from putting this colour upon it.

The other thing I want to shew you is, how very little calm consideration you have given to my suggestion before pronouncing such a sentence of absurdity & self conceit upon it. You assume that after the proposed vote of want of confidence, the Whigs are to resign, & sit still till a Tory ministry is formed. They are not such fools. They would *not* resign, but would, the very next day, move, in some parliamentary form, that the House would have no confidence in any Tory ministry. There would be ways enough of wording it. Of course I am supposing that the Court is with them, & would not seek an excuse to turn them out. Nay, I have not the least doubt that the mere fact that forty or fifty radicals were known to be *ready* to vote for want of confidence, would effect the desired object without an actual vote, & without their losing ten of their supporters. By "the desired object" I mean, a modification of the *personnel* of the ministry; not even a Durham ministry, but a *Whig* ministry unfettered on the finality of the reform bill.

I have nothing further to say, except that for a person who complains of "imputations" you are very profuse of them.

ever yours truly

J. S. MILL

235. TO ALBANY FONBLANQUE[1]

I.H.
Wednesday
[Feb. 7, 1838]

MY DEAR FONBLANQUE

I am glad you are not angry & I am not conscious of being so—& it is some evidence of my not being angry, that I can bear to be called so, for I have generally observed that when any one is just hovering on the verge of anger, *calling* him angry invariably *makes* him so.

You are of course not to blame if you really think, & have thought all the

1. *Addressed*: Albany Fonblanque Esq. / 48 Connaught Square. *Postmark*: ???? / FE 7 / 1838. MS at LSE. One excerpt published in *Life and Labours of Albany Fonblanque*, ed. E. B. de Fonblanque, p. 31.

years you have known me, that I agree in my opinions with Grote or with any of those whom you allude to. I thought you had known me better: but if you did not, I certainly did not expect that your tone towards me would be altered merely by my writing to you a letter. What I will make you ashamed of is, having forgotten, or mistaken my opinions & feelings so long.

I cannot however admit your doctrine that one ought to treat any person or thing which one is opposed to, as it appears to the public, without regard to anything one may personally know, which places it in a different light. If I dealt in that way with you, I am sure you would have reason to complain of very gross injustice.

With regard to "the Grote conclave" there may be such a conclave, but I know nothing of it, for I have never been within the doors of Grote's house in Eccleston Street[2] & have been for the last few years completely estranged from that household. Surely there never was so surprising a proposition gravely advanced as that my saying that Roebuck (who was known to be the author of the former articles) was not privy to this, implied "that they were privy to it." If those are your rules of evidence I am not surprised at any false judgment you make.

How can you say the Review "countenances & agrees with" those people with the single exception of the suspension of the Canadian constitution, when it has been attacking them for inefficiency & for being unequal to their position for years, & most notably in the very last number? I tell them the same things to their faces whenever I see them. Immediately after Lord J.R.'s declaration[3] I tried to rouse them, & went to a meeting of most of the leading parliamentary radicals at Molesworth's[4] from which I went away *they* thinking me, I fancy, almost mad, & *I* thinking them craven. I do not except Grote, or Warburton, or Hume, all of whom were there. I except none but Molesworth & Leader, two raw boys. I assure you, when I told them in the review what I thought would be done by men of spirit & *real* practicalness of character I had perfect ground for feeling well assured that they would not do it. You have therefore no earthly reason for considering me "dangerous."

I am certain that in the concluding part of your article which you say refers "exclusively to the Grote conclave" there is no human creature who would not suppose that you were pointedly & determinedly & whether I would or not, including me—i.e. the review in general, & the writer of that article in particular.

ever yours truly

J. S. MILL

2. No. 3 Eccleston Street, to which Mr. and Mrs. Grote had moved in Oct., 1836. See Mrs. Grote, *The Personal Life of George Grote* (London, 1873), p. 108.
3. Lord John Russell's declaration of Nov. 20, 1837, as to the finality of the Reform Act of 1832. See Letter 225, n. 4.
4. See Letter 228.

236. TO THE SECRETARY OF UNIVERSITY COLLEGE[1]

India House.
13th Feb[y]
1838

MY DEAR SIR

I do not know whether the appointment to the professorships of languages at the University College is referred by the Council to the consideration of the Professors, but if it is I hope you will excuse my saying a word to you in favour of a candidate for the Italian Professorship, Count Pepoli,[2] a member of the Provisional Government of Bologna. I know nothing of him personally, but I can vouch for his high literary reputation & acquirements on the authority of one of the most competent witnesses living, though not a very producible one perhaps, Mazzini,[3] the celebrated President of La Jeune Italie who appears to me one of the most accomplished & every way superior men among all the foreigners I have known, & profoundly versed in his country's literature. As you probably have not Mazzini's testimony before you, I have thought it but right to tell you what I have learned from him. I should consider his testimony sufficient by itself to warrant any such appointment.

Ever yours truly

J. S. MILL

237. TO GUSTAVE D'EICHTHAL[1]

27 February 1838

MY DEAR GUSTAVE

The presents constitution of our sinking fund is this: there is no fixed appropriation of annual revenue to it, but the *surplus* revenue, whatever it happens to be, is always paid over to the Commissioners of the Sinking

1. MS at UCL. Published in M. C. W. Wicks, *The Italian Exiles in London, 1816–1846* (Manchester, 1937), p. 288. Dr. Wicks reports (p. 176) that JSM's and other testimonials "were first sent to Carlyle and in his absence forwarded to the Secretary by Erasmus Darwin."
2. Count Carlo Pepoli (1796–1881), formerly professor of philosophy at the University of Bologna, at this time in exile in England. Pepoli received the appointment at University College and held it until 1847.
3. Giuseppe Mazzini (1805–1872), Italian patriot and revolutionary, was in exile in England from 1837 to 1848. He became a close friend of the Carlyles and contributed to the *LWR* as well as other English periodicals.

*   *   *   *

1. *Addressed*: Monsieur / M. Gustave d'Eichthal / 14 Rue Lepelletier / à Paris. MS at Arsenal.

Fund (at the end of every quarter I belive) so ——[2] the amount continually
varies— —— last quarter (1837) is the first in —— payment at all
was ——? ——re happened to be n—— that quarter, Besides u——
deemed debt continues till ——mption of more. This ——ng fund was
establish—— ministry, not long after —— into office: in 1831 or 1832
—— amount of redeemed d—— I do not know, but if you wish for the
exact figures, I will procure them for you. The unredeemed debt on the
5th January 1831 was £757,486,997, besides exchequer bills £27,278,-
400. At present the debt is rather greater, on account of the 20 millions
compensation to the slave owners, which exceeds the amount of debt since
redeemed. In 1816, when the debt was at its highest, the unredeemed
debt, independently of exchequer bills, was £816,311——. so that there
must have b—— re—— in the meanwhile, —— is there were redu—— me
£90,538,701, to —— s, *per contra*, in —— 13,759 by funding [?] ——
& by different operatio—— of conversion, reducing the interest but aug-
menting the capital

If these facts are not sufficient for your purpose, write to me immediately & I will get a complete & accurate statement. You may rely upon
the correctness of all I have now stated.

If I were not so extremely busy I would write you a —— letter: I was
very glad —— from you again & —— w that you wi——.[3]

ever yours fai——

J.S.M——

238. TO EDWARD LYTTON BULWER[1]

India House
3[d] March
1838

MY DEAR SIR—I have read the Monthly Chronicle with deep interest & I
hasten to make my acknowledgments to you for the feeling which prompted
the very complimentary expressions with which you have accompanied
your strictures on my article in the L. & W. R.[2]

2. Page torn. The double dashes throughout the remainder of the letter indicate
missing portions.
3. What remains of the last line is crossed through, and illegible.

* * * *

1. *Addressed*: Edward Lytton Bulwer Esq. MP. / 8 Charles Street / Berkeley
Square. *Postmark*: 6E6 / MR3 / 1838. MS in the possession of Lady Hermione
Cobbold. Collated by Dr. Eileen Curran. Published in Elliot, I, 107–9.
2. Bulwer's leading article, "The Position and Prospects of the Government,"
Monthly Chronicle, I (March, 1838), 1–15, discusses JSM's "Lord Durham and the

I agree entirely in the greater part of the views set forth in the first article of the Monthly Chronicle, & especially in the general character you have given of the policy suited to the middle class. On the points in which I differ from you, or perhaps I should rather say, on which I would add to or qualify what you say, there would be much to be discussed between us at a suitable time & place. But I am much more desirous at present to express my great delight at the complete recognition which I find in that article, of its being advisable for the moderate radicals to form themselves openly & avowedly into a distinct body from the whigs—to shake off the character of a *tail*—& to act together as an independent body. My only quarrel with the parliamentary radicals has hitherto been, that they have not done this, nor seemed to see any advantage in doing it. But whenever I see any moderate radical who recognizes this as his principle of action, any differences which there can be between me & him cannot be fundamental, or permanent. We may differ as to our views of the conduct which would be most expedient at some particular crisis, but in the main principles of our political conduct we agree.

I have never had any other notion of practical policy, since the radicals were numerous enough to form a party, than that of resting on the *whole body* of radical opinion, from the whig-radicals at one extreme, to the more reasonable & practical of the working classes, & the Benthamites, on the other. I have been trying ever since the reform bill to stimulate, so far as I had an opportunity, all sections of the parliamentary radicals to organize such a union, & such a system of policy: not saying to them, Adopt my views, do as I bid you—but, Adopt *some* views, do *something*. Had I found them acting on any system, aiming at any particular end, I should not have stood upon any peculiar views of my own as to the best way of attaining the common object. The best course for promoting radicalism is the course which is pursued with most ability, energy, & concert, even if not the most politic, abstractedly considered, and for my own guidance individually, my rule is—whatever power I can bring in aid of the popular cause, to carry it where I see strength—that is, where I see, along with adequate ability & numbers, a definite purpose consistently pursued. Therefore if I find all that among you—& if I do not, I am quite aware that I shall find it nowhere else—you will find me quite ready to cooperate with you, if you

---

Canadians." "In the last number of the London and Westminster Review, we find the following advice: Turn out the Whigs, to bring in the Tories: turn out the Tories, in order to bring in the Radicals. With all due respect to the distinguished propounder of this doctrine [JSM], we must say that his device seems to have been pre-allegorized by Pope, in the Apologue to Sir Balaam:—

'Asleep and naked as an Indian lay,
An honest factor stole a gem away;
He pledged it to the knight—the knight had wit,
So kept the diamond—and the rogue was bit.' "

think my cooperation worth having. I am no "Impracticable," & perhaps the number of such is smaller than you think. As one of many, I am ready to merge my own views, whatever they may be, in the *average* views of any body of persons whom I may chuse to ally myself with: but not unless I have full opportunity of bringing my own views before the body, & giving to those views any degree of influence which their own intrinsic character may obtain for them, over its collective deliberations. You cannot wonder that having always been obliged to act alone, I act in my own way. As long as that is the case, I must struggle on, making mistakes & correcting them, doing the best I can under all the disadvantages of a person who has to shift for himself—& raising up allies to myself, where & how I can, as I have already done & am doing with a success that shows that I cannot be altogether in a wrong way. You have seen, in Robertson, no bad specimen, I think, of my *practicalness* in finding men suitable to my purpose. But enough of this.

Robertson requests me to put you in mind of his request to you, in which I most heartily join, on the subject of an article for our next number (*a propos* of Knighton,[3] the "Diary," &c.) on the social influence &c. of the Court. Such an article from you, would be a great treasure to us, & specially valuable in our next number as it is the best time of the year for such a subject.

Ever yours truly

J. S. MILL.

239. TO EDWARD LYTTON BULWER[1]

India House
5th March
1838

MY DEAR SIR

In answer to your question as to what I would be ready to do if my friends, as you call them, will not consent to what I think reasonable,—if a party can be formed, for the Durham policy, including such men as yourself & those whom you mention, & pursuing its objects by means which I think likely to be effectual, even though not exactly those I should myself

3. *Memoirs of Sir William Knighton*, ed. Dorothea Lady Knighton (2 vols., London, 1838). Knighton (1776–1836) was physician, private secretary, and keeper of the Privy Purse to George IV as Regent and King. Bulwer's review, "Courts of British Queens," appeared in the Aug. number of *LWR*, XXIX, 281–308.

* * * *

1. *Addressed*: Edward Lytton Bulwer Esq. M.P. / 8 Charles Street / Berkeley Square. Postmark illegible. MS in the possession of Lady Hermione Cobbold. Collated by Dr. Eileen Curran. Published in Elliot, I, 110–12.

have preferred—I am ready to give such a party all the aid I can, & as a necessary consequence, to throw off, so far as is implied in that, all who persevere in conduct either hostile to the party, or calculated to diminish its strength. But I do not think that any liberal party, out of office, can be strong enough to beat the Tories, without a degree of popular enthusiasm in its favour, which could not be had without the support of some of the men who, in the same proportion as they are thought impracticable, are thought honest. I have a personal knowledge of the men, far exceeding any which I believe you have, & from that knowledge I have no doubt that such a party as I am supposing could carry with it all of those men who are worth having, if in the first place real evidence is afforded them that popular objects, to the extent of those to which Lord Durham is pledged to are sincerely pursued, & if, secondly, their *amour propre* is not irritated by personal attacks—such for instance as that in the Chronicle[2] of this morning, or some recent ones in the Examiner. I think such attacks good policy in the Whigs, but in the moderate radicals as bad tactics almost as Thompson's insane conduct in Marylebone,[3] though I admit there are considerable palliations both for the one & the other. Both on public & private grounds I am not only precluded from joining in such attacks, but must defend them against any such, & I must do so all the more, in proportion as I separate myself from them in my political course. The October number of the review was the first in which I systematically advocated a moderate policy,[4] and it was consequently the first in which I personally complimented the extreme politicians. The Canada question then in an evil hour crossed the path of radicalism, & my difference of opinion from you on the course of conduct required by Lord John Russell's declarations made me again apparently one of them; which I regretted at the time, but could not help. But I have never swerved from my intention of detaching the review, and myself, from all coterie or sectarian connexion; & making the public see that the review has ceased to be Benthamite; & throwing myself upon the *mass* of radical opinion in the country. All this I determined to do when I had no hope of a radical party in parliament—& if such a party be formed I would of course prefer to ally myself with, rather than run a race against it for the moderate radicals. I could only enter into such a party as a representative, in it, of opinions more advanced in radicalism than the average opinions of the party—but, in my idea of the principles on which such a party ought to be constituted, it cannot do without the

2. A leading article attacking Molesworth, Leader, and the extreme Radicals, *Morning Chronicle*, March 5, 1838, p. 3. See also "The Position and Prospects of the Government," presumably by Bulwer, in his *Monthly Chronicle*, I (March, 1838), 1–17.

3. Col. T. Perronet Thompson on March 2 was badly defeated by the Tory Lord Teignmouth. For Thompson's behaviour, see *Spectator*, March 3, 1838, pp. 200–201.

4. In his article "Parties and the Ministry." See Letter 217, n. 7.

support of persons considered ultra in opinion, provided they are not impracticable in conduct.

With regard to Molesworth's motion,[5] we shall so soon know what comes of it, that there is little use in speculating about its probable effects, for the next two days I shall only say, that I neither counselled it nor knew of it till the notice was given; and when I first heard of it, disapproved of it. The position I have since taken about it is a sort of neutral one. I feel quite unable to foresee whether in the end its consequences will be good or bad. But one of those consequences, the division of the radical body, I feel all the evil of, & I regret much that such a union as we are discussing, earlier adopted, did not prevent such a division from arising. In the present state of matters, were I to urge Molesworth to turn back, I should only compromise my influence wi[th] him, without attaining the object. The division thus brought to a [cri]sis, some new state of things will arise, which we must work [to] the best ends we can.[6]

Thanks for your kind expressions about the Westminster. I need hardly say how much I value your assistance as a contributor & I shall be much disappointed if an article which would be of peculiar value to the review at present,[7] should, from the engagements you mention, be unavoidably lost to it.

I shall set about my political article for the next number[8] the moment I have made up my mind what the relations of the review are likely to be[9] to parties in parliament.

ever yours faithfully

J. S. MILL.

240. TO LEIGH HUNT[1]

India House
11ᵗʰ May
1838

MY DEAR SIR

Mr. Robertson, who goes out of town today for a few days, requests me to remind you of the proposition he made to you concerning an article on

5. On Feb. 20 Sir William Molesworth had fixed March 6 for his motion for an address to the Crown expressing no confidence in the Secretary of State for the Colonies, Lord Glenelg. Molesworth's speech on March 6 was a sharp attack on the government's colonial policy; his motion was defeated.
6. Brackets in this sentence indicate where page is torn.
7. See preceding letter, n. 3.
8. No political article appeared in the next (the April) number of *LWR*.
9. JSM originally wrote, "what my relations are likely to be," and then amended it as shown.

* * * *

1. MS at LSE.

the Tower of London[2]—which I hope it will not be inconsistent with your engagements to undertake. The subject is attractive, & treated by you, would be excellent for the light readers & would add to the sort of reputation we most want & are only beginning to acquire.

Robertson tells me you have a copy of Mr. Milnes' volume[3] of poems: if you are not needing it for a day or two, would it be too much to beg the favour of a sight of it? Something relating to the next number of the Review may depend upon the opinion we form of it—if left at Hooper's or sent by omnibus or parcel company to the I.H. I should receive it.

Ever yours truly

J. S. MILL

241. TO JOSEPH BLANCO WHITE[1]

India House
17th May 1838

MY DEAR SIR

I have been extremely concerned to hear from your friend Mr Thom[2] the form which your complaints have assumed & the increase of your infirmities. It grieves me to think that living alone as you do & at such a distance from most of your friends, they cannot know how you are attended, & have it little in their power to do anything that might promote your comfort. I do hope you will consider me as one of those whom it would most gratify to be of any use to you or to shew in any way my deep respect & regard for you. Pray do not hesitate a moment in letting me know of anything you need, & I should consider it a great favour if Mr Thom or some other friend would now & then write me word to tell me how you are.

It was hardly needful to ask permission of the review for the publication of the article which you were so kind as to write for us—we cannot of

2. Hunt contributed the article to the Aug., 1838, *LWR*, XXIX, 433–61.
3. Richard Monckton Milnes, *Poems of Many Years*, privately printed, 1838, reviewed by JSM in *LWR*, XXIX, 308–20.

* * * *

1. MS in Liverpool University Library. Excerpts published in J. H. Thom, "Archbishop Whately and the Life of Blanco White," *Theological Review*, IV (Jan., 1867), 112.
2. John Hamilton Thom (1808–1894), Unitarian minister, editor of the *Christian Teacher*, and editor of the life of White.

course derive anything but pleasure from seeing it in print & in the hands of every one who can be induced to read it, & I regret much that we could not with safety to the circulation of our review, make it the vehicle for sentiments so much bolder than any large class of readers can yet bear.

I have not yet thanked you for your notes on the Oxford Theology & on Sewell's article.[3] We have not yet been able to take up the subject, but we hope to do so in our October number,[4] & both those notes & those on Oxford itself will be of great assistance to us in treating those subjects which are of a kind that is more & more superseding in importance politics & everything else.

I assure you it is only my multiplied & multiplying occupations & cares that prevent me from being a much less infrequent correspondent of yours—they prevent me indeed from writing almost any letter without some special object—but to be of any use to you is an object for which I should easily find time.

Ever faithfully yours

J. S. MILL

242. TO JOHN ROBERTSON[1]

[June or July, 1838(?)]

DEAR ROBERTSON,

I cannot bestow upon Bulwer's article[2] any milder name than despicable, & nothing could reconcile me to inserting it in any shape but the absolute impossibility of finding any substitute for it in time. I have drawn my pen through some of the stupidest & most conceited things, and sent the rest to press—and God grant that nobody may read it, or that whoever does, will instantaneously forget every word of it.

Ever yours

J. S. MILL.

3. Probably the article "Memorials of Oxford," *QR*, LXI (Jan., 1838), 203–38, which has been identified as by the Rev. William Sewell (1804–1874), who was later to break with the Tractarians because of the Romanizing tendencies of their movement.
4. No such article appeared.

* * * *

1. Published by Towers, p. 65. MS at LSE.
2. Probably Bulwer's "Courts of British Queens," *LWR*, XXIX (Aug., 1838), 281–308.

243. TO JOHN ROBERTSON[1]

[July (?), 1838]

DEAR R.,—

I shall not be in town this evening, but will meet you at Hooper's to-morrow. I wish you would verify two queries of mine in the second sheet of Montaigne.[2] You will see them in a corrected proof which I have returned to Reynell's,[3] and from which, when that is done, it may be printed off. S[terling] has overlooked some bad mistakes.

I send the Arctic[4] with my corrections. They relate solely to small matters, but I do not think you are aware how often your sentences are not only unscholarlike, but absolutely unintelligible, from inattention to ambiguities of small words and of collocation. This article is a splendid instance of it.

Simpson[5] has made all his corrections in such a manner that the printers are sure not to attend to them, but I have left this to you to remedy when you have determined how far to adopt them.

J. S. MILL.

If we are *much* above our fourteen sheets, I think H.M.[6] ought to wait till October. It will do as well then, if not better, and I am very anxious to save expense of that kind.

244. TO HENRY COLE[1]

Kensington
Friday evg.
[July (?), 1838]

DEAR COLE,

It was provoking that they did not get the revise[2] ready for you, nor did I get mine till about six o'clock & I have been obliged to return it finally corrected for the press.

1. Published by Towers, p. 62. MS not located. Dated by Mrs. Towers as "Probably September, 1837," but the letter concerns the Aug., 1838, number of the *Review*.
2. John Sterling's "Montaigne and his Writings," *LWR*, XXIX (Aug., 1838), 321–52.
3. The printing office at 16 Little Pulteney St., Westminster, of Charles Reynell, printer of both the *LWR* and the *Examiner*.
4. "The Arctic Discoveries," signed S.R., *LWR*, XXIX (Aug., 1838), 373–92.
5. Sir George Simpson (1792–1860), administrator of the Hudson's Bay Company's territory. He had evidently been asked to check the accuracy of Robertson's article.
6. Harriet Martineau. Her article, "Domestic Service," did appear in the Aug. number, pp. 405–32.

* * * *

1. From copy supplied by Professor J. M. McCrimmon, University of Illinois, of the MS in his possession.
2. Cole's "Modern Wood Engraving," *LWR*, XXIX (Aug., 1838), 265–80.

We have said all that Jackson[3] wanted, in his note which I return herewith. We have also put in Branston's[4] name beside Vizetelly's[5] & have adopted several of your minor suggestions. I did not on consideration think it worth while to say anything more about [handbills?], when there was nothing to talk of but initial letters—nor to give a statement of the publications for which Orrin Smith[6] inquires, when our illustrations & the list annexed to them already do it sufficiently. Jackson's case was different, as he was passed rather slightly over. But Smith I am sure has nothing to complain of now.

I have put X (by itself) as the signature at the end.

Ever yours,

J. S. MILL.

245. TO AN UNIDENTIFIED CORRESPONDENT[1]

13 Pall Mall East
12th Sept' 1838

MY DEAR SIR

According to Sterling's directions I send the proof of his very interesting article[2] to you—having first made two or three alterations which he desired me to make.[3] There is one further alteration which I asked him to consent to, but my letter did not reach Hastings till he had left it—& as he gave you full power to make alterations I venture to submit the expediency of doing so in this instance, to your judgment. The questionable point is, the intimation that Simonides may possibly have had some supernatural monition at the feast of Scopas.[4] I know all that may be said in favour of such a supposition—I know that D' Johnson believed in ghosts, & Wesley said he could not positively refuse his belief to the *convulsionnaire* miracles at Paris. But these reasons do not at all convince me, & if it be necessary to stand up against the almost unanimous opinion both of the believing & unbelieving world, (who would agree in considering it impossible that a miracle should have been wrought in the name of false gods) I should like it to be on some occasion which required it & on which my own convictions went with it.

3. John Jackson (1801–1848), wood engraver.
4. Allen Robert Branston (1778–1827), wood engraver.
5. James Henry Vizetelly (d. 1838), publisher, father of Henry Vizetelly (1820–1894), pioneer of the illustrated press.
6. John Orrin Smith (1799–1843), wood engraver.

* * * *

1. MS at LSE.   2. "Simonides," *LWR*, XXXII (Dec., 1838), 99–136.
3. In a letter of Sept. 4, as yet unpublished; MS at King's.
4. See Sterling's article (cited in n. 2 above), p. 112.

I do not feel that I am at liberty to make any alteration myself, but you are, & to your discretion I refer it.

I shall be out of town for the next four weeks, during which time please direct to John Robertson Esq 13 Pall Mall East instead of me—& believe me

Most truly yours

J. S. MILL

246. TO SIR WILLIAM MOLESWORTH[1]

October, 1838.

[In a later letter from John Mill to Sir William, October 1838, there is a passage about a sum of £17 which Mill said was on "every account" Molesworth's and he adds:] If you get it, let Woolcombe[2] know that he may include it in the statement of your disbursements for the Review, which I am sorry to say it goes but a little way to liquidate.

247. TO JOHN ROBERTSON[1]

Axminster
2ᵈ October 1838

MY DEAR ROBERTSON

I duly received your letter, but I had so little to say in answer to it that I delayed from day to day until now in conscience I cannot delay any longer writing to tell you not to address any more letters to Torquay. I hope the one I received is the only one you have sent there, but as I left that neighbourhood two days ago I may perhaps have missed one. I am now going to Weymouth where I expect to stay about a week and shall be in town about the 15th as I intended.

I have been thinking very little about the review but a good deal about my Logic, of which I have, since I left town, completely planned the concluding portion & written a large piece of it which I hope I shall add to during my stay at Weymouth. I have also read the third (newly pub-

1. Excerpt published by Fawcett, p. 65. MS not located. The portion in brackets is Mrs. Fawcett's summary.
2. Thomas Woollcombe, Sir William's solicitor and friend. Molesworth, not wholly in agreement with JSM's political views and wearied of the financial burden of the *Review*, had yielded the proprietorship to JSM. See Letter 231.

* * * *

1. *Addressed*: John Robertson Esq. / 13 Pall Mall East / London. *Postmarks*: B / 4 OC 4 / 1838, and Axminster / 150. Published, with omissions, by Towers, pp. 66–67. MS at LSE.

lished) volume[2] of Comte's book, which is almost if not quite equal to the two former. This is much pleasanter work than planning the next number of the review—for which I have not a single idea beyond what we had when we last talked on the subject. Our not coming out in October is of no consequence at all,[3] for people will hardly say after our last brilliant number and our second edition,[4] that the review is dropped.

I have seen scarcely any newspapers, and none which contain reports of the Palace Yard meeting.[5] Those particulars about the arming are very ominous of important results at no long distance, but I cannot see in the menacing attitude of the working classes anything to prevent a Tory ministry and the middle classes are still very far indeed from the time when they will cry *Concede*—they will be much more likely to cry *Resist*!

Your idea about Mazzini's article seems to me good.[6] If Carlyle cannot take to either of the subjects we had in view for him we must be thankful for anything he can take to. I am sorry James Martineau has given up the Catholic subject. What answer have you given to Lucas?[7] As for the American Slavery article I think it a good subject for making the number interesting and saleable & as more likely to be well treated by H.M.[8] than [any] subject on which she has yet written for us, [but] it must be a condition that she shall not be sentimental, which she has more tendency to than any other writer we have.[9] You do not think of it for this number I believe. I cannot judge of the other two subjects you mention & as I said before I have not a single idea of my own—& am too glad at not having to think on the subject for a fortnight yet to come.

I am sorry you have been unwell—I have not been quite well myself, but am getting better. It was only a cold.

Ever yours,

J. S. MILL.

P.S. I think we are bound to give some answer to the Globe man,[10] driveler or not. I have no doubt he is a driveler or in the hands of drivelers on that subject.[11]

2. *La Philosophie chimique et la philosophie biologique* (Paris, 1838), Vol. III of his *Cours de Philosophie positive*.

3. The next number of the *LWR* is dated Dec., 1838.

4. The publication of a second edition of the Aug. number had permitted JSM to add his timely article, "Lord Durham and his Assailants," XXIX, 507–12.

5. A Chartist meeting on Sept. 17, 1838, addressed by, among others, William Lovett, Henry Hetherington, Ebenezer Elliott, and Feargus O'Connor.

6. Mazzini's article, "Prince Napoleon Louis Bonaparte," appeared in the Dec. *LWR* (XXXII, 85–98).

7. Probably Samuel Lucas (1811–1865), journalist and politician.

8. The leading article of the Dec. number was Harriet Martineau's "The Martyr Age of the United States."

9. Brackets in this sentence indicate where page is torn, but printed in Towers.

10. Not identified.

11. The postscript is written at the top of the first page.

248. TO SIR WILLIAM MOLESWORTH[1]

[Oct. 19, 1838]

The present turn in Canada affairs brings Lord Durham home, incensed to the utmost (as Buller writes to me)[2] with both Whigs and Tories—Whigs especially, and in the best possible mood for setting up for himself; and if so, the formation of an efficient party of moderate Radicals, of which our Review will be the organ, is certain—the Whigs will be kicked out never more to rise, and Lord D. will be head of the Liberal Party, and ultimately Prime Minister.

I am delighted with Buller; his letters to his father and mother and to me show him in a nobler character than he ever appeared in before, and he and Wakefield[3] appear to be acting completely as one man, speaking to Lord D. with the utmost plainness, giving him the most courageous and judicious advice, which he receives both generously and wisely. He is the man for us, and we shall have him and make a man of him yet. . . . There is a great game for you to play in the next session of Parliament. Buller has the best cards in the House of Commons, and I think he will play them well, but yours are the next best. As for me, this has awakened me out of a period of torpor about politics during which my Logic has been advancing rapidly. This winter, I think, will see me through the whole of it except the rewriting.

—Yours most truly,

J. S. MILL

249. TO SIR WILLIAM MOLESWORTH[1]

India House,
Nov. 14, 1838.

DEAR MOLESWORTH,—What think you of all this rumpus in Canada? I find all the Whigs and Moderates here blame Lord Durham for the Proclamation,[2] and he has already the greater part of the real Radicals

1. Published by Fawcett, pp. 203–4. MS not located.
2. Charles Buller had served as Chief Secretary to Lord Durham in Canada.
3. Edwin Gibbon Wakefield accompanied Durham to Canada as an unofficial adviser; he and Buller were responsible for much of Durham's famous Report.

* * * *

1. Published by Fawcett, p. 204. MS not located.
2. On learning that the government had disallowed his ordinance banishing to Bermuda some of the leaders of the Canadian revolt, Durham on Oct. 9 issued a proclamation of the act of indemnity passed by Parliament and of the disallowance of his ordinance. He further made the proclamation a defence of his policy in Canada.

against him for the Ordinance. But I think the Liberal party in the country generally is with him. I mean to stand by him, as my letters from Buller[3] and Rintoul's from Wakefield convince me that he was quite right in resigning, and that he comes home fully prepared (if the damned pseudo-Radicals do not get round him and talk him over) to set up for himself. For the purpose of acting at once upon him and upon the country in that *sens* I have written an elaborate defence of him, which will be published in the Review next week,[4] and will be in the newspapers before that. I hope exceedingly that you will approve of it, for if this man really tries to put himself at the head of the Liberals, your standing by him will do a world of good[. . . .] Write to me sometimes to say how you are[. . . .] Ever yours,

J. S. MILL

250. TO JOHN ROBERTSON[1]

13, Pall Mall, East, Monday.
[Nov., 1838]

DEAR ROBERTSON,

The inclosed is from Bulwer, and is exactly what we would expect from him. In the meantime Rintoul has shown me a letter from Wakefield, enthusiastic about Lord Durham, and full of the predictions respecting him which we most wish to see realized, though in general terms.

There is no concealing from ourselves that there is almost an equal chance of Lord D. acting either way,[2] and that his doing the one or the other will wholly depend upon whether Wakefield, we ourselves, and probably Buller and his own resentment, or Bulwer, Fonblanque, Edward Ellice, the herd of professing Liberals, and the indecision and cowardice indigenous to English noblemen, have the greatest influence in his councils.

3. A letter of Buller's to JSM, dated Quebec, Oct. 13, 1838, is published in the Dominion of Canada's *Report of the Public Archives for the Year 1928* (Ottawa, 1929), App. F, pp. 74–77. The MS of another, dated Oct. 19, is at LSE.

4. The *LWR* for Dec., containing JSM's "Lord Durham's Return" (XXXII, 241–60), was published Nov. 26, 1838.

* * * *

1. Published by Towers, p. 68. MS not located. Dated by Mrs. Towers as of "1837 during the Canada coercion and rebellion," but the reference to Wakefield's letter to Rintoul seems to establish approximately the same date as the preceding letter to Molesworth.

2. I.e., joining with the Radicals to form a new Liberal party or continuing with what JSM in the preceding letter called the "pseudo-Radicals" of the Whig party.

Give us access to him *early* and I will be d——d³ if we do not make a hard fight for it.

Ever yours,

J. S. MILL.

251. TO MRS. JAMES MILL¹

Paris

28th Decr 1838

DEAR MAMMY

Please send the first page of this scrawl to Robertson²—it saves double postage.

I am about as well, I think, as when I left London. I had a wretched passage—for want of water the boat could not get into Boulogne till half past two in the morning—it set off at ½ past eight & spent the whole 18 hours in going as slowly as it could. My already disordered stomach stood the sickness very ill & I arrived very uncomfortable & was forced to start for Paris a very few hours afterwards. The first day I was uncomfortable enough, but as the effect of the sea went off I got better & arrived at Paris after 30 hours of the diligence much less unwell than I thought I possibly could. Unless I could have got to Marseilles by the 30th it was of no use getting there before the 9th so I do not start till Sunday morning & shall not travel any more at night, but post to Chalons (expensive as it is) & then go down the Saone & Rhone to Avignon. Letters put in the post on the 2nd directed to M. J.S. Mill Poste Restante à Marseille France, will be sure to reach me in time. After that direct Poste Restante à Pise, Italie.—I cannot tell if I shall have time to write to you from Marseille but I will endeavour. The weather has not got very cold yet & I dare say I shall get into the mild climate first.

They call England's a bad climate but the north and east of France have certainly a worse. What I most dread is the sea passage from Marseille to Leghorn—seasickness is so bad with me now. Love to all—

yours affectionately

J. S. MILL

3. It is improbable that JSM wrote the word thus.

* * * *

1. MS at LSE. *Addressed*: Mrs. Mill / 18 Kensington Square / Kensington / London / Angleterre. *Postmarks*: PARIS / 29 / DEC / 1838, and LONDON / 31 / DEC / 1838. Published, with minor variations, in Hayek, p. 106.

JSM had again been directed by his physician to take a medical leave of absence and go to the Continent for his health. Mrs. Taylor, who was also in poor health, arrived in Paris shortly ahead of JSM, but subsequently accompanied him to Italy. For an account of this period, see Packe, pp. 238–40.

2. See following letter.

252. TO JOHN ROBERTSON[1]

[Paris,] 28th December, 1838.

DEAR ROBERTSON,

The steamboat by which I shall go from Marseilles[2] does not leave till the *tenth*; therefore you may direct to me there as late as the 2d, or you may risk even the 3d, if there be any reason for it.

Use Browning's means of conveyance as much as you can, but if he sends Sordello we must not let him suppose that we can promise a review of it in the February number.[3]

I cannot, on looking forward to my movements, and the time it will take before I feel settled enough to write, feel it at all likely, if even *possible*, that I can do more than the organization in time to send you for publication in February. When we asked him for Sordello, it was in hopes of finishing it before I set out.

If it must be reviewed in the February number, somebody else must do it; and perhaps that is best, at any rate, for I *cannot* honestly give much praise either to Strafford or Paracelsus. Yet I do not know whom we could get to do it.

Is the account I have seen copied from the English papers of Lord D[urham]'s Canada plans authentic? They seem good mostly, but the notion of a separate colonial office for North America seems rather foolish in itself (as if, instead of curing the defects of the whole system, we were to try to get one set of colonies *excepted* from it) and quite unpractical to propose, because impossible to carry out, or even to make acceptable to anybody.

The idea of adding British America to the Queen's title is laughably pedantic and absurd, and the notion of giving the colonies representatives in the H. of C. cannot be entertained by anybody who has one grain of statesmanship in his head.

I do hope the report will contain no such nonsense, and if you think there is the slightest chance of it pray tell me, that I may write strongly to Buller[4] against it.

1. Published by Towers, pp. 69–70. MS not located. Presumably the first page of JSM's preceding letter of same date and place to his mother, which he asks her to detach and send to Robertson.
2. See preceding letter.
3. No review of Browning's *Sordello* appeared. The next number of the *LWR* was not published until April.
4. Charles Buller, as Lord Durham's secretary, played an important (some say the major) role in the composition of the famous Report, which was published early the next year: *Report on the Affairs of British North America from the Earl of Durham, Her Majesty's High Commissioner.* Ordered, by the House of Commons, to be printed (London, 1839).

I have inquired yesterday morning and this morning for letters, but found none. I doubt not I shall find some from you (if not from other people) at Marseilles.

Yours ever truly,

J. S. MILL.

Write fully to me on the reception Lord D.'s plans meet with, if these *be* his plans, and the sort of attacks made on them.

Write long letters and often,—you will have so much to write about. Your letters will be a great pleasure to me, as I expect from them the particulars of a game well played in which I have a deep stake.

J. S. MILL.

1839

253. TO AN UNIDENTIFIED CORRESPONDENT[1]

[Rome, March 11, 1839]

I have returned here after passing about three weeks very pleasantly in Naples, and the country about it. I did not for some time get any better, but I think I am now, though very slowly, improving, ever since I left off animal food, and took to living almost entirely on macaroni. I began this experiment about a fortnight ago, and it seems to succeed better than any of the other experiments I have tried. [The remainder of the letter describes Naples and the neighbourhood—"Pompeii, Baiæ, Pæstum, &c."]

254. TO AN UNIDENTIFIED CORRESPONDENT[1]

[March 21, 1839]

As for me I am going on well too—not that my health is at all better; but I have gradually got quite reconciled to the idea of returning in much the same state of health as when I left England; it is by care and regimen that I must hope to get well, and if I can only avoid getting worse, I shall have no great reason to complain, as hardly anybody continues after my age (33)[2] to have the same vigorous health they had in early youth. In the meantime it is something to have so good an opportunity of seeing Italy.

1. Excerpt published by Bain, *JSM*, p. 45. MS not located. Bracketed portion is Bain's summary.

* * * *

1. Excerpt published by Bain, *JSM*, p. 45. MS not located. Bain notes that the letter was written ten days after the preceding one.
2. The parenthesis is probably by Bain.

255. TO JOHN ROBERTSON[1]

[Italy, April (?), 1839]

DEAR ROBERTSON,

I have been very much annoyed by seeing announced in the advertisement of the Review the article[2] which, in a letter that must have reached you in time, I so very particularly requested you to omit; and my annoyance has not been diminished by the manner in which the announcement is made, which is fitter for the Satirist or the Age than for any periodical which lays claim either to a literary character or a gentlemanly one.

I certainly never contemplated making any work in which I was engaged a vehicle for either attacking or defending the reputation of women, and in whatever way it has been done, it must make the Review consummately ridiculous. However, it is of no use writing more about what is past mending.

256. TO JOHN ROBERTSON[1]

Rome, 6th April, 1839.

I have, as you see, taken plenty of time to consider about the manner in which what you told me about Lord Durham in your last letter affects the position of the Review and the question of continuing or not to carry it on.

The result is to strengthen very greatly the inclination I had before to get it off my hands. I shall form no sudden resolution, and above all shall wait till I see Lord Durham myself before I make up my mind finally. But if his purposes are such as he appears to have declared to you, I do not feel myself particularly called upon to tender him any other aid than that of my good wishes. He may be quite right, and there may be no better course to be taken than the one he means to take, but it cannot lead to the organization of a radical party, or the placing of the radicals at the head of

1. Published by Towers, p. 67. MS not located.
2. The April number (XXXII, 459–75) contained an article by Robertson, "Criticism on Women," a defence of women in general but in particular of women writers like Mrs. Norton, Lady Morgan, Miss Edgeworth, and Miss Martineau against the satirical, critical assaults which Robertson labels "Crokerism."

* * * *

1. Published by Towers, p. 70. MS not located.

the movement,—it leaves them as they are already, a mere appendage of the Whigs; and if there is to be no radical party there need be no Westminster Review, for there is no position for it to take, distinguishing it from the Edinburgh.

For my own part, I feel that if the time is come when a radical review should support the Whigs, the time is come when I should withdraw from politics. I can employ myself much better than in conducting a ministerial review, and should think my time and money ill spent in doing only what the Examiner and the Chronicle and all that class of publications can do and are doing much more effectually. In short, it is one thing to support Lord Durham in *forming* a party; another to follow him when he is only joining one, and that one which I have so long been crying out against.

If he shows any desire to cultivate my acquaintance I shall respond to it, shall give him my opinion freely whenever he asks it, and any help in a private way which he may think that he needs and that I can give; but as for the Review, even if he would bear the whole expense and leave me the entire control, I doubt *now* whether I should accept it. On the other hand, any chance of the Review's paying its expenses without being considered as his organ, or that of persons who are acting in concert with him, is still farther off than before.

I am sorry that my political article should have been inserted in any shape in a posture of affairs so unsuitable to it, and as I am sure it must have been very much altered to be put in at all, I do hope you have not put my signature to it.[2]

I do not feel clear about publishing even another number.[3] I have not put pen to paper except to write letters since I left Pisa, and I do not intend to do so: when I reach England I shall for some time be extremely busy; and to work hard for a thing one has almost determined to give up seems waste of labor. I shall be glad if you can avoid entering into any *positive* engagements about articles for the July number till I return and can look about me.

I have begun to improve in health (I think so, at least) since the weather grew hot,—it is now complete summer here,—and I expect much more benefit from the three months to come than I have derived from the three that are past. When will you write again?

Ever yours,

J. S. MILL.

2. "Reorganization of the Reform Party," *LWR*, XXXII (April, 1839), 475–508, bore JSM's usual signature, A.

3. Another number did not appear until Oct.; it carried no article by JSM.

257. TO MRS. JAMES MILL[1]

Venice
19th May 1839

MY DEAR MOTHER—I have been some days in this strange & fine old place, the most singular place in Italy—& I write to say that I am going to set out almost immediately on my return. I shall go by the Tyrol, & through Germany, slowly; if you write very soon, write to Mannheim; if not, to Brussels. As to how far the object of my journey has been attained, that is rather difficult to say, & I shall probably be able to say more about it after I have been for some time returned & have resumed my regular occupations. I certainly have not recovered my former health; at the same time I have no very troublesome complaint & no symptoms at all alarming & I have no doubt that by proper regimen & exercise I shall be able to have as good health as people generally have, though perhaps never again so good a digestion as formerly. In this however I shall be no worse off than three fourths of all the people I know. I am not the least liable to catch cold—I never was less so in my life, & all idea of the English climate being dangerous for me may be entirely dismissed from all your minds. I shall in time find out how to manage myself—indeed I think I have in a great measure found it out already.—I have found no letters at Venice except one old one from Robertson. I do not know if any have been written but I shall leave word to send them after me to Munich where at any rate I hope to find some. Will you shew this or tell the contents of it to Grant[2] & thank him warmly from me for his unwearied obligingness & kindness—& will you or the boys tell Mr. Robertson that his letter without date, but bearing I think the postmark 1st April, & directed to Rome, did not for some reason or other reach me there, but has followed me here, & is the last I have had from him & I am hoping for another with fresher news about himself & all other matters—also that I have not yet seen the review, for although they take it at the reading room in Florence, they had not yet got the last number. I have been unusually long without English news having neither had any letters nor seen any newspapers but of very old date. But I shall make it all up six weeks hence.—I have had a most pleasant stay in Italy & may say that I have seen it pretty thoroughly—I have left nothing out except Sicily, & a few stray things here & there. I have been last staying at the baths of Abano in the Euganean hills, not far from Padua—most lovely country, more of the English sort than Italy generally is—but the weather

1. MS at LSE. *Addressed*: Mrs Mill / 18 Kensington Square / Kensington / London / Inghilterra. *Postmarks*: VEN / . . . . / and LONDON / 29 / MAY / 1839. Published, with minor variations, in Hayek, pp. 108–9.
2. Horace Grant.

for a month past has been as bad as a wet English summer except that it has never been cold. Italy is a complete disappointment as to climate—not comparable as to brightness & dryness to the South of France, though I can easily believe that some parts of it are more beneficial to certain complaints. Among other fruits of my journey I have botanized much, & come back loaded with plants. By the bye among those I want Henry to dry for me, I forgot to mention the common elder. Italy is no disappointment as to beauty, it is the only country I have ever seen which is more beautiful than England—& I have not seen a mile of it that is not beautiful. I expect to enjoy the passage of the Alps exceedingly if the weather will let me, & there seems to-day some chance of its clearing—it is the first day without rain for a fortnight past.—Let me hear from some of you soon.

affectionately

J. S. MILL

258. TO JOHN ROBERTSON[1]

Munich, 31st May, 1839.

DEAR ROBERTSON,

On arriving here I found your letter of the 13th of May from Edinburgh.

Another letter had followed me from Rome to Venice, though it must have reached Rome in time to have been given to me there.

I hope by this time you see your way through your troubles and annoyances, and are in better spirits and health.

About the state of politics and about the Review it is of no use writing much when we shall see each other so soon. I have seen no English papers since the turn-out and turn-in of the ministry,[2] and what I know of it is chiefly from letters, the latest and most explicit of which is from Buller.[3] But I expect no change whatever in the politics of the ministry as long as Melbourne is at their head; and when a change does come it will be so gradual and imperceptible that the Review will not profit much by it. I must get rid of the Review not only on account of the expense, but the time and exertion. I think myself, and still more everybody else, including the doctors and the India House people, will think, that I must not undertake so much work; especially when I first come back and have a long arrear of business at the I.H. It will be quite impossible for me to write *anything* for the Review, and the next number must certainly appear without anything of

1. Published by Towers, pp. 71–72. MS not located.
2. On May 7 the Melbourne ministry resigned but within forty-eight hours, after Sir Robert Peel's failure to form a government, was reinstated.
3. See Buller's letter of May 21 to Robertson, published by Towers, p. 71.

mine in it. I can better spare even money than time and labor for that number.

And I see no prospect of Lord Durham or anybody else taking it off my hands, as matters stand at present. I ought not to drop it without trying to preserve an organ for radicalism by offering it to any radical who would carry it on, on radical lines. Do you think Dilke[4] would now be willing to take it, and would you sound him on the subject? I have not yet seen the last number, for though the reading-room at Florence takes it, everything is so long in coming that they are always far behind. I shall probably see it at Brussels. Will you thank Buller for his letter, and say I would answer it if I were not likely to see him so soon?—but I am so little able to judge of the present state of the public mind in England that I cannot judge whether he or the ten radicals who voted against the ministry[5] were in the right. I think it likely that I should have done as he did, because the ministerial measure was probably right in itself, however absurdly defended; but if Grote and Molesworth thought the measure bad, I think they were right in voting against it. Buller's remarks on the general state of politics seem to me sensible and right; whether his practical views are right or not will depend very much on the conduct of the ministry, which I feel persuaded will entirely disappoint both him and you. The radicals will not insist on any conditions, and if they did the ministry would reject them.

I shall leave this place in a day or two for Mannheim and the Rhine, from whence I shall go to Brussels, where I hope to find a letter from you. I shall be in London at latest on the 30th of June. I am coming back not at all cured, but cured of caring much about cure. I have no doubt I shall in time get accustomed to dyspepsia, as Lafontaine hoped he should to the regions below.

Ever yours,

J. S. MILL.

259. TO AN UNIDENTIFIED CORRESPONDENT[1]

[Munich, May 31, 1839]

I am not at all cured, but I cease to care much about it. I am as fit for all my occupations as I was before, and as capable of bodily exertion as I have been of late years—only I have not quite so good a stomach.

4. Charles Wentworth Dilke.
5. The desertion of ten Radical members from the Whigs on the Jamaica bill division on May 6 led to the temporary dissolution of the Melbourne government.

* * * *

1. Excerpt published by Bain, *JSM*, p. 45. MS not located.

260. TO JOHN STERLING[1]

I.H.
24th July 1839

MY DEAR STERLING

I did not need the arrival of the second packet to know whether the article[2] would suit me or not—& if I could have had any doubts, that packet would have removed them—the contents of that same not being liable to even the minor objections which I might have raised to the first.

There are, as you surmised, (but confined almost entirely to the introductory part) many opinions stated in which speculatively I do not agree; but the time is long gone by when I considered such differences as those are, matters of first rate moment; & if I have a fault to find with your Introduction—it is a fault only with respect to *my* readers—viz. that it gives an account of the transcendental part (if I may so call it) of Carlyle's opinions in somewhat too transcendental a manner; & not interpreting his views in language intelligible to persons of opposite schools, will scarcely serve to recommend him to any (some of the religious excepted) who are not already capable of appreciating him in his own writings. But "I speak as to the wise—judge ye what I say."

In the passage on Superstition, I think you hardly do justice to Carlyle's meaning. When he called Voltaire the destroyer of European superstition,[3] I do not think he meant by superstition those fears & anxieties respecting the invisible world, which I understand you to mean that nothing but religion can save a meditative & sensitive character from—I think he meant by superstition, all such dogmatic religious belief as is not well grounded, & will not bear a close investigation, & especially, in his view, any religious belief resting on logic, or external evidences. If this be his meaning, what you say on the subject is scarcely in place—& the more commonplace meaning which I suppose him to have had, is perhaps maintainable, viz. that the first acute sceptic whose writings obtained European popularity, was thereby the destroyer for ever in the European mind of the absurdities which had entwined themselves with religion & the groundless arguments which were currently used in its support.

1. *Addressed*: Rev. John Sterling / Manor House / Clifton Place / Clifton / near Bristol. *Postmark*: LS / 24 JY 24 / 1839. MS at King's. Published in Elliot, I, 112–13. Sterling had moved his family from London to Clifton the preceding month.

2. Later note in JSM's hand: "The article on Carlyle ['Carlyle's Works,' *LWR*, XXXIII (Oct., 1839), 1–68], republished in Sterling's collected writings."

3. In his essay on Voltaire, first published in the *Foreign Review*, III (April, 1829), 419–75.

I have not a word more to say in the way of criticism—I am delighted with the article, & so I am persuaded will almost everybody be, whose good opinion is desirable—

ever truly yours

J. S. MILL.

261. TO EDWIN CHADWICK[1]

I.H.
Tuesday
[Aug. 6, 1839]

DEAR CHADWICK

I have not yet been able to manage a visit to you—& I do not like a flying visit, especially when it is also a *first* visit[2]—*shall* you be able to go down on Saturday? We all hope so very much.

Ever yours

J. S. MILL

262. TO JOHN ROBERTSON[1]

13 Pall Mall, East, Friday.
[Sept., 1839]

DEAR ROBERTSON,

Though I cannot find fault with you for not coming to town this week, it has happened unluckily, as I was waiting impatiently to talk with you about Horne's article and Mrs. Hall's.

The former I send. You will hardly believe that the fellow has not even *mentioned* any *one* of the plays he pretends to review. It is a mere dissertation (though for him tolerably well done) on his dreadful *ennuyeux* subject of the "precarious state of the drama," which nobody on earth cares for except playwriters by profession, and which he and a few others have made so dreadfully vulgar by their raving about it that the very sight of the words is disgusting to everybody of common good taste. Will you decide

1. *Addressed*: Edwin Chadwick Esq. / Poor Law Commission Office / Somerset House. *Postmarks*: TP / Leadenhall St. and 2 AN2 / AU6 / 1839. MS at UCL.
2. "*First* visit," i.e., to the newly established home of Chadwick, who had married Rachel Dawson Kennedy on July 23.

* * * *

1. Published by Towers, pp. 65–66. MS not located. Not dated by Mrs. Towers, but the reference to Mrs. Hall's article seems to establish the approximate date.

as to this article as you like, and write to Horne about it?[2] He has already been at the printer's, it seems.

As for Mrs. Hall's,[3] I have not yet dared to touch it. It is beyond all measure bad, and impossible to be made better. It has no one good point but a few of the stories towards the end, and those are told cleverly and with sprightliness, no doubt, but in the tone of a London shopkeeper's daughter.

If I have my way we shall reject it totally, but if you could possibly suggest to me any means of making it endurable I should be happy to try them.

One thing I am determined on: nothing shall go to Paris under my sanction and responsibility showing such ignorance and such cockney notions of France and French matters as this does.

J. S. M.

Leigh Hunt's article[4] is with the printers, and with some leaving out it does very well.

263. TO GUSTAVE D'EICHTHAL[1]

India House
14th September
1839

MY DEAR GUSTAVE

I am happy to hear from you again after so long an intermission of our correspondence.

I have received your little pamphlet[2] and have read it with the interest

2. The decision was evidently in the negative, for no such article appeared. R. H. Horne was apparently continuing on the theme of one of his earliest books, *The Exposition of the False Medium and Barriers Excluding Men of Genius from the Public* (London, 1833).

3. Anna Maria Hall (1800–1881), editor and novelist, wife of Samuel Carter Hall (1800–1889), editor and miscellaneous writer. Her one article published in *LWR* seems to have been the one referred to here: "Heads of the People," XXXIII (Oct., 1839), 162–81.

4. "New Translations of the Arabian Nights," *ibid.*, pp. 101–37.

* * * *

1. *Addressed*: Monsieur / M. Gustave d'Eichthal / 14 Rue Lepelletier / à Paris. *Postmarks*: LONDON / 14 / SEP / 1839 / F.B.O., and ANGL / 16 / SEPT / 39 / CALAIS. MS at Arsenal. Published in *Cosmopolis*, IX, 368–69, and in *D'Eichthal Corresp.*, pp. 171–73.

2. *Lettres sur la race noire et la race blanche* (Paris, 1839), in collaboration with Ismayl Urbain.

with which I always read anything of yours. I find in it, as I did in Les Deux Mondes,[3] a foundation of what seems to me important truth—I have long been convinced that not only the East as compared with the West, but the black race as compared with the European, is distinguished by characteristics something like those which you assign to them; that the improvement which may be looked for, from a more intimate & sympathetic familiarity between the two, will not be solely on their side, but greatly also on ours; that if our intelligence is more developed & our activity more intense, *they* possess exactly what is most needful to us as a qualifying counterpoise, in their love of repose & in the superior capacity of animal enjoyment & consequently of sympathetic sensibility, which is characteristic of the negro race.

I have even long thought that the same distinction holds, though in a less *prononcé* manner, between the nations of the north & south of Europe; that the north is destined to be the workshop, material & intellectual, of Europe; the south, its "stately pleasure-house"[4]—& that neither will fulfil its destination until it has made its peculiar function available for the benefit of both—until our *work* is done for their benefit, & until we, in the measure of our nature, are made susceptible of their luxury & sensuous enjoyment.

Thus you see I am very well prepared to give a favorable reception to your speculations & to join in your aspirations—& I am not less desirous than at any former period to keep up that sort of intellectual communion with you which I have already enjoyed. I do not find my enjoyment of speculation at all abated though I see less & less prospect of drawing together any body of persons to associate in the name & behalf of any set of fixed principles. Still, no good seed is lost: it takes root & springs up somewhere, & will help in time towards the general reconstruction of the opinions of the civilized world, for which ours is only a period of preparation, but towards which almost all the things & men of our time are working; though the *men*, for the most part, almost as unconsciously as the things. Therefore "cast ye your bread on the waters, & ye shall find it after many days."

I am much concerned to hear of your father's late illness & Adolphe's indisposition—pray assure them both, Adolphe especially, of my affectionate regards & tell me when you next write, very particularly, how they are.

ever truly yours,

J. S. MILL.

3. See Letter 197, n. 2.
4. Cf. Tennyson, "I built my soul a lordly pleasure-house" ("The Palace of Art").

264. TO JOHN STERLING[1]

India House
28 September 1839

MY DEAR STERLING

I have done by the separate copies[2] according to your directions, except that Carlyle having called on me the day I received your letter, I gave him the copy destined for him. He expressed great interest about it—& seemed to expect something much less favorable than he will probably find it. Putting together my idea of the man & of the thing, I cannot think but that he must be on the whole greatly pleased with it.

I would have written to you immediately after receiving your answer to my last if it had occurred to me that there could be any doubt about the satisfactoriness to me of that answer. I felt that you were quite right & I wrong about the way in which that part of the article would be taken by the majority of English religious people[3]—I though your corrections as far as they went diminished the force of my objections even in regard to the non-religious—& though I continued to think that there would have been a better way of stating Carlyle's creed, I felt quite unable to state what that better way would be, or to satisfy myself that it would be a better way from your point of view. Taking the article altogether, & notwithstanding that those of its thoughts to which I subscribe with a heartiness of assent & sympathy that I seldom feel in reading any speculations ancient or modern, are inseparably interwoven with views of the fundamentals of philosophy which I am unable rather than unwilling to adopt—I yet think there has been nothing published for many years so likely both to fix the attention of the best spirits & to be a source of light & warmth to them—& instead of thinking of it as you say you do with little pleasure, it will always be one of the most agreeable facts in my connexion with the review that this article appeared in it. I am even now not alone in thinking that it will be received by many as the appearance of a not insignificant new element in the present chaos of English opinion—& that many will look out eagerly for the future manifestations of the same.

If I carry on the review to another number it will be partly in order to publish in it an article on Coleridge[4] which I have always thought desirable as a counter-pole to the one on Bentham. I shall write the article whether

---

1. *Addressed*: Rev. John Sterling / Manor House / Clifton Place / Clifton / near Bristol. *Postmark*: LS / 28 SP 28 / 1839. MS at King's. Two paragraphs published in Elliot, I, 113–14.
2. Of Sterling's review of Carlyle in the Oct., 1839, *LWR*.
3. See Letter 260.
4. JSM did publish his article on Coleridge, in the last number of the *LWR* under his proprietorship, March, 1840, XXXIII, 257–302.

it appear in the review or elsewhere—& have begun a fresh study of Coleridge's writings for that purpose—but as there is so much of Coleridge which is not to be found except by implications in his published works, which are only one of the channels through which his influences have reached the age, I am fearful of understating both his merit & his importance —or rather of not producing sufficient detailed evidence to bear out my general estimate. I should have much preferred to see the subject treated by some one better versed in Coleridge, did it not seem essential to my purpose that the likeness should be taken from the same point of view as that of Bentham. It would be of most essential service to me to receive any suggestions or warnings from you, which may occur to you as needful, & especially such as would preserve me against overlooking any of the great thoughts, (whether general *philosophic* conceptions or single truths leading to important consequences) which he has contributed to the philosophy either explicit or implicit of the age, or which he has powerfully aided in deepening or diffusing. (I am ashamed of all this clumsy expression but you will understand what I mean). One essential part of my notice of him will be an attempt to enumerate & appreciate the principal of those thoughts, & perhaps that will be the only valuable part of the article. I hope therefore that I may be able to make it not absurdly incomplete.

I quite think with you that it is no part of my vocation to be a party leader, but at most to give occasional good advice to such as are fitted to be so. Whether I have any better vocation for being a philosopher, or whether you will think so when you see what I am capable of performing in that line, remains for the future to decide. I hope to give materials for the decision before long, as I can hardly fail I think to finish my Logic in the course of next year. I have endeavoured to keep clear so far as possible of the controversy respecting the perception of the highest Realities by direct intuition, confining Logic to the laws of the investigation of truth by means of extrinsic evidence whether ratiocinative or inductive. Still, I could not avoid conflict with some of the subordinate parts of the supersensual philosophy, which for aught I know may be as necessary to it as what may appear to me its fundamental principles & its only important results. I doubt therefore whether I can expect anything but opposition from the only school of metaphysical speculation which has any life or activity at present. But *nous verrons.* I have at all events made many things much clearer to myself than they were before—& that is something, even if I am destined to be my only disciple.

I am very far from agreeing, in all things, with the "Analysis,"[5] even on its own ground—though perhaps, from your greater distance, the interval between me & it may appear but trifling. But I can understand your need

5. James Mill's *Analysis of the Phenomena of the Human Mind* (1829).

of something beyond it & deeper than it, & I have often bad moods in which I would most gladly postulate like Kant a different ultimate foundation "subjectiver bedürfnisses willen" if I could.

I have left till the last what I have now barely room for—I consider myself your debtor not only in gratitude but pecuniarily for all that you have written in the review except the article on Montaigne[6]—that I as willingly accepted as you kindly offered. I hoped however that the profits of the review might some time or other enable it to pay its debt to you for that article too; but for the others you ought to be & must be paid now; gratuitous assistance to such an extent ought neither to be received nor given except where the giver is at least as well able to do without payment as the receiver is able to pay: what I have lost by the review is not so much as to be of importance to me, & this will not make any material addition to it. When I asked you to write I fully contemplated payment & would gladly have obtained cooperation like yours at any price I could afford. So when you next write pray tell me where & to whom I shall pay what is your due for this article & Simonides[7]—& now adieu—

Yours affectionately

J. S. MILL

265. TO JOHN STERLING[1]

India House
2ᵈ October
1839

MY DEAR STERLING

I am very happy that you have put it in my power to acquit myself of a small part at least of the obligation I owe you. I know where I can get a copy of the Biographie Universelle at a very reasonable price—as well as Guizot's writings; & those you mention of my father's of course. But all these together are such a very small set off against two such articles as those, that you must really tell me of some other books that would be useful or pleasant to you, so that I might add them to the packet—& tell me where they should be sent.

---

6. See Letter 243, n. 2.   7. See Letter 245, n. 2.

* * * *

1. *Addressed*: Rev. John Sterling / Manor House / Clifton Place / Clifton / near Bristol. *Postmark*: LS / 2 OC 2 / 1839. MS at King's. Published in part in Elliot, I, 114–15.

I suppose you have got the review by this time—at least your father has, whom I saw yesterday & with whom I had some talk about your article[2]— he likes it very much but thinks you pass too lightly over Carlyle's faults— which as was to be expected, he exaggerates.—There is nothing of mine in the review except a few words of note at the end of your article. There is on the whole little in this number to interest you. The best thing is an article on Oliver Cromwell[3] by the editor, Robertson, which I should like you to read because I think it the first thing he has written which does anything like justice to his sentiments & capacity. Your very kind offer about reviewing Gladstone[4] I will think about. In reviewing Coleridge I cannot help going over much of the same ground, as his "Church & State" must of course be very prominent in any such view of him as I should take —this however is partly a reason *for*, as well as partly *against*, the treatment of the subject by you in the same number. I see no reason at all for your depreciating comments on the article on Carlyle—not that there are not things to be said against it, but I am convinced no competent judge except yourself, will see those things in as strong a light as you do—one naturally is a severe critic upon oneself. There *is*, no doubt, occasional looseness of expression—but also, frequently, great aptness & even condensation of it; & even something exceedingly like the stile of Coleridge himself, of whom I have been reading sentences which I could easily have mistaken for yours. I have come to this conclusion about your writing, that the more important & universal the subject, the better you treat it.

I have read through with great interest the little volume lately published by Pickering containing the Church & State & the Lay Sermons.[5] In the former I see more & more to admire, though I think, there & elsewhere, he runs riot with the great historical conception of a certain idea of the scope & fitting attributes of some social elements working in the minds of people from age to age without distinct consciousness on their part. This I am aware is the natural result of his system of metaphysics, but I who do not believe in pre-existent ideas see in as much as is true of this doctrine (& that much of it is true I contend as strongly as he) only the first confused view, suggested by our various instincts, of the various wants of society & of the mutual correlation of these.—On the particular doctrines of his political philosophy—it seems to me that he stands almost alone in having seen that the foundation of the philosophy of the subject is a perception what are those great interests (comprehending all others) each of which

---

2. "Carlyle's Works." See previous letter, and Letter 260.
3. *LWR*, XXXIII (Oct., 1839), 181–256.
4. W. E. Gladstone's *The State in its Relations with the Church* (London, 1838); no review of it appeared in *LWR*. See Letter 267.
5. *On the Constitution of Church and State* [3rd ed.], and *Lay Sermons* [2nd ed.], ed. H. N. Coleridge (London: William Pickering, 1839).

must have somebody bound & induced to stand up for it in particular, & between which a balance must be maintained—& I think with him that those great interests are two, *permanence & progression*. But he seems to me quite wrong in considering the land to be essentially identified with permanence & commercial wealth with progression. The land has something to do with permanence, but the antithesis, I think is rather between the contented classes & the aspiring—wealth & hopeful poverty—age & youth —hereditary importance & personal endowments.—As I think the Church & State the best, so the Lay Sermons seem to me the worst of Coleridge's writings yet known to me—though there are excellent passages in them.

I think exactly as you do about the doctrine which resolves the pleasure of music into association. I seem to myself to perceive clearly two elements in it, one dependent on association, the other not—& those elements combine in very varying proportions, as e.g. the former predominating in Gluck & Beethoven, the latter in Mozart.

I heard from Mr Sterling yesterday more than I liked to hear about the state of your health, though I trust not enough to inspire any serious apprehension. *Do* take care of yourself for you can ill be spared publicly or privately & by few (out of your own family) so ill as by

yours affectionately

J. S. MILL

As I finish this letter, behold a note from Carlyle.[6] He says "Sterling's is a splendid article: in spite of its enormous extravagance some will like it; many are sure to talk of it & on the whole to be instructed by it. No man in England has been better reviewed than I,—if also no one worse."—So far so good: & as for the "extravagance" I doubt not his modesty applies that appellation mainly to the praise.

The Moral Philosophy Chair at Glasgow is vacant, & my friend Nichol has written to me about finding some fit person to fill it—it is in the gift of the Professors & any good man would be sure of all that Nichol & Lushington[7] could do for him. Can you recommend any one? Alas that you are not in a condition to take it yourself.

It is worth, Nichol tells me, about £700 a year, & gives employment only for six months.[8]

---

6. In A. Carlyle, pp. 169–70, but dated Monday night [Oct. 7, 1839]; a more likely date for Carlyle's letter is Sept. 30, 1839. See also Carlyle's letter to Sterling, Sept. 29, 1839, in A. Carlyle, pp. 222–27.
7. Edmund L. Lushington (1811–1893), professor of Greek at Glasgow University; later the brother-in-law of Alfred Tennyson.
8. The last two paragraphs of the postscript are written at the top of the first page.

266. TO JOHN MITCHELL KEMBLE[1]

India House
14th October 1839

MY DEAR SIR,

There would be very great weight in the objections which you state to a junction of the two reviews[2] if the L. & W. really represented the sentiments of the great majority of those who buy it—but I do not believe this to be the case—I believe that the buyers of the L. & W. buy it only because it is the radical review & because they are radicals, i.e. people who wish to carry their changes beyond those which would be consented to by Whigs or Tories, & in particular who would widen the basis of the representative system. Provided these are the conclusions arrived at, I believe they will allow the writer to chuse his own premises. Among the points of principle which you enumerate, the Ballot is the only one which might threaten to set the readers of the L. & W. at variance with you, but I think rather because opposition to the ballot is interpreted as opposition to all radicalism. When the repudiation of the ballot is construed with a large declaration in favour of extension of the suffrage, yet on principles quite opposite to those of Chartism I do not think it would be found a very serious obstacle. The ballot though in my opinion necessary, & but little objectionable, is passing from a radical doctrine into a Whig one as will be seen the moment it is carried. It is essentially a juste milieu, middle class doctrine.

If I thought I could do better for my principles, different as they are in some important respects from yours, than by placing my review under your guidance, I would do so: but as in the present state of affairs in this country I know of no disposal I could make of it, without having to get over objections fully as strong and even stronger, I accept your offer of writing to Mr. Beaumont[3] on the subject although I can hardly expect that your unfavourable opinion, if it should continue, will not turn the scale against me. I do not utterly despair of your ultimately taking a more favourable view of the position, because I firmly believe that any set of writers promulgating extensive views of political & social improvement, freed from party trammels & exhibiting an example of superiority to the littlenesses of

1. From copy supplied by Professor Ney MacMinn of MS in his possession.
John Mitchell Kemble (1807–1857), philologist and historian; editor of the *British and Foreign Review*, 1835–44.
2. The *British and Foreign* and the *London and Westminster*. The merger was not effected.
3. Thomas Wentworth Beaumont (1792–1848), politician, and owner of the *British and Foreign Review*.

the age & of its notions of statesmanship, may obtain all the support which it possessed or can be hoped for by the L. & W. as at present conducted.

Yours very truly

J. S. MILL

267. TO JOHN STERLING[1]

India House
4ᵗʰ November
1839

MY DEAR STERLING

I am truly sorry that you have found it necessary to renounce your project of reviewing Gladstone, but I cannot contest the reasons you assign for giving it up. I wish most heartily that there were any other channel through which you could conveniently do it, as I am sure it would do much good & for myself I feel a special desire to have your view of the matter in print. The British & Foreign Review has already had a tolerable article on Gladstone & Maurice[2]—otherwise that might have been a less exceptionable vehicle under the circumstances you mention, than, I feel, mine would be likely to be.

I imagine your books must have reached Clifton by this time—they are certainly on the way—at least they were all at Hooper's some days ago.

I have set to work upon an article on Coleridge, partly in consequence of the encouragement you gave me. It will not be a popular article; & perhaps not one person who reads it will like it; probably few will derive much benefit from it; but if I do what I have thoughts of doing, viz. to collect the few things I have printed which are worth preserving & republish them in a volume,[3] I shall be glad to have this among them because some of the others, without this, would give a false view of my general mode of thinking —& besides I sometimes think that if there is anything which I am under a special obligation to preach, it is the meaning & necessity of a catholic spirit in philosophy, & I have a better opportunity of shewing what this is, in writing about Coleridge, than I have ever had before.

Touching your question to me, whether I think that we know a sufficient number of Laws of particular Phenomena to be able to mount up to the Laws of the whole system of which they are a part—if you mean, to such laws as that which Coleridge ascribes to Heraclitus & Giordano Bruno, the

---

1. *Addressed*: Rev. John Sterling / Clifton / near Bristol. *Postmark*: LS / 4 NO 4 / 1839. Part published in Elliot, I, 116. MS at King's.

2. "The State and the Church," *BFR*, IX (Oct., 1839), 433–66.

3. This plan was eventually carried into execution with the publication of his *Dissertations and Discussions*, vols. I and II, 1859; vol. III, 1867; vol. IV, 1875.

essential polarity of all power[4]—I do not think that the time is come for such wide generalizations, though I do not consider the attainment of them hopeless at some future period. I am afraid that the only principles which I should at present recognize as laws of *all* Phenomena, are some of those which for that very reason are classed by Kant as laws of our perceptive faculty only—subjective, not objective—as for instance the subjection of all phenomena to the laws of Time & Space. But it would require a good deal of explanation before we could make ourselves understood by each other on this matter, & for my part I dare say I may have something to learn on this subject from the German philosophers when I have time to read them. You may think it presumptuous in a man to be finishing a treatise on logic & not to have made up his mind finally on these great matters. But mine professes to be a logic of *experience* only, & to throw no further light upon the existence of truths not experimental, than is thrown by shewing to what extent reasoning from experience will carry us. Above all mine is a logic of the indicative mood alone—the logic of the imperative, in which the major premiss says not *is* but *ought*—I do not meddle with.

My notion, a *vague* one enough, about the reason of Charles's consent to Strafford's death[5] is that he was frightened at the discovery of the "army-plot" just at that time—I have no recent familiarity with the details of the history, & Robertson is in the country.

ever yours faithfully

J. S. MILL

268. TO GUSTAVE D'EICHTHAL[1]

India House

12th Nov. 1839

MY DEAR GUSTAVE

I can answer your two questions. Buxton,[2] a rich brewer, is the head of the English Abolitionists—the principal supporter, & present successor, of Wilberforce:[3] & like him, a leader in what is called the religious world. He is, I believe, a very honest & well-meaning man. The object of the last bill relating to the Portuguese slave trade[4] (the legality of which on prin-

4. S. T. Coleridge, *The Friend* (1818), I, 155–56, footnote.
5. Sterling was working on his tragedy, *Strafford*, published in 1843.

* * * *

1. *Addressed*: Monsieur / Gustave d'Eichthal / 14 Rue Lepelletier / à Paris. *Postmark*: LONDON / 12 / Nov / 1839 / F.B.O. MS at Arsenal.
2. Sir Thomas Fowell Buxton (1786–1845), philanthropist.
3. William Wilberforce (1759–1833), the great Evangelical abolitionist.
4. A bill enacted Aug. 19, 1839, because of Portugal's failure to abolish the slave trade in accordance with treaties of 1810, 1815, and 1817. See *Annual Register*, LXXXI (1839), 242 ff.

ciples of international law is very doubtful) was to assume the right of search, capture, & condemnation of Portuguese vessels in our own Admiralty Courts, in all cases in which the same rights could be exercised over English vessels; including cases in which the only proof of a ship's being destined for the slave trade, is the appearance & fitting-up of the vessel itself. How far this bill will be executed time must shew. It goes much beyond anything warranted by existing treaties, & is justified only by the disregard which the Portuguese government has systematically shewn towards those treaties.

There is no later edition of my father's history[5] than the third, which I believe was that of 1826; & it is not often I think, to be met with under the full publishing price. But a bookseller, who has lately bought the copyright, has announced a new edition,[6] with a continuation; & this, no doubt, will bring down considerably the price of the old editions. Your friend therefore will be likely to have a better bargain by delaying his purchase for some months.

I have read with interest the two notices you sent me, of your little tract,[7] & I will not lose any opportunity of getting it noticed here; but I am not sanguine of doing any good by it. Our people are not ripe for any generalizations of so wide & ambitious a kind—for which even *you* have only been prepared by St Simonism. And you know very well that large ideas must be made to look like small ones *here*, or people will turn away from them. This is not a place for speculative men, except (at most) within the limits of ancient & traditional Christianity. The chief recent development of scientific speculation here is one of reaction, similar to that of De Maistre.[8] Have you heard of the new Oxford school?[9] If not, I shall have much to tell you when I have time to write you a long letter.

To whom, at the Ambassador, here, shall I address the letters which are to be under cover to M. Armand Lefebvre?[10]

ever yours

J. S. MILL

My kindest remembrances to your father & Adolphe.

5. *The History of British India*, first published in 1817.
6. The fourth edition, with notes and continuation by H. H. Wilson (9 vols., London, 1840–48).
7. Probably D'Eichthal's *Lettres sur la race noire et la race blanche*. See Letter 263, n. 2.
8. Joseph de Maistre (1754?–1821), leader of Neo-Catholic and anti-revolutionary movement in France.
9. See Letter 270 for JSM's description of the Oxford or Tractarian movement.
10. Armand E. Lefebvre (1800–1864), diplomatist and writer.

269. TO THOMAS CARLYLE[1]

[Early Dec., 1839]

It is a glorious piece of work,[2] & will be a blessed gospel to many, if they read it & lay it to heart.

I took a great piece of paper, to make notes upon, but found scarcely any to make. When I had done reading, the scrap which accompanies this[3] was all I had written. But I would strongly recommend the omission of much of the quotation from Sauerteig,[4] not because it is not true & good & beautiful in itself, but because much of it is not at all, or in a very inferior degree, pertinent to the subject. The historical view of the "eras" serves, I think, merely to interrupt the flow of the thoughts & feelings, & to make the conclusion comparatively flat. Yet what is said of the two tasks of England, & especially the *constitutional* task, must stand in some shape or other, though I think rather as your own than as Sauerteig's.

I incline to think that the condition of the working classes has not deteriorated; but all that you say on the matter, ought to be said by those who think it, & the far greater part of it, I think too. And the tone in which it is said, does not assume more certainty than the case admits of—while all the practical conclusions hold equally, howsoever the fact stands in that respect.

I should be very averse to disturb any other arrangement you may have made, or may wish to make—but it would delight me much to let this be the last dying speech of a Radical Review. I do not think a radical review *ought* to die without saying all this—& no one else could say it half as well. Any number of copies of it might be printed in pamphlet form from the same types.[5]

J.S.M.

1. MS at NLS. Part published as note to Carlyle's letter of Dec. 6, 1839, to JSM, in A. Carlyle, pp. 171–72.

2. Carlyle's *Chartism*, the MS of which he had sent JSM to read. Pencilled note on MS: "Enclosed in an ms of T. Carlyle marked 'Rejected fragments of Chartism.' (Ms. taken out long ago. A.C.)"

3. A copy of this letter, also at NLS, includes the following scraps of criticism: "page 9. Not just, I think, to the Poor Law. All this would be true of it if it only proceeded by refusing relief. But it gives relief, on terms which would hardly ever be refused, if ever, by the absolutely destitute. There cannot be more *absolute* destitution in the country, than the workhouses show.

"31. The relation between the higher & lower orders in the feudal times requires *more* developement and illustration."

4. Like Professor Teufelsdröckh in *Sartor Resartus*, Sauerteig, another mythical German professor. Carlyle disregarded JSM's advice; chap. viii, "New Eras," of *Chartism* consists almost wholly of quotations from Sauerteig's supposed *History of the Teuton Kindred*. Sauerteig also appears in Carlyle's *Past and Present* (1843).

5. Carlyle rejected JSM's offer; the pamphlet was published before the end of Dec., 1839, by James Fraser. See also Carlyle's contemptuous remarks on the subject of JSM's offer, in J. A. Froude, *Thomas Carlyle: A History of His Life in London, 1834–1881* (2 vols., New York, 1884), I, 148.

270. TO GUSTAVE D'EICHTHAL[1]

18 Kensington Square
27th December 1839

MY DEAR GUSTAVE

I have been a long while without answering your last letter—which I should not have been if I could have given you any information worth sending on African affairs. I do not believe there has been any voyage on the Niger since Laird & Oldfield:[2] if there has, I am sure you will find references to it in Buxton's book.[3] It is said that there is to be another expedition soon to ascend the river in steamboats, but I do not know whether it is to be fitted out by Government or by individuals. I am very little conversant with the affairs of Western Africa or I could perhaps tell you more.

The continuation of my father's history[4] will come down to the last renewal of the Company's charter, in 1833. The whole, continuation & all, will be contained in eight volumes, which will cost 10s. 6d. or 12 shillings each, & will be published, it is hoped, monthly, beginning next February or March, so as to be completed within the year. But I think it very doubtful whether they will be able to complete it within so short a time.

You have not told me what information you wish for about Ireland, or our Asiatic affairs. As for the Oxford School, it is a new Catholic school without the Pope. It has revived & reasserted the *old* Anglican doctrine, that the English Church is the Catholic Church—that the Church of Rome since the Council of Trent is schismatic—& it claims in behalf of the Church, a real Spiritual Power, similar & almost equal to that which was exercised by the Catholic Church before the Reformation. The depositary of this Spiritual Power is, according to them, the body of *ordained* Clergy, that is, ordained by Bishops deriving their authority by apostolic succession from Jesus Christ. The principal peculiarity of this school is hostility to what they call ultra-Protestantism. They recognise tradition, & not the scriptures merely, as one of the sources of Christianity. They dislike the word Protestant altogether, as a word which denotes only negation and disunion. And they urge all the arguments of the 19th century against the 18th, of the St Simonians against the *école critique*, all these they urge against Protestantism of the common English kind. Some of them have even revived prayers for the dead, keeping saint's days, &c., & one of their

1. *Addressed*: Monsieur / Gustave d'Eichthal / Rue Lepelletier à Paris. Published, with omissions, in *Cosmopolis*, IX, 369–71, and in *D'Eichthal Corresp.*, pp. 174–77. MS at Arsenal.
2. See Macgregor Laird and R. A. K. Oldfield, *Narrative of an Expedition into the Interior of Africa, by the River Niger . . . in 1832, 3, 4* (2 vols., London, 1837).
3. Sir Thomas F. Buxton, *The African Slave Trade* (London, 1839).
4. See Letter 268.

leaders has published a book of Latin hymns,[5] including some to the Virgin. They reprobate the "right of private judgment" & consider *learning* rather than original thinking the proper attribut[ion][6] of a divine. They discourage the Methodistical view of religion which makes devotional feeling a state of strong *excitement*, & inculcate rather a spirit of humility & self-mortification. This is a very vague description of them but I have not studied them sufficiently yet to give a better. It is one of the forms, & the best form hitherto, of the *reaction* of Anglicanism against Methodism, incredulity & rationalism. They hold many of the opinions of Laud[7] & the semi-Catholic high-church divines of Charles the First's times, & their doctrine, which is spreading fast among the younger clergy, is giving great offence to the evangelical part of the Church (you know the Calvinistic part of it, who fraternize with the Dissenters, take that name) which had previously been increasing very much in numbers & influence. They are passive obedience men, & one of their chiefs preached a sermon on the 5th of November in which he said that we ought to beg forgiveness of God for the sin of our ancestors in turning out James the Second.[8] Among others of their proselytes it is said that Gladstone, the only rising man among the Tories, is one; the man who will probably succeed Peel as the Tory leader, unless this prevents him. The principal chiefs are Dr Pusey, an Oxford Professor, & Mr. Newman.

ever yours faithfully

J. S. MILL.

5. Probably Isaac Williams' *Hymns Translated from the Parisian Breviary* (1839).
6. Page torn.
7. William Laud (1573–1645), Archbishop of Canterbury.
8. Presumably the sermon by Edward Bouverie Pusey (1800–1882), Regius Professor of Hebrew at Oxford, *Patience and Confidence the Strength of the Church. A Sermon preached on the fifth of November before the University of Oxford, at St. Mary's* . . . (Oxford, 1837). The sermon was reprinted several times. It was attacked in *ER*, LXVI (Jan., 1838), 396–415. For a discussion of the sermon and the subsequent controversy, see Henry P. Liddon, *Life of Edward Bouverie Pusey* (4 vols., London, 1893–97), II, 16–20.

271. TO LEIGH HUNT[1]

I.H.
Wed[y]
[Feb. 12, 1840]

MY DEAR SIR

Many thanks for the letter which is very interesting & does great honor to the writer. As to the review however it will either cease or go out of my hands after the forthcoming number which will be out in a few days.

It must be some namesake of mine who sent the congratulations, unless it so happen that Robertson sent them in my name which he was well warranted in doing. Ill health & family distresses have come in aid of other causes which keep me away from the theatre but I read the announcement of your brilliant success[2] with no ordinary pleasure & I trust it is the commencement of a new era of prosperity for you. It is time that the world began to pay off its long arrear of debt for your services to it.

ever faithfully yours
J. S. MILL

272. TO CLARA MILL[1]

I.H.
Saturday
[Feb. 15, 1840]

MY DEAR CLARA

There is nothing new to tell you since my letter to Derry of yesterday.

1. *Addressed*: Leigh Hunt Esq. / 4 Upper Cheyne Row / Chelsea. *Postmark*: FE 12 / 18 ... 0 /. MS in Brit. Mus.
2. Hunt's verse drama, *A Legend of Florence*, was first performed at Covent Garden on Feb. 7, 1840.

* * * *

1. MS at LSE. *Addressed*: Miss Mill / Post Office / Falmouth. *Postmark*: PAID / 15 FE 15 / 184?.
Earlier this year it had become evident that JSM's nineteen-year-old brother Henry

I understand from Oliver Grant[2] that you will still have to buy bedding, or at least mattresses & bolsters—he has undertaken to enquire whether they provide sheets & blankets or not. Whatever money you require at Falmouth Mess[rs] Fox[3] will readily advance to you having been asked to do so in the letter from Capt. St Croix.[4] One advantage of your going by the Florence instead of the packet, will be, that as the Florence is not going any farther than Madeira, there will be no hurry about your landing—& you had better write from the vessel to Mr Innes,[5] that he may make the necessary arrangements—since he will have expected you by the packet & finding you not come by it, will not know when to expect you. We will probably have to provide a palankeen for Derry as well as to take lodgings or rooms at a hotel &c &c.

The Florence may be expected I presume at Falmouth by the end of the week. I am heartily glad we have been able to make so good an arrangement.

We have all written to James.[6] I hope some of you will write to give him the latest news of Derry.

I do not wonder that you find Falmouth beautiful. I wish there were a railroad that I might come down & see you for a day or so before you go.

I have been so busy I hardly knew which way to turn, & have not been well, besides—but I think I am getting better again. I shall write often while you remain at Falmouth.

Ever affectionately

J.S.M.

I have written to Sterling. As he was not to be at Madeira I am heartily glad for the sake of all of you that he was at Falmouth.[7]

("Derry") was in an advanced stage of consumption. A family decision was reached to try a warmer climate, and in the first week of Feb. Mrs. Mill, Clara, and Henry went to Falmouth, hoping to catch a mail packet to Madeira. They arrived too late for the packet, however, and at this point they were planning to go by the ship *Florence*. See *Pym*, I, 102–3, and Wilson Harris, *Caroline Fox* (London, 1944), p. 64 n.

2. Unidentified.
3. G. C. Fox and Co., shipping agents.
4. Unidentified.
5. Unidentified.
6. JSM's younger brother James had been in India since 1836.
7. Ever since 1836, when he first discovered that he had tuberculosis, Sterling had been obliged to spend winters in warmer climates: in southern France (1836–37), Madeira (1837–38), and Italy (1838–39). In the summer of 1839 he had moved his family from London to Clifton, near Bristol, hoping that its milder climate would permit him to remain in England, but by the end of the year he had to seek a still milder climate. In Jan., 1840, he went to Falmouth to embark for Madeira, but instead stayed on in Falmouth until spring.

273. TO HENRY COLE[1]

I.H.
Thursday
[Feb. (?), 1840]

DEAR COLE,

The review has been altogether so expensive an affair to me, & I am at present drained so dry by that, by my own journey,[2] by this new call upon me for Madeira,[3] etc., that I cannot incur the smallest extra expense on account of the next number of the review, and, all things considered, I would not recommend your doing so.

Unless the number sells more than 1,200, the article will do no good, as that has been for a long time the ordinary number sold—though I believe the *last* number sold rather fewer.

The conditional authority you mention I readily give—subject to the chance of Beaumont's[4] accepting.

Ever yours,

J. S. MILL

274. TO CLARA MILL[1]

I.H.
Wednesday
[Feb., 1840]

DEAR CLARA

We received your yesterday's letters. What may have been received at Kensington today I do not know.

After full consideration Harriet[2] prefers fatigue to the probability of seasickness & thinks that it will probably less unfit her for what she will have to do when she arrives. Her place has therefore been taken by the Falmouth mail for Thursday (tomorrow) & she anticipates being able to go right through at once & arrive on Saturday morning. You of course will know at what time the mail may be expected to come in & will do whatever is advisable.

1. MS in the possession of Professor J. M. McCrimmon, University of Illinois.
2. On the Continent for six months the previous year.
3. See preceding letter.
4. See Letter 266.

* * * *

1. MS at LSE. No address, postmark, or signature. Perhaps only a part of the letter.
2. JSM's sister, who was to join their mother and their sister Clara in Falmouth to help care for Henry. See Letter 272.

I shall send money by her sufficient for a present supply.

I will write tomorrow either to you or to poor dear Derry—& Harriet will of course know anything that I may have to say.

Arnott[3] has told both Harriet & me since you were at Falmouth that it was not a case in which a medical man would have recommended going to Madeira, & that the chief reason was that I so much wished it.[4] So far therefore he is not in fault—& he has shewn much real feeling through it all —but why was he not sincere with me sooner, so as to enable ourselves to judge? Why did he continue to do all he possibly could to persuade us that his not getting rid of the cough was quite an ordinary & not an alarming thing?

275. TO HENRY COLE[1]

Friday
[Feb. (?), 1840]

MY DEAR COLE,

Robertson tells me of a mode of carrying on the review with you and him combined which he says you are willing to agree to[2]—on which however it is quite impossible for me to decide unless I first see you. I waited till rather late at Kensington this morning thinking you might possibly come— & should then have gone to your house if I had thought I should find you there. This misadventure makes it impossible to terminate matters immediately, as I go out of town this afternoon & cannot return till Monday. But I think you may proceed with *your* arrangements on either supposition. I am more annoyed about Hickson,[3] who has reasons for wishing for a speedier decision.

Ever yours,

J. S. MILL

3. Neil Arnott (1788–1874), physician and philosopher; author of *Elements of Physics* (London, 1827–29). Arnott had been a close friend of James Mill in his latter years (see Bain, *James Mill,* pp. 338–39).

4. The proposed trip to Madeira for Henry Mill's health had had to be abandoned.

* * * *

1. MS in the possession of Professor J. M. McCrimmon.

2. This was probably the proposal described in an unpublished letter (n.d., owned by Professor McCrimmon) from Cole to JSM: "I had much talk with Hickson last night about the Review. He is most decidedly averse to Robertson's having the Editorship. . . . R. asked me whether I was willing to become the sole proprietor—he remaining the Editor under certain conditions to be agreed upon between us. . . . R. proposes to me. . . . that I should have the unconditional control of the Management or business part of the Review."

3. William Edward Hickson (1803–1870), educational writer, editor of the *Westminster Review,* 1840–52 (see Letter 278).

276. TO HENRY COLE[1]

India House
Saturday
[Feb. or March (?), 1840]

MY DEAR COLE,

I am afraid you will think me very changeable, but since I saw you last I have thought a good deal more about the proposed arrangement concerning the review, & have heard the opinion of one or two friends on the matter (I had consulted nobody before) & I find their opinion to be exceedingly strong that if the review goes on at all under the same name it will not be possible for me to destroy the connexion in people's minds between it and myself—& that it is much more to my credit that it should cease entirely than that it should be continued as anything else than the philosophical & political organ it was designed to be. I am not sure that after what has passed between us you have not a right to hold me to what was conditionally agreed upon but I hope you will not think it necessary to do so. Of course I hold myself responsible for the expense of the Postage article[2] & will pay for any work that you have entered into engagements for, & I hope that by laying all the blame, where alone it can justly fall, on me, you will be able to terminate the thing without any unpleasantness.

Ever yours truly,

J. S. MILL

277. TO HENRY COLE[1]

I.H.
Thursday
[Feb. or March (?), 1840]

MY DEAR COLE,

If you are willing to carry on the review under the name of *Westminster,* & with some slight alteration in the cover, I am willing to make it over to you, without requiring that it should be a new series or new numbering— unless before the present number comes out I receive some communication, at this eleventh hour, from Beaumont,[2] or from another quarter almost as improbable.

1. MS in the possession of Professor J. M. McCrimmon.
2. Cole's article, "The Postage Stamp," *LWR,* XXXIII (March, 1840), 491–505.

* * * *

1. MS in the possession of Professor J. M. McCrimmon.
2. See Letter 266.

It will give me still greater satisfaction to deliver it over to you & Hickson jointly, as he proposes, as it will both diminish your risk & aid you very much in the management.

Ever yours,

J. S. MILL

278. TO JOHN ROBERTSON[1]

[March (?), 1840]

I am exceedingly grieved by the consciousness that I must appear to you (what I never have been nor could be intentionally) unkind to you. The thought of this matter has been, ever since it was first mentioned by you in a letter last July, but especially of late, no small addition to the burthens of various sorts that have lain upon me.

I feel, however, that I have meant rightly to you and to every other interest concerned, and that I have acted to the best of my judgment; and though I feel painfully the impossibility of my convincing you that I am right, I am sure you will respect me more for acting upon my own conviction than for giving way, from feelings of friendship and confidence, without being convinced.

Cole repeatedly expressed his wish not to stand in the way of any arrangement more beneficial to you and independent of him; but we seemed to have already exhausted the possibilities of such, and as it was impossible to keep Hickson any longer without an answer, I have told Cole that I considered the Review as made over to them, although the formal transfer has not yet taken place.[2]

I am sure you have that in you which a disappointment in so poor a hope as this cannot unnerve or permanently discourage.

Ever yours,

J. S. MILL

279. TO JOHN ROBERTSON[1]

Kensington, Monday
[March, 1840?]

DEAR ROBERTSON,

Some points in your letter positively require from me a few words to set right a few matters in which you have quite misunderstood me,

1. Published by Towers, p. 72. MS not located.　　　2. See Letter 280.

* * * *

1. Published by Towers, pp. 72–73. MS not located.

and in which it would be very unpleasant to me that you should continue to do so.

First. I did not allude to that number of the Review for any purpose of disparagement. Why should I? It has fully less of the defects to which I alluded than I thought it would have. I referred to it *bona fide*, as I professed to do, namely, as evidence you could appeal to in contradiction to my opinion if I was wrong.

Second. When I spoke of unconciliativeness to contributors, I never meant that you were in the wrong in your disputes with them, but that you gave them unnecessary offense by matters of mere manner, and did not spare their vanity, which I am sure I have often said to you before; and also that I think you, in that particular, extremely unpractical, since no one can use others as instruments unless he makes them like his service.

Third. When I spoke of subserviency, I carefully explained that I was not speaking of your intentions or feelings, but of *their* expectations.

Fourth. I never said that *you* would get a character like Fonblanque's, but that the *Review* would. I have distinctly said to you several times that *you* personally would not suffer in any way, and I said it most distinctly in the very same sentence by saying I should be glad to aid you in a ministerial course by any other means than the Review.

Fifth. Finally, I *do* feel that I can and ought to support the ministry, but not connect myself with them (unless I had a voice in their councils); that is, I can neither take their money nor make over power which is in my hands and put it into theirs, though any power in my own hands I would, while I see as much cause as I now do, use in their support.

Having endeavored to put myself right in these points, I will now say that your readiness to give up a project, in my objections to which you do not at all concur, is a thing which, you may rely upon it, I shall not forget.

I think your letter to Lord N[ormanby][2] in perfectly good taste, as well as right feeling towards him.

Ever yours,

J. S. MILL.

2. Sir Constantine Henry Phipps, first Marquis of Normanby and second Earl of Mulgrave, prominent Whig leader.

Mrs. Towers (p. 72) explains that Robertson had hoped to get into Parliament, "and he would have used the Review, had he continued his editorship, to support the Whigs. . . . Lord Normanby had had one interview, if not more, with Robertson with reference to this subject."

280. TO HENRY COLE[1]

India House
12th March
1840

MY DEAR COLE,

I hereby make over to you & Mr William Hickson my whole interest in the London & Westminster Review—the work hereafter to be called the *Westminster Review* & the change of proprietorship to be announced in the next number.

Yours very truly

J. S. MILL

281. TO RICHARD MONCKTON MILNES[1]

India House
Saturday
[March, 1840]

MY DEAR SIR

My course on Monday morning next will be not anti-solar but at right angles to the sun's course, as I shall be on my way from Sussex. & even on other days I can seldom manage to stop on my way, as I do not like to arrive here much after ten. We keep earlier hours here both in the morning & in the afternoon, than the Government offices at the West End. Therefore I am obliged to renounce the pleasure, which would have been a great one, of breakfasting with you.

I cannot omit this opportunity of thanking you for the very interesting & valuable article you have contributed to this number of the London & Westminster,[2] & which I am very happy to have been the means of publishing before the termination of my connexion with the review.

Every truly yours

J. S. MILL

1. MS in the possession of Professor J. M. McCrimmon.

* * * *

1. MS at Trinity College Library, Cambridge.
Richard Monckton Milnes, later first Baron Houghton (1809–1885), writer and politician, author of *The Life, Letters, and Literary Remains of John Keats* (1848).
2. "American Philosophy.—Emerson's Works," signed R.M.M., *LWR*, XXXIII (March, 1840), pp. 345–72. This was the last number under JSM's proprietorship of the Review.

282. TO ROBERT BARCLAY FOX[1]

India House
16th April
1840

My dear friend (if you will allow me to adopt this "friendly" mode of address) your kind & sympathizing letter has given me great pleasure. There is no use in my saying more than has been said already about him who has gone before us where we must so soon follow—the thought of him is here & will remain here, & seldom has the memory of one who died so young, been such as to leave a deeper or a more beneficial impression on the survivors. Among the many serious feelings which such an event calls forth, there is always some one which impresses us most, some moral which each person extracts from it for his own more especial guidance—with me that moral is, "work while it is called today—the night cometh in which no man can work." One never seems to have adequately *felt* the truth & meaning of all that is tritely said about the shortness & precariousness of life till one loses some one whom one had hoped not only to carry with one as a companion through life, but to leave as a successor after it. Why he who had all his work to do has been taken, & I left who had done part of mine and in some measure as Carlyle would express it "delivered my message," passes our wisdom to surmise. But if there be a purpose in this, that purpose it would seem can only be fulfilled in so far as the remainder of my life can be made even more useful than the remainder of his would have been if it had been spared. At least we know this that on the day when we shall be as he is, the whole of life will appear but as a day, & the only question of any moment to us then will be, Has that day been wasted. Wasted it has not been by those who have been, for however short a time, a source of happiness & of moral good even to the narrowest circle. But there is only one plain rule of life eternally binding, & independent of all variations in creeds & in the interpretations of creeds & embracing equally the greatest moralities & the smallest—it is

1. *Addressed*: R. Barclay Fox Esq. / Neath Abbey / Glamorganshire. *Postmark*: B / 16 AP / 1840. Published in Pym, I, 173–79. MS in 1944 in the possession of Mr. W. H. Browning, of Eltham, Surrey.

Robert Barclay Fox (1817–1855), son of the scientific writer Robert Were Fox (1789–1877), and brother of Anna Maria Fox (1816–1897) and of Caroline Fox (1819–1871), diarist.

JSM on March 16 had joined his mother and his sisters Clara and Harriet in their attendance upon the last illness of Henry Mill (see Letters 272 and 274). After Henry's death on April 4, JSM had returned to London on April 10. During their stay in Falmouth the Mills had become intimately acquainted with the Foxes, a prominent Quaker family.

this—try thyself unweariedly till thou findest the highest thing thou art capable of doing, faculties & outward circumstances being both duly considered—and then DO IT—

You are very kind to say what you have said about those reviews[2]— the gift of unsold copies of an old periodical could under no circumstances have called for so warm an expression of thanks, & would have deserved an opposite feeling if I could not say, with the utmost sincerity, that I do not expect you to read much of it, or any of it unless you feel thereunto moved. My principal feeling in the matter was this—You are likely to hear of some of the writers, & judging of your feelings by what my own would be, I thought it might be sometimes agreeable to you to be able to turn to something they had written & imagine what manner of persons they might be. As far as my own articles were concerned there was also a more selfish pleasure in thinking that sometimes, however rarely, I might be conversing with my absent friends at 300 miles distance—We scribblers are apt to put not only our best thoughts but our best feelings into our writings, or at least if the things are *in* us they will not *come out of us* so well or so clearly through any other medium—& therefore when one really wishes to be *liked* (it is only when one is very young that one cares about being admired) it is often an advantage to us when our writings are better known than ourselves.

As for these particular writings of mine, all in them that has any pretension to permanent value will I hope during the time you are in London be made into two little volumes[3] which I shall offer to no one with greater pleasure than to you. The remainder is mostly politics—of little value to any one now—in which, with considerable expenditure of head & heart, an attempt was made to breathe a living soul into the Radical party— but in vain—there was no making those dry bones live. Among a multitude of failures I had only one instance of brilliant success—it is some satisfaction to me to know that, as far as such things can ever be said, I saved Lord Durham—as he himself, with much feeling, acknowledged to me, saying that he knew not to what to ascribe the reception he met with on his return from Canada, except to an article of mine[4] which came out immediately before. If you were to read that article now you would wonder

2. Caroline Fox noted in her journal on April 5 (Pym, I, 158): "A great parcel arrived in the evening with John Mill's kind regards, containing all the *London and Westminster Reviews* from their beginning, with notes in his own hand, and the names of the writers attached to the articles—a most valuable and interesting gift." Efforts to trace this set of volumes have thus far proved unavailing.

3. Not until 1859 were these articles republished, in the first two volumes of *Dissertations*. See Letter 267, n. 3.

4. "Lord Durham's Return." See Letter 249, n. 4.

what there was in it to bear out such a statement—but the *time* at which it appeared was everything—every one's hand seemed to be against him, no one dared speak a word for him, the very men who had been paying court & offering incense to him for years before (I never had) slunk away, or ventured only on a few tame & qualified phrases of excuse—not, I verily believe, from cowardice so much as because, not being accustomed to think about *principles* of politics, they were taken by surprise in a contingency which they had not looked for, and feared committing themselves to something they could not maintain—& if this had gone on, opinion would have decided against him so strongly that even that admirable Report of his & Buller's could hardly have turned the tide & unless some one who could give evidence of thought & knowledge of the subject, had thrown down the gauntlet at that critical moment, & determinedly claimed honour & glory for him instead of mere acquittal, & by doing this made a diversion in his favour & encouraged those who wished him well to speak out, & so kept people's minds *suspended* on the subject, he was in all probability a lost man, & if I had not been the man to do this nobody else would. And three or four months later the Report came out & then everybody said I had been right, & now it is being acted upon.

This is one of only three things, among all I attempted in my reviewing life, which I can be said to have succeeded in. The second was, to have greatly accelerated the success of Carlyle's French Revolution,[5] a book so strange & incomprehensible to the greater part of the public, that whether it should succeed or fail seemed to depend upon the turn of a die—but I got the first word, blew the trumpet before it at its first coming out & by claiming for it the honours of the highest genius frightened the small fry of critics from pronouncing a hasty condemnation, got fair play for it & then its success was sure.

My *third* success is that I have dinned into people's ears that Guizot is a great thinker & writer, till they are, though slowly, begining to read him—which I do not believe they would be doing, even yet, in this country but for me.

There, I think, is a full account of all the world has got by my editing and reviews.

Will you pardon the egotism of this letter? I really do not think I have talked so much about myself in the whole year previous as I have done in the few weeks of my intercourse with your family—but it is not a fault of mine generally, for I am considered reserved enough by most people— & I have made a very solemn resolution when I see you again to be more

5. By his review, "The French Revolution." See Letters 208, n. 5, and 209.

objective and less *subjective* in my conversation (as Calvert[6] says) than when I saw you last.

Ever yours faithfully,

J. S. MILL

It seems idle to send remembrances—they saw enough to know I am not likely to forget them.

283. TO JOHN STERLING[1]

I.H.

22[d] April

1840

MY DEAR STERLING

Your letter should have been answered when I first received it, which was just before I left Falmouth. The bustle & turmoil of London when one comes back to it, & the accumulation of different sorts of business which I have had to dispose of, are very uncongenial to the mood in which such a letter is read or in which it should be responded to.

I rejoice greatly that we met at Falmouth; independently of the good, of many kinds, which your presence did, it is very much to me now, & more than I thought it would be, that my last recollections of Henry are shared with you. If he had lived he would certainly have been an additional bond between us, & now that he is dead his memory will be so—& perhaps as you say he is conscious of it. I do feel as you do that we have been more to each other lately than ever before, & I think on one side this is easily to be explained, for it is natural to you to feel more affectionately in proportion as you have shewn more kindness—that is one of the ways in which acts of love fructify & yield a large increase. On my own side less explanation is needed, for it seems to me that you have at all times been giving more & more to me—though there have been times when the contrary may have seemed to be the case—in consequence partly of constitutional or habitual defect of quickness of sensibility, but much more of the jarring elements both in my own character & in my outward circumstances which I have had to reconcile, as indeed is the case with most

6. John M. Calvert (1801–1842), physician. A fellow-victim of tuberculosis, Dr. Calvert had first met Sterling in Madeira in 1838. They had become close friends, and after giving up their plans to spend the winter again at Madeira they had stayed on together at Falmouth. Caroline Fox's journals recount numerous meetings with Calvert and Sterling.

* * * *

1. MS at Leeds. Published in Elliot, I, 116–18.

people, but I think both in an unusual degree and in an unusual manner with me—& which have made me describe an orbit very different from the direction of any one of the forces which urged me. And even now I am very far from appearing to you as I am—for though there is nothing that I do not desire to shew, there is much that I never do shew, & much that I think you cannot even guess.

My mother & sisters & George[2] have returned, & George is certainly better, not worse, for his journey. I have much anxious thought about him—to him the loss of Henry is a greater calamity than he can yet feel.

As for me, I have begun to get ready my reprint—but I find some difficulty in finding enough for two volumes.[3] I have softened the asperity of the article on Sedgwick,[4] & cut out whatever seemed to take an unfair advantage against his opinions, of his deficiencies as an advocate of them.

ever affectionately

J. S. MILL.

284. TO MACVEY NAPIER[1]

India House
22^d April
1840

MY DEAR SIR

It is just possible you may have heard—though it is most likely you have not—that my connexion with the Westminster Review has terminated. The review has gone into other hands, & although I wish well to the new proprietors & think they will conduct it creditably & usefully, I do not feel myself in such a manner bound to them that I should wish to exclude myself from the power of addressing a larger auditory. This is also the feeling of several of the best of my late coadjutors in the Westminster, to whom, as well as to myself, it would be agreeable, if you give any encouragement to the proposition, to establish a connexion with the Edinburgh. I believe it is the feeling of nearly all Reformers that this is not

2. George Grote Mill (*ca.* 1825–1853), youngest of JSM's brothers, had been at Falmouth since April 2.
3. See Letter 267, n. 3.
4. "Professor Sedgwick's Discourse.—State of Philosophy in England," *London Rev.*, I (April, 1835), 94–135, eventually reprinted in *Dissertations* as "Professor Sedgwick's Discourse on the Studies of the University of Cambridge."

* * * *

1. MS in Brit. Mus. Published, except for last paragraph, in *Napier Corresp.*, pp. 325–26.
Macvey Napier, editor of the *Edinburgh Review*, 1829–47.

a time for keeping up a flag of disunion among them—& even I who have been for some years attempting it must be owned with very little success, to induce the Radicals to maintain an independent position, am compelled to acknowledge that there is not room for a fourth political party in this country—reckoning the Conservatives, the Whig-Radicals, & the Chartists as the other three. Of a clear view of this fact a natural consequence is, a different notion of what my own course ought to be—if I can hope to do any good it can only be by merging in one of the existing great bodies of opinion; by attempting to gain the ear of the liberal party generally, instead of addressing a mere section of it. There seems no longer any reason why my little rivulet should continue to flow separate, little as it can contribute to decide the colour or composition of that great stream.

Among those contributors to the Westminster who would like to become contributors of yours, those who I think would be of most use to you (besides Charles Buller with whom I believe you are already in communication) are Robertson, the late editor, & writer of many articles and George Fletcher,[2] the author of two very interesting papers, one in the number for December, 1838, on Heloisa & Abelard,[3] the other (in the last number) on Robin Hood.[4] If you have not seen these articles I am sure it would give you pleasure to read them especially the former.

Of Robertson's articles some were hastily got up under many disadvantages & he did himself scanty justice in them—but others I think are sufficient proof that he can do something considerable especially those on "Cromwell" "Caricatures" "Statistical Society" "Congregational Dissenters" & one or two others.

Ever yours truly

J. S. MILL

285. TO MACVEY NAPIER[1]

India House
April 27, 1840

MY DEAR SIR,

Permit me in the first place to make my acknowledgments for the extremely kind & flattering manner in which you have received my propo-

2. Otherwise identified only as the author of *Studies in Shakespeare* (London, 1847), which contains essays contributed originally to the *Athenæum* in 1843–44 and to the *Westminster Review* in 1844–45. He also contributed to *Fraser's Magazine* in 1850.

3. *LWR*, XXXII, 146–219.   4. *LWR*, XXXIII (March, 1840), 424–91.

* * * *

1. MS in Brit. Mus. Published, except for last paragraph, in *Napier Corresp.*, pp. 326–27. (See preceding letter.)

sition for becoming a contributor to the Edinburgh. You have done me only justice in supposing that the idea of any compromise of the principles of the E. Review never entered into my mind—it did not occur to me even to disavow such a thought. Of course I did not expect to have the same range of subjects as I had in a review under my own exclusive control, nor to be allowed to commit the review to opinions which would be obnoxious to its other writers & its supporters. I look for no other latitude than that commonly allowed by periodical works to the individual modes of thinking of their various contributors. There will be no difficulty in our understanding one another, since the principles of the review are public property, & what I have written in the last year or two, or what I may now write will soon shew you what are the points if any, on which mine are irreconcileable with them. I am myself under an impression that there is very little of what I should now be inclined to say to the public in a review, which would be at all in contradiction to the established character & purposes of the Edinburgh.

As you conjecture, it is only occasionally that I should find time to write for you, especially at present, as I am desirous of finishing a book I have in hand. But the subject you suggest, my friend Tocqueville's book, is so very attractive to me that if the other arrangement you mention should not take effect, I would make an effort to get an article ready on Tocqueville for your October number.[2] With regard to other subjects, one thing which I should like very much, & on which I should not interfere with any of your existing contributors, would be to write occasionally on modern French history & historical literature, with which from peculiar causes I am more extensively acquainted than Englishmen usually are. If I had continued to carry on the London & W. review, I should have written more than one article on Michelet[3] a writer of great & original views, very little known among us. One article on his history of France, & another combining his Roman history with Arnold's,[4] might I think be made very interesting & useful. Even on Guizot[5] there may be something still to be written. I mention these things only that you may know the course my thoughts have taken in regard to future articles.

2. The review of Tocqueville's *Democracy in America* appeared, as here projected, in the Oct., 1840, number of *ER*, LXXII, 1–47; it was reprinted in *Dissertations*, II, 79–161.
3. Jules Michelet (1798–1874). JSM's review of the first five volumes of his *Histoire de France* (Paris, 1833–42) eventually appeared in *ER*, LXXIX (Jan., 1844), 1–39. It was reprinted in *Dissertations*, II, 198–259.
4. Michelet, *Histoire romaine: republique* (2nd ed., 3 vols., Paris, 1833). Thomas Arnold, *History of Rome* (3 vols., London, 1838–43).
5. JSM's review of "M. Guizot's Essays and Lectures on History" appeared in *ER*, LXXXII (Oct., 1845), 381–421; it was reprinted in *Dissertations*, II, 297–362.

I will immediately make known to Robertson & Fletcher your answer in respect to them & I have no doubt that you will find them valuable auxiliaries.

> Ever my dear Sir
> Truly yours,
>
> J. S. MILL

286. TO GUSTAVE D'EICHTHAL[1]

> India House
> 7th May
> 1840

MY DEAR GUSTAVE

I have been very long in answering your letters, having been absent from London for some weeks attending the deathbed of a brother, who was the pride & hope of our whole family & whose loss I shall have cause to regret as long as I live. This absence occasioned my losing the opportunity of seeing MM Stéphane Mony & Isaac Pereire,[2] both well known to me by their *antécédents* & the former personally. I have to thank you for a letter I have received from M. Michelet accompanying two volumes of his admirable history,[3] & which as I had not time to answer immediately I shall now defer answering until I have read the new volume. I was already intimately acquainted with the former volumes as well as with all his other works, & I beg of you to tell him that I have long felt the warmest admiration for them & have expressed it publicly on several occasions before the one which attracted your notice. I had long meditated reviewing his Roman history in the Westminster, & now that I am no longer connected with that review it is probable that I shall have the satisfaction of making both that, & his History of France still more widely known by means of the Edinburgh review in which I have engaged to write some articles on the new French historical school.[4] Would you oblige me with M. Michelet's address?[5]

1. *Addressed*: Monsieur / Gustave d'Eichthal. Published, with omissions, in *D'Eichthal Corresp.*, pp. 178–80. MS at Arsenal.
2. Isaac Péreire (1806–1880), French banker, earlier associated with the Saint-Simonians.
3. His *Histoire de France* in 17 volumes was published at intervals between 1833 and 1867. His letter of April 7 to JSM is at LSE.
4. See preceding letter.
5. Eugène d'Eichthal in *D'Eichthal Corresp.*, p. 179, appends as a note this part of a letter from Michelet to Gustave d'Eichthal:
"J'aurais voulu vous dire un mot de mon 5e volume qui va être attaqué de deux côtés opposés. J'espère pour le défendre (ce volume si peu favorable aux Anglais),

I have no doubt that the two books which you mention, Lyon's Voyage[6] & Crawfurd's History,[7] may be obtained here by watching an opportunity, at a tolerably cheap rate, but it is impossible to say how cheap, as it depends on accident. I would recommend to you for such commissions a bookseller named Edward Rainford, 86 High Holborn, & if you will communicate with him the first time through me you will have no difficulty with him afterwards. He is a most deserving person, & manages to get books exceedingly cheap.

I have not yet seen M. Guizot,[8] though I have been very near seeing him several times—& should have ventured to call on him if I were not so circumstanced as to hours, that it is impossible for me to call at any time of the day suitable to a civilized being.

Your opinion on the decisive character of the late triumph of parliamentary government[9] (ostensibly) & of democracy really, in France, is very interesting to me. It is a great event, & makes me recur to what I have so often thought, *les choses marchent vîte en France* (& in this age, altogether one may add)

ever yours

J. S. MILL

287. TO ALEXIS DE TOCQUEVILLE[1]

11th May, 1840

MY DEAR TOCQUEVILLE,

I shall have the greatest pleasure in owing to your friendship a copy of the second part of your great work. I had already possessed myself of it

---

dans la haute impartialité d'un Anglais, de M. Mill, qui m'a écrit cette belle lettre que nous avons admirée ensemble. Vous avez trouvé, je pense, son exemplaire joint au vôtre?
    . . . Si vous écrivez à M. Mill, veuillez lui faire considérer avec quelle méthode sévère, dans l'affaire de la Pucelle et dans bien d'autres j'ai écarté les *chroniques* pour m'en tenir aux *actes.* . . . Si M. Mill me fait l'honneur de parler de mon livre dans une revue anglaise, il m'obligera fort de faire remarquer combien cet historien qu'on traite trop aisément comme un homme d'*imagination*, a été dominé par la passion de la *vérité.*"
    6. Probably *The Private Journal of Captain G. F. Lyon During the Voyage of Discovery under Captain Parry* (London, 1824).
    7. Probably John Crawfurd's *History of the Indian Archipelago* (London, 1820).
    8. Guizot had been appointed ambassador to London the preceding February. JSM would have met Guizot on March 17 at the Grotes' had he not been detained at Falmouth by his brother Henry's illness. See Pym, I, 134. But see Letter 291.
    9. The return of Thiers to power in March, 1840, as Premier was regarded as a triumph for the liberals.

* * * *

    1. Published in Mayer, pp. 327–29. MS in Tocqueville archives.

& have now finished one careful perusal of it: several more will be required before I can master it, for although my own thoughts have been accustomed (especially since I read your First Part) to run very much in the same direction, you have so far outrun me that I am lost in the distance, & it will require much thought & study to appropriate your ideas so completely as to be qualified to say what portion of them I shall at last feel to be demonstrated & what, if any, may seem to require further confirmation. In any case you have accomplished a great achievement: you have changed the face of political philosophy, you have carried on the discussions respecting the tendencies of modern society, the causes of those tendencies, & the influences of particular forms of polity & social order, into a region both of height & of depth, which no one before you had entered, & all previous argumentation and speculation in such matters appears but child's play now. I do not think that anything more important than the publication of your book has happened even in this age of great events—& it is truly happy that it was produced in France & is therefore sure of being read by every thinking person both *in* France and *out* of it. Even in this stupid island where Guizot's Lectures[2] had scarcely penetrated until Guizot himself came here as ambassador—& when hardly anybody knows that there is a French philosophy subsequent to Voltaire—even here your book, *par exception*, is read, because luckily Sir R. Peel praised it,[3] & made the Tories fancy it was a Tory book: but I believe they have found out their error. It could only have been written in France or in England, & if written in England it would probably never have been known beyond a small circle.

Among so many ideas which are more or less new to me I have found (what I consider a very great compliment to the justness of my own views) that one of your great general conclusions is exactly that which I have been almost alone in standing up for here, and have not as far as I know made a single disciple—namely that the real danger in democracy, the real evil to be struggled against, and which all human resources employed while it is not yet too late are not more than sufficient to fence off—is not anarchy or love of change, but Chinese stagnation & immobility. Finding this view of the matter to have presented itself with the same strength of evidence to you, who are the highest living authority (& therefore the highest that has ever lived) on the subject, I shall henceforth regard it as the truth scientifically established, and shall defend it *envers et contre tous* with tenfold pertinacity.

2. The lectures printed in his *Cours d'Histoire moderne* (6 vols., Paris, 1829–32).

3. Peel had praised Tocqueville's book in his inaugural speech as Lord Rector of the University of Glasgow on Jan. 11, 1837, and again at the public dinner at Glasgow on Jan. 13, 1837 (see *A Correct Report of the Speeches by . . . Sir R. Peel . . . on January 11, 1837; and . . . January 13, 1837* (London, 1837).

When I last wrote to you I lamented that from having terminated my connection with the London & Westminster Review I should not have the opportunity of reviewing your book there, but I have now the pleasure of telling you that I am to have the reviewing of it in the Edinburgh Review which as you know is much more read, and which has never had a review of your First Part—I suppose none of the writers dared venture upon it, and I cannot blame them, for that review is the most perfect representative of the 18th century to be found in our day, & that is not the point of view for judging of your book. But I & some others who are going to write in the Ed. Review now, shall perhaps succeed in infusing some young blood into it. They have given me till October for this article.[4]

I received a long & most acceptable letter from Beaumont,[5] when I was 300 miles off, attending a very dear brother in his last illness. I owe him a long letter in return which shall be paid very shortly.

Though I am not a very regular correspondent you may believe me when I say that there is no living man in Europe whom I esteem more highly or of whose friendship I should be more proud than I am of yours. Unfortunately I have only one means of shewing it, but that I have used pretty freely, for your name somehow finds itself under my pen almost whenever I write—.

Ever affectionately yours

J. S. MILL.

India House.

288. TO ROBERT BARCLAY FOX[1]

I.H.
Friday [May 22, 1840][2]

Pray do not think of Saturday for the Museum if you have any other day disposable. My concern for your welfare bids me assure you that it is much pleasanter to go to such places when there is no crowd: besides which I have a secret reason which I do not mean to tell you, viz. that Saturday week is the only possible day on which I could not be there to welcome you, as I am inexorably bound to pass that Saturday and Sunday more than thirty miles from town. Woe is me—but the case is such that there is no help for it.

4. See Letter 285, n. 2.   5. Gustave Beaumont.

* * * *

1. MS in the possession of Mr. W. H. Browning.
2. The Fox family had come to London for a visit of several weeks, in part no doubt to attend the Yearly Meeting of the Society of Friends. The visit to the Museum at the India House, to which this and the following letter refer, took place on Thursday, May 28, 1840. See Pym, I, 197.

If however your ill fortune will have it that you are to see the Museum and Dulwich without my agreeable society, various topics of consolation suggest themselves, as for instance that it will be all the same thing a hundred years hence, that what can't be cured must be endured &c. &c. These & similar reflections I hope will enable you to bear your affliction with becoming fortitude & I will endeavour to support mine with antique heroism, that is to say as the antique heroes always did, by trying all they could to remove the cause of it. As a first step to which I send you an admission for Mondays & Thursdays that you may have no excuse for going on Saturday. Please to fill up the blank with some name or other before you go.

I am glad you are going to Carlyle's[3]—if your sisters can go you should ask leave to bring them.

J.S.M.

289. TO ROBERT WERE FOX[1]

India House
Tuesday
[May 26, 1840]

MY DEAR SIR

I will not take so ungenerous an advantage as not to tell you that Nichol[2] is *not* coming today & that he *is* coming on Thursday. If this should prevent you from coming this evening, the loss is ours—but at least I hope it will not unless you can come on Thursday instead, either to dinner or in the evening.

Mrs. Nichol & I hope Nichol also, will be of the party to the Museum here; & to Dulwich afterwards if what we are hardly allowed to think possible, should come to pass—but if it should not, & if Saturday is the most convenient day to your party, being also as convenient for my sisters as any other, I am not such a dog in the manger as not to protest in the most earnest manner against any consideration being had of me in the matter—especially as I am so much hampered as to hours.

Ever yours faithfully

J. S. MILL

3. Caroline Fox records that on May 19 while attending Carlyle's lecture on "The Hero as Man of Letters" with some of her family they had been introduced to Mrs. Carlyle by Harriet Mill, and had been invited to call. See *ibid.*, p. 182. JSM evidently did not know that Barclay Fox's sisters had already been invited when he wrote this letter. On June 3 both the Foxes and the Carlyles spent the evening at the Mills' home.

* * * *

1. *Addressed*: R. W. Fox Esq / London. MS at LSE.   2. John Pringle Nichol.

290. TO ROBERT BARCLAY FOX[1]

I.H.
Thursday
[June 4, 1840]

MY DEAR FRIEND   As you say you reached home "this morning" I perceive you made no more haste than good speed—indeed to make the former compatible with the latter seemed, under the aspect of affairs last night, rather hopeless.[2] Let me congratulate you on the fact that the safe preservation of all of you was, under these somewhat inauspicious circumstances, achieved. As for us we have none of us experienced anything unpleasant except the remembrance of the shortness of your visit, & the uncertainty which as yet hangs over the next.

You might well doubt whether I had received your note, for such a note surely merited some acknowledgment—however not being able to respond to it in the only suitable manner viz. in verse, I left it without any response at all—feeling all the while a vast respect for you, for being able to write such good verses. But the feelings towards myself which they express require me to say once more how highly I value your friendship & how unexpectedly gratifying it is that in me, seen as you have seen me, you have found as much to like, as these verses seem to indicate. For you have not, nor have even those of your family whom I have been so fortunate as to see more of, as yet seen *me*, as I really & naturally am, but a *me* artificially made self-conscious, egotistical, & noisily demonstrative by having much feeling to shew & very little time to shew it in. If I had been looking forward to living peaceably within a stone's throw or even a few hours' walk or ride of you, I should have been very different. As it is, that poor little sentence of the poor Ashantee[3] really expresses the

1. *Addressed*: R. Barclay Fox Esq. / S. Gurney Esq. / Ham House / West Ham. *Postmark*: JU 4 1840. Published by Pym, II, 333–34, but dated "probably July 1842." MS in the possession of Mr. W. H. Browning.
2. This refers to an episode on the Foxes' return from a party at the Mills', described by Caroline Fox in her journal (Pym, I, 204), under June 3, 1840: "At last we were going, but our postillion was fast asleep on the coach-box. Barclay gave him an intimation of our presence, to which he languidly replied, 'All right,' but in a voice that showed clearly that it was all wrong. We asked for a hackney coach, but J. S. Mill was delightfully ignorant as to where such things grew, or where a likely hotel was to be found; and as our culprit was now a little sobered by fright and evening air, and passionately pleaded wife and children, we ventured forward, Barclay and J. Mill walking for a long way beside us."
3. Probably a reference to a remark of one of two young princes of Ashantee, William Quantamissa and John Ansah, who with their tutor, the Rev. T. Pyne, visited Falmouth in April, 1840 (see Pym, I, 168–72, and *The Times*, April 25, 1840, p. 5). In July the princes visited Wordsworth in the Lake Country (see Mrs. [Eliza] Fletcher, *Autobiography* [Edinburgh, 1875], 247–48).

spirit of all I have said & done with regard to any of your party, almost from the beginning until now, when one is to be but a remembrance, it is difficult to refrain from even awkward attempts to make the remembrance last for more than a few days or weeks.

And now till I have the opportunity of doing it myself, will you express for me, my warmest regards to your father & mother—& for your sisters & yourself, remember that you have not only as many additional "blessings in disguise" as there are sisters at Kensington, but also (unless it be peculiarly a feminine designation) one more, namely, yours affectionately

J. S. MILL

291. TO GUSTAVE D'EICHTHAL[1]

India House
17th June 1840

MY DEAR D'EICHTHAL

Your very interesting letter came in due course. As the prices of the books seemed to me reasonable, & quite as low as it was likely Mr Rainford[2] could procure them for without waiting, perhaps a considerable time, for an opportunity, I sent your note at once to Mr Russell Smith.[3] On receiving your subsequent note I called on Mr Smith who told me that the books were sent to Paris, in a parcel along with other books, on the 7th of this month, & that as soon as they arrived, you would receive a letter by the petite poste informing you where to send for them.

Since I received your letter I have written to M. Michelet. I addressed my letter *aux archives du royaume*. If you have an opportunity perhaps you would ask him whether it arrived properly. But it did not require nor did I expect any answer.

I dined last Saturday with M. Guizot whose conversation quite corresponds to the high idea I had formed of him from his writings. He was very kind & gave me a general invitation to call upon him. His having come here as ambassador is a real *événement*, for it makes our stupid incurious people read his books. You would be astonished how few here, even yet, know that there is such a thing as a philosophy of the 19th century in France, different from the 18th. We are certainly an ignorant nation, with all our self-conceit —& by reason of it. Still, we are improving—the best ideas of the age are

1. *Addressed*: Monsieur / Gustave d'Eichthal / 14 Rue Lepelletier / à Paris. *Postmarks*: G / JU 17 / 1840 and LONDON / 17. Published in part in *Cosmopolis*, IX, p. 372, and in *D'Eichthal Corresp.*, pp. 181–82. MS at Arsenal.
2. See Letter 286.
3. Probably R. Smith, bookseller at 25 Foley St., Portland Place, London.

in some degree insinuating themselves into our minds, though we in general are very little aware how or from whence they come to us.

You may measure the distance between France & England by that between Guizot & Peel, each the leader of the Conservative party in their respective countries. Happily though we are slow we are sure. We are the ballast of Europe, France its sail.

ever yours truly

J. S. MILL.

292. TO JOHN MITCHELL KEMBLE[1]

India House
26th June 1840

MY DEAR SIR

I know you will not consider it an intrusion on my part to ask you whether among the many persons of mental cultivation & attainments with whom you must necessarily be acquainted, who have the world still "before them where to choose"[2] & perhaps nothing very promising as yet offered for their choice, there be any one whom you could recommend as tutor to the eldest son (about twelve years old) of a person of very high rank[3] & of ideas & aspirations on the subject of education, considerably above what are common in any rank? I am not yet at liberty to say who the party is— it has only been told to me in confidence, because if it were to transpire there would be a troublesome quantity of applications & a corresponding number of disappointments. But there is, probably, no situation of the kind in England in respect to which more important consequences may depend on its being well filled.

Do you think your friend Mr. Edgeworth[4] would accept such a situation? & do you think him qualified for it? I only mention him because his writings prove him to be a man of considerable powers & accomplishments, & I think I have understood that he is not in such circumstances as would prevent his taking employment of this kind.

Ever truly yours

J. S. MILL

1. *Addressed*: J. M. Kemble, Esq. MS in the possession of Professor Ney MacMinn, Northwestern University.
2. Milton, *Paradise Lost*, Book XII, l. 646.   3. Unidentified.
4. Francis Beaufort Edgeworth (1809–1846), half-brother of the novelist Maria Edgeworth; he had been a student with Kemble and Sterling at Cambridge and had contributed to Kemble's *British and Foreign Review*. He had at one point set up a school at Eltham (see *Letters and Literary Remains of Edward Fitzgerald*, ed. W. A. Wright [London, 1889], I, 36). For a sketch of Edgeworth, see Thomas Carlyle, *Life of John Sterling* (London, 1851), Part II, chap. 4.

293. TO [JOHN MITCHELL KEMBLE?][1]

I.H.
Thursday
[July, 1840?]

MY DEAR SIR

It would seem that Mr Edgeworth[2] is still at Edgeworthstown, but I know that he is, or was till lately, often in or near London. I wait for your further instructions before authorizing any communication to him.

From the little I know or have heard of the Mr Thompson[3] whom you speak of, I should think his recommendation a valuable one.

Ever yours truly
J. S. MILL

294. TO ROBERT BARCLAY FOX[1]

Kensington 3d August 1840

MY DEAR FRIEND   Your letter came & was most welcome, & the same may be said of certain other missives[2] which I had the pleasure of despatching to Guildford. It was very pleasant to be able to figure to oneself your mode of existence at Penjerrick[3]—I often think one never knows one's friends or rather they are not properly one's friends until one has seen them in their home, & can figure to oneself some part at least of their daily existence. I am sure we all feel much nearer to all of you by having become so familiar with your local habitation or I may say habitations, & with so many of your haunts on that lovely coast—how often I fancy myself looking through the transparent spring air across the lovely blue bay to Pennance[4]—nor are reminiscences of Penjerrick either unfrequent or faint.

1. MS at LSE. No indication of person addressed. Paper bears watermark, 1838.
2. See preceding letter.   3. Unidentified.

* * * *

1. *Addressed*: R. Barclay Fox Esq. / Falmouth. *Postmark*: AUG 4 1840. Partly published by Pym, II, 313–15. MS in the possession of Mr. W. H. Browning.
2. Probably letters by Caroline and Anna Maria Fox to JSM's sisters, who were evidently spending part of the summer at Guildford, as they did in 1841 (see Letter 324).
3. The summer home of the Foxes, several miles from Falmouth.
4. *Sic*. Possibly *Penzance*, but Caroline Fox refers several times to walks to Pennance (see Pym, I, 109, 111, 119, 153).

It is curious that your letter about Tocqueville & Brown[5] found me also occupied with both of them—reviewing the one,[6] & reading the other once again after an interval of many years. I have not however yet got to his theory of the moral feelings, & though I remember that I did not like it, & took great pains, as I fancied quite successfully, to refute it, I cannot say I remember what it is—& so many of my philosophical opinions have changed since, that I can trust no judgment which dates from so far back in my history. My renewed acquaintance with Brown shews me that I was not mistaken in thinking he had made a number of oversights, but I also see that he has even more than I formerly thought of these characteristic merits which made me recommend him as the best *one* author in whom to study that great subject. I think you have described his book by the right epithets, & I would add to them that it seems to me the very book from which to learn both in theory & by example the true *method* of philosophising—the analysis in his early lectures of the true nature & amount of what we can learn of the phenomena of the world, seems to me perfect, & his mode of inquiry into the mind is strictly founded upon that analysis.

As for Tocqueville I do not wonder that you should find him difficult, for in the first place the philosophical writers of the present day have made almost a new French language, & in the next place he is really abstruse— by being so abstract, & not sufficiently (especially in the 2d part) *illustrating* his propositions. I find it tough work reviewing him, much tougher than I expected, especially as I was prevented from beginning so soon as I ought.

So you are now all or nearly all reassembled & we again see or fancy the family picture in its accustomed & original frame. That is much, although not so much as it would have been if we had not seen you in the opposite circumstances of London—I was going to say the *uncongenial* circumstances, but you are all so happily constituted that no circumstances are uncongenial to you—still some are more congenial than others & I can fancy for instance that if you were standing beside Sterling in one of Raphael's *stanze* in the Vatican you would find the situation very congenial *indeed*.

I cease to regret Sterling's sudden departure when I learnt that your party had had so much more of him & he of them in consequence of it.[7] What a pleasant winding up of their "mankind" tour.

5. Thomas Brown, author of *Observations on the Nature and Tendency of the Doctrine of Mr Hume concerning the relation of cause and effect* (Edinburgh, 1805), and *Lectures on the Philosophy of the Human Mind* (4 vols., Edinburgh, 1820).
6. See Letter 285, n. 2.
7. Sterling had returned to his family at Clifton, where the Foxes were visitors in July. See Pym, I, 206–15.

I return the old Michelet[8] with my prayer that your youngest sister whom I have hardly yet forgiven for not taking it & who must by this time be weary of the sight of it, will make haste to lay it up in some crypt of her autograph-cabinet & let the world see no more of it. I trust she is satisfied, for I have now kept it till another came—which proves to me by the extravagance of its compliments upon the letter I wrote to him, that if one gives a man exactly the sort of praise he wants to receive, one is sure of getting into his good graces.

The knowledge that an autograph of Guizot has probably reached you or will reach you from other quarters consoles me for not having one to offer—for his invitations to dinner are printed forms. I have dined with him again but one gets so little real conversation with any one who has to attend to his guests. The last time it was a most successfully made up party, I mean that fortune was most propitious to me in particular for of six guests three were persons I always like to meet & two of the other three were the two persons I most wished to meet—Thirlwall,[9] with whom I renewed an acquaintance of which the only event was a speech he made in reply to one of mine when I was a youth of nineteen—(it has remained impressed upon me ever since as the finest speech I ever heard)—& Gladstone whom I had never seen at all—and with both these I hope I have laid the foundation of a further knowledge especially as Thirlwall will now be in town in parliament time. How delighted Sterling must be at finding him a bishop—but hardly more so than I am.

Have you heard yet that Cunningham after all will only let us have *one* likeness of the present deponent[10]—so how my mother & Sterling are to settle it I do not know, as Mammy resolutely declines the equitable method of tossing up a halfpenny.

My sisters I dare say have written this very day. Pray tell us how your Aunt at Clifton[11] goes on & when your mother returns.

Your message to Carlyle shall be delivered—ever faithfully

J. S. MILL

8. Evidently an autograph of the French historian. JSM had contributed other autographs to Caroline Fox's collection.

9. Connop Thirlwall had recently been raised to the Bishopric of St. David's. His speech to the Co-operative Society in 1825 in reply to one of JSM's is also referred to in similar terms in the *Autobiog.*, pp. 87–88.

10. JSM had his portrait painted while in Falmouth by a painter named Cunningham. Caroline Fox describes the portrait as "very beautiful; quite an ideal head, so expanded with patient thought, and a face of such exquisite refinement" (journal, April 10, 1840, in Pym, I, 168). Efforts to trace this portrait have not been successful.

11. Not identified.

295. TO MACVEY NAPIER[1]

India House
5th September
1840

MY DEAR SIR

My article[2] has gone to Longman's this day. Whether it will answer your expectation I cannot venture to predict—but you will not find me, (as I have generally found those who have themselves conducted periodicals) an intractable contributor. If you were to bid me cancel the whole article & begin again, it would be no more than I have done before now with other articles of mine at the instigation of my own editor.

If the article suits you & it is not inconsistent with the practice of your Review, I should like to have half a dozen or at most a dozen separate copies chiefly to send abroad (of course I will readily pay the expense of them)—& I should also like to reserve the power of reprinting my articles & particularly this one, as I intend next spring to publish a collection of the few things I have written which either I or any one else thinks worth preserving, & I should like to include this in it as forming a sort of completion & winding up of the view which the publication will exhibit of my present opinions & modes of thinking.

With regard to alterations I repeat that you will not find me troublesome, but I should like, whenever time permits, to have the making of them myself. I do not mean that I object to your making any alteration in the first instance, since it often happens that the shortest & best way of making the nature of an objection intelligible is to suggest the *exact* change which would remove it.

Ever my dear Sir
Yours truly

J. S. MILL

296. TO MACVEY NAPIER[1]

India House
21st September
1840

MY DEAR SIR

Allow me to thank you for your kind compliance, & more than compliance, with my wishes about the separate copies & the power of reprinting

1. MS in Brit. Mus.   2. On Tocqueville's *Democracy in America*.

* * * *

1. MS in Brit. Mus. Published, with one omission, in *Napier Corresp.*, pp. 327–29.

& to express the pleasure it gives me that you should have found reason to think favorably of my article.[2] Of course I cannot have the slightest objection to the omission of the sentence you mention, & am only glad that it is the only one upon which you feel it necessary to exercise your editorial scissors. I was prepared to find that there were parts of the article in which you could not agree, but on the points you mention I think a little explanation would remove most of the difference between us. I did not mean to class the power of combination as an element (except in a certain limited sense) of *fitness* for political power but only as one of the causes which actually *create* a political power whether the parties are fit for it or not. And my argument requires no more. My remarks also on Tocqueville's opinion that democracy does not bring to the helm the fittest persons for government, were only intended to moderate the strength with which he claims admission for that opinion, & to suggest grounds of hesitation & further examination; not to contradict the opinion itself for on the whole I to a great degree coincide in it, though not to the extent to which he carries it.

On the possibility of a mixed government it is probable that you & I & Tocqueville would on explanation agree. I agree & have long agreed in all you say on the point, but he would say that one of the three powers always *could* by constitutional means, carry any point it was in earnest about, if it chose to encounter the consequent odium & that the other two could *not* unless aided by the *one* or by a portion of it.

About future articles—those which I have chiefly thought about would require a good deal of reading & reflection, & considering that I have a book to finish I could hardly venture to name any particular time for their being ready. They are mostly historical—for instance one on the Romans & their history, a propos of Arnold's History and Michelet's—or, if you think the French Revolution not too stale a subject, I could write an article on Alison's book,[3] or on the Histoire Parlementaire[4] that would perhaps have still something of novelty in its views. But I should not like to undertake either of these if it were necessary to appoint any time within a year for their being ready—though they might *possibly* be finished much sooner. If I am to undertake anything soon it must be something requiring less time & research.

I have been much pressed to write on the Report (or rather Minutes of Evidence) of the Committee on Currency & Banks—especially by Mr. Tooke[5] with whom I agree on the subject more than with anybody else who has written on it—but I suppose you would look to McCulloch[6] on

2. See preceding letter, n. 2.
3. See Letter 72, n. 13.   4. See Letter 101, n. 12.
5. Thomas Tooke.   6. John Ramsay McCulloch.

that question, and even if he were not likely as I suppose he is, to write on it himself, you would probably hardly think it fair to him to put in an article which would contain what he would consider heresies. Mr. Tooke says he has no doubt the *Quarterly* would take it, & perhaps it would, but I think liberal writers ought to stick to liberal reviews, & my adhesion to the Edinburgh is in a certain sense political as well as literary.

Believe me, with much satisfaction at the new connexion which is now formed between us,

Yours ever faithfully

J. S. MILL

297. TO JOHN STERLING[1]

I.H.

1st Oct. 1840

MY DEAR STERLING

Döring's Life of Goethe[2] is a little book, about as long as one of the thicker volumes of the small edition of Goethe's works: therefore unless by a really first rate hand it is likely to be but meagre. The booksellers say it is thought well of but I can learn nothing specific about it. They know of no other Life. Nutt[3] says the price is six sh^s but offered me for four sh. the only copy he had, a worn one. A bookseller named Senior says the price is 4 s. but he had sold all his copies. Shall I order one from him? & shall it be sent to Knightsbridge?

I am to have a dozen separate copies of my review of Tocqueville & I will send you one. There is a review of him in Blackwood,[4] cleverish but hollow. What an antigallican tone in this whole number of Blackwood: & not a man among the writers who is not persuaded that he knows the whole French people, intus et in cute.[5] There is much more danger of war than people are aware of.[6] More than one credible testimony of Frenchmen now in Paris or lately there, assures me that the war feeling there is uni-

1. In reply to Sterling's letter from Clifton, Sept. 21, 1840 (MS at King's). MS at Leeds. Part published in Elliot, I, 118.
2. J. M. H. Döring, *J. W. v. Göthe's Leben* (Weimar, 1828), about which Sterling had inquired.
3. David Nutt (1810–1863), bookseller in Fleet Street, of whom Sterling had asked JSM to make inquiries.
4. *Blackwood's*, XLVIII (Oct., 1840), 463–78.
5. "inside and out." Cf. Persius, Satire III, 30.
6. In the autumn of 1840 there were widespread fears that Palmerston's policies with respect to intervention in the Levant to support Turkey against Mohammed Ali of Egypt might bring war between England and France. Thiers, the French Premier, who threatened war, was ousted in Oct. and succeeded by Guizot. By the end of the year Palmerston was widely credited with a great triumph. Liberals and Radicals in general, however, opposed him for aligning England with Russia, Prussia, and Austria. See also Letters 300 and 303.

versal, & has for the time silenced all others, that even those whose personal interests are opposed to it share the feeling, & that there is not now one voice against the fortifying of Paris which excited such clamour a few years ago. And that this is not from love of war, for they dislike it, but because they feel themselves *blessé* & humiliated as a nation. This is foolish, but who can wonder at it in a people whose country has within this generation been twice occupied by foreign armies? If that were our case we should have plenty of the same feeling. But it is melancholy to see the rapid revival of hatred on their side & jealous dislike on ours.

I am curious to see the review of Carlyle in the Quarterly.[7] From extracts I have no doubt it is by the author of the article on Socialism.[8] Merivale's article[9] has many sound criticisms, as much of appreciation as you can expect from an Edinburgh reviewer, & a few damnable heresies. Carlyle's dislike of it seems to me excessive, & nothing that he says surprises me more than that he should think Macaulay would have done it better. Macaulay would not have had half as much appreciation of him.

What you say about the absence of a disinterested & heroic pursuit of Art as the greatest want of England at present, has often struck me, but I suspect it will not be otherwise until our social struggles are over. Art needs earnest but quiet times—in ours I am afraid Art itself to be powerful must be polemical—Carlylean not Goethian—but "I speak as to the wise—judge ye what I say."—

Ever yours,

J. S. MILL

298. TO SIR WILLIAM MOLESWORTH[1]

19th November 1840

Your Leeds demonstration seems to me a very proper thing, done in the very best way, and I think that is the general impression about it. I cannot but think it has done, and will do, good both in France and here, and I am sure it has had a good effect in raising your public character.

7. "Carlyle's Works," *QR*, LXVI (Sept., 1840), 446–503. The review was by the Rev. William Sewell. See Francis Espinasse, *Literary Recollections* (London, 1893), p. 77 n.

8. "Socialism," *QR*, LXV (March, 1840), 484–527.

9. Herman Merivale (1806–1874), then professor of political economy at Oxford, later Under-Secretary for India. His article on Carlyle's *French Revolution* (2nd ed.) had appeared in *ER*, LXXI (July, 1840), 411–45.

* * * *

1. Excerpt published in Fawcett, p. 217. MS not located.

On Nov. 7, 1840, at the height of the war scare, Molesworth addressed a large audience of his constituents at Leeds, attacking Palmerston's policies and urging the maintenance of peace with France. The meeting, which passed a resolution heartily endorsing Molesworth's position, was reported in the *Examiner*, Nov. 15, 1840, p. 729.

299. TO MACVEY NAPIER[1]

India House
23[d] Nov[r] 1840

MY DEAR SIR

Many thanks for the very handsome payment which reached me this morning.

I have not yet seen Fletcher since I returned to town, but I am in daily expectation of doing so. He is unfortunately apt to be behind his time & though he was particularly anxious not to be so in this instance he was also particularly desirous to do his very best which may perhaps cause him to be behindhand—but I hope not.

I will keep Arnold in view[2] & set to work upon him as soon as I can. How soon that will be I do not precisely know: but it may very possibly be in time for your spring number. I feel much obliged for the latitude you give me.

Ever yours
in haste

J. S. MILL

300. TO ROBERT BARCLAY FOX[1]

I.H.
25 Nov. 1840

MY DEAR FRIEND It is very long since I either heard from you or wrote to you, but the correspondence between your sisters & mine, which is considerably more active than ours, has kept up a sort of communication between us, which though very agreeable I do not find entirely to supply the place of direct correspondence. I am not, I know, entitled to expect frequent letters while I shew myself so remiss in fulfilling my own part of the implied contract between absent friends. But we people whose whole life is passed in writing either to "Our Governor General of India in Council" or to everybody's governor general the English public, are I believe excusable if we like better to receive letters than to write them. I enclose a copy of a recent epistle of mine[2] to the latter of those great authorities. It will reappear as part of two little volumes which although you already have nearly all the contents of them, will some time or other in the course of next year appear before you as suppliants for a place on your shelf. About

1. MS in Brit. Mus.   2. See Letter 285, n. 4.

* * * *

1. *Addressed*: R. B. Fox Esq. Published with omissions by Pym, II, 316–17. MS in the possession of W. H. Browning.
2. Presumably his review of Tocqueville in the Oct., 1840, *ER*.

the same time I hope to have finished a big book[3] the first draft of which I put the last hand to a few weeks ago. I do not know whether the subject of it will interest you—but as you have been so much pleased with Brown,[4] many of whose views I have adopted, perhaps it may.

We have all of us been in great trepidation about the state of affairs in Europe. It would have been too bad if the two most lightheaded men in Europe, Palmerston[5] and Thiers, had been suffered to embroil the whole world[6] & do mischief which no one now living would have seen repaired. I do not know which of the two I feel most indignant with. The immediate danger is I hope over, but the evil already done is incalculable—the confidence which all Europe felt in the preservation of peace will not for many years be re-established & the bestial antipathies between nations & especially between France & England have been rekindled to a deplorable extent. All the hope is that founded on the French character which as it is excitable by small causes may also be calmed by slight things—& accordingly alternates between resentment against England and Anglomania.

You know of course that George[7] is at Torquay & also that Sterling is there, perhaps for the winter, perhaps only till he sets out for Italy. With kind regards to all, ever faithfully yours,

J. S. MILL.

301. TO GEORGE HENRY LEWES[1]

I.H.
Thursday
[probably late 1840]

MY DEAR SIR

I lost no time in setting about your paper on Shelley.[2] It abounds in true & important things & yet (for I know you want me to tell you exactly the impression it has made upon me) there is something about it which satisfies me less than is usually the case with your writings. It is easier however to say this, than to tell exactly what that *something* is, or to point out how the article could have been or could now be improved. After thinking a good deal about it I can get no nearer than this—that you do

---

3. The *Logic*, not published until 1843.   4. Thomas Brown. See Letter 294, n. 5.
5. Henry John Temple, third Viscount Palmerston (1784–1865), Secretary of State for Foreign Affairs (1830–41) and later Prime Minister.
6. See Letter 297, n. 6.
7. JSM's youngest brother. The reason for George's visit to Torquay can only be surmised; perhaps he was already manifesting symptoms of the family disease, tuberculosis, which was to lead to his early death, and the milder climate of Torquay had been recommended.

*   *   *   *

1. Published in Kitchel, p. 28. MS at Columbia University.
George Henry Lewes (1817–1878), writer, later the husband of George Eliot.
2. The paper appeared in *WR*, XXXV (April, 1841), 303–44, signed G.H.L.

not seem to me to have laid down for yourself with sufficient definiteness, what precise impression you wished to produce, & upon what class of readers. It was particularly needful to have a distinct view of this sort when writing on a subject on which there are so many rocks & shoals to be kept clear of. For example I think you should have begun by determining whether you were writing for those who required a *vindication* of Shelley or for those who wanted a *criticism* of his poems or for those who wanted a biographic Carlylian *analysis* of him as a *man*. I doubt if it is possible to combine all these things, but I am sure at all events that the unity necessary in an essay of any kind as a work of art requires at least that one of these should be the predominant purpose & the others only incidental to it. If I can venture an opinion on so difficult & delicate a matter, I would say that the idea of a *vindication* should be abandoned. Shelley can only be usefully vindicated from a point of view nearer that occupied by those to whom a vindication of him is still needed. I have seen very useful and effective vindications of him by religious persons, & in a religious tone: but *we*, I think, should leave that to others, & should take for granted, boldly, all those premisses respecting freedom of thought & the morality of acting on one's own *credo*, which to anyone who admits them, carry Shelley's vindication with them. By descending into that other arena I think we only spoil what is already going on much better than anything we can do in that way can possibly mend.

I intended to say but a word now, & more when we meet, but I have run on to this length—I will add that there are several things in the article which Hickson could not, I am sure, with any common prudence print in his review.

You are certainly a conjurer, in finding out my old obscure articles. The only valuable thing in these two[3] is I think the distinction between poetry & oratory. The "Genius"[4] paper is no favorite with me, especially in its boyish stile. It was written in the height of my Carlylism, a vice of style which I have since carefully striven to correct & as I think you should do— there is too much of it in the Shelley. I think Carlyle's costume should be left to Carlyle whom alone it becomes & in whom it would soon become unpleasant if it were made common—& I have seen as you must have done, grievous symptoms of its being taken up by the lowest of the low.

As to my Logic, it has all to be rewritten yet.

ever yours,

J. S. MILL

come soon.

---

3. "What is Poetry?" (in which appears the distinction between poetry and oratory) and "The Two Kinds of Poetry" (which compares Wordsworth and Shelley), *MR*, VII (Jan. and Oct., 1833), 60–70, 714–24. See Letter 85, n. 3.
4. "On Genius," *MR*, VI (Oct., 1832), 649–59. See Letter 49, n. 2.

302. TO JOHN STERLING[1]

3rd December, 1840.

MY DEAR STERLING—I suppose this will reach you although directed only to the Torquay Post Office. I write only to keep up the thread of our correspondence, as I have nothing very particular to say.

When I advised you, if you go to Italy, to see Genoa and the Corniche, I forgot that you had not seen Venice and Munich. You certainly ought by no means to miss the pictures, of course, better than anything you would see there, though I cannot help thinking that the Venetian school is but the Flemish "with a difference"—that difference being chiefly the difference between Italian physique and Belgian or Dutch. But then again some of the sculptures at Munich are among the very first extant—and *you* will be interested in the modern German art; it is probably from knowing nothing of the subject, that what I saw of it appears to me a feeble, hot-house product. But *quære* whether anything so essentially objective as painting and sculpture can thrive in Germany—any more than Shakespeare or Beethoven could have been produced in Italy. This, however,[2] is *sus Minervam.*[3]

Have you any idea who that Fellow of St John's is, who publishes in the Monthly Chronicle his notes on Italy?[4] He has something in him but seems, as yet, very [low?] & inexperienced. Have you read either of Laing's books?[5] You should read his defence of them in the said Monthly Chronicle.[6]

I have been considering whether I ought to postpone revising my Logic in order to read the German books you mention. On the whole I think not,—their way of looking at such matters is so very different from mine, which is founded on the methods of physical science, & entirely *a posteriori.*—

Ever yours faithfully

J. S. MILL

I suppose George has seen you though we have not heard from him since—

1. *Addressed*: Rev. John Sterling / Post Office / Torquay. *Postmark*: PAID / DE 3 / 1840. In reply to Sterling's letter of Nov. 20, 1840 (MS at King's). Part of letter at LSE. Published with omissions in Elliot, I, 118–19.
2. The portion of the original letter which is at LSE begins with this word.
3. "A sow teaching the Goddess of Wisdom," a saying of ancient Greek origin (cf. Plutarch, *Demosthenes* 11, and Cicero, *De Oratore* 2.57.233 and *Academica* 1.5.18.
4. "Letters from the Continent," *Monthly Chronicle*, VI(July-Dec., 1840), 196–224, 289–315, 399–433, 505–31, and VII (1841), 11–37.
5. Samuel Laing (1780–1868), traveller and author of *A Journal of a Residence in Norway* (London, 1836); and *A Tour in Sweden* (London, 1839).
6. "Sweden and Norway," *Monthly Chronicle*, VI (Nov., 1840), 385–97.

303. TO JOHN STERLING[1]

I.H.
19th Dec[r]
1840

MY DEAR STERLING

In consequence of what you wrote about Ritter's book[2] I have, after two unsuccessful attempts to get it in London, ordered it from Germany.

I think & feel very much as you do on the subject of the bad spirit manifested in France by so many politicians & writers & unhappily by some from whom better things were to be expected. But this does not appear to me to strengthen Palmerston's justification.[3] I do not believe that Thiers would have acted, in power, in a manner at all like his braggadocio afterwards when he knew that he had only the turbulent part of the population to throw himself upon, & no watchword to use but the old ones about making the Mediterranean a French lake, getting rid of the treaties of 1815, &c. I have no doubt that he would have attempted to make such an arrangement as should leave a powerful state at that end of the Mediterranean under French influence & I think he had a good right to attempt this, & we no right at all to hinder it if the arrangement was not objectionable on any other account. It appears to me very provoking treatment of France that England & Russia should be extending their influence every year till it embraces all Asia & that we should be so indignant at the bare supposition that France wishes to do a little of what we do on so much larger a scale. It is true we do it almost in spite of ourselves, & rather wish to keep others out than to get ourselves in; but we cannot expect France to think so, or to regard our professing it as anything but attempting to humbug them & not doing it well. I believe that no harm whatever to Europe would have resulted from French influence with Mehemet Ali,[4] & it would have been easy to *bind* France against any future occupation of the country for herself. We should then have avoided raising this mis-

1. In reply to Sterling's letter of Dec. 9, 1840 (MS at King's; part published in Tuell, *John Sterling*, pp. 72–74 and 131–32). MS at Leeds. Part published in Elliot, I, 119–20.
2. August Heinrich Ritter, *Vorlesungen zur Einleitung in die Logik* (Berlin, 1823). Sterling had also recommended books by Twesten, Schleiermacher, and Hegel.
3. See Letter 297, n. 6. Sterling on Dec. 9 had written: "Lord Palmerston went on much stronger grounds than I supposed in his bellicose policy. Thiers clearly meant himself and expected the support of the country in designing to frustrate any arrangement that would not leave Egypt strong & independent & Turkey nearly impotent—in order that France might at the first opportunity seize for herself the possessions that she thus would have detached even with an absolute certainty that Russia would in consequence obtain all the rest of Turkey." (Tuell, *John Sterling*, pp. 131–32.)
4. Mehemet (or Mohammed) Ali (1769–1849), Viceroy of Egypt.

chievous spirit in France—the least evil of which will be what Lord P.'s supporters no doubt think a great one, viz. that in another year France will be in strict alliance as to all Eastern matters with Russia as the only power who will give her anything for her support & moreover as her only means of retaliating upon England.

No one seems to me to have raised himself by this but Guizot, & he has done what perhaps no other man could have done & almost certainly none so well.

I am extremely grateful for your attentions to George & glad that you give so good an account of him. I wish you had been able to give a better one of the health of your own family. I have not seen either Carlyle or Mrs. Austin (I think) since I last wrote to you. Calvert I have heard nothing of for a long time except the rather indifferent news of him in your letter.

This is only an apology for a letter but for the present it must serve—

ever faithfully

J. S. MILL

304. TO ROBERT BARCLAY FOX[1]

Kensington
23d Decr 1840

MY DEAR FRIEND

I return with many thanks what I ought to have returned much sooner, the notes of the Welsh sermon. It is a really admirable specimen of popular eloquence, of a rude kind—it is well calculated to go to the very core of an untaught hearer—I believe there is much preaching of that character among the Methodists & more perhaps among their still wilder kindred the Ranters &c. Do you know Ebenezer Elliott's poem of *the Ranter?*[2] This might be such a man—I believe even this does good when it really penetrates the crust of a sensual & stupid boor who never thought or knew that he had a soul or concerned himself about his spiritual state. But in allowing that this may do good I am making a great concession, for I confess it is as revolting to me as it was to Coleridge[3] to find infinite justice represented as a sort of demoniacal rage that must be appeased by blood & anguish but provided it has that, cares not whether it be the blood &

1. Published, with omissions, in Pym, II, 317–21. MS in the possession of Mr. W. H. Browning.
2. In *The Splendid Village; Corn Law Rhymes; and Other Poems* (London, 1834), I, 141–56.
3. Cf. his *Aids to Reflection* in *The Complete Works of Samuel Taylor Coleridge*, ed. W.G. T. Shedd (New York, 1853), I, 277.

anguish of the guilty or the innocent. It seems to be but one step farther, & a step which in spirit at least is often taken, to say of God what the Druids said of their gods that the *only* acceptable sacrifice to them was a victim pure & without taint. I know not how dangerous may be the ground on which I am treading, or how far the view of the Atonement which is taken by this poor preacher may be recognised by your Society or by yourself; but surely a more christianlike interpretation of that mystery is that which—believing that Divine Wisdom punishes the sinner for the sinner's sake & not from an inherent necessity, more heathen than the heathen Nemesis—holds as Coleridge did[4] that the sufferings of the Redeemer were (in accordance with the eternal laws on which this system of things is built) an indispensable means of bringing about that change in the hearts of sinners, the want of which is the real & sole hindrance to the universal salvation of mankind.

I marvel greatly at the accuracy of memory which could enable Mrs Charles Fox[5] to write down from recollection so wonderfully vivid and evidently almost literally correct report of this sermon. I know that Friends cultivate that kind of talent but I should think few attain so high a degree of it.

The Testimony of the Yearly Meeting[6] I have read with great interest & though I had read several similar documents before I do not remember any in which the peculiarities of the Society in reference to the questions of Church Government &c which agitate the present day, are so pointedly stated & so vigorously enforced.

I am glad you have seen Molesworth. He is genuine, & *is perfectly* the thing he is; complete within his limited sphere. One ought to be satisfied with that; so few are as much & so very, very few are more. A man of Molesworth's sort of limitation has a natural tendency to be intolerant, because unappreciative of ideas & persons unlike him & his ideas—I knew how to excuse all that because I have been just like him myself & I believe knowing me keeps him out of much intolerance & prejudice because he sees that many things which are nothing to him are much to one whom he allows to be fully a match for him in the things in which his strength lies. I believe if I have done any good a large share of it lies in the example of a professed logician & political economist who believes there are other things besides logic & political economy. Molesworth in spite of his bluster, at least half believes it too, on trust from me. *Par exemple* one that will never be made to believe it at all, least in the sense I do, is one of the best of men & a highly instructed man too, Mr Grote—of whom Mrs Grote,

4. Cf. *ibid.*, pp. 303, 307. Punctuation has been supplied in this sentence.
5. Sarah Fox (née Hustler), wife of Charles Fox of Trebah (near Falmouth) and aunt of Robert Barclay, Caroline, and Anna Maria Fox.
6. Of the Society of Friends.

with more natural quickness & natural liveliness, is in point of opinions the caricature.

I am glad you like my article. I have just had a letter from Tocqueville[7] who is more delighted with it than I ventured to hope for. He touches on politics, mourning over the rupture of the Anglo-French alliance & as the part he took in debate has excited much surprise & disapproval here it is right to make known what he professes as his creed on the matter, viz. that if you wish to keep any people, especially so mobile a people as the French, in the disposition of mind which enables them to do great things you must by no means teach them to be reconciled to other people's making no account of them. They were treated, he thinks, with so great a degree of slight (to say the least) by our government that for their public men not to shew a feeling of *blessure* would have been to lower the standard of national pride which in the present state of the world he thinks almost the only elevated sentiment that remains in considerable strength. There is really a great deal in this although it does not justify & scarcely excuses the revival of the old national animosity or even the warlike demonstrations & preparations. A nation can shew itself offended without threatening a vengeance out of proportion to the affront & which would involve millions that never offended them with units that did, besides ruining themselves in the end, or rather in the beginning. And the tricky policy of Thiers, which is like the whole character of the man, is not in the least palliated by the offence given. But I do think it quite contemptible in England to treat the bare suspicion of France seeking for influence in the East as something too horrible to be thought of; England meanwhile progressively embracing the whole of Asia in her own grasp. Really to read our newspapers any one would fancy such a thing as a European nation acquiring territory & dependent allies in the East, were a thing never dreamt of till France perfidiously cast a covetous eye on the dominions of Mehemet Ali. I cannot find words to express my contempt of the whole conduct of our government or my admiration for the man who has conjured away as much as was possible of the evil done & has attained the noblest end, in a degree no one else could, by the noblest means. Of course, I mean Guizot who now stands before the world as immeasurably the greatest public man living. I cannot think without humiliation of some things I have written years ago of such a man as this, when I thought him a dishonest politician.[8] I confounded the prudence of a wise man who lets

---

7. Dated Dec. 18, 1840; in Mayer, pp. 329–31.

8. Despite his earlier distrust of Guizot as a politician (see Letter 35), JSM had at the same time expressed his admiration for Guizot as historian. Cf. the summary of French news in the *Examiner*, Oct. 21, 1832, p. 680, and the review (partly written by JSM), "Guizot's Lectures on European Civilization," *London Review*, II (1836), 306–36. For a later revision of JSM's view of Guizot as a politician, see Letter 501.

some of his maxims go to sleep while the time is unpropitious for asserting them, with the laxity of principle which resigns them for personal advancement. Thank God I did not wait to know him personally in order to do him justice, for in 1838 & 1839 I saw that he had reasserted all his old principles at the first time at which he could do so with success & without compromising what in his view were more important principles still. I ought to have known better than to have imputed dishonourable inconsistency to a man whom I now see to have been consistent beyond any statesman of our time & altogether a model of the consistency of a statesman as distinguished from that of a fanatic.

You have been a little premature in saying anything to a bookseller about my Logic for no bookseller is likely to hear anything about it from me for many months. I have it all to rewrite completely & now here is Sterling persuading me that I must read all manner of German Logic which though it goes much against the grain with me, I can in no sort gainsay. So you are not likely to see much of my writing for some time to come except such scribble as this—

All send love to all. Pray write soon—

Yours always—

J. S. MILL

305. TO GUSTAVE D'EICHTHAL[1]

Kensington
25th Decr 1840.

MY DEAR D'EICHTHAL

I did not write to you when I received the mournful & to me quite unexpected news of the loss of your father—not that I did not feel with you & for you, but I knew how little comfort words can give in such a case —& if they could, how many you have who are nearer & more efficacious consolers than I can be. There is certainly something in a father's death (quite independently of personal affection) more solemn & affecting than in any other loss. It closes the past, & as it were severs the connexion between oneself & one's youth. The only still worse loss is that which closes the future, as the death of a beloved wife or child, because *there* disappointed hopes are superadded. I had something like this to bear when I lost, less than a year ago, a brother only in his twentieth year who was likely if he had lived to be one of the most valuable men of our time as he was already one of the most loveable. But *allah akhbar* as your friends the Mussulmans say.

1. Published in *D'Eichthal Corresp.*, pp. 182–87, and in *Cosmopolis*, IX, 373–75. MS at Arsenal.

I received duly your letter to Sir T. Buxton[2] & forwarded it to him & I have since received the pamphlet[3] for which I thank you very much. What prospect is there of the appearance of the work itself? One of our principal papers, the Times I think, inserted the account which appeared in the Moniteur. There is every appearance that you have made out your case, & if you have it is a very important thing to have done. Islamism is a fortunate thing for the Africans & I sometimes think it is very unfortunate for the Indians of America that Mussulmans did not land there instead of Christians, as they would have been much more likely to adopt that type of religion & civilization than the other. You are very usefully employed in throwing light on these dark subjects—the whole subject of the races of man, their characteristics & the laws of their fusion is more important than it was ever considered till of late & it is now quite *a l'ordre du jour* & labour bestowed upon it is therefore not lost even for immediate practical ends.

I am out of heart about public affairs—as much as I ever suffer myself to be. I never thought that in our day one man had the power of doing so much mischief as that shallow & senseless coxcomb Palmerston has done.[4] Half the Liberal party, even many of the old Whigs, are against him, & it is most mortifying to think if the Tories had been in power & had done this (which they never would have dared) how gloriously we should have turned them out upon it & thereby cemented the friendship of France & England for generations to come. But the ten years of Whig administration have entirely demoralized our Liberal party. Lord Holland certainly died of it,[5] so old Rogers[6] says who you know is the familiar of the Whig houses & he adds that it will kill him too. The worst is that with all the good will in the world I can only palliate, not excuse the conduct of France & the spirit displayed by the French press & much of the French public. And this display you may believe me when I say it, has made numbers of our best & most thinking persons think Palmerston in the right who would otherwise have been grievously incensed against him. It is *that* which has done the mischief here. I fear the present generation of English will never again feel confidence in the French people. They are now convinced that the spirit of military & Bonapartist aggression & the bitterness of resentment against England are still alive—that France *cannot* be conciliated to England &

2. Sir Thomas Fowell Buxton.

3. Presumably an offprint of D'Eichthal's article, "Recherches sur l'histoire et l'origine des Foulahs ou Fellans," which appeared in the Nov., 1840, *Bulletin de la Société de géographie*. The "work" referred to in the next sentence was the longer treatise, *Histoire et origine des Foulahs ou Fellans*, published in the *Mémoires de la Société ethnologique* (Paris, 1841).

4. See Letters 297, 303, and 306.

5. Henry Richard Vassall Fox, third Baron Holland (1773–1840), prominent Whig leader, pro-French in his sympathies, had died on Oct. 22.

6. Samuel Rogers (1763–1855), poet, man of wealth, an intimate in the highest circles of the Whig party.

that the only chance for peace in Europe is in a strong conservative government which shall keep down the democracy & the public feeling for its own sake. I do assure you that until the French journalists & orators irritated & alarmed our public there was not a particle of feeling here against France or of interest one way or the other in the Egyptian question. The whole was a wretched freak of Palmerston for which God reward him instead of us—but *quicquid delirant Whigges plectuntur Achivi.*[7]

It is impossible not to love the French people & at the same time not to admit that they are children—whereas with us even children are care-hardened men of fifty. It is as I have long thought a clear case for the *croisement des races.*

It is really quite time that I should see & converse with you again, & with my dear & most valued friend Adolphe.[8] We are both of us much changed since we last met, you & I I mean, for Adolphe I should think is much the same as before. You probably have found out by experience as I have the meaning of growing "sadder & wiser" as one grows older & that too without growing at all unhappy but on the contrary happier. And you have felt as I have how one's course changes, as one gets experience but changes by *widening* & therefore still keeps the same direction as before only with a slower movement as attempting to hit more points at once. There is so much to say if one begins to let oneself go that I must not go on. Pray write soon & tell me among other things whether Guizot is likely to stand & what you now think of him. As for me I honour and venerate him, (it is but little to say) before all living statesmen though I differ from many of his opinions.

ever affectionately yours

J. S. MILL

306. TO ALEXIS DE TOCQUEVILLE[1]

30th December 1840.

MY DEAR TOCQUEVILLE,

You may imagine how much pleasure it gave me to find that you were pleased with my review of your Second Part. I can very easily believe that many of those who had ventured to give an opinion upon your speculations had not taken so much pains or so conscientiously striven to understand & enter into the spirit of your speculations as I did, & many doubtless were

---

7. Cf. Horace (*Epistles* I.2.14): *Quicquid delirant reges, plectuntur Achivi* (Whatever folly the kings commit, the Achaeans pay the penalty).
8. Gustave d'Eichthal's brother.

* * * *

1. Published in Mayer, pp. 331–33; in reply to Tocqueville's of Dec. 18, *ibid.*, pp. 329–31. MS in Tocqueville archives.

not so well prepared for doing so by the previous direction of their thoughts and studies. And it is no more than natural to a mind like yours to be much more gratified by any evidence of your book's having worked in another mind & given birth to thought than by any amount of eulogy, or by a much more unqualified expression of concurrence, when not accompanied by such evidence.

It does not surprise me that this second part should be less popular than the first. The reason you assign, no doubt is partly the true one, but besides this, the thoughts in the second part are much more recondite, & whether one assents to them or not, are brought from a much greater depth in human nature itself, than those in your first publication. It constitutes still more than the other did, an era in science. I know how much thought it calls for from the reader when I remember how long it was before I could make up my mind about it, although few of my countrymen are so much accustomed to that kind of speculation and also I had previously thought that if there was any one of the leading intellects of this age to which I could flatter myself that my own had a kind of analogy it was probably yours. I therefore cannot wonder at the smaller extent of immediate popularity, especially as the most competent judges are exactly those who are not in a hurry to express any opinion on thoughts for the most part so entirely new.

Your observation that you do not believe in the errors of the public judgment as to literary works will be assented to by few Englishmen, and that such a thing should be said by a philosopher so much in advance of his countrymen is a high compliment to the French public which is certainly the cleverest public in the world, & as M. de Stendhal says, can understand everything, so far as intellect goes, even what they would have been quite incapable of originating. That is far from being the case with either the German or the English; who probably have more original genius than the French have hitherto manifested, but whose ideas seldom make much way in the world until France has recast them in her own mould & interpreted them to the rest of Europe & even sometimes to the very people from whom they first came. It is my belief however that in political & social philosophy the French are not only original but the *only* people who are original on a large scale & that as soon as they shall have appropriated, & fitted into their theories, the stricter & closer deductions of the English School in political economy & in some other matters of comparative detail they will give the law to the scientific world on these subjects. I do wish they would thoroughly master Ricardo & Bentham. Tanneguy Duchâtel did the former. They need not for that reason contract their telescopic view to our microscopic one, but they could and would combine the two & make them reconcilable.

I am very glad to have had from yourself your view of the unhappy embroilment between our two countries & I have shown that part of your letter to several people who had received a painful impression from your speech in the Chamber.[2] I agree with you in thinking our ministry very culpable, but our people are not to blame. You know that the English public think little & care little about foreign affairs & a ministry may commit them beyond redemption before they are aware. If the Tories had been in power they would have been suspected of anti-French predilections, they would have been watched, & would never have dared as these men have, or if they had, we should have gloriously turned them out on this question. But the ministry being liberal, and at a moment too when the liberal party has become entirely demoralised by seven years of a weak whig government, the public looked on in confidence that all was right, and that Palmerston knew more about the matter than they did, never dreaming that they had been brought to the brink of a war until it was revealed to them by the manifestations of feeling in France. Then, however, I firmly believe that the reaction you speak of in favour of the French alliance would have taken place, if there had not been such a lamentable want both of dignity & of common sense on the part of the journalists & public speakers in France. The whole of the feeling which has arisen since in this country, has arisen, you may believe me on such a subject, from the demonstrations since made in France—from the signs of rabid eagerness for war, the reckless hurling down of the gauntlet to all Europe, the explosion of Napoleonism and of hatred to England, together with the confession of Thiers & his party that they were playing a double game, a thing which no English statesman could have avowed without entire loss of caste as a politician. All this has made the most sober people here say openly that from the feeling which has shown itself in France, Palmerston must have had stronger grounds for his conduct than appear on the surface —never considering that Palmerston's conduct has revivified morbid feelings that were dying away. You know how repugnant to the English character is anything like bluster, & that instead of intimidating them, its effect when they do not treat it with calm contempt is to raise a dogged determination in them not to be bullied. All these feelings are decidedly beginning to abate since the peace party has had so strong a majority in the chamber of deputies, but the mischief is that the distrust will continue for a long time on our side as well as the resentment on yours. Palmerston supported by all the Tories and by half the Liberals will carry all before him in our Parliament but the opinion of most wise men here is that the Whig party have really destroyed themselves in the country by this. For

2. His speech, delivered on Nov. 30, 1840, was reported at length in *The Times* for Dec. 2 and 3, 1840, p. 5.

my part, I would walk twenty miles to see him hanged, especially if Thiers were to be strung up along with him. Do pray write to me again & at more length about this matter as I am most anxious to know your whole mind upon it—*en attendant* our meeting at Paris which I hope will be in the coming year.

Ever faithfully yours,

J. S. MILL.

India House.

1841

307. TO JANE WELSH CARLYLE[1]

India House
Saturday
[1841?]

DEAR MRS CARLYLE

I was prevented by want of time from writing to you yesterday as I said I would—but I believe it comes to the same thing.

Of all Balzac's things the Medecin de Campagne is the best, at least it is that which exhibits him in the best light: the Scenes Parisiennes are the very worst. But the Scenes de la *Vie Privée*, 5 vols. & Scenes de la Vie de Province, 4 vols. are a fair specimen of all he has done, & whoever has read them can judge of him. I would add to these, "Un grand homme de province à Paris" which is a continuation of a story in the Vie de Province, & "Le Lys dans la Vallée."

As for Sand I believe you know all she has written: those I like best are Valentine, the Lettres d'un Voyageur & the new one "Le Compagnon du Tour de France."

so now goodbye & a pleasant journey to you.

J.S.M.

308. TO JOHN STERLING[1]

India House
5 Jan. 1841.

MY DEAR STERLING

Thanks for Twesten[2] which I will certainly read. I am now reading an older book, Lambert's Neues Organon,[3] of which Austin[4] speaks favorably

1. MS at the Pierpont Morgan Library, New York. The approximate date is established by the reference to George Sand's "new one," *Le Compagnon du Tour de France*, published late in 1840.

* * * *

1. Part published in Elliot, I, 120–21. MS at Leeds. In answer to unpublished letter of Jan. 4, 1841, by Sterling; MS at King's.
2. August D. C. Twesten, *Die Logik, insbesondere die Analytik* (Schleswig, 1825).
3. Johann Heinrich Lambert, *Neues Organon, oder Gedanken über die Erforschung und Bezeichnung des Wahren* . . . (Leipzig, 1764).
4. John Austin.

& which is certainly an able book though I do not know whether I shall find much in it that I had not found out myself or obtained from other sources.

I am glad you have been able to work, & glad you have left off working at least in the way which gave you a fever. I am glad too that it is a Tragedy. By the bye I never told you how very good I thought your lines in the Times on Acre & Napoleon.[5] I think I have seen nothing of yours yet, in a versified form at least, that seems to me equal to them.

About the war matters, I suspect we shall not make much of our discussion till we can carry it on by word of mouth. When I spoke of binding France,[6] I meant engaging her as a party in a general compact of European powers, which she could not afterwards have ventured to infringe. And the aggressions I meant are the proceedings by which we are gradually conquering all Asia, from Pekin to Herat—I did not mean that they were either aggressions in any bad sense, or provoking to France in themselves, but I do think it provoking that France should see England & Russia adding every year on a large scale to their territory & dependent alliances in the East & then crying out at the suspicion of her wishing to do something of the same kind as if it were an enormity never before heard of among the nations of Europe. But you must not think I defend France or would even excuse or palliate her conduct except so far as attacked by people themselves liable to the same accusations in all respects, except (so far as Thiers is concerned) that of duplicity.

I have had a letter from Tocqueville[7] which I put under this cover as you may like to see what he has to say for the part he has taken in this matter & how he connects it with his philosophic ideas. I have written to him a long letter[8] in reply to which I rather expect from him a long & controversial answer.[9] At all events I thought it right to try the chance of doing some good with him by speaking out with entire frankness, which his personally kind feelings towards me & his knowledge of my sentiments about France both in itself & in relation to England, gave me the power of doing without

5. "The Egyptian Vision," *The Times*, Dec. 9, 1840, p. 5.
6. In Letter 303. Sterling in his letter of Jan. 4 had disagreed with JSM: "Your argument on the Egyptian question I am sorry to say does not convince me. France had I think no right to insist on the independence of Egypt if that was likely to derange the actual relations of the European nations to each other & I do not perceive to what you allude when you say that we might bind France not to avail for her own advantage—the only way I can conceive of binding her or indeed any nation in such a matter is by making the intended step impossible which is what we have done. . . . What the aggressions are which you say naturally provoke France I do not know. We have done nothing at least since the peace at all resembling the conquest of Algiers & its occupation."
7. Of Dec. 18, 1840; in Mayer, pp. 329–31.
8. Letter 306.
9. Answer dated March 18, 1841; in Mayer, pp. 334–36.

offence. If he sends me an answer I will send that also to you. Please return this when you next write. You will see also how pleased he is with my review of him which considering how much of controversy there is in it, is an honour to him; & how complimentary he is upon it, which is an honour to me.

I need hardly say how earnestly I feel with you about the Corn Laws[10] & I therefore think the Anti Corn Law League right at Walsall.[11] To let in for a manufacturing town any man not an out & out opponent of the Corn Laws would I think have been a folly & something worse.

That you were able to bear this weather even at Torquay is very satisfactory &, no doubt, made it right for you to return to Clifton. Tell me how Mrs Sterling & your children are & give my kind remembrances to her.

ever yours faithfully

J. S. MILL

I had a long walk with Carlyle on Xmas day—he is as usual—Austin, I think, rather better than usual. I have not heard lately of Calvert.

309. TO GEORGE HENRY LEWES[1]

I.H.
Wed^y.
[Feb.?, 1841]

MY DEAR SIR,

Excuse my breaking in upon you at such a time as this,[2] but I think it best to write while the impression is fresh. Of course I do not expect any answer. I have read your MS. which I think very well done, & likely when finished & finally revised to be quite suitable to the Edinburgh.[3] You have not however yet convinced me that the line between poetry, & passionate writing of any kind, is best drawn where metre ends & prose begins. The

---

10. Sterling had written: "The iniquity of those Corn Laws & their widespread mischievousness made me rage. . . . Is there any chance of getting rid of them?"

11. At Walsall on Dec. 30, 1840, one Spencer Lyttleton, after refusing to pledge his support for immediate repeal of the Corn Laws, had withdrawn his candidacy for Parliament. The Anti-Corn-Law League sought pledges from parliamentary candidates. For details on the Walsall election, see Archibald Prentice, *History of the Anti-Corn-Law League* (2 vols., London, 1853), I, 176–84.

* * * *

1. Published in Kitchel, pp. 30–31. MS at Yale.

2. I.e., that of his marriage, on Feb. 18, 1841, to Agnes Jervis (1822–1902), daughter of Swinfen Jervis (1798–1867), MP for Bridport.

3. The article, "The Philosophy of Art: Hegel's Æsthetics," eventually appeared, not in the *Edinburgh*, but in the *BFR* for Oct., 1842 (XIII, 1–49).

distinction between the artistic expression of feeling for feeling's sake & the artistic expression of feeling for the sake of compassing an end, or as I have phrased it between poetry & eloquence, appears to me to run through all art; & I am averse to saying that nothing is poetry which is not in *words*, as well as to saying that all passionate writing in verse is poetry. At the same time I allow that there is a natural, not an arbitrary relation between metre & what *I* call poetry. This is one of the truths I had not arrived at when I wrote those papers in the Repository[4] but what afterwards occurred to me on the matter I put (in a very condensed form) into the concluding part of an article in the L. & W. on Alfred de Vigny.[5] I wish you would look at that same when you have time, (I will shew it to you) & tell me whether what I have said there exhausts the meaning of what you say about the *organic* character of metre, or whether there is still something further which I have to take into my theory.

I will carefully read your papers a second time and note down anything I have to remark, in the manner you suggested.

And now without any more on these rather untimely matters let me conclude by wishing you as I do most cordially all possible prosperity & happiness in your new condition, which all I have heard of the lady inclines me to regard as an enviable one.

ever yours

J. S. MILL

310. TO GUSTAVE D'EICHTHAL[1]

India House

23^d February 1841

MY DEAR D'EICHTHAL

I should not have delayed so long replying to your two letters if I had not been hoping every day that the pamphlets would arrive—but neither the two which you sent by the ambassador nor the six through the booksellers have reached me. I have always found that things sent through Paris booksellers were delayed for months & that it was of no use enquiring about them & that things sent by the ambassador generally came sooner or later without being enquired for & as it is very inconvenient to me to go or send to Manchester Square I have not hitherto done it, but if the packet does

---

4. See Letter 301, n. 3.

5. *LWR*, XXIX (April, 1838), 1–44, and reprinted in *Dissertations*, I, 312–54.

* * * *

1. Published in part in *D'Eichthal Corresp.*, pp. 188–90, and in *Cosmopolis*, IX, 375–76. MS at Arsenal.

not arrive I must do so. The Journal des Débats reached me & gave me great pleasure. The idea of your pamphlet[2] is so appropriate to the present time that it could not fail to excite attention. The Quarterly Review not long ago made a suggestion of a similar tendency for securing religious liberty &c at Jerusalem by placing it under the protection of *Austria*[3] (a not uninteresting *rapprochement* with your view of the mission of that power in "Les Deux Mondes.")[4] But the time is not yet come when the public mind can be drawn to the settlement of Syria nor will that time come until the apprehension of a European war is at an end, & that apprehension is now, in England, much more serious than it has ever yet been. The fortifications, & the arming, appear to most people here impossible to be accounted for except by aggressive designs on the part of France; it is in vain to say as those who know the state of the French mind do, that the purpose is merely defensive, because to every Englishman the idea that there is the least disposition anywhere to commit aggression against France appears so utterly senseless that no one can believe such an idea to be sincerely entertained in France. There is something exceedingly strange & lamentable in the utter incapacity of our two nations to understand or believe the real character & springs of action of each other. I am tempted to write a pamphlet or a review article on that very subject, but that I fear it would produce no effect. There will be much to discuss between you & me on that subject as well as on so many others when we meet.

Thanks my dear friend to you & Adolphe for your kind propositions respecting my visit to Paris. I have a very serious intention of going there, but there are things that may prevent me from doing so this next summer & if I do it will probably be under engagements which will prevent me from being able to make use of your kind & friendly offers to the extent I otherwise might—but neither those engagements nor anything else could or should prevent me if your & Adolphe's engagements do not, from seeing I hope very much of both of you & renewing our former intimate intercourse. I doubt not from what you say that you will by that time be married & though that is not likely to be the case with me I can yet very heartily congratulate you, more heartily than I generally can venture to congratulate an Englishman on a similar event which in nine cases out of ten changes a man of any superiority very much for the worse without making him happy. I do not believe that this is commonly the case in France & I would attempt to shew why, if the considerations entering into the question were not far

2. *De l'Unité européenne* (Paris, 1840, 35 pp.). See Letter 312. D'Eichthal had sent JSM a copy of the *Journal des Débats* for Jan. 18, 1841, which carried an article on the pamphlet.

3. In an article on "Foreign Policy," LXVII (Dec., 1840), 301.

4. See Letters 197, n. 2, and 215.

more complicated than most people have reflected upon. Excuse this poor letter—I will write again & I hope better when I have read your pamphlet.

yours affectionately

J. S. MILL

311. TO GEORGE HENRY LEWES[1]

18 Kensington Square

1st March 1841

MY DEAR LEWES

I suspect the difference between us is a difference of classification chiefly. I accept all your inferences from my definition & am willing to stand by them. I do *not* think that epos *quâ* epos, that is, quâ narrative, is poetry, nor that the drama *quâ* drama is so. I think Homer & Aeschylus poets only by virtue of that in them which might as well be lyrical. At the same time you have just as much right to use the word Poetry in a different extension & as synonymous with "Art by the instrument of words" as music is Art by the instrument of rhythmic sounds, & painting, Art by the instrument of colours on canvas. Taking Poetry in this sense I admit that metre is of the essence of it or at least necessary to the higher kinds of it. In that case I claim the privilege of drawing within this large circle a smaller inner circle which shall represent poetry κατ' ἐξοχήν[2] or poet's poetry as opposed to everybody's poetry & of that I think mine the right definition. But "I speak as to the wise, judge ye what I say."

I return your Ms. with a good deal of pencil scratching at the back, for I have been, & intended to be, *hyper*critical. I have *studied* to find fault insomuch that you are to assume that I like & admire whatever I have not directly or by obvious implication objected to.

Your notion of the essentially religious nature of poetry seems to me to need a world of explanation. I think it will give entirely false ideas to English readers, & is only true in *any* degree if we, *more Germanico*, call every idea a religious idea which either grows out of or leads to, feelings of infinity & mysteriousness. If we do this, then religious ideas are the *most* poetical of all, an inmost circle within my inner circle; but surely not the *only* poetical, especially if your other definition of poetry be right.

I am afraid Mrs. Lewes will by this time find out that instead of being the *boree* on the subject of an unfinished article I have a strong vocation for being the bor*er* in respect of it. By the way, will you kindly make my

1. Published in Kitchel, pp. 31–32. MS at Yale.
2. *Par excellence.*

acknowledgements to her for an invitation I have been favoured with, & the *spirit* of which I most cordially accept (I never go to evening parties in the *flesh*) and believe me ever yours (and hers too)

J. S. MILL

312. TO GUSTAVE D'EICHTHAL[1]

India House
9th March
1841

MY DEAR GUSTAVE

I have received your letter of the 2d of March & also the *second* packet (but not the first) of two copies of "l'Unité Européenne" one of which I have sent to Carlyle. I will get the six copies from Messrs Belizard. Certainly the article in the Débats[2] could give no idea of the comprehensive & decided views taken in the pamphlet & altogether it does not seem to me, any more than the article in the Univers,[3] worthy of the subject. I am not surprised that such a paper as this should have given you *le caractère politique* for it is admirably suited to the moment & nothing could be better calculated to do good in France. It is much to be hoped & is in itself probable that the French Government will propose to itself as an object to reenter into the association of European nations & reassert its just influence in their deliberations by some such means as you suggest. The danger, I am sorry to say, is that *our* Government will not be prompt to seize this mode of reestablishing friendship & calming irritated susceptibilities. By most stupid & *grossier* mismanagement our Government has got itself committed to treating the affair of Syria as a mere question between a sovereign & a rebel governor, & has made all manner of unnecessary declarations, which will preclude it from entering, I fear into any proposition for superseding the authority of the Porte in what is absurdly called our territory. Wait a little & the Porte will get into such terrible embarrassments & will prove itself so utterly incapable of bringing the country into order and tranquillity that the necessity of a joint intervention of the European powers will become apparent to everybody, & then France will be able if she chuses to gain the well merited credit of intervening on a basis of enlightened philan-thropy & enlarged views of futurity instead of leaving all to the other powers who would certainly continue to drag in the *ornières* of the old notions of government & international relations.

1. Published in *D'Eichthal Corresp.*, pp. 191–93, and in *Cosmopolis*, IX, 376–78. MS at Arsenal.
2. See Letter 310, n. 2.
3. Not located.

What you say on the character of the present state of feeling in France is most powerfully & vividly conceived & recommends itself to me as conformable to all that I in a more confused manner thought of it. But in this country everybody imagines that the French are far more warlike than they were in the time of M. Thiers, & it is of no use telling people the contrary. It must be left to time & events to correct the error. I have always thought that the events which have so deplorably resuscitated the old feelings of alienation between the two nations would produce an effect less sudden & violent on our people than on yours but more deeply rooted & more durable.

I have bought Salvador's last book & ordered the previous one.[4] I have not yet read either. I wish I had time to write to you a whole volume on the unheard of *travail d'esprit* which is pervading all branches of society & shades of opinion among us. We are in a curious time of the world.

ever yours

J. S. MILL

There is nothing recent about the Red Sea & the Euphrates.

313. TO ROBERT BARCLAY FOX[1]

India House
12th March
1841

MY DEAR FRIEND

I feel somewhat ashamed of having allowed two months to elapse since your last letter especially when I consider the inclosure which it contained, respecting which however I sent you a message by one of my sisters (a *verbal* message which she doubtless transmuted into a written one) which a little lightens the weight on my conscience. As there is a good side to everything bad (& not solely to the misfortunes of one's friends as La Rochefoucault would have it)[2] this tardiness on my part has had one good effect, viz. that on reading your little poem once more after a considerable

---

4. Joseph Salvador, *Jésus-Christ et sa doctrine. Histoire de la naissance de l'Eglise, de son organisation et de ses progrès pendant le premier siècle* (2 vols., Paris, 1838); and *l'Histoire des Institutions de Moïse et du peuple hébreu* (3 vols., Paris, 1828).

* * * *

1. *Addressed*: R. Barclay Fox Esq. / Falmouth. Published by Pym, II, 321–23. MS in the possession of Mr. W. H. Browning.

2. "Dans l'adversité de nos meilleurs amis, nous trouvons toujours quelque chose qui ne nous déplaît pas." *Reflexions, Sentences et Maximes morales de La Rochefoucauld* (Paris, 1853), p. 260.

interval I am able to say with greater deliberation than I could have said at the time, that I think your verses not only good, but so good, that it is no small credit to have done so well on so *extremely* hacknied a subject— the *great* simple elemental powers & constituents of the universe have how- ever inexhaustible capabilities when any one is sufficiently fitted by nature & cultivation for poetry to have felt them as *realities*, that which a poet alone does habitually or frequently, which the majority of mankind never do at all & which we of the middle rank perhaps have the amazement of being able to do at some rare instants when all familiar things stand before us like spectres from another world—not however like phantoms but like the real things of which the phantoms alone are present to us or appear so in our common everyday state. That is truly a revelation of the seen, not of the unseen—& fills one with what Wordsworth must have been feeling when he wrote the line "filled with the joy of troubled thoughts."[3]

I cannot undertake to criticise your poem for I have no turn for that species of criticism, but there seems to me enough of melody in it, to justify your writing in verse, which I think nobody should do who has not music in his ear as well as "soul." Therefore if it were at all necessary I would add my exhortation to that which you have no doubt received from much more competent & equally friendly judges, Sterling for instance, to persevere. You have got over the mechanical difficulties which are the great hindrance to those who have feelings & ideas from writing good poetry— therefore go on & prosper.

I congratulate you on having Dr Calvert with you. Sterling you may or may not have for I had a letter from him yesterday dated at Clifton, on Thursday, & he had said if he went at all it would be on Wednesday. It would be a pleasure to us all to think of him as in the midst of you.

I have been doing nothing worth telling you for a long time for I cannot count among such things the rather tiresome business of reading German books of logic. It is true I have diversified that occupation by reading Euripides about whom there would be much to say if one had time & room. Have you ever read any of the great Athenian Dramatists? I had read but little of them before now & that little at long intervals so that I had no very just & nothing like a complete impression of them—yet nothing upon earth can be more interesting than to form to oneself a correct & living picture of the sentiments, the mode of taking life & of viewing it, of that most accomplished people. To me that is the chief interest of Greek poetic literature, for to suppose that any modern mind can be satisfied with it as a literature or that it can, in an equal degree with much inferior modern

3. Inaccurately quoted? Presumably, in view of the context, the reference is to the "Lines Composed a Few Miles Above Tintern Abbey": "And I have felt / A presence that disturbs me with the joy / Of elevated thoughts."

works of art (provided these be really genuine emanations from sincere minds), satisfy the requiremen[ts][4] of the more deeply feeling, more introspective, & (above even that) more genial character which Christianity & chivalry & many things in addition to these have impressed upon the nations of Europe, it is if I may judge from myself quite out of the question. Still, we have immeasurably much to win back as well as many hitherto undreamed of conquests to make & the twentieth & thirtieth centuries may be indebted for something to the third century before Christ as well as to the three immediately after him—

Here is a long letter full of nothing but the next shall be better. With kindest regards to your delightful circle—

yours ever,

J. S. MILL.

314. TO GEORGE HENRY LEWES[1]

I.H.
24 April 1841

MY DEAR LEWES

I have read the article[2] once but I should like to keep it, if you will permit me, long enough to read it again.

I see nothing fundamental in it that requires alteration though I would recommend a careful revision of the details, chiefly for the purpose of weeding out quaintnesses of expression, which find less favour in Edinburgh eyes than anywhere else—& perhaps I may add that the article strikes me, on a first reading, as being a little rambling. I do not know how the Edinburgh will like such severe diatribes against English criticism, which fall heavier on the Ed. itself than on anything else, but if it were my own case & I were sending such matter to the editor of the Edinburgh I should feel as if I were civilly giving him a thump on the face. In revising, it might be well to make it look as little German as possible—& I recommend, as you are so long in coming to Hegel & say so little about him, that you should stick a few titles of other books also at the beginning of the article.

You have come a little way to meet me, I see, & I believe I have come about as far, meanwhile, to meet you. As one hint among many towards a definition of poetry that has occurred to me, what do you think of this—

4. Page torn.

* * * *

1. Published in Kitchel, pp. 34–35. MS at Yale.
2. See Letter 309, n. 3.

"feeling expressing itself in the forms of thought." (That serves for *written* poetry, grammatical language being the form of *thought* not feeling) & it denotes that oh! & ah! are not poetry though Körner's[3] battle songs are. Then for the poetry of painting, sculpture &c. we have "feeling expressing itself in symbols" a definition which though often given for *all* poetry really serves very ill for the poetry of written or spoken language.

That article in the Edin. is not mine but Palgrave's,[4] & not the thing. I am too busy finishing my book to write articles. Anything I can do for you with Kemble I shall be glad of. Can you give me, that is him, any idea of the shape into which you will throw the subject?[5]

Ever yours

J.S.M.

Vive, vale, et *scribe.*

315. TO GEORGE HENRY LEWES[1]

[April, 1841?]

There need no more titles.[2] I had overlooked the fact that there were already several, but I would not call it an article on *Hegel*. I have marked quaintnesses with crosses, & made a few other remarks.

I like it better & better. But I fear the *Ed.* will find it too German. Still it ought to go there.

I did not give that phrase as a definition,[3] but as a contribution towards one. In turning over the thing to be defined, one feature after another turns up—& from the whole, a definition will one day or other emerge.

Should not your historical article[4] be on some *one* particular book? Editors are rather shy of such comprehensive plans of articles, especially with new contributors.

J.S.M.

3. Karl Theodor Körner (1791–1813), German poet, best known for his patriotic lyrics, *Leier und Schwert* (Berlin, 1814).

4. Sir Francis Palgrave (1788–1861), historian. The article referred to was "Progress of Historical Enquiry in France," *ER*, LXXIII (April, 1841), 84–120, reprinted in *The Collected Historical Works of Sir Francis Palgrave, K.H.*, ed. Sir R. H. Inglis Palgrave, F.R.S. (10 vols., Cambridge, 1919–22), X, 1–40.

5. See Letter 319.

* * * *

1. Undated fragment, but must refer to preceding letter. Published in Kitchel, p. 35. MS at Yale.

2. See last sentence of second paragraph of preceding letter.

3. See third paragraph of preceding letter.

4. Probably his article "Modern French Historians," a review of Augustin Thierry's *Récits des temps mérovingiens* (3 vols., Bruxelles, 1840), in *WR*, XXXVI (Oct., 1841), 273–308.

316. TO GUSTAVE D'EICHTHAL[1]

[Early May (?), 1841][2]

. . . to procure them for you.

I am truly glad that you & that M. Guizot expect from the fortifications a result so much the contrary of what everybody out of France expects from them. Englishmen of all parties, thinking it entirely frantic to suppose that any power whatever has, or is likely to have, a design of invading France, will be very long before they can be persuaded to look upon these measures of defence as proceeding from any other spirit than one of *offence*. I agree with you that the discussions[3] do honour to France, but I say so only because there were so many good speeches *against* a measure which had the popular cry in its favour. As to the speeches *for* it at least those of Thiers & his friends I only express the universal opinion here when I say that there has been no public exhibition for many years so discreditable to the country producing it.

As for us, we are entering into a new epoch: the proposition of our ministry respecting the tariff[4] & especially the corn laws, coming after many smaller measures of internal improvement, will rally the whole liberal party to the present ministry & will keep them in office for a long time to come.[5] Except our Chartists all the radicals will now be one with the Whigs, & I expect & believe that out of this crisis will arise a situation of things which will render the Whig Ministry what they have never been before, real mediators between the new & the old ideas & interests, and real preparers & softeners of the change to a new & better social organization. But I will write to you more at length about these matters soon. Meanwhile, adieu—With kind regards—

J. S. MILL.

I can tell you nothing certain yet about my own movements—

1. Published in *D'Eichthal Corresp.*, pp. 194–95, and in *Cosmopolis*, IX, 378–79. MS at Arsenal. The beginning of the letter has been lost.

2. Eugène d'Eichthal dates the letter 1841. The May date would seem to be justified by the reference in the second paragraph to the Melbourne government's espousal of a lowering of the duties imposed by the Corn Laws. Melbourne announced his change of policy on May 3, 1841.

3. The debate on the fortification of Paris took place in the Chamber of Deputies in Jan., 1841, and in the Chamber of Peers in March.

4. See n. 2 above.

5. JSM's prophecy proved false. On June 4 the Whig government lost on a vote of no confidence; in the ensuing election in the summer the Tories were returned to power under Sir Robert Peel.

317. TO EDWIN CHADWICK[1]

I.H.
Monday [May, 1841]

DEAR CHADWICK

Can you in any way help my cousin Harriet Burrow, a sister of Mr. Burrow who is a clerk in your office, to obtain the situation of matron to the Union Workhouse of Saffron Walden? It is a kind of thing which of course she would not seek if she had found it possible to do anything better for herself but for which she is more than qualified by experience & character, although only 25 years of age which I fear would be a presumption against her.

I inclose the advertisement.

Ever yours

J. S. MILL

318. TO ROBERT BARCLAY FOX[1]

India House
6th May 1841

MY DEAR FRIEND—I will be more prompt this time in contributing my part towards keeping the thread of our correspondence unbroken.

I am glad that you do not write *only* poetry—for in these days one composes in verse (I don't mean *I* do for I don't write verses at all) for oneself rather than for the public—as is generally the case in an age chiefly characterized by earnest practical endeavour. There is a deep rooted tendency almost everywhere, but above all in this England of ours, to fancy that what is written in verse is not meant in earnest, nor should be understood as serious at all (for really the common talk about being *moral* & so forth means only that poetry is to treat with respect whatever people are used to profess respect for, & amounts to no more than a parallel precept not to play at any indecent or irreverent *games.*) Prose is after all the language of *business*, & therefore is the language to do good by in an age when men's minds are forcibly drawn to external effort—when they feel called to what my friends the St Simonians not blasphemously call "continuing the work of Creation" i.e. cooperating as instruments of

1. Endorsed in another hand: "J. S. Mill / May / 41 / . Assistance of Mr. C. requested to obtain his cousin an appt as School Mistress of a W.H." MS at UCL.

* * * *

1. *Addressed*: R. Barclay Fox Esq. / Falmouth. *Postmark*: 6 MAY 1841. Published with omissions in Pym, II, 323–26. MS in the possession of Mr. W. H. Browning.

Providence in bringing order out of disorder. True, this is only a part of the mission of mankind & the time will come again when its due rank will be assigned to Contemplation, & the calm culture of reverence and love. Then Poetry will resume her equality with prose, an equality like every healthy equality, resolvable into reciprocal superiority. But that time is not yet, & the crowning glory of Wordsworth is that he has borne witness to it & kept alive its traditions in an age which but for him would have lost sight of it entirely & even poetical minds would with us have gone off into the heresy of the poetical critics of the present day in France who hold that poetry is above all & preeminently a *social* thing.

You ask my opinion on the punishment of death. I am afraid I cannot quite go with you as to the abstract right—for if your unqualified denial of that right were true, would it not be criminal to slay a human being even in the strictest self defence—if he were attempting to kill or subject to the most deadly outrages yourself or those dearest to you? I do not know whether the principles of your Society go this length: mine do not; & therefore I do hold that society has or rather that Man has a right to take away life when without doing so he cannot protect rights of his own as sacred as the "divine right to live." But I would confine the right of inflicting death to cases in which it was certain that no other punishment or means of prevention would have the effect of protecting the innocent against atrocious crimes, & I very much doubt whether any such cases exist. I have therefore always been favorable to the entire abolition of capital punishment though I confess I do not attach much importance to it in the case of the worst criminals of all, towards whom the nature of the punishment hardly ever operates on juries or prosecutors as a motive to forbearance.

Perhaps this view will afford you matter to confute in your essay—but indeed it is so trite that you have no doubt anticipated it.

There is nothing of mine in the Edinburgh this time—nor is it likely there will be till I have finished my book—the big book I mean, the Logic. I think I told you that the first draught was finished last autumn. I have now got to work on the rewriting & have just completed, tolerably to my own satisfaction, the first of the Six Books into which it will be divided. I don't suppose many people will read anything so scholastic, especially as I do not profess to upset the schools but to rebuild them—& unluckily everybody who cares about such subjects nowadays is of a different school from me. But that is the concern of a higher power than mine: my concern is to bring *out* of me what is *in* me, although the world should not find even after many days that what is cast on the waters is wholesome bread—nay even although (worst of all) it may happen to be, in reality, only bread made of sawdust.

So you are really to have Sterling always with you.[2] I congratulate you heartily—there is no place where I would rather wish him—except with me.—Carlyle is in the country roaming about, at least I have not heard of his being yet returned.[3] I quite agree with you as to his Lectures.[4] That little book contains almost all his best ideas in a particularly attractive shape, & with many explanations which he has not given elsewhere or has given only by way of allusion.

We have not heard from George for more than a fortnight—up to that time all was well with him & we shall soon have him with us again.[5]

Clara & Harriet will write soon—for aught I know they are writing to-day.

With kindest regards to Mr & Mrs Fox & your sisters & to all relations whom I have the good fortune to know (except those at Perran whom I trust soon to see), believe me, ever yours

(in no merely polite sense)

J. S. MILL.

319. TO JOHN MITCHELL KEMBLE[1]

India House
7th May 1841

MY DEAR SIR

A young friend of mine, by name Lewes, would like to write an article for your review[2] on the modern French Historians,[3] a propos of Buchez' Introduction à la science de l'histoire[4] or Michelet, Introduction à l'Histoire Universelle.[5] He is willing to take the risk of your not liking his article, but he is not willing to take, in addition, that of the subject's not suiting you. What say you?

He is rather a good writer, has ideas (even in the Coleridgian sense) &

2. Sterling moved his family from Clifton to Falmouth in June, 1841, where they lived until the spring of 1843.
3. He returned from Scotland on the day of this letter.
4. *On Heroes, Hero-Worship, and the Heroic in History*, delivered in 1840 (the Foxes had attended some of them), and published in 1841.
5. George Mill had probably spent the winter at Torquay for reasons of health. See Letter 300, n. 7.

* * * *

1. *Addressed*: J. M. Kemble Esq. MS in the possession of Professor Ney MacMinn.
2. The *British and Foreign Review*, of which Kemble was editor.
3. See Letter 315, n. 4.
4. P. J. B. Buchez, *Introduction à la science de l'histoire, ou science du développement de l'humanité* (Paris, 1833).
5. Jules Michelet, *Introduction à l'histoire universelle* (Paris, 1831).

much reading, & altogether I think he is a contributor worth having. You may have seen some papers of his in the Monthly Chronicle[6] & an article on the French Drama in the Westminster.[7]

Ever yours

J. S. MILL

320. TO JAMES MARTINEAU[1]

May 21, 1841

[When Dr. Martineau was in 1840 appointed Professor of Mental and Moral Philosophy and Political Economy in Manchester New College, he sent to Mr. Mill a copy of his Introductory Lecture and the Syllabus of his Course. On the 21st of May, 1841, Mill in acknowledging the volume, indulged "the happiest forebodings" of the work of the institution, from the soundness of its fundamental principles and the qualifications of its professors. He offered to ensure insertion in the "Westminster Review" for any article which Mr. Martineau might write in exposition and vindication of the principle of free teaching and free learning, of which Manchester New College was the unique representative.]

I had not been an uninterested observer of the affiliation of Manchester New College with the University of London; but I was not aware till I read your letter that the plan of instruction was founded upon the principle which I have always most earnestly contended for as the only one on which a University suitable to an age of unsettled creeds can stand, namely, that of leaving each Professor unfettered as to his premises and conclusions, without regard to what may be taught by the rest. Besides all the other important recommendations of this principle, it is the only one which in our time allows such professorships to be filled by men of real superiority, whose speculations have the power of exciting interest in the subject. Such men can less and less endure to be told what they are to teach.

[After referring to the near approaching completion of his own important work on "Logic," Mr. Mill, in a passage which Dr. Martineau has in part reproduced in the preface to the "Types of Ethical Theory," ex-

---

6. Not identified.
7. *WR*, XXXIV (Sept., 1840), 287–324.

* * * *

1. Excerpts published by James Drummond and C. B. Upton, *Life and Letters of James Martineau* (2 vols., London, 1902), II, 276–77. MS not located. The passages in brackets are the editors' summaries of parts of the letter, I, 111–12, and II, 276–77.

presses his desire that his friend, if satisfied with the "Logic," would himself take up, systematically, some other part of the great subject of philosophy.]

As a Professor, you will, I know, take up the whole; but I do not want to have to wait for your Lectures, which, like Brown's,[2] will no doubt be published some day; but before that time I may very likely be studying them in another state of existence. I have been very much interested by your Introductory Lecture and Syllabus. I shall never forget the time when I was myself under that awful shadow[3] you speak of, nor how I got from under it, but it is all written down in my book.[4] Are not your general metaphysical opinions a shade or two more German than they used to be?

321. TO JOHN HAMILTON THOM?[1]

India House
21st May 1841

MY DEAR SIR

Permit me to thank you for so promptly communicating to me the intelligence of our poor friend's death.[2] The accounts I had received of his condition from various friends during the last two or three years had led me to expect an earlier dissolution but I was not aware that his sufferings had been so severe.

Is there any prospect of a biography? It would be a most interesting life to write and most valuable to read—& so noble a spirit ought not to pass away from us & leave no record of what it was.

ever yours truly

J. S. MILL

2. Thomas Brown.
3. The editors point out that this refers to the following sentence in Martineau's Introductory Lecture: "It is probable that in the secret history of every noble and inquisitive mind there is a passage darkened by the awful shadow of the conception of Necessity; and it is certain that in the open conflict of debate, there is no question which has so long served to train and sharpen the weapons of dialectic skill."
4. Book VI, chap. 2 ("Of Liberty and Necessity"), *A System of Logic* (London, 1843).

* * * *

1. MS in Liverpool University Library. The MS bears no indication of the person addressed, but the ascription of it to Thom seems plausible since he had previously communicated with JSM about White (see Letter 241). Thom did publish a life of White.
2. Joseph Blanco White died on May 20, 1841.

India House
Thursday
[June 17, 1841]

MY DEAR FONBLANQUE

I understand from Chadwick that he has said something to you about the probability of my being disposed to write on the free trade measures & that you were kind enough to say you should like to have an article from me on the subject. The fact however is that I am very hard at work finishing a book[2] of considerable labour and magnitude which unless I stick to it I cannot be sure of getting ready for the next publishing season, & it is therefore very inconvenient for me to allow any other subjects to divert me from that. Unless the call upon me were such as to make it worth while to throw aside every other pursuit & devote my whole thoughts & exertions to the cause for the next two or three months I should lose more than the cause would gain by any merely occasional assistance that I could give it: & I have not hitherto seen any necessity or opportunity for such a decided step. In the meantime I have been doing my part, like other people, in my own neighbourhood. The Kensington petition, printed in the Chronicle today,[3] is of my writing, & I had a great share in getting up the public meeting, which, though in a very unpromising neighbourhood, was a very striking demonstration.

As I am writing to you I will not omit, what I have never had a good opportunity of doing before, namely to express the great admiration I have felt for the writing and conduct of the Examiner during the last year & especially on the Eastern question on which it alone resisted an almost universal madness, & did so with an ability & in a spirit which seemed to me quite perfect.

I believe there is nothing of any importance in practical politics on which we now differ for I am quite as warm a supporter of the present government as you are. Except Lord Palmerston's Syrian folly,[4] I have seen nothing in their conduct since the last remodelling of the ministry two years

1. MS in 1961 in the possession of Major General E. B. de Fonblanque, The Cottage, Bank, Lyndhurst, Hants. Transcript supplied by Mr. William E. S. Thomas. Last paragraph published in *Life and Labours of Albany Fonblanque*, ed. E. B. de Fonblanque (London, 1874), p. 32.

2. The *Logic*.

3. *Morning Chronicle*, June 17, 1841, p. 6. The Kensington petition for free trade was adopted at a public meeting of the inhabitants of Kensington at the King's Arms on Tuesday, June 15. William Prescott presided.

4. See Letters 297, 298, 300, and 303–306.

ago, but what is highly meritorious; & now after this great act[5] a radical, unless he be a chartist, must be worse than mad if he does not go all lengths with them for men who are capable of doing what they have done on this occasion, & of supporting it moreover by speeches shewing so thorough a knowledge of the principles of the subject, will certainly bring forward any other great improvements which the time is or becomes ripe for. The moderate radical party, & moderate radical ministry, which I so much wished for & of which I wished that poor Lord Durham[6] would have made himself the leader, were merely a party & a ministry to do such things as they are doing, & in the same manner. They have conformed to my programme, they have come up to my terms, so it is no wonder that I am heart & soul with them.

ever yours

J. S. MILL.

323. TO MACVEY NAPIER[1]

India House
23^d July 1841

MY DEAR SIR

A friend of mine who formerly wrote an article for your Supplement to the Encyclopedia, Mr. Weir,[2] is inclined to offer his services to you for the Edinburgh if they would be acceptable. He is an able & instructed man & a good writer, & could write valuable articles on many subjects but there are two kinds of subjects which he has chiefly in view: namely, the recent historical labours of the Germans, with which he is extensively & accurately acquainted; & Geography, of which he has made a systematic study, with a view to produce an elaborate work which from unforeseen circumstances it is probable will not be gone on with. You know how much of the reputation & popularity of the Quarterly has been owing to its articles of this sort & it strikes me as being a department which, in the Edin. is not systematically occupied. I think you would have every reason to be satisfied with what Mr. Weir would supply to you. If you are inclined to look favorably upon the project he would propose to furnish an article on Röppel's[3] Travels in Abyssinia, lately published in Germany & not at all

---

5. The Whig ministry's move in May, 1841, to lower the duties on grain. See Letter 316.
6. Lord Durham had died on July 28, 1840.

* * * *

1. MS in Brit. Mus.
2. William Weir (1802–1858), journalist, editor (1854–58) of the *Daily News*.
3. In Letter 326 JSM spells the name correctly as Rüppell.

known here. He says they are very interesting & important—& you might perhaps get the start of the Quarterly.

We are soundly thrashed in the Elections—but it is perhaps better so, for the ultimate interests of the party. It is the nature of Liberalism to require to be often reunited in opposition: liberalism always loses ground when in power, because in the first place it has to bear the brunt of that resistance to the pressure from without, the responsibility of which both when right & when wrong, should naturally fall upon Conservatism, & also because the impression of weakness is always given by the purely defensive position of a liberal government unable to carry its own liberal measures.

The 290 liberals in the new parliament, united as they have never been before, will be much more powerful, as well as more respectable, than a majority not exceeding 330 or 335.

ever yours truly

J. S. MILL

324. TO ROBERT BARCLAY FOX[1]

India House

24th July 1841

MY DEAR FRIEND

Have you not thought that I was dead, or gone mad, or had "left my home" like the "unfortunate gentlemen" who are advertised (or as Dickens expresses it, 'tized) in every day's newspaper—for none of my friends have heard of me for months past; not even Sterling, who of all men living had the strongest claim not to be so treated. But I meditate an ample reparation to him so far as a long letter can be so—& in the mean time I steal a moment to pay to you a small instalment of the debt which is due to you.

I suppose the most interesting subject to you as to most other people at this particular moment, is politics,—& in the first place I must say that your (or let me venture to say *our*) Falmouth is a noble little place for having turned out its Tory & elected two Liberals at the very time when it had received from the liberal government so severe a blow as the removal of the packets. If there had been many more such places the Tories would not have been, for another ten years, where they will be in half as many weeks. I cannot say however that the result of the elections has disappointed me. The remarkable thing is that the Corn Law question, *as such*, should have told for so little, either one way or the other. I expected that it would give us all the manufacturing places, instead of which we have *lost ground,*

1. Published with omissions in Pym, II, 326–28. MS in the possession of Mr. W. H. Browning.

even there! while it has not prevented us from turning out Tories from many small & purely agricultural towns. Now the only explanation which is possible of these facts, is one which reflects some light on the causes of the general result. The people of Leeds, Wigan, &c. cannot be indifferent to the Corn question; Tory or Liberal, it is a matter of life & death to them, & they know it. If they had thought that question depended on the result of the present elections, they *must* have returned Liberals. But their feeling was, that the Whigs cannot carry the Corn question, & that it will be as easily, if not more easily extorted from the Tories. And the agriculturists think the same[;] most likely we should have lost as many counties at the next general election even if the Corn question had not been stirred.

The truth is, & everybody I meet with who knows the country says so; the people had ceased to hope anything from the Whigs; & the general feeling among reformers was either indifference, or desire for a change. If they had not proposed, even at the last moment, these measures they would have been in a miserable minority in the new parliament. As it is, their conduct has to some extent reanimated radical feeling, which will now again resume its upward movement & the Whigs having put themselves really at the head of the popular party, will have an opportunity, which there seems considerable probability that they will use, of making themselves again popular. For my part they have quite converted me to them; not only by the courage & determination they have shewn (though somewhat too late) but by the thorough understanding they have shown of so great a subject. Their speeches in the great debates were really the speeches of philosophers.

I most entirely agree with you about the sugar question, & I was delighted to see that the anti slavery party in the country generally did not follow the aberrations of their parliamentary leaders. This part of the subject is admirably argued in an article in the Ed. Rev. just published.[2]

Have you yet resumed your speculations on capital punishment? As for me I have been quite absorbed in my Logic, which indeed it is necessary I should lose no time about, on pain of missing the next publishing season— when I hope to publish that & my reprint too.

With kindest regards to all your family (& apologies for so meagre a letter) believe me

yours ever

J. S. MILL.

My mother & sisters are at Guildford, some of them rather unwell with colds—George not being an exception.

2. "Grounds and Objects of the Budget" [by Nassau Senior], *ER*, LXXIII (July, 1841), 502–59. See F. W. Fetter, "The Authorship of Economic Articles in the *Edinburgh Review*, 1802–47," *Journal of Political Economy*, LXI (June, 1953), 257.

325. TO JOHN BLACK[1]

Kensington
Wed[y]
[July 28 (?), 1841]

DEAR MR. BLACK

I have just been reading again that poem I told you of and I liked it so much that I could not help sitting down and scribbling off a hurried notice of it for you. Do with it as you please—I shall be glad to see either that or any other notice of the book in the Chronicle.[2]

Ever yours,

J. S. MILL

326. TO MACVEY NAPIER[1]

I.H.
Friday [July 30, 1841]

MY DEAR SIR

Mr Weir will immediately set about the article on Rüppell[2] (as I now find the name should be spelt) and send it to be disposed of at your pleasure & in your own time.

Though he has lived for some time in Germany a few years ago, neither his opinions nor his stile are at all of the Germanic order, & you need be under no apprehension of any unsuitableness on that score. I told him of your *caveat*, & he said there was perhaps more danger of a few Scotticisms.

Fletcher[3] is pretty well again & has been long busy on his article, which I think you will have before long—but he is so slow a workman that it is hazardous to make any promises in his behalf.

I think the present number of the Edinburgh the best you have published for some time, & altogether an admirable one—both solid & brilliant. The

1. *Addressed*: John Black. Esq. MS in the possession of Professor Jacob Viner, Princeton University.
2. JSM's review of Sterling's poem *The Election* appeared in the *Morning Chronicle* on July 29, 1841.

* * * *

1. In another hand on the verso: John S. Mills Esq / July 30th / 1841. MS in Brit. Mus.
2. Weir's review of Eduard Rüppell's *Reise in Abyssinien* (2 vols., Frankfurt am Main, 1838–40) appeared in *ER*, LXXIV (Jan., 1842), 307–28.
3. George Fletcher.

three articles by Stephen,[4] Mangles,[5] & Senior,[6] seem to me almost perfect, each in its way—& they are three men exactly suited to take a leading part in the literary & philosophical organ of the Liberal party being three of the most distinguished men of our time for an ardent spirit of improvement combined with good sense, & for the capacity of moulding philosophical truths into practical shapes. It is from such men that the party ought to take its tone & I am really proud of being enrolled in the same corps with them.

We are entering upon times in which the progress of liberal opinions will again, as formerly, depend upon what is *said* & *written*, & no longer upon what is *done*, by their avowed friends. Many things are often occurring to me which seem at the time, to be worth saying, respecting the modes in which a review like yours might, in the peculiar circumstances of the present time, forward this progress—but the thoughts generally die or remain dormant for want of an opportunity of discussing them. If I were living near you I dare say I should often teaze you with more suggestions than you have any need of. But at this distance I am obliged to keep my wisdom to myself, for like some kinds of wine it is not of quality to bear so long a journey.

ever yours truly
J. S. MILL

327. TO GEORGE HENRY LEWES[1]

I.H.
Wed^y
[Aug., 1841]

MY DEAR LEWES,

There is little use in detailed remarks on an unfinished article[2]—and in the absence of the extracts it is difficult to judge of the effect of the paper on the whole. There are a great number of good things in it, & I have no doubt of its ripening into a good article. Its deficiencies, as is usually the case with an *ébauche*, are chiefly in the introductory part. I think you should dwell much more, & in a more explanatory manner on the *idée mère* of

4. Sir James Stephen's "The Port-Royalists" was the leading article in the July, 1841, *ER*, LXXIII, 309–65.
5. Ross Donnelly Mangles (1801–1877), expert on Indian affairs; liberal MP for Guildford, 1841–58; chairman of the East India Company, 1857–58. His article in the July *ER*, LXXIII, 425–60, was on "Administration of Justice in India."
6. See Letter 324, n. 2.

* * * *

1. Published in Kitchel, pp. 37–38. MS at Columbia University.
2. This may have been an early version of "The State of Criticism in France," eventually published in the *BFR*, XVI (Dec., 1844), 327–62.

Nisard & of the article, the necessity of considering literature not as a thing per se, but as an emanation of the civilization of the period. The idea is one which it is of great importance to impress upon people. A writer in Blackwood this month,[3] on German literature, has said some things on the subject, not badly.

The concluding part, also, from the first mention of Lucan, seems too slight.

There is nothing Germanic in the style, but an occasional Gallicism or so.

The reviews generally give their extracts from foreign books translated— no doubt the editor would get that done, but woe betide the reviewer whose passages from a French or German xotbetic writer are translated by an English or Scotch hack.

ever yours

J.S.M.

328. TO GEORGE HENRY LEWES[1]

I.H.
Saturday
[Aug., 1841?]

MY DEAR LEWES,

The differences of opinion I alluded to chiefly related to the character of the Romans. In the matter of "beauty, religion, form, or art" I objected to the assertion as too sweeping—you would not be understood if you said that there was no beauty in Lucan—& *beauty* altogether means with you only a *part* of poetic merit, while it would be understood as meaning the whole. Then the word *form* which in that sense is not English, & I think scarcely deserves to be so, would have suggested no idea to an editor but that of Germanism. But of all this, more another time.

I will make no more crusty tea for the incarnate solecism if she calls me a w—— but I will not write the atrocious word. No one is *that* but from consciousness of being hated by women & deserving to be so.

Ever yours

J.S.M.

3. "Traits and Tendencies of German Literature," *Blackwood's*, L (Aug., 1841), 143–60.

* * * *

1. Published in Kitchel, p. 38. MS at Yale.
The letter may refer to the article discussed in the preceding letter (see n. 2).

329. TO JOHN ROBERTSON[1]

September 7, 1841

I am doing and thinking of nothing but my Logic, which I shall soon have re-written the first half of, ready for press.

330. TO EDWIN CHADWICK[1]

I.H.
Friday
[Sept. 21, 1841]

DEAR CHADWICK—I go out of town this afternoon & do not return till Monday, when I will endeavour to call upon you on my way home, as I am very busy in the evenings on my Logic & do not like to interrupt it. However it is very possible I may be unable to call upon you on Monday, & if so I will try Tuesday.

Ever yours

J. S. MILL

331. TO SARAH AUSTIN[1]

India House
4th October 1841

DEAR MRS AUSTIN

I ought to have written to you & Mr Austin long ago, but I never felt myself so little inclined to write a single line that could possibly be put off, for ever since you left England every moment almost that I could spare for writing has been employed upon my Logic which I am determined to finish in time for next publishing season. I find the rewriting harder work still than I had anticipated. I knew that the whole business of arranging it & of making it readable was yet to come, but the thoughts themselves I find were much more crude & imperfect than I fancied, & those only who have tried to write a systematic treatise on anything, know what the difficulty is of keeping the whole of a subject before one at once. However I believe

1. Excerpt published in Alexander Bain, *Autobiography* (London, 1904), p. 111. MS not located.

* * * *

1. Endorsed in another hand: "J. S. Mill / Sept 21 / 41." MS at UCL.

* * * *

1. *Addressed*: A Madame / Madame Austin / Poste Restante / à Dresden. *Postmarks*: PAID / OC 4 / 1841 and POST / 11 OCT / U. MS at King's.

I have now broken the neck of the thing—about half of it, & the most difficult half, being finished, some parts of which I have had to rewrite three or four times.

I have watched constantly for American news but have seen nothing either good or bad worth writing about. You no doubt either saw or heard of what was stated by the American correspondent of one of the English papers in the very week you set out—that both the rival parties in Mississippi had put up candidates for the approaching election of Governor, who had voted for the measure which the present Governor refused to pass.[2] I have never had much apprehension about that matter ultimately going right. What do you mean by "this last blow"? Surely not anything still more recent than those which you told me of in London? And yet when I remember that you did not then think it impossible that you might return to England this winter—I am afraid.

As for politics, free trade & so forth, which you ask me about, things appear to me to be going on as well as can be expected. Peel gives every indication that his own inclinations are towards liberal measures both in commerce & in many other things, & next spring will most likely see him either bring forward some considerable improvement in the corn laws or quarrel with his party & resign, in which case the victory in a year or two will be still more complete, for the Peel Tories & the Liberals together can carry any thing. The serious part of the matter is that every year of delay does permanent mischief by its effect on the policy & feelings of other countries, & there is danger that free trade like Catholic emancipation & other Tory concessions will come too late for some of the good effects expected from it. The Tory writers here affect to think the ministry very strong but there is evidently a terrible storm brewing against them which they could, no doubt, succeed in weathering if they were not likely to fall to pieces in the attempt.

I have not taken any holidays this year, & do not intend. They are however, I hope, only postponed, not lost, as I shall claim a longer leave of absence some other year in consequence.

Mrs Taylor bids me tell you how one fine day (it was really not more than a week) she suddenly & with hardly any warning lost the use of her

2. JSM and the Austins, like many in England at this time, were concerned over the possible loss of their investments in American State bonds because of repudiation movements in some of the states. JSM's information about the situation in Mississippi was not wholly accurate, and his optimism proved unfounded. The retiring Governor, Alexander G. McNutt; the successful Democratic candidate, Tilghman M. Tucker; and the Whig candidate, David O. Shattuck, were all in favour of the repudiation of the Mississippi Union Bank bonds, and on Feb. 26, 1842, the bonds were finally repudiated by the State. See "Banking and Repudiation in Mississippi," *Bankers' Magazine* (N.Y.), XVIII NS (Aug., 1863), 89–109; and R. C. McGrane, *Foreign Bondholders and American State Debts* (New York, 1935), chap. x.

legs almost entirely—this was in June, & since, the little power of moving them that was left has become still less, in spite of all manner of remedies.[3] If the present system of treatment continued through the winter is ineffectual, she talks of trying Franzensbad (near Eger I think) next spring. Do you know anything of that place, or of the medical personages there?

I hope you will let me know immediately if there is anything I can do for you here which would not be better done by some of the many others who would be glad to make themselves of use, though few would be *so* glad as I should.

ever affectionately

J.S.M.

332. TO ALEXANDER BAIN[1]

[Autumn, 1841]

Have you ever looked into Comte's *Cours de Philosophie Positive*? He makes some mistakes, but on the whole, I think it very nearly the grandest work of this age.

333. TO GUSTAVE D'EICHTHAL[1]

India House
8th Nov[r] 1841

My dear d'Eichthal

I have long been a letter in your debt, & have remained so because I have not had a moment of leisure lately to think on the different matters on which I should wish to write to you. I do not think I have written once since I finished reading Salvador's two works,[2] & I certainly have not time to write at present the long letter which I felt a desire to write to you while I was reading them.

I cannot however longer delay telling you that I received the fifth volume

3. Mrs. Taylor eventually recovered from the paralysis, but her health thereafter was usually precarious.

* * * *

1. Excerpt published in Bain, *Autobiography*, p. 112. MS not located.

Alexander Bain (1818–1903), philosopher, first biographer of JSM. Bain had been encouraged by his friend John Robertson to begin a correspondence with JSM in Sept., 1841. They did not meet until the following spring, when Bain visited London.

* * * *

1. *Addressed*: Monsieur / M. Gustave d'Eichthal / 14 Rue Lepelletier / à Paris. *Postmark*: LONDON / [8?] NOV / 1841. MS at Arsenal.

2. See Letter 312, n. 4.

of M. Michelet's History of France & that it appears to me worthy of those which preceded it. Pray, when you see him, give him my very sincere thanks for it & say that as soon as I have finished a book which I have in hand & which is now very nearly ready for the press I will not only write *to* him but I will endeavour to write something to the public *concerning* him.[3]

I have not been in very good health lately, although my complaints are not serious—& the little time & thought that I had to spare from my occupations have been taken up by various cares. I hope my friends at Paris will consider these excuses sufficient for my apparent neglect of them. Next year I hope to be both in better health & with less work on my hands.

As for the state of public affairs here, I can make no prediction about it, except that I am fully satisfied it will go well. In what manner the good results will be brought about I cannot tell, but every contingency which can [occur?] appears to me to be the [bearer?] of good in some very important shape.[4] I rather think this is also the case with affairs in France & that you will agree with me. The only serious mischief which I am at all apprehensive of is foreign intervention in Spain & of that I trust there is very little chance.

With kind regards to Adolphe & all friends

ever yours affectionately

J. S. MILL.

334. TO AUGUSTE COMTE[1]

India House, London
8 Novembre 1841.

Je ne sais, Monsieur, s'il est permis à un homme qui vous est totalement inconnu, d'occuper quelques moments d'un temps aussi précieux que le vôtre en vous entretenant de lui et des grandes obligations intellectuelles dont il vous est redevable; mais encouragé par mon ami M. Marrast,[2] et pensant que peut-être au milieu de vos grands travaux philosophiques il ne

3. A promise eventually fulfilled in 1844 with the publication of his review of the first five volumes of Michelet's *Histoire de France*. See Letter 285, n. 3.
4. Brackets in this sentence indicate where page is torn.

* * * *

1. *Addressed*: Monsieur / M. Auguste Comte / à l'Ecole Polytechnique / à Paris. *Postmark*: LONDON / 8 NOV / 1841 / FBO. Published in Lévy-Bruhl, pp. 1–4; Comte's answer of Nov. 20, 1841, *ibid.*, pp. 4–11. All the MSS of JSM's letters to Comte are at Johns Hopkins.
2. Armand Marrast (1801–1852), journalist and politician; editor of the *Tribune* until 1834; when the paper was suppressed and he was imprisoned in 1835 he escaped and fled to England; upon return to France he became editor of the *National*; after the Revolution of 1848, he became President of the Assemblée Constituante.

vous serait pas complètement indifférent de recevoir d'un pays étranger des témoignages de sympathie et d'adhésion, j'ose espérer que vous ne trouverez pas déplacée ma démarche actuelle.

C'est dans l'année 1828,[3] Monsieur, que j'ai lu pour la première fois votre petit Traité de *Politique Positive*; et cette lecture a donné à toutes mes idées une forte secousse, qui avec d'autres causes mais beaucoup plus qu'elles, a déterminé ma sortie définitive de la section benthamiste de l'école révolutionnaire, dans laquelle je fus élevé, et même je puis presque dire dans laquelle je naquis. Quoique le Benthamisme soit resté, sans doute, très loin du véritable esprit de la méthode positive, cette doctrine me paraît encore à présent la meilleure préparation qui existe aujourd'hui à la vraie positivité, appliquée aux doctrines sociales: soit par sa logique serrée, et par le soin qu'elle a de toujours se comprendre elle même, soit surtout par son opposition systématique à toute tentative d'explication de phénomènes quelconques au moyen des ridicu[les][4] entités métaphysiques, dont elle m'a appris dès ma première jeunesse à sentir la nullité essentielle.

Depuis l'époque où j'ai pris connaissance de la première ébauche de vos idées sociologiques, je crois pouvoir dire que les semences jetées par cet opuscule ne sont pas restées stériles dans mon esprit. Ce n'est pourtant qu'en 1837[5] que j'ai connu les deux premiers volumes de votre Cours, à l'appréciation duquel j'étais heureusement assez bien préparé, n'étant resté totalement étranger à aucune des sciences fondamentales, dans chacune desquelles au reste j'avais toujours surtout recherché les idées de méthode qu'elle pouvait fournir. Depuis l'heureuse époque où ces deux volumes me sont connus, j'attends toujours chaque volume nouveau avec une vive impatience et je le lis et le relis avec une véritable passion intellectuelle. Je puis dire que j'étais déjà entré dans une voie assez voisine de la vôtre, surtout par l'impulsion que m'avait donnée votre ouvrage précédent; mais j'avais encore à apprendre de vous bien des choses de la première importance, et j'espère vous donner à quelque temps d'ici la preuve que je les ai bien apprises. Il reste quelques questions d'un ordre secondaire sur lesquelles mes opinions ne sont pas d'accord avec les vôtres; un jour peut être ce désaccord pourra disparaître: au moins je ne pense pas trop me flatter en croyant qu'il n'y a pas chez moi d'opinion mal fondée qui soit assiz enracinée pour résister à une discussion approfondie, telle qu'elle pourrait peut être se trouver dans le cas de subir si vous ne me refusez pas la permission de vous soumettre quelquefois mes idées et de vous demander des explications sur les vôtres.

Vous savez, Monsieur, que les opinions religieuses ont jusqu'ici plus de racine chez nous que dans les autres pays de l'Europe, quoiqu'elles aient

3. Actually it appears that he first read Comte in 1829. See Letters 26 and 27.
4. MS torn.   5. See Letter 228.

perdu depuis longtemps, ici comme ailleurs, leur ancienne valeur civili-satrice: et il est, je crois, à regretter pour nous que la philosophie révolu-tionnaire qui était encore en pleine activité il y a une douzaine d'années soit aujourd'hui tombée en décrépitude avant d'avoir fini sa tâche. Il est d'autant plus urgent pour nous de la remplacer en entrant à pleine voie dans la philosophie positive: et, c'est avec grand plaisir que je vous le dis, malgré l'esprit ouvertement anti-religieux de votre ouvrage, ce grand monument de la vraie philosophie moderne commence à se faire jour parmi nous, moins pourtant parmi les théoriciens politique que parmi les dif-férentes classes de savants. Il se montre d'ailleurs depuis quelque temps, pour la premiére fois chez nous, dans les cultivateurs des sciences physiques, une tendance assez prononcée vers les généralités scientifiques, qui me paraît de très heureux augure, et qui porte à croire qu'il y a aujourd'hui pour nous plus à espérer de leur part que de la part des hommes politiques soit de spéculation soit d'action. Ceux-ci, en effet, sont tombés dans un affaissement pareil à celui qui s'est si fortement déclaré en France depuis 1830, et chacun voit qu'on ne pourra faire des choses nouvelles que par une doctrine nouvelle; seulement la plupart ne croient pas à l'avènement d'une telle doctrine et restent par conséquent dans un scepticisme de plus en plus énervant et décourageant.

Veuillez, Monsieur, me pardonner cette tentative un peu présomptueuse de me mettre en relation intellectuelle immédiate avec celui des grands esprits de notre temps que je regarde avec le plus d'estime et d'admiration —et croyez que la réalisation de ce vœu serait pour moi d'un prix immense.

J. S. MILL

335. TO JOHN MITCHELL KEMBLE[1]

India House
15th Nov.
1841

MY DEAR SIR

Mr. Weir, a friend of mine, of whom both as a man & as a thinker & writer I can speak very highly, has written me a note of which I inclose a portion. Would you be kind enough to send a line either to himself or to me, to say whether the article he proposes to undertake would suit you.

Ever yours

J. S. MILL

Mr. Weir has been for sometime engaged in extensive & accurate geo-graphical researches.

1. MS owned by Professor Ney MacMinn.

336. TO AUGUSTE COMTE[1]

India House,
18 Décembre, 1841

MON CHER MONSIEUR COMTE—

Je suis vraiment honteux en me rappelant le temps qui s'est écoulé depuis que j'ai reçu la réponse, aussi bienveillante qu'honorable pour moi, que vous avez bien voulu faire à ma première lettre. Mais si j'ai paru montrer peu d'empressement à profiter d'une relation que j'ai si vivement désirée, cela n'a tenu qu'à des occupations urgentes, et dont la principale était précisément de nature à établir entre nous deux plus promptement que par toute autre voie, l'échange d'idées philosophiques dans lequel je compte trouver pour tout le reste de ma vie une si précieuse source soit d'instruction soit de stimulation intellectuelle. Je viens dans ces derniers jours d'achever un ouvrage assez volumineux qui va être livré à l'impression pour paraître, je crois, au printemps prochain. Si après sa publication vous daignez en prendre connaissance, ce que le prix que vous avez bien voulu mettre à la sympathie si fortement prononcée entre nos tendances intellectuelles, me permet seul d'espérer, l'exposition détaillée que j'y ai donnée d'un nombre assez considérable de mes idées vous indiquera jusqu'à un certain point les questions sur lesquelles il n'y a plus lieu à aucune discussion entre nous, et celles où je puis encore profiter de la maturité plus complette de vos conceptions philosophiques. Je vous soumettrai cet ouvrage avec d'autant plus de crainte, que le but même vous en sera certainement suspect, puisque c'est enfin un traité de logique, ou de méthode philosophique. Je suis certainement bien loin d'être insensible aux motifs qui vous ont porté à nier la possibilité, au moins dans la phase scientifique actuelle, d'une théorie de méthode, abstraction faite de la doctrine; même en se conformant à la condition à laquelle je me suis toujours fidèlement soumis de ne puiser la méthode que dans la doctrine même. Aussi je n'attribue nullement au travail que j'ai fait un caractère philosophique permanent, mais tout au plus une valeur transitoire, que je crois pourtant réelle, du moins pour l'Angleterre. Quant aux divergences partielles qui existent jusqu'ici entre ma manière de concevoir certaines questions philosophiques et la vôtre, je crains surtout que si vous en jugez par l'écrit en question vous ne soyez exposé à les croire plus grandes qu'elles ne sont, en ne faisant pas suffisamment la part des concessions que je me suis cru forcé de faire à l'esprit dominant de mon pays. Vous n'ignorez pas sans doute que chez nous l'écrivain qui avouerait hautement

---

1. *Addressed*: A Monsieur / M. Auguste Comte / 10 Rue Monneur le Prince / près l'Odéon / à Paris. *Postmark*: LONDON / 18 / DEC / 1841. MS at Johns Hopkins. Published in Lévy-Bruhl, pp. 11–15; in reply to Comte's letter of Nov. 20, 1841, *ibid.*, pp. 4–11.

des opinions anti réligieuses, ou même anti-chétiennes, compromettrait non seulement sa position sociale, que je me crois capable de sacrifier à un but suffisamment élevé, mais aussi, ce qui serait plus grave, ses chances d'être lu. Je risque déjà beaucoup en mettant soigneusement de côté, dès le commencement, le point de vue religieuse, et en m'abstenant des éloges déclamatoires de la sagesse providentielle, généralement usités parmi les philosophes, même incrédules, de mon pays. Je fais rarement allusion à cet ordre d'idées, et, tout en tâchant de ne pas éveiller, chez le vulgaire des lecteurs, des antipathies religieuses, je crois avoir écrit de manière à ce que nul penseur, soit chrétien soit incrédule, ne puisse se méprendre sur le caractère véritable de mes opinions: me fiant un peu, je l'avoue, à la prudence mondaine, qui chez nous empêche en général les écrivains religieux de proclamer sans nécessité l'irréligion d'un esprit d'une valeur scientifique quelconque.

Un même motif, quoique moins fort, m'a fait quelquefois conserver (ce que je n'aurais probablement pas fait en France) certaines expressions d'origine métaphysique, en m'efforçant toujours d'y attacher un sens positif, et en éliminant autant que possible toutes les formules qui ne paraissent pas susceptibles aujourd'hui d'être envisagées seulement comme les noms abstraits des phénomènes. Je dois m'avouer, en même temps, suspect à vos yeux de tendances métaphysiques, en tant que je crois à la possibilité d'une psychologie positive, qui ne serait certainement ni celle de Condillac, ni celle de Cousin, ni même celle de l'école Ecossaise, et que je crois toute comprise dans cette analyse de nos facultés intellectuelles et affectives qui entre dans votre système comme destinée à servir de vérification à la physiologie phrénologique, et qui a pour but essentiel de séparer les facultés vraiment primordiales de celles qui ne sont que les conséquences nécessaires des autres, produites par voie de combinaison et d'action mutuelle.

Je vois que mon ami M. Marrast vous a donné sur mon compte quelques renseignements qui ne sont pas d'une exactitude complète. D'abord, je ne suis pas chargé des travaux statistiques de la Compagnie des Indes, mais bien d'une partie de l'administration politique de l'Inde, surtout en ce qui regarde les relations extérieures, y compris le contrôle général des nombreux rois ou roitelets indigènes qui sont dans notre dépendance, et dont la civilisation peu avancée nous donne souvent des embarras. Ensuite je dois vous dire que mon abstinence de la vie parlementaire ne peut pas être pour moi un titre de louanges, ayant toujours été nécessitée par l'incompatibilité de cette vie avec l'emploi dont je retire mes moyens de vie. Je puis d'autant moins vous laisser dans l'erreur à cet égard, que des occasions ont existé où si ma position personnelle ne m'avait pas interdit l'action politique directe, je crois que je m'y serais lais[sé][2] entraîner. Les

2. MS torn.

motifs auxquels j'aurais crû obéir eûssent été d'abord la difficulté, beaucoup plus grande ici qu'en France (vû la moindre activité spéculative de mes compatriotes) d'attirer l'attention même d'un public d'élite sur les idées théoriques d'un homme qui n'aurait pas fait ses preuves dans la vie active; et ensuite la considération, certainement bien fondée, que la véritable émancipation des spéculations sociologiques soit de l'empirisme, soit de la tutelle théologique ne saurait avoir lieu chez nous, tant que nous n'avons pas encore fait notre 1789, ce qu'il devient tous les jours plus difficile de faire au nom et par les moyens de la doctrine purement négative; et je crois même qu'une réaction durable ne tarderait pas à se déclarer en faveur des doctrines rétrogrades, sans l'influence des divers intérèts personnels qui se trouvent aujourd'hui froissés par les institutions que ces doctrines tendent à consacrer: intérêts qui pourtant seront bientôt frappés d'impuissance, même dans le sens subversif, s'ils ne trouvent quelque part, et même dans la vie politique, un point de ralliement spéculatif tel que les doctrines simplement révolutionnaires ne sont plus capable aujourd'hui d'offrir. Sentant au reste comme je le fais très sincèrement, jusqu'à quel point on est porté à se faire des illusions sur tout ce qui peut intéresser, même médiocrement la vanité personnelle, je dois probablement me féliciter de ce que la direction spéciale de mon activité a été principalement déterminée jusqu'ici par des causes indépendantes de ma propre sagesse.

J'attends avec impatience la publication du volume qui complètera votre grand ouvrage, et celle ensuite du traité spécial de politique qui doit le suivre, et où je compte trouver des éclaircissements sur bien des questions posées dans les 4me et 5me volumes et qui n'ont fait jusqu'ici qu'éveiller chez moi des besoins intellectuels sans y satisfaire complètement mais sur tout cela je compte à vous entretenir plus au long dans mes lettres à venir.

Votre bien dévoué

J. S. MILL.

337. TO JOHN MURRAY[1]

India House
20th Dec 1841

MY DEAR SIR

I have just finished preparing for the press a book of which I enclose the Preface and Table of Contents.[2] It will make two good-sized octavo

1. MS in the possession of Sir John Murray.
2. The *Logic*. JSM's friend John Sterling had written Murray on Dec. 16, 1841, reporting the completion of the book and describing it as "the labour of many years of a singularly subtle, patient, and comprehensive mind. It will be our chief speculative monument of this age." (Samuel Smiles, *A Publisher and His Friends* [2 vols., London, 1891], II, 499.)

volumes. I should like it to have the benefit of being published by you, but it does not suit me if I can do otherwise, to print it at my own risk, and I cannot tell whether it will suit you to do so at yours. I however request your consideration of the subject, and should be much obliged by an early determination, as I should wish at all events that it should be published in the approaching season.

Very truly yours

J. S. MILL

The whole or any part of the manuscript shall be sent for your inspection whenever you may require it, or at least as soon as I have finished reading it through and making the few final corrections.

1842

338. TO ALBANY FONBLANQUE[1]

India House
Saturday
[Jan. 1, 1842]

MY DEAR FONBLANQUE

Soon after the Copyright Bill was thrown out,[2] there appeared in the Examiner a very able article[3] in answer to Macaulay's speech[4] which appeared to many persons the best thing yet written on the subject & which as such has been inserted entire in an article of Lockhart,[5] published in the Quarterly this day.[6] Some of the supporters of Talfourd's Bill have thought that it would be useful to do with this question what is done with other questions by commercial and other bodies interested in them, namely to get a statement of the case drawn up by a competent person to be published & circulated as a pamphlet & I have been asked to ascertain whether the writer of that article in the Examiner would be willing to undertake this, being properly remunerated for which purpose a subscription is spoken of. I have not the least idea who the writer is, nor of course do I ask it, but if you would communicate with him, that is, if you would communicate *to* him what I have now written, & to me what he says about it, you will oblige the persons in question & perhaps do some considerable good to the cause.

ever yours truly

J. S. MILL

1. MS in the possession of Lady Hermione Cobbold. Collated by Dr. Eileen Curran.
2. Feb. 5, 1841.
3. "The Defeated Copyright Bill," *Examiner*, Feb. 28, 1841, pp. 130–31. Since this letter to Fonblanque is preserved in Bulwer's papers, the inference seems fair that the article was by Bulwer.
4. On Feb. 5, 1841. Reprinted in *Miscellaneous Works of Lord Macaulay*, ed. Lady Trevelyan (6 vols., New York, 1880), V, 228–43.
5. "The Copyright Question," *QR*, LXIX (Dec., 1841), 186–227. J. G. Lockhart was editor of the *Quarterly Review*, 1825–53.
6. The Dec., 1841, *QR* was published on Jan. 1, 1842. See *Spectator*, Jan. 1, 1842, p. 24.

339. TO GUSTAVE D'EICHTHAL[1]

I.H.
10ᵗʰ Janʸ 1842

My dear Gustave—I am really ashamed to see that your last letter, one of the most interesting I ever received from you, has remained more than six weeks unanswered. My only excuse is that I was & still am busy making the final revision of a book which is to be published this spring[2] & in which I have said all that I can find to say on Methods of Philosophic Investigation. I do not expect to find many readers for this book, but I had things to say on the subject, & it was part of my task on earth to say them & therefore having said them I feel a portion of my work to be done.

With regard to Salvador's two books,[3] the earliest made a very mixed impression upon me, the latest one wholly favourable: it seems to me that he has better understood the spirit of the times in which Christianity arose, & the nature of Christianity itself as a phenomenon in the history of the ancient world than anybody else, & that he is nearer the truth than even Strauss.[4] Altogether it is a grand book & I have instigated several people to read it. As for the first, it has also thrown much new light upon history & has made me think in a manner I never expected to do of the Hebrew people & polity, mais cela se ressent horriblement des quinze dernières années de la restauration—I could hardly help laughing at the manner in which he strains everything to recommend poor Moses to the Constitutional Opposition & to shew that the Jews were Liberals, political economists & Utilitarians, that they had properly speaking no religion, or next to none, & were altogether à la hauteur de l'époque, worthy sons of the 18ᵗʰ century. I would very strongly advise him to cancel the whole book & write it over again in a spirit worthy of his second work, written ten or twelve years later & for a public much more advanced. He is quite right for instance in saying that the liberty of prophesying was equivalent in the Jewish polity to the liberty of the press & the point is a new & striking one, but it really is not necessary to tell us that the prophets did not *pretend to be*, nor were supposed to be, specially accredited from God, that all the expressions implying them to be such are a mere façon de parler, meaning only that they were very clever fellows, & to fortify this by philological arguments from the usages & phrases of the Hebrew tongue. Why not say

---

1. *Addressed*: Monsieur / Gustave d'Eichthal / 14 Rue Lepelletier / à Paris. *Post-marks*: LONDON / 8 / JAN / 1842 and 10 / CALAIS. Published in *D'Eichthal Corresp.*, pp. 196–200, and in *Cosmopolis*, IX, 379–81. MS at Arsenal. The first postmark would seem to indicate that JSM had misdated his letter.
2. The *Logic* did not appear until 1843.
3. See Letter 312, n. 4.
4. D. F. Strauss (1808–1874), German rationalist theologian, author of *Das Leben Jesu* (2 vols., Tübingen, 1835), and *Christliche Glaubenslehre* . . . (2 vols., Tübingen, 1840–41).

at once that all persons of genius, inspired persons in the modern sense, poets & persons of imagination & eloquence who had great & wonderful powers not derived from teaching, were believed to derive these powers straight from God & were in consequence of that religious belief, permitted from religious motives to exercise that right of free speech & free censure of powerful persons, which certainly would not in that age have been conceded to any one who spoke merely as from himself?

I have been reading at odd times your old friend Leroux's book, De l'Humanité:[5] the historical part I like; those few pages on the schools & Greek philosophy are quite perfect; but when we come to his own theory, did ever mortal man write such intolerable nonsense! There are ideas in that too about Moses, but qui ne valent pas celles de Salvador.

I long to see your speculations on the subject but I would not advise your publishing a translation here, at least in the first instance: even Salvador has not been translated nor heard of, & nobody here is yet ripe for reading a serious philosophical discussion on the Bible. We are all either bigots or Voltairians. But we are improving. In ten years I think we shall have made some way, between our neo-Catholic school at [Oxf]ord[6] & the German Rationalists who are beginning to be *secretly* read here.

All you say on politics in your letter is extremely interesting & *evidently* true. You are the only person whose opinion on the political state & prospects of France I always feel that I can rely on. As for us, I believe that we are about to have a real *juste milieu* ministry & that things will go on tolerably smoothly till the grande question sociale des ouvriers becomes imminent, which it is rapidly becoming, perhaps more rapidly here than even with you. What will happen then, heaven knows. Il nous manque *un homme*, tout comme à vous.

Give my kindest regards to Adolphe & remembrances to all friends.

Ever yours,

J. S. MILL.

340. TO JOHN MURRAY[1]

India House
31st Jany 1842

MY DEAR SIR

I have now finished revising my Manuscript, and the remaining three Books shall be sent to you if you think fit. I believe I have already men-

---

5. Pierre Henri Leroux, *De l'Humanité, de son principe et de son avenir* . . . (2 vols., Paris, 1840).
6. Page torn. The Tractarian or "Puseyite" movement led by John Henry Newman.

* * * *

1. MS in the possession of Sir John Murray. See Letter 337.

tioned that they are of a rather more popular character than the three preceding.

You would oblige me very much, if you cannot give me an affirmative answer, by giving me a negative one as early as possible, since any other publisher to whom the MS. might be referred would probably also require some time for making up his mind and in that way the season might be lost.

Very truly yours

J. S. MILL

341. TO MACVEY NAPIER[1]

India House
8ᵗʰ Febʸ 1842

MY DEAR SIR

Having now my hands clear of all other literary occupation, except in the matter of correcting proofs, I am at liberty to resume & strengthen my incipient connexion with the Ed. Rev. if it continues to be agreeable to you that I should do so. I have not at present any particular subjects in view, except those which we formerly spoke of[2] Michelet's Histories of Rome & France. If those subjects will still suit you I will begin preparing myself for them, but as this will necessarily require a good deal of reading & thought, indeed I might say a gradual crystallization of many thoughts at present held in a state of suspension, it may be some time before I am able to produce anything fit for you on these topics, while the process of preparation would not be interfered with by my writing something else for you in the meantime if you should have any subject in view on which I could write with less previous study. I am therefore open to any proposition you may be inclined to make.

I am glad to say that my friend Fletcher after a tedious & harrassing illness of a year in duration, is now tolerably recovered & at work vigorously on Cervantes—he says his article will soon be ready.[3]

ever yours

J. S. MILL

1. MS in Brit. Mus.
2. See Letter 285.   3. No such article appeared.

342. TO MACVEY NAPIER[1]

I.H.
18th Feb[y]
1842

MY DEAR SIR

Your opinion & the prospects you hold out respecting Bain[2] & Lewes[3] are quite as favourable as I had any reason to expect. They are both very young men, the former in particular almost a youth, & they have the full measure of the defects natural in the one case to a young littérateur, in the other to a young metaphysician. I myself wrote a long letter to Bain about his article on Toys[4] pointing out some of the graver defects in it which he at once saw & admitted & neither he nor I ever supposed for a moment that that particular article would have been admissible into the Edinburgh. I only mentioned it to you or rather to your son in order to shew what the young man can already do & how much he has in him.

In one respect I think you judge both of them too severely. I do not think they are either of them coxcombs although Lewes at least is very likely to be thought so. But what gives him that air is precisely the buoyancy of spirit which you have observed in him, & he is so prompt & apparently presumptuous in undertaking anything for which he feels the slightest vocation, (however much it may be really beyond his strength) only because he does not care at all for failure, knowing & habitually feeling that he gets up stronger after every fall & believing as I do that the best way of improving one's faculties is to be continually trying what is above one's present strength. I should say he is confident but not at all conceited, for he will bear to be told anything however unflattering about what he writes—& when I say *bear*, I do not mean that he is so well fortified in self conceit as to bear with temper what he does not believe to be just—no, but to be convinced at the very first suggestion, that it *is* just & to betake himself without delay to correcting it. As for Bain, I can completely understand *him*, because I have been, long ago, very much the same sort of person, except that I had not half his real originality. I should have been thought quite as presumptuous if the things I wrote had found any body to publish them. When one is so young, & writes out one's thoughts exactly as they have grown up in one's own mind without reference to other people & without seizing the connexion between them & what others have previously written, one always seems to be laying the most unbounded &

1. MS in Brit. Mus.
2. Alexander Bain.
3. George Henry Lewes.   4. "On Toys," *WR*, XXXVII (Jan., 1842), 97–121.

groundless claims to discovery, when really one is not consciously making such claims to any extent at all, or not to any considerable extent.

I am very glad that I sent you the extract from Comte's letter.[5] I have no doubt he would be much gratified by a letter from Sir D. Brewster,[6] but I throw that out only as a suggestion.

ever yours truly

J. S. MILL.

343. TO JOHN MURRAY[1]

India House
24th Feb[y]
1842

MY DEAR SIR

Being prevented by official occupation from having the pleasure of calling upon you at any hour at which it is usually agreeable to discuss matters of business, I write to you again[2] to solicit an answer on the subject of my MS *on Logic*—not from any impatience but because the delay in signifying your intentions leads me to presume that you would rather not publish the book and therefore I am desirous of saying that although I should have been glad if you could have done so, I am not disappointed having never thought it very likely that you would. As however I should not like either to postpone the publication to another year or to hurry the printing, I should wish to try some other publisher as soon as possible and therefore if I have rightly conjectured your own feeling on the matter, I should be much obliged by your returning the MS.

very truly yours

J. S. MILL

---

5. Which letter has not been ascertained.
6. Sir David Brewster (1781–1868), Scottish scientist and educator.

* * * *

1. MS in the possession of Sir John Murray.
2. See Letters 337 and 340. Samuel Smiles in his memoir of John Murray, *A Publisher and His Friends* (2 vols., London, 1891), II, 499, notes that Murray was very ill at this time and could not give attention to the work.

344. TO AUGUSTE COMTE[1]

India House
25 février 1842

MON CHER MONSIEUR COMTE—

Je ne crois pas nécessaire de vous faire de nouvelles excuses sur le retard que je mets à répondre aux lettres si aimables et si instructives dont vous voulez bien m'honorer. Ce ne sont pas, cette fois-ci, des occupations qui m'ont empêché de vous écrire, mais plutôt des préoccupations. Je n'ai pas besoin de dire que des lettres telles que les vôtres ne doivent pas seulement être bien et mûrement pesées, mais aussi que pour y répondre dignement on a besoin de se trouver dans une disposition d'esprit tout à fait convenable.

Je dois commencer par vous témoigner la vive satisfaction avec laquelle j'ai appris la prochaine terminaison de l'ouvrage que j'ai si longtemps suivi avec une admiration toujours croissante. Ce travail est un exemple qui me confirme dans l'idée déjà ancienne chez moi, que les plus grandes choses sont faites le plus souvent par ceux qui ont le moins de loisir. Je sais trop ce que doivent être les pénibles travaux journaliers de votre état, pour ne pas m'étonner que vous ayez osé entreprendre et que vous soyez parvenu à accomplir une tâche si immense, et exigeant une si grande concentration d'esprit ainsi qu'une si rare dépense de forces intellectuelles. Je sais d'ailleurs combien au milieu de tout cela vous payez noblement votre tribut aux intérêts philanthropiques du moment, par le cours scientifique que vous faites chaque année aux ouvriers de Paris. C'est une manière de participation aux affaires du jour, bien plus féconde sans doute en résultats bienfaisants, que celle des stériles discussions de la presse périodique ou de la tribune parlementaire, au moins en France.

Quant à vos remarques sur l'incompatibilité, même en Angleterre, de l'action politique directe avec une influence réelle sur la rénovation philosophique qui seule aujourd'hui peut être d'une importance majeure, je ne suis déjà pas très éloigné de votre opinion, à laquelle je me rendrai peutêtre tout entier après la lecture, si vivement désirée, de votre 6me volume. Je puis du moins indiquer comme étant pour moi le résultat jusqu'ici le plus positif et le plus certain de l'étude du 5me volume, une conviction complète du grand principe que seul entre les philosophes contemporains vous avez énoncé, celui de la séparation définitive des deux pouvoirs, temporel et spirituel. Ces pouvoirs doivent incontestablement s'organiser d'une manière totalement distincte, ce qui au reste n'implique pas pour moi l'impossibilité

---

1. MS at Johns Hopkins. Published in Lévy-Bruhl, pp. 26–32. In answer to Comte's of Jan. 17, 1842, *ibid.*, pp. 16–25.

que le même individu puisse participer jusqu'à un certain point aux travaux de tous les deux. Je pense au contraire qu'une éducation partiellement active est nécessaire à la perfection de la capacité spéculative, ainsi qu'une éducation spéculative l'est, de l'aveu de tous les philosophes, à celle de la vie active. Je n'en suis pas moins radicalement guéri, et cela par votre ouvrage, de toute tendance vers les doctrines utopistes qui cherchent à remettre le gouvernement de la societé entre les mains des philosophes, ou même de le faire dépendre de la haute capacité intellectuelle, envisagée plus généralement. Comme la plupart des libres penseurs nourris dans les idées françaises du 19ᵐᵉ [sic] siècle, je n'ai pas toujours complètement évité cette erreur irrationnelle; mais le sens commun et l'histoire en avaient jusqu'à un certain point fait justice chez moi, même avant la lecture des arguments irrésistibles par lesquels vous soutenez si victorieusement la doctrine contraire. Outre l'altération grave que la suprématie politique ne tarderait pas à produire dans les habitudes morales et intellectuelles de la classe spéculative, il me semble que cette domination ne serait nullement favorable au progrès intellectuel, en vue duquel, sans doute, elle a été surtout rêvée. Je trouve dans l'exemple de la Chine un grand appui à cette opinion. Dans ce pays-là, la constitution du gouvernement se rapproche autant peutêtre que cela se peut, du principe saint-simonien, et qu'est-ce qui en est résulté? le gouvernement le plus opposé de tous à toute sorte de progrès. La majorité d'une classe lettrée quelconque est peutêtre moins disposée que celle de toute autre classe, à se laisser mener par les intelligences les plus développées qui s'y rencontrent; et comme cette majorité ne pourrait, sans doute, se composer de grands penseurs, mais simplement d'érudits, ou de savans sans véritable originalité, il ne pourrait en résulter que ce qu'on voit dans la Chine, c'est à dire une pédantocratie.

Vous voyez donc que nous sommes tous deux en sympathie complète, quant à nos principes généraux sur ce sujet. Ce que je dois, là-dessus, à votre livre, c'est surtout d'avoir formulé dans le principe de la séparation des pouvoirs temporel et spirituel et de l'organisation de chacun sur les bases qui lui sont propres, une doctrine plus vague que j'avais moi-même tirée de l'histoire et que j'avais jetée dans les discussions du jour comme réponse décisive à tout système politique démocratique ou Benthamiste. Cette doctrine la voici: Que dans toutes les sociétés humaines où l'existence des véritables conditions du progrès continu a été prouvée *a posteriori* par l'ensemble de leur histoire, il y a eu, du moins virtuellement, un antagonisme organisé. Puisque dans nulle société le pouvoir dominant n'a pu résumer en soi tous les intérêts progressifs et toutes les tendances dont la réunion est nécessaire à la durabilité indéfinie de la marche ascendante, il a fallu partout aux intérêts et aux tendances plus ou moins antipathiques à ce pouvoir, un point de ralliement assez fortement constitué pour les pro-

téger efficacement contre toute tentative soit réfléchie, soit seulement instinc-
tive, de les comprimer; tentative dont le succès amènerait, après un temps
ordinairement très court, soit la dissolution sociale, comme à Athènes, soit
l'état stationnaire bien caractérisé de l'Egypte et de l'Asie. J'avais toujours
ressenti une grande difficulté à concevoir la forme dans laquelle ce principe
nécessaire au progrès devait trouver son application définitive à la politique
moderne. Mais je vois dans la doctrine de la séparation des pouvoirs
spirituel et temporel, une fois posée par vous, la solution de cette difficulté,
puisque cette théorie réunit toutes les conditions de l'antagonisme indispensable, avec des recommandations qui lui sont propres et qui en font
évidemment la forme théoriquement parfaite de l'application de ce principe.

Pour en revenir aux considérations personnelles; la question de participation au moins directe, au mouvement politique, se trouve pour moi à peu
près décidée par ma position individuelle. Je remettrai à un autre temps
l'exposition de mes vues sur les circonstances politiques de mon pays, qui
malgré la force incontestable de vos objections, font encore à mes yeux de
la tribune parlementaire la meilleure chaire d'enseignement public pour un
philosophe sociologiste convenablement placé, et qui chercherait peut être
à faire des ministères ou à les diriger dans sons sens, mais en s'abstenant
d'en faire partie, sinon probablement dans des moments critiques que je
ne crois pas, chez nous, très éloignés. Mais au lieu de parler de ces choses
qui ne me regardent nullement, je m'autoriserai de votre sympathie bienveillante pour vous entretenir de celles qui me regardent, et je dirai que
j'entre dans une époque de ma vie qui me mettra pour la première fois à
même de savoir jusqu'à quel point l'activité purement philosophique, dirigée
dans le sens de mes opinions et avec le dégré de capacité dont je puis
disposer, est capable de donner dans notre pays une influence réelle sur la
marche des idées, au moins chez les hommes les plus avancés. Jusqu'ici
quoique plus connu qu'on ne l'est ordinairement lorsqu'on n'a jamais
exercé aucune fonction publique évidente et qu'on n'a rien publié qu'anony-
mement, je suis totalement inconnu du public ordinaire et par conséquent
je n'ai pas le moindre commencement d'autorité morale. Ceux d'ailleurs
qui ne sont pas totalement étrangers à mes travaux ne me connaissent que
comme une sorte d'homme politique, appartenant au parti révolutionnaire
modéré, et qui a quelquefois écrit en philosophe sur les questions de la
politique actuelle. Mais aujourd'hui je livre mon nom à la publicité, par un
ouvrage purement philosophique et en même temps par la réimpression des
meilleurs de mes écrits antérieurs dont pour la première fois je prends sur
moi la responsabilité. Je ne me fais aucune illusion sur le dégré de succès
dont l'une ou l'autre de ces publications est susceptible, mais quel qu'il
puisse être il me donnera probablement une place quelconque parmi les
supériorités intellectuelles reconnues, et me permettra jusqu'à un certain

point d'apprécier le degré d'influence que je suis capable d'exercer sur le mouvement spirituel, ainsi que les meilleurs moyens de m'en servir.

Je regrette de vous avoir involontairement donné l'idée que l'ouvrage philosophique dont il est question avait pour but l'analyse de nos facultés mentales et de nos tendances morales. J'ai seulement entendu exprimer ma croyance à la possibilité et à la valeur scientifique d'une psychologie ainsi entendue; mais dans ma Logique, je ne m'occupe que de méthode, c'est à dire des actes intellectuels, en faisant autant que possible abstraction des facultés. Il n'est pourtant pas impossible que je m'occupe un jour de cette autre tâche, et afin d'y être mieux préparé je vous engage très fortement à m'indiquer les lectures les plus propres à me donner une véritable connaissance de la physiologie phrénologique. Chez nous la phrénologie n'a guère été cultivée que par des hommes d'une intelligence moins que médiocre, si j'en juge par ce que j'ai lu de leurs écrits, et je vous avouerai que j'ai longtemps regardée cette doctrine, au moins dans son état présent, comme indigne d'occuper l'attention d'un vrai penseur, idée dont je ne suis revenu qu'en apprenant par votre 3me volume que vous y adhériez au moins dans ses principales bases. Je suis donc resté fort arriére sur ce sujet important, ce à quoi je désire promptement remédier, et me faire le plus tôt possible, sur une question qui doit nécessairement exercer une grande influence sur mes spéculations à venir une opinion mûre, et aussi bien fondée qu'elle peut l'être.

Tout à vous de cœur

J. S. MILL,
(John Stuart)

345. TO MACVEY NAPIER[1]

I.H.
3^d March
1842

MY DEAR SIR

I do not doubt that I could easily have an article on Michelet's Hist. of France ready for your October number, but as there will probably be another volume published before that time it is of no use setting about the article just yet, & as the book will extend to twelve volumes of which only five are yet published the subject will be good for a long time to come.[2]

I should have preferred if it had been possible to begin with the Romans

1. MS in Brit. Mus.
2. JSM's review did not appear in the *Edinburgh* until Jan., 1844.

because I think I can make a better, & certainly a more original article on them than on the middle ages, my acquaintance with which is not derived from the original authorities. The article on Michelet's France would be essentially an article on the middle ages, not on France & I may as well mention that my views of that portion of history are strongly Guelphic, that is I am almost always with the popes against the Kings. That is a view very seldom taken in this country, & I do not know how it would suit the Edinburgh Review. But the principles it involves lie at the heart of all my opinions on politics & history.

If there were any suitable peg on which to hang an article on the Romans, I should be much obliged by your suggesting it since Michelet's History is too old. I cannot help thinking that if you were fully aware of the importance of Michelet as a European thinker you would consider a book of his even if not quite recent (provided it is not previously much known in this country) as a better occasion for an article than a production of little value in itself even if fresh. I should have thought, too, that in regard to *foreign* books the question was not so much when they were published, as whether they are a fresh subject to the English reader. But you are the best judge of the principles & rules for conducting your review.

ever yours truly

J. S. MILL.

346. TO JOHN WILLIAM PARKER[1]

Kensington
Monday
[March, 1842]

MY DEAR SIR

I send the portions of MS. which your friend[2] wishes to see—together with some other chapters or portions of chapters which from the manner in which the papers are stitched together, cannot conveniently be separated from them.

I fear some parts are by no means so legible as I could wish, owing to the number of interlineations & erasures. The portions moreover of the Third Book,[3] will scarcely perhaps be intelligible without the chapters which are intended to precede them. However they must take their chance

1. MS at LSE. No date [paper watermarked 1841].
John William Parker (1792–1870), publisher and printer.
2. Presumably the referee whom Parker had asked to see the manuscript of the *Logic*. See Letter 351, n. 2.
3. Book III of the *Logic*, "Of Induction."

& perhaps on the whole these fragments are as fair a specimen of the book as any others would be.

Ever yours truly

J. S. MILL

347. TO SARAH AUSTIN[1]

India House
11th March
1842

You must, both of you, have thought me very negligent or very indifferent, but it is not so. I have delayed writing from day to day in hopes that I might be able to tell you something or other about your own affairs, about America of course I mean. I watch very sedulously & interestedly, on your account, every indication of future events there, but without any result worth communicating. It seems to me however, as far as I have the means of observing, that the expectation *here* among people who attend to the matter, is that the debts, Mississippi included, will be *ultimately* recognised & paid.[2] It is certainly difficult to believe that prosperous & improving communities can go on long without feeling the inconvenience of not being trusted in pecuniary transactions.—Failing anything on this subject I was in hopes of being able to tell you something decisive about my own affairs, namely about my book—but all I have to tell is that I have only just succeeded in extorting a negative answer from Murray after a consideration or at least a delay which endured from the middle of December to last Tuesday. I am now in treaty with Parker, with whom Lewis[3] has placed me in communication but I know not yet what will be the result. I have not begun to print, as my object is if possible to induce somebody to take the risk—a thing I confess if I were myself a publisher I should hesitate to do. The book is all finished, however, revision and all, & has been so nearly two months & if Parker is tractable there will still be time to print it & bring it out this season. I am on the whole quite as well satisfied with the book as I ever thought I should be—perhaps more so. In any case it is the best I can do, & others must judge of it now, & make what they can of it, or leave it alone if it so pleases them.

I was very glad to hear from Stephen[4] the other day that an article is in preparation for the Edin. Rev. on a book[5] the nature of which I well

1. *Addressed*: Madame Austin / Poste Restante / Dresden. *Postmark*: LONDON / 11 / MAR / 1842. MS in Goldsmiths' Library, University of London.

2. Both JSM and the Austins suffered losses by the repudiation of the debts of some of the American states. See Letter 331, n. 2.

3. George Cornewall Lewis.   4. James Stephen.

5. Austin's review of Friedrich List's *Das nationale System der politischen Oekonomie* (Stuttgart and Tübingen, 1841), in *ER*, LXXV (July, 1842), 515–56.

remember though I have forgotten the author. Stephen took credit to himself for having instigated Mr. Austin to write & publish the things which he had already spoken to him (Stephen) on the subject & of which he appeared to have a most genuinely *sentie* admiration. I hardly know anything more likely to be of use here in making people think, & in putting the best views into the best minds, than that subject treated as Mr. Austin is sure to treat it—& the more nearly he writes as he would talk, the better in point of popular impressiveness it is sure to be. The only real danger is lest he should attempt to make it *too* good.

Politics here are going smoothly enough. Peel is making a considerable number of petty improvements, such however as would not have been thought petty formerly, while his corn law has at least the negative merit of doing so very little that it has no tendency to slacken the agitation. The most remarkable recent indication perhaps of the decay of prejudice is that a bill[6] has been brought into the H. of Lords to take away nearly all the disqualifications of witnesses, except that of the parties to the suit, & this is most strenuously supported by Lyndhurst[7] & all the Law Lords, old Wynford[8] being even eager to admit the parties too. At the present moment however nobody is thinking of anything but the Afghanistan disasters.[9] Everybody now condemns the folly of involving ourselves in that *galère* & nobody knows how we are now to get out of it. The thing will end in our exacting at immense cost some signal reparation for the treacherous menace & then evacuating the country, & that is the best end it can have. The feeling in France towards England seems as bad as ever and that in England towards France worse than ever. If the anti English feeling continues to grow in Germany also, things will be in a hopeful condition—

What are to be your movements this year? is there any chance of your coming here, even for ever so short a time? if not, how are you to be communicated with, & in particular how shall I send a copy of my Logic when it is printed? Whenever there is anything to be done for you here which cannot be done better by somebody else, do let me know & let me do it.

yours affectionately

J. S. MILL

6. The second reading of this bill for the improvement of the law of evidence was heard in the House of Lords on March 8, 1842.

7. John Singleton Copley, first Baron Lyndhurst, Lord Chancellor.

8. William Draper Best, first Baron Wynford (1767–1845), Deputy Speaker of the House of Lords.

9. An insurrection against the British in Afghanistan had arisen in Nov., 1841. In Jan. the British had been forced to evacuate Kabul and their forces were subsequently annihilated. News of the disaster at Kabul reached England early in March.

348. TO AUGUSTE COMTE[1]

India House
22 mars 1842

Mon cher Monsieur Comte—

Je me félicite toujours de plus en plus des rapports de correspondance qui se sont si heureusement établis entre nous deux, en attendant, j'espère, des rapports personnels, qui me seraient encore plus précieux. Votre dernière lettre me fait sentir plus que jamais combien notre sympathie philosophique est déja intime, en montrant qu'elle ne se borne pas aux principes fondamentaux, mais qu'elle s'étend jusqu'aux questions secondaires de manière à indiquer que dans la suite elle se prononcera constamment de plus en plus. Non seulement les divergences qui semblaient d'abord exister dans notre manière d'envisager les relations mutuelles des deux puissances élémentaires, ont à peu près disparu par les explications que vous avez bien voulu me donner de votre opinion; non seulement vous avez donné votre sanction philosophique au principe de l'antagonisme continu comme condition de la progression humaine, principe qui faisait le terme le plus avancé du développement sociologique auquel j'étais parvenu par mes propres réflexions; mais aussi je retrouve chez vous une autre idée à laquelle j'ai toujours tenu beaucoup, et peutêtre seul parmi mes compatriotes. Je suis comme vous intimement persuadé que la combinaison de l'esprit français avec l'esprit anglais est un des besoins les plus essentiels de la réorganisation intellectuelle. L'esprit français est nécessaire afin que les conceptions soient générales, et l'esprit anglais pour les empêcher d'être vagues, défaut prédominant en France chez les intelligences secondaires, tandis que chez nous les généralisations quelconques ne trouvent guère d'accueil, en matière morale ou sociale, que de la part d'hommes très avancés. Je crois que c'est Voltaire qui a dit: "Quand un français et un anglais s'accordent, il faut qu'ils aient pleinement raison":[2] cela serait encourageant pour nous deux si nous en avions besoin, avec la conviction profonde que nous avons déjà. Il est au reste fort à regretter que les

1. *Addressed*: Monsieur / M. Auguste Comte / 10 Rue M. le Prince / près l'Odéon / à Paris. *Postmark*: LONDON / 22 / MAR / 1842. MS at Johns Hopkins. Published in Lévy-Bruhl, pp. 40–45. In answer to Comte's letter of March 4, 1842, *ibid.*, pp. 32–40.
2. JSM's quotation is not wholly accurate: "Quand un Français et un Anglais pensent de même, il faut bien qu'ils aient raison" (Lettre XXII, "Sur M. Pope et quelques autres poëtes fameux," *Lettres philosophiques*, in *Œuvres complètes de Voltaire*, ed. Louis Moland, XXII [Paris, 1879], 178).

penseurs de nos deux pays soient loin d'avoir les uns pour les autres l'estime qu'ils méritent. En mathématique, en physique, en chimie, en biologie même, les savants français et anglais se rendent justice mutuellement, et il en était ainsi même au plus chaud de la guerre révolutionnaire et napoléonienne. Il n'en est malheureusement pas de même en ce qui concerne les questions morales et sociales; et c'est ici l'angleterre qui est le plus en défaut. Le mouvement intellectuel français postérieur à la révolution est encore aujourd'hui pour la plupart des anglais même instruits, comme s'il n'avait pas existé. Vous me croirez à peine quand je dis que même les travaux de la nouvelle école historique sont à peine connus ici; que les écrits par exemple de M. Guizot ne commencent à être un peu lus que depuis qu'il a passé ici comme ambassadeur, et que ceux qui savaient devoir se rencontrer avec lui dans le monde ont trouvé convenable de connaitre au moins les noms de ses principaux écrits. Les anglais cherchent plus volontiers des idées nouvelles chez les allemands que chez les français et bien du monde a lu non seulement Kant, mais encore Schelling et Hegel sans même avoir lu Cousin, qui présente les mêmes idées ténébreuses avec une lucidité et un esprit de systématisation tout français. Dans cette inattention au mouvement philosophique de la france, il se rencontre toutefois de singulières exceptions. Je ne sais si je vous ai encore parlé d'une nouvelle école de philosophie théologique qui s'est élevée dans ces derniers temps à Oxford et qui me paraît destinée à remplir dans la régénération sociologique de l'Angleterre un rôle tout pareil à celui de l'école de De Maistre, dont elle partage essentiellement les doctrines. Comme cette école, elle juge la crise actuelle d'une manière à peu près vraie, se trompant seulement sur les remèdes; elle réhabilite le catholicisme et le moyen âge; elle s'appelle catholique, et prétend que l'église anglicane est toujours restée telle (à la vérité sans le pape, mais en transportant le pouvoir spirituel dans le corps des évêques) elle soutient le principe de l'autorité contre celui de la liberté illimitée de conscience, principe qui est encore plus fortement accrédité ici par les préjugés protestants qu'il ne l'a pu être en France par la philosophie de Voltaire et de Diderot, justement parce que sa victoire moins complète n'a pas permis qu'il se réduisît à l'absurde par le plein développement de ses conséquences antisociales. Cette école resemble aussi à l'école française catholique en ce qu'elle a été la première à fonder dans ce pays-ci une sorte de philosophie historique, tout à fait semblable, au reste, à celle de l'auteur du *Pape*,[3] que je doute pourtant si ces écrivains ont lu. Malgré cela ils ne laissent pas de jeter les yeux de temps en temps sur l'autre côté de la Manche, et il leur est arrivé une fois de prôner assez singulièrement la

3. Joseph de Maistre, *Du Pape* (2 vols., Lyon, 1819).

ridicule école de Buchez,[4] qui a parodié d'une manière si baroque les formes de la positivité, et dont les chefs se recommandent surtout à nos catholiques anglicans en ce que d'athées qu'ils étaient ils sont devenus catholiques romains.

J'attends avec un vif intérêt le jugement sur l'Angleterre qui se trouvera dans votre 6me volume. En tant que je connais votre opinion, elle s'accorde complètement avec la mienne, et je serais bien étonné d'une si grande justesse d'appréciation d'un pays ordinairement si mal connu en france si je n'y voyais pas un exemple de la grande puissance d'interprétation à l'égard des faits généraux et patents, qu'un esprit vraiment scientifique puise dans la connaissance approfondie des grandes lois sociologiques. Malgré la brièveté de la vie humaine, nous pouvons l'un et l'autre espérer de voir la position sociale et le caractère national de chaque portion importante du genre humain rattachés aux lois de la nature humaine et aux propriétés du milieu organique général ou particulier par une filiation aussi certaine sinon aussi complète que celle qui existe aujourd'hui dans les sciences les plus avancées. Je serais bien heureux si je me croyais capable de prendre une part vraiment importante, bien que secondaire, à ce grand travail.

Ce que vous me dites sur votre position personnelle, et sur la manière dont elle pourra être compromise par la liberté de discussion dont vous avez usé à l'égard du régime scientifique actuel, est de nature à ajouter une certaine inquiétude au plaisir avec lequel j'envisage la prochaine terminaison de votre mémorable travail. Il est certainement dans l'ordre que les philosophes soient aujourd'hui persécutés par les savants comme ils l'ont été autrefois par les prêtres, comme ils le seront probablement un jour par les industriels, et cela manquait peut être au cercle de l'enseignement sociologique à tirer de l'histoire des persécutions. Mais il est à espérer que vous au moins n'en serez pas la victime[5] et que lors même que vous éprouveriez de l'amour propre blessé d'un corps savant l'injustice infâme qui ne vous parait pas impossible, cela déterminerait de la part de toutes les personnes impartiales un sentiment contraire et qui pourrait exercer une influence plus qu'équivalents sur votre position même matérielle. Je crois avoir entendu

4. Philippe Joseph Benjamin Buchez (1796–1865), physician, politician, and writer. Originally, along with Comte, he had been associated with the Saint-Simonians. Comte had left them because they were too mystical; Buchez, because they were not spiritual enough. He subsequently developed a Neo-Catholic doctrine which attempted to reconcile Christianity and the ideals of the Revolution.

5. Comte in his letter of March 4 had predicted that the final volume of his great work might so offend the professional hierarchy as to cause him to lose his teaching position at the Ecole Polytechnique, an appointment that had to be renewed annually by vote of the professors. See Letter 377, n. 3.

dire à M. Marrast que vous aviez éprouvé aussi de la part du gouvernement de graves injustices; sans cela j'aurais cru que malgré la critique sévère que vous avez faite de l'ordre de choses actuel, le gouvernement d'aujourd'hui pourrait avoir été capable de vouloir utiliser votre capacité dans des fonctions d'enseignement supérieures à celles qui vous ont occupé jusqu'ici; d'autant plus que M. Guizot, avec qui pendant son séjour ici je me suis un peu entretenu de vous, s'est exprimé d'une manière honorable sur votre compte, et que, malgré les passions haineuses, dont on ne peut le disculper, il ne me parait pas dénué d'une certaine magnanimité.

Je vous remercie grandement des renseignements que vous avez eu la bonté de me donner sur les ouvrages phrénologiques à lire,[6] et je me propose de m'en occuper incessamment.

tout à vous

J. S. MILL.

349. TO ALBANY FONBLANQUE[1]

I.H.
5th April
1842

MY DEAR FONBLANQUE

I do not know whether the play[2] which accompanies this has been sent to your paper but in any case I send it to you because it is written by a friend of mine who is very highly deserving of notice & encouragement if you can honestly give him any. He has written very good things of other kinds, among others an excellent pamphlet on law reform[3] & one of the best extant defences of utilitarianism.[4] *I* like his tragedy also though I

---

6. Comte had recommended works by Spurzheim and Gall.

* * * *

1. MS at LSE.
2. *Athelwold; A Tragedy in Five Acts,* published in March, 1842, by William Henry Smith. The play was greatly admired by Mrs. Taylor. G. S. Merriam, *The Story of William and Lucy Smith* (Boston, 1899), p. 110, reports that JSM wrote to the author quoting the favourable opinion of Mrs. Taylor; no such letter has been found. The *Examiner,* which Fonblanque was editing, seems to have carried no review of *Athelwold.*
3. *Remarks on Law Reform* (London, 1840).
4. *A Discourse on Ethics of the School of Paley* (London, 1839).

can see faults in it, but of course I have not the impertinence to wish to impose my opinion upon you.

It has been rather scornfully cut up in the Spectator.[5]

ever yours

J. S. MILL

350. TO ROBERT BARCLAY FOX[1]

India House
5th April
1842

MY DEAR FRIEND

I am really ashamed to think of the time which has elapsed since I wrote to you or gave the smallest indication of remembrance of a family whom I have so much cause never to forget. I beg that you will all of you ascribe this omission on my part to any other cause than want of remembrance or of frequent thought of you—& I believe I could assign such causes as would go far towards palliating it. Now however I feel impelled to write to you by two feelings—one is the wish to condole with you on the loss which Sterling's going abroad[2] is to you & on the anxiety which after so much longer and more intimate knowledge of him than you had had when I last saw you, I am sure you must feel about a life and health so precious both to all who know him & to the world. It is a cruel thing that the hope of his being able to live even at Falmouth & be capable of work, without the periodical necessity for going abroad, should be thus blighted when it seemed to be so fortunately realised.[3] I fear not so much for his bodily state as for his spirits—it is so hard for an active mind like his to reconcile itself to comparative idleness & to what he considers as uselessness—only however from his inability to persuade himself of the whole amount of the good which his society, his correspondence, & the very existence of such a man diffuses through the world. It he did but know the moral & even intellectual influence which he exercises without writing or publishing any-

5. For March 5, 1842, p. 234.

* * * *

1. *Addressed*: R. Barclay Fox Esq. / Falmouth. *Postmark*: FALMOUTH / 6 APRIL 1842. Published with omissions in Pym, II, 329–31. MS in the possession of Mr. W. H. Browning.

2. Because of continuing slight haemorrhages, Sterling had been obliged to accept medical advice to take a trip to the Mediterranean.

3. The remainder of this paragraph was first published by Julius Hare in his memoir of Sterling in the latter's *Essays and Tales* (London, 1848), I, cxciii.

thing, he would think it quite worth living for, even if he were never to be capable of writing again.

Do, if you have a good opportunity, tell Mrs Sterling how truly I sympathise with her, although I do not intrude upon her with a direct expression of it.

My other prompting to write to you just now comes from the approach of spring, & the remembrance of what this *second* spring *ought* to bring, & I hope will.[4] Surely there is not any doubt of your all coming to London this year? There seemed some shadow of an uncertainty in one of the last letters which my sisters shewed me but I hope it has all cleared off.

Carlyle is in Scotland owing to the almost sudden death of Mrs Carlyle's mother. Mrs Carlyle was summoned too late to see her mother alive. She has returned & seems to have suffered much. Carlyle is still there, having many affairs to arrange. It is said & I believe truly that they will now be in much more comfortable circumstances than before. They heroically refused to receive anything from Mrs Welsh during her lifetime.

I have little to tell concerning myself. My book will not be published till next season for which I may thank Murray. He kept me two months waiting for the negative answer which I at last extorted from him, & which it is evident could as well have been given the very first day.[5] I could have accelerated the matter if I had chosen to dun him more, but I committed the mistake of treating him as a gentleman—& besides I really did not care enough about it. I am now in treaty with Parker & with considerable hope of success. Does it not amuse you to see how I stick to the high-church booksellers. Parker also publishes for Whewell with whom several chapters of my book are a controversy, but Parker very sensibly says he does not care about that. The book is now awaiting the verdict of a taster unknown to whom several chapters of his own choice have been communicated: & he gave so favourable a report on the table of contents, that one may hope he will not do worse by the book itself. If Parker publishes the book, he shall have my reprint too, if he will take it—but I am afraid he will not like anything so radical & anti-church as much of it is.[6]

Do, if you have time, write to me, & tell me your recent doings in the way of poetry or prose, together with as much of your thoughts & feelings respecting this little earth & this great universe as you are inclined to communicate—& in any case do not forget me.

ever yours

J. S. MILL

4. The Yearly Meeting of the Society of Friends in May, which the Foxes usually attended.
5. See Letter 343, n. 2.
6. See next letter, n. 3, and Letter 357, penultimate paragraph.

351. TO JOHN WILLIAM PARKER[1]

India House
6th April
1842

My dear Sir

I am very much indebted to your referee[2] for so favorable an opinion, expressed in such complimentary terms, & am much gratified by the result. I will keep his observations in view in finally reading through the manuscript before it goes to press, but I fear I am nearly at the end of my stock of apt illustrations. I had to read a great deal for those I have given, & I believe that the chapters on Fallacies which preceded those that were submitted to your friend's judgment, are considerably richer than those he has seen, in examples selected as he recommends from eminent writers.

With respect to your very handsome offer of half profit, my feeling is that if I were to take advantage of your liberality in any manner, the shape in which I should most like to do so would be by a certain latitude in giving away copies—chiefly to foreigners or persons who would not be likely to buy the book although they would like to read it & who would therefore be more likely by making it known, to attract buyers to it than to interfere with its sale. I have not in view any alarming number, some 25 or 30 copies being as far as I can now judge, the extreme limit.

In reference to the contingency of a future edition, it is I think very unlikely that I should be inclined to change my publisher, especially when he is as I believe you to be, the most desirable one in England for the kind of book.

I have another publication in view which I should like to bring out about the same time with this book, as they might serve to advertise one another—a selection from a great number of articles, political literary & philosophical which I have published in different periodicals during the last eight or ten years, concluding with an article on Tocqueville's Democracy in America, in the Edinburgh Review for October 1840. It would be a sort of collection something like Carlyle's Miscellaneous essays, but extending only to two small volumes instead of five. I should be very glad if it suited you to publish this also,[3] but I have my doubts whether it would, as some of the opinions are likely to be considered ultra-liberal,

---

1. MS at King's.
2. The referee was William Cooke Taylor (1800–1849), miscellaneous writer and historian. Parker had sent the opinion in the referee's own handwriting but had withheld the name. "He forgot," said JSM, "that I had been an Editor, and knew the handwriting of nearly every literary man of the day" (Bain, *JSM*, p. 66 n.).
3. Parker declined. See Letter 357.

although (in the later papers especially) rather anti-democratic, so much so indeed as to have given great offence to many of the radicals. If you should be inclined to take this into consideration I should be happy to send you the collection.

yours very truly

J. S. MILL.

352. TO JOHN MITCHELL KEMBLE[1]

India House
13th April 1842

MY DEAR SIR

The accompanying paper is written by a clergyman of the Church of England, who has long quitted the Church on account of conscientious scruples. If his paper on Socrates should suit you he will be glad to follow it up by another on Plato & a third on Philo & the Platonisms of Christianity. He is a very sincere Christian & much respected by all who know him.

In case you should wish to communicate directly with him, his address is Rev. J. P. Potter[2] 8 Boyne Terrace Notting Hill.

Yours very truly

J. S. MILL

353. TO GEORGE CORNEWALL LEWIS[1]

I.H.
Wed^y
[April, 1842]

MY DEAR LEWIS

I am glad to tell you that Parker having received a very favourable answer from his referee has consented to publish an edition of 750 copies of the Logic at his own risk.

I have just received a long letter from Mrs. Austin.[2] She bids me give their love to you & say that M. de Lindenau[3] has your book[4] & that she shall see what he says of it—also to ask what you think of Otfried Müller's

1. MS in the possession of Professor Ney MacMinn.
2. Rev. John Philips Potter (1793–1861), who later published *Characteristics of the Greek Philosophers, Socrates and Plato* (London, 1845).

* * * *

1. MS at LSE.   2. The Austins were still in Germany.
3. Bernhard August von Lindenau (1779–1854), astronomer and statesman.
4. Probably *A History of the Literature of Ancient Greece; translated from the German Manuscript of Karl Otfried Müller* by G. C. Lewis (2 vols., London, 1840–42).

Nachlass[5] as a subject for translation. It seems to consist of three little books, on Rome, Naples & Venice. She says Mr Austin's article[6] is going on, but slowly & interruptedly & with terrible *anstrengung* & on the whole she writes in miserable spirits about him & about their present position.

How much I wish that any way could be found such as he would not reject, in which those here who are deeply interested in him might combine to make it possible for him to live in this country, at least during the uncertainty of American matters. Could nothing be thought of? I would cheerfully take upon myself a second income tax to aid towards such an object—& I should think there are quite enough of those who would gladly do so & who could without inconveniences.

ever yours

J. S. MILL

354. TO EDWIN CHADWICK[1]

Monday
[April, 1842]

MY DEAR CHADWICK,

I have read through your report[2] slowly & carefully. I do not find a single erroneous or questionable position in it, while there is the strength & largeness of practical views which are characteristic of all you do. In its present unrevised state it is as you are probably aware, utterly ineffective from the want of unity and of an apparent thread running through it and holding it together. I wish you would learn some of the forms of scientific exposition of which my friend Comte makes such superfluous use, & to *use* without *abusing* which is one of the principal lessons which practice & reflexion have to teach to people like you & me who have to make new trains of thought intelligible.

yours ever

J. S. MILL

5. The literary remains of the great German archaeologist, Karl Otfried Müller (1797–1840). Mrs. Austin appears not to have undertaken the translation.

6. See Letter 347, n. 5.

* * * *

1. MS at UCL. Endorsed in another hand: "John Mill Esq / on the Sanatory [*sic*] Report / April / 42."

2. Evidently a draft of *Report of the Poor Law Commissioners to the Secretary of State, on an inquiry into the sanitary condition of the labouring population of Great Britain*, 1842, XXVI (House of Lords).

355. TO VICTOR COUSIN[1]

India House, 27 avril 1842

Monsieur,

Je ne sais pas trop comment je trouve en moi-même, après une si longue interruption de notre correspondance, la hardiesse de vous adresser par mon jeune ami, M. G. H. Lewes, et en sa faveur, une lettre de recommandation. Mais vous savez que ceux de mes compatriotes qui s'occupent de haute philosophie sont malheureusement très peu nombreux; et comme M. Lewes est de ce petit nombre d'exceptions honorables, j'ai pensé que vous le verriez peut-être avec quelque plaisir. J'ai donc cru pouvoir me permettre de faire ce qui dépendait de moi pour lui procurer l'honneur et l'avantage de votre connaissance.

Ce n'est pas M. Cornewall Lewis, que vous connaissez probablement, et dont au moins vous avez entendu parler notre amie Mme Austin. Celui que je vous adresse est beaucoup plus jeune: mais il a des connaissances et une capacité qui donnent de grandes espérances, et il commence déjà à se faire connaître par ses écrits.

Moi-même, je viens de terminer un travail philosophique assez étendu, dont je compte vous faire l'hommage quand il sera imprimé. Je n'ose espérer de votre part, pour cet ouvrage, qu'une approbation très modérée, puisqu'il appartient plutôt a l'école de Locke qu'à la vôtre; mais je crois avoir profité, plus que ne l'a fait jusqu'ici cette ancienne école anglaise, des critiques et même des principes de la philosophie du XIXe siècle.

Veuillez agréer le témoignage de mes sentiments respectueux.

J. S. Mill

356. TO AUGUSTE COMTE[1]

India House
6 mai 1842

Mon cher Monsieur Comte

D'après ce que vous m'avez indiqué dans une de vos lettres, ce qui restait à faire de votre dernier volume doit être aujourd'hui à peu près terminé. J'en attends la lecture avec une impatience que tout tend à accroître, et j'espère en retirer quelquavantage pour mon propre livre, dont l'impression, retardée par des délais de libraire, n'a pas encore commencé

1. Published in J. Barthélemy–Saint Hilaire, *M. Victor Cousin, Sa Vie et Sa Correspondance* (3 vols. Paris, 1895), II, 456–57. MS not located.

* * * *

1. MS at Johns Hopkins. Published in Lévy-Bruhl, pp. 53–57. In answer to Comte's letter of April 5, 1842, *ibid.*, pp. 45–53.

et qui ne paraîtra que sur la fin de l'année. Quels que puissent être à tout autre égard les résultats de cet ouvrage, je me flatte qu'il ne sera pas sans valeur comme œuvre de propagande et que les idées importantes que j'ai tirées de votre grand travail, en reconnaissant comme je le devais, la source d'où elles m'étaient venues, contribueront, avec la manière dont j'ai parlé de ce travail, y compris la partie sociologique, à attirer sur lui l'attention d'un certain nombre de lecteurs les mieux préparés et à provoquer leur adhésion au seul moyen d'étudier les phénomènes sociaux qui soit aujourd'hui au niveau de l'état intellectuel de l'humanité.

Vous devez sentir, du reste, sans aucune difficulté, que l'esprit anglais se trouve nécessairement moins préparé que celui des autres peuples avancés, à suivre et à perfectionner la science positive de l'histoire. La physique sociale devait certainement naître et grandir en france, et ne s'étendre que plus tard à ce pays ci, par la raison surtout que la civilisation française se rapproche de plus près que toute autre du type normal de l'évolution humaine, tandis que l'histoire anglaise s'écarte, comme vous l'avez si bien remarqué, très loin de la marche ordinaire. De ce caractère exceptionnel du développement anglais, ainsi que de la tendance éminemment insulaire que cette évolution anormale a imprimée à notre caractère national, il en est résulté chez nous une grande indifférence envers l'histoire européenne, dont nous avons l'habitude anti-scientifique de regarder la nôtre comme essentiellement séparée: et comme personne ne saurait parvenir à comprendre et à expliquer les anomalies sans avoir préalablement etudié le cas normal, les recherches qu'on a faites sur notre histoire nationale ne nous ont donné qu'un petit nombre d'érudits et pas un seul philosophe même du troisième ou quatrième ordre.

Quant à la tâche honorable que vous avez bien voulu me désigner, celle de rattacher la marche sociale de l'angleterre à la théorie sociologique fondamentale, je ne puis évidemment me dispenser de cette tentative, ne fût-ce que pour mieux affermir mes propres convictions sociales. Mais dans le cas même d'un succès complet, je crois que je ferais mieux de soumettre le résultat de mes travaux à vous-même et au public continental qu'à celui de mon pays, qui certainement ne saurait ni le juger ni en profiter convenablement, faute de connaître, je ne dis pas seulement les lois générales, mais les faits généraux eux-mêmes, sources des inductions dont ces lois sont tirées. Aujourd'hui même, ce que nous avons encore de mieux en fait de spéculation historique sur notre pays, c'est l'Essai de Guizot sur le système représentatif en angleterre,[2] et vous conviendrez que ce n'est pas là grand'chose.

Puisque je suis sur le chapitre de M. Guizot, je vous dirai que tout en

2. Presumably his lectures published in the *Journal des cours publics de jurisprudence, histoire et belles lettres* (2 vols., Paris, 1820–22), which were later revised

ayant toujours jugé comme vous ses spéculations politiques et sa métaphysique doctrinaire, j'ai éprouvé une impression pénible en apprenant
l'idée désavantageuse que vous avez de son caractère[3] et qu'il ne mérite
vraisemblablement que trop bien. On n'apprend pas sans peine qu'un
homme en qui il faut reconnaître une véritable capacité scientifique, ait
porté l'esprit de secte jusqu'à manquer de magnanimité envers un philosophe qui n'en a jamais manqué envers personne, et dont les écrits ont un
charme particulier par l'admiration noble et profonde qu'il y témoigne à
toute occasion pour tous ceux qui ont fait honneur à l'humanité, quelque
éloignées qu'aient été leurs croyances des siennes propres. Il faut avoir
le cœur bien petit pour ne pas trouver un attrait irrésistible dans cette
noble sympathie avec tous les genres de grandeur morale et intellectuelle
que je regarde au reste comme une des conditions essentielles de la vraie
capacité philosophique, au moins de nos jours. Sans cela on ne peut être
tout au plus que l'homme d'une spécialité, et les spécialités n'ont en
sociologie, comme vous l'avez si bien établi, qu'une valeur provisoire.
M. Guizot n'est certainement pas autre chose, quoique je croie que si
vous aviez pris connaissance de son Cours d'Histoire,[4] vous y auriez
reconnu, avec les mêmes intentions de positivité que dans son premier
ouvrage, une capacité spéculative plus générale. Si mes compatriotes
avaient une connaissance réelle de ce Cours, ils seraient beaucoup mieux
préparés qu'ils ne le sont à la positivité sociologique.

J'ai commencé l'étude de Gall:[5] il me paraît un homme d'un esprit
supérieur. Je le lis avec plaisir et j'espère aussi avec fruit. Dès que je serai
à même de juger sa théorie, je vous écrirai ce qui m'en semble.

Je regrette d'autant plus vivement que les devoirs de votre position vous
empêchent de faire un voyage, même court, dans ce pays-ci, attendu que
moimême, par des circonstances particulières, je suis au moins pour cette
année dans une situation à peu près pareille et que je serai probablement
dans l'impossibilité de quitter Londres. La rélation personnelle que je
désire si vivement établir avec vous se trouve par là ajournée, mais je ferai
de mon mieux pour que ce retard dure le moins possible.

tout à vous

J. S. MILL.

for his *Histoire des origines du gouvernement représentatif en Europe* (2 vols., Paris,
1851).
3. In his letter of April 5 Comte had been bitterly critical of Guizot.
4. *Cours d'Histoire moderne* (6 vols., Paris, 1829–32).
5. Franz Joseph Gall, *Sur les fonctions du cerveau et sur celles de chacune de ses
parties* . . . (6 vols., Paris, 1825). Gall (1758–1828), anatomist, physiologist, was
the founder of phrenology. JSM had heard of Gall's theories as early as 1821 in a
lecture at Montpellier (see *John Mill's Boyhood Visit to France*, ed. Anna Jean Mill
[Toronto, 1960], pp. 110 ff.).

357. TO ROBERT BARCLAY FOX[1]

I. H.
10th May
1842

Many thanks my dear friend for your letter & its inclosures—& still more for the very agreeable intelligence that we may hope to see you all, & *expect* to see some of you very soon.

I have had much pleasure in reading both the prose & the verse which you sent me. I think I can honestly give downright straightforward praise to them both. The poetry has both thought & music in it, & the prose seems "to me much reflecting on these things" to contain the real pith of the matter, expressed "simply" & "perspicuously" & with the kind of force which so purely intellectual a subject required & admitted of.[2] If it were shewn to me as the production of a young writer whom I knew nothing of I should say at once that he was of the right school & likely to go far.

I have not time to enter upon metaphysics just now or I might perhaps discuss with you your curious speculation respecting a duality in the hyperphysical part of man's nature. Is not what you term the mind as distinguished from the spirit or soul, merely that spirit looking at things as through a glass darkly compelled in short by the conditions of its terrestrial existence to see & know by means of media, just as the mind uses the bodily organs, for to suppose that the eye is *necessary* to sight seems to me the notion of one immersed in matter. What we call our bodily sensations are all in the mind & would not necessarily or probably cease because the body perishes. As the eye is but the window *through* which, not the power *by* which, the mind sees, so probably the understanding is the bodily eye of the human spirit, which looks through that window, or rather which sees (as in Plato's cave) the camera-obscura images of things in this life while in another it may or might be capable of seeing the things themselves.

I do not give you this as my opinion but as a speculation, which you will take for what it is worth.

Thanks for your interest about my books. Parker has proved genuine & has behaved so well altogether that I feel twice as much interested as I ever did before in the success of the Logic for I should really be sorry if he were to lose money by it. He proposes to bring it out about Christmas. He will not publish the reprint as he makes a point of not publishing

---

1. *Addressed*: R. Barclay Fox Esq. / Falmouth. *Postmarks*: 10 MAY 1842 and FALMOUTH / 11 MAY 1842. Published, except for last paragraph, in Pym, II, 331–32. MS in the possession of Mr. W. H. Browning.
2. A lecture on modern British poets. See Pym, I, 292.

politics or polemics, so I shall print it myself in time for next season, & perhaps shall have a copy for you before that.

Give all kind remembrances from all to all—& to your sisters special ones from me for their kind wishes respecting my mental offspring. Please tell them also that I have lately seen for the first time their friend Henrietta Melvill[3] whose appreciation of & attachment to them were very pleasant to see.

ever yours
J. S. MILL.

358. TO SARAH AUSTIN[1]

India House
22d May 1842

You are most probably at Bonn & the agonies of the article for the Edinburgh[2] are over. I know what those agonies must have been but I think I also know what must be the relief from them & from that relief conjointly with the coming of a German summer, so much warmer than ours, dryer & less variable than ours, one may hope good results for his health: but above all from the consciousness of having *achieved* something, & he is sure to find by its reception that he has not toiled in vain, for he never wrote anything which did not satisfy all whom he would wish it to satisfy, except himself. I suppose there is something physical & organic in that incapacity of persuading himself that anything he does is done sufficiently well. Everybody who hears him talk on any subject in which he is interested would be quite satisfied if he would write the very words which he talks; almost any framework would serve to hold them together & that is exactly what Stephen expressed to me about the article now in question, he wished that the two lectures, as he called them, which he *heard* could be merely put on paper. By the bye I have no reason to believe that Mr Stephen was in any misapprehension about the subject of the article, although I was. About your own literary projects—I hope the article or articles for the Edin.[3] have come *zu Stande* as I think it is a kind of writing which suits you, & which is likely to be a better speculation than translating. For a translation to succeed, unless it be of something merely trumpery &

---

3. Henrietta Melvill (1816–1900), daughter of Sir James Cosmo Melvill (1792–1861), official of the East India Company.

* * * *

1. MS in the possession of Mr. Gordon Waterfield.
2. See Letter 347, n. 5.
3. Her next article in the *Edinburgh* appears to have been, "On the Changes of Social Life in Germany," LXXVII (Feb., 1843), 138–69.

gossiping there must be some peculiarly English interest involved in it, as in the case of Ranke[4] the interest of Protestantism. If those German selections[5] have done no more than pay their expenses I do not know what on the score of intrinsic merit could have any better chance. Of the books you mention I should think those on Rome, Naples & Venice[6] would have the best. Are they by Otfried Müller? His name is known here, which is seldom the case with any Germans not of the very first rank but I fancy I was wrong in concluding as I did at first from your letter that these books were by him. I know how much better suited the business of translating must often be to the state of your occupations & spirits than the more continuous exertion of even a review article & it is very desirable that you should have something of the kind in hand. You might finish Egmont[7] which would not take you very long & then *offer* it to Macready,[8] he is, from what I hear, exceedingly on the alert for any new theatrical speculation which has even a chance of *taking* & surely that would have a considerable chance. At any rate it might be published either alone or as part of a little volume of dramatic translations.—It is very dreary to think of you remaining in exile —the only thing which could make it *not* exiled would be your having friends near you, in the sense of real intimacy & that I thought it possible *you* & even *he* might have in Germany, but it seems not at Dresden: & although the German people are much more to your taste (as to mine) than the English, you seem to have fallen upon a time when all sorts of odious feelings are rife among them & besides as one grows older one is less & less capable of taking the species in general as an equivalent for the two or three whom one knows well enough to value them most in it. But I doubt if you would be better off in this respect anywhere in England, except London & its immediate neighbourhood, than in Germany. You ask me about the cheapness of living. The experience of all whom I am able to speak of, is that in such places as Dorking there is no advantage whatever in cheapness, over London, but rather a disadvantage. Of Selborne & such little places off the high roads I am unable to speak, but that would be a still more complete isolation than you are in at present. There *is* cheapness in remote parts as for example in Wales or Cornwall. The best place I know of the kind is Falmouth, because there are really interesting & superior

4. Mrs. Austin in 1840 had published her translation of Leopold von Ranke as *The Ecclesiastical and Political History of the Popes of Rome during the sixteenth and seventeenth centuries* (3 vols., London).

5. Her anthology of translations, *Fragments from German Prose Writers* (London, 1841).

6. See Letter 353, n. 5.

7. She had published her translation of two scenes from Goethe's *Egmont* in her *Fragments from German Prose Writers*.

8. William Charles Macready (1793–1873), actor, at this time manager of the Drury Lane Theatre.

people there, even without counting Sterling who is now fixed there. Whether this would be better or worse than the Continent you can best judge. I have very little to tell you about myself. The book is to be published by Parker who has in every respect behaved so well about it that I really begin to care a little about its chances of sale, as I should be sorry that he lost any money by the speculation. It is some encouragement to know that Deighton, the Cambridge bookseller (whom Parker very much consults) thinks that a book of the kind if competently executed *may* sell. I am sure I did not expect any such opinion from any publisher. Murray's procrastination lost the present season & Parker proposes to publish the book about Christmas & to begin printing it in July. You have I suppose more news of most of your friends here through other channels than I could give. The Grotes are just returned from Italy. Sterling was obliged to go there two months ago on account of a return of his usual spring symptoms but they went off before he reached Gibraltar & he will soon I suppose return. The black seal of my letter indicates no death that I care about. George has had to pass the winter at Clifton but his state has really improved—he has been with Dr. Carpenter[9] the physiologist, son of Dr. Lant Carpenter & a man whom I have a great esteem for, & I have no doubt he will have been much improved by it. Mrs Taylor is no better, but she means to try all remedies that are practicable here before going abroad.

Yours ever affectionately

J. S. MILL.

359. TO EDWIN CHADWICK[1]

I.H.
Thursday
[June 8, 1842]

DEAR CHADWICK

I should have written yesterday by post if you had not said you would send. I have read the whole report[2] carefully through again. The defects of arrangements are now corrected & I have nothing to suggest except that it be carefully revised by yourself or some other person to correct the

9. William Benjamin Carpenter (1813–1885), prominent physician and scientist (see Letter 386), son of Dr. Lant Carpenter (1780–1840), Unitarian minister.

* * * *

1. MS at UCL. Endorsed in another hand: "J. Mill Esqʳ / On the Sanatory [*sic*] Report / May [crossed out], June 8 / 42."
2. See Letter 354, n. 2.

numerous typographical errors & occasional ungrammatical sentences. I think it all excellent & shall be glad to write about it for any newspaper as you suggest.[3]

yours

J. S. MILL

360. TO AUGUSTE COMTE[1]

India House
9 juin 1842

MON CHER MONSIEUR COMTE—

Pour commencer par le sujet le plus spécial, bien que sans doute le moins important, de la lettre si honorable pour moi qui vous a été dictée par notre sympathie non seulement philosophique, mais j'ose le dire, personnelle; je vous donne, puisque votre délicatesse en a besoin, l'autorisation pleine et entière d'user à volonté du mot de pédantocratie[2] qui vous a tant souri, et même de tout autre mot et de toute idée que vous puissiez trouver chez moi. Je ne tiens pas assez au mérite aujourd'hui si répandu, d'une expression heureuse, la fût-elle beaucoup plus qu'elle ne l'est, pour penser que ceux qui la trouvent commode ne doivent pas s'en servir sans ma permission préalable, ou qu'ils doivent s'assujettir à l'obligation de me nommer. Toutefois c'est avec un plaisir véritable que je verrai mon nom associé au vôtre à l'occasion d'une doctrine fondamentale, que nous seuls peutêtre parmi les hommes de spéculation reconnaissons dans sa plénitude. L'assentiment fortement prononcé d'un second penseur peut effectivement comme vous l'avez senti, n'être pas inutile au progrès d'une opinion contraire aux idées régnantes, et naturellement repoussée par les propagateurs ordinaires de doctrines nouvelles. Il serait en même temps de votre prudence de ne pas vous servir à mon égard d'expressions trop flatteuses, et je le dis sans aucune affectation, par la seule considération que vous n'avez pas pû jusqu'ici suffisamment apprécier le degré de ma capacité réelle, pour vous en porter garant auprès du monde scientifique, et que la lecture de mon livre pourra rabaisser considérablement le jugement anticipé que vous voulez bien me témoigner si aimablement.

3. JSM kept his promise; he wrote the greater part of the article on Chadwick's Report in the *Examiner*, Aug. 20, 1842, pp. 530–31.

* * * *

1. MS at Johns Hopkins. Published in Lévy-Bruhl, pp. 64–69. In answer to Comte's of May 29, *ibid.*, pp. 57–64.

2. Comte had been much impressed with this coined word of JSM in his letter of Feb. 25, 1842 (Letter 344), and had asked permission to use it. Years later JSM again employed the word, in the penultimate paragraph of his *On Liberty*.

Je vous remercie infiniment des détails que vous m'avez donnés sur l'état actuel de la grande opération philosophique qui doit compléter votre immense travail. Chaque nouvelle indication des choses que ce volume contiendra, augmente encore l'impatience avec laquelle je l'attends et si malheureusement la publication se trouvait ajournée jusqu'au mois de décembre, j'éprouverais un regret que je n'ai nullement ressenti au délai de la publication de mon propre ouvrage. Il est d'ailleurs convenable que vous passiez le premier, afin que je puisse profiter pour mon travail de votre exposition finale des principes de la logique positive, exposition que je regrette de n'avoir pas eue sous les yeux dès le commencement d'une tentative semblable au fond quoique souvent différente par les formes.

J'ai lu les six volumes de Gall[3] avec une attention sérieuse, et je me trouve tout aussi embarrassé qu'auparavant pour bien juger sa théorie. Je suis à peu près persuadé qu'il y a quelque chose de vrai là-dedans, et que les penchans et les capacités élémentaires, quels qu'ils soient, se rattachent chacun à une portion particulière du cerveau. Mais j'éprouve de très grandes difficultés. D'abord, vous convenez de la prématurité de toute localisation spéciale, et en effet les preuves ne manquent pas pour montrer l'inexactitude de celles qu'on a tentées jusqu'ici. Je me citerai moi-même comme exemple. La seule chose que je sais avec certitude de mon développement craniologique, c'est que le prétendu organe de la constructivité est chez moi très prononcé. Un phrénologue très décidé s'est écrié au moment de me voir pour la première fois: *Que faites-vous de votre constructivité?* ("What do you do with your constructiveness?") Or je manque presque totalement de la faculté correspondante. Je suis dépourvu du sens da la mécanique, et mon inaptitude pour toute opération qui exige de la dextérité manuelle est vraiment prodigieuse. En accordant la futilité de la plupart des essais de localisation particulière, vous trouvez suffisamment établie la triple division du cerveau, correspond[ant][4] à la distinction des facultés animales, morales et intellectuelles. Je suis bien loin de prétendre que cela n'est pas; cependant à en juger par l'ouvrage de Gall, il me semble qu'il y aurait autant de preuves à donner pour un grand nombre des organes spéciaux que pour le résultat général. J'admets que la spécialisation des organes appropriés aux plus hautes facultés intellectuelles et morales doit par sa nature même, reposer sur une base inductive bien moins large que celle des organes que nous partageons avec les animaux inférieurs. Mais je ne vois pas très bien comment l'anatomie et la physiologie comparée puissent fournir une preuve concluante de la théorie générale sans en fournir pour une grande partie des détails. Gall me paraît avoir raison lorsqu'il dit que toute classification des animaux inférieurs, fondée sur le

3. See Letter 356, n. 5.
4. MS torn.

degré supposé de leur intelligence générale, est vague et anti-scientifique, vu que les espèces animales se distinguent entr'elles bien moins par l'étendue de leurs facultés mentales considérées dans leur ensemble, que par le degré très prononcé de telles ou telles capacités spéciales, dans lesquelles les différences d'intensité sont ordinairement si immenses que la plupart des cas sont réellement des cas extrêmes; en sorte qu'on devrait s'attendre à trouver plus facilement les conditions anatomiques par exemple de la constructivité chez le castor ou chez l'abeille, du sens local chez le chien ou chez les oiseaux voyageurs, que celles de l'intelligence en général. J'ajoute que si j'en juge par ma propre expérience, et par la comparaison que j'en ai faite avec celle d'autres observateurs meilleurs que moi et également dépourvus de toute préoccupation métaphysique ou théologique, la correspondance des facultés supérieures de l'homme avec le développement de la région frontale supérieure se trouve fort souvent en défaut. J'ai souvent vu une intelligence remarquable réunie à une petite tête ou à un front fuyant en arrière, tandis qu'on voit tous les jours des têtes énormes et des fronts bombés, avec une intelligence médiocre. Je ne donne certes pas ceci comme décisif, car je sais qu'il faut faire attention non seulement comme vous l'avez vous-même remarqué au degré d'activité de l'organe, mais aussi à l'ensemble de l'éducation, (envisagée dans la plus grande extension du mot) que l'individu a reçue, et à laquelle Gall n'a certainement pas fait une part suffisante. Les exagérations d'Helvétius[5] ont eu au moins l'avantage de donner une forte impulsion à la théorie difficile de l'éducation théorie qu'aujourd'hui on néglige à tel point d'approfondir, que la plupart des penseurs ignorent jusqu'où les circonstances extérieures combinées avec le degré de sensibilité nerveuse générale peuvent d'après les lois physiologiques mentales, non seulement modifier le caractère mais quelquefois même en déterminer le type. Des diversités de caractère individuel ou national, qui admettent une explication suffisante par les circonstances les mieux connues, se trouvent tous les jours résolues par la ressource facile d'une différence inconnue d'organisation physique, ou même, chez les métaphysiciens par des diversités primordiales de constitution psychique. Je pense au reste qu'on finira par rattacher tous les instincts fondamentaux, soit à la moelle épinière, soit à des ganglions cérébraux déterminés. Mais c'est encore pour moi un grand problème s'il existe peu ou beaucoup de ces instincts primitifs. Gall et Spurzheim[6] prononcent par exemple très décidément que le sentiment de la propriété est instinctif et primordial: mais de même que vous rejetez le sentiment de la justice du nombre des facultés spéciales, la fesant dériver de la bienveillance associée avec les diverses facultés intellectuelles,

5. Claude Adrien Helvétius (1715–1771), philosopher and psychologist.
6. Johann Caspar Spurzheim (1776–1832), a disciple of Gall in the development of phrenology.

de même ne devrait-on pas décider que le désir de s'approprier une chose susceptible de satisfaire à ses besoins quelconques, dérive naturellement et sans qu'il y ait lieu à une faculté spéciale, de l'ensemble de nos désirs, combinès avec l'intelligence, qui relie la conception du moyen à celle du but? Je n'ai pas besoin sans doute de vous dire que je vous soumets mes difficultés comme questions seulement, et non pas comme arguments.

Je vous sais beaucoup de gré de votre aimable bienveillance envers mon jeune ami Lewes, qui se réjouit très vivement de vous avoir vu. Je n'ai pas osé demander pour lui cet avantage parce que je savais qu'avec d'excellentes dispositions, et une certaine force d'esprit, il manque des bases essentielles d'une forte éducation positive. Je trouve très honorable à son caractère et à son intelligence la vive admiration qu'il éprouve pour vous, avec des moyens si imparfaits d'apprécier votre supériorité scientifique.

tout à vous

J. S. MILL.

361. TO JOHN AUSTIN[1]

India House
7th July 1842

DEAR MR AUSTIN

The book[2] you so kindly enquire about would have been in your hands by this time if I had decided to publish it this season. But the publisher, Parker, to whom by the advice of Lewis I had recourse on being rejected by Murray, & who has behaved so very well in the matter as to make me much more solicitous than I was before about the saleability of the book, thought it best to publish about Christmas next & to begin printing about this time: & I expect daily to hear that he is ready to commence. If you would like me to send you the sheets & Sir A. Gordon[3] would be so kind as to let me know when he has good opportunities I will do so.

I did not at all look forward to such good fortune as being reviewed by you, but I do not know of anything in the book to prevent it. It is true that the part relating to Induction is *not* "more occupied with the mental & social than with the mathematical & physical sciences" because it was more convenient to illustrate inductive methods from those subjects on which the conclusions elicited by them are undisputed. But I have chosen almost exclusively the simplest & best known cases, partly because my knowledge

1. In reply to letter by John Austin, June 27, 1842, at LSE. MS in Brit. Mus.
2. The *Logic*.
3. Sir Alexander Duff-Gordon (1811–1872), who had married Austin's only child, Lucie.

did not enable me to venture on any others without risk of making blunders, & partly because I did not wish to be unread by all who are not profoundly versed in physics. I do not think I have made much more use of mathematical & physical principles than Dugald Stewart & Brown.[4] I have, besides, endeavoured whenever I could, to make my examples carry their own explanation with them, & to give, as I went on, the knowledge necessary for understanding my meaning. The scientific examples are for those who have not already scientific habits of mind, but those who have, will be enabled by those habits, to understand the examples themselves.

If you do not review the book it will probably fall into the hands either as you suggest, of Sir W. Hamilton, or of Brewster.[5] The first would be hostile, but intelligent, the second, I believe, favourable, but shallow: neither, therefore, would exactly suit me. I have hopes of a review in the Quarterly, grounded on the fact that Herschel[6] writes in it, & his review of Whewell[7] contains so much that chimes with my comments on the same book that he would probably like to lend a helping hand to a writer on the same side with him. If so, such ample justice will be done to the book in so far as it is connected with physical or mathematical subjects, that it is much more important to have an article in the Edinburgh, strong on the other & more difficult parts of the investigation.

I have read the article on List[8] & find it as good as even I expected. I have had no opportunity yet of knowing what other people think of it as it is not yet in the hands of the general public—but I will watch the impression it makes & let you know. List seems to have as much confusion in his head as the advocates of prohibition[9] generally have, but the state of public feeling to which such a book recommends itself is a very serious consideration. What chance there is of a change of policy here, no one can foresee. But it seems to me that the more any person knows of the state of the country, both as to men's circumstances & their minds, the more doubtful he feels of the possibility of going on as we are. There is a speech of Lord Howick[10] in this very day's paper which dwells upon what is becoming

4. Thomas Brown.   5. Sir David Brewster.
6. Sir John Frederick William Herschel (1792–1871), astronomer.
7. The review of William Whewell's *History of the Inductive Sciences* (3 vols., London, 1837) and *The Philosophy of the Inductive Sciences* (2 vols., London, 1840) appeared in *QR*, LXVIII (June, 1841), 177–238.
8. See Letter 347, n. 5.
9. I.e., prohibitory tariffs.
10. Sir Henry George Grey, Viscount Howick, later third Earl Grey (1802–1894), statesman. The occasion of the speech was a parliamentary debate on the public distress. Much of his speech was devoted to the Corn Laws, but towards the close he remarked, as reported in *The Times* (July 7, 1842, p. 2), "he was induced to believe that a very different temper and spirit than had hitherto existed were fast springing up, that such a temper and spirit were no longer confined to the meetings of Chartists, but were rapidly gaining ground in the country."

daily more apparent, the spread of Chartism among the middle classes: & there is certainly alarm in the Tory camp: Lockhart the editor of the Quarterly said to Sterling a day or two ago "we do not know that we shall not have a French Revolution this very winter." Everybody thinks that the time is out of joint but nobody feels "born to set it right." Lockhart says the landlords are mad if they think they can go on as they do, but the only remedy he dreams about is "home colonization." He thinks if the parks were all cut up into square patches of arable & *let* (not given) to the labourers, things would go right, not seeing that it would be merely turning England into another Ireland. It makes one sick to see full grown men such babies— afraid to look the only real remedy in the face.

I may as well inclose you my table of contents[11] as it will shew you the arrangement of the topics.

ever yours

J. S. MILL

If the titles of my chapters should suggest to you any good examples, it is not too late for me to profit by them—

Do you know of any good German book on Roman history, subsequent to Niebuhr?[12] I have engaged to write something for the Ed. on the Romans & their place in history & in civilization.

362. TO AUGUSTE COMTE[1]

India House
le 11 juillet
1842

MON CHER MONSIEUR COMTE

Quand cette lettre vous parviendra, les doutes que vous aviez sur l'époque de la terminaison de votre grand travail seront déjà levées, et vous saurez si l'impatience de vos lecteurs doit se prolonger pendant quatre mois de plus. Il y avait pour moi une sorte de volupté intellectuelle dans l'idée de savourer ce dernier volume, comme il m'est arrivé a l'égard des autres, dans les beaux jours de l'été ou de l'automne, époque où l'on se trouve ordinaire-ment plus susceptible à toute sorte de stimulations agréables, et où ma tête

11. The accompanying table of contents of the *Logic* has been omitted here.
12. The first two volumes of Barthold Georg Niebuhr's famous *Römische Geschichte* had been published in Berlin in 1812; the third volume in 1832.

* * * *

1. MS at Johns Hopkins. Published in Lévy-Bruhl, pp. 76–81; in answer to Comte's of June 19, *ibid.*, pp. 69–76.

travaille toujours, sinon mieux, au moins avec une conscience plus joyeuse de son activité. Mais si je dois renoncer à cette satisfaction luxurieuse [*sic*], et à celle beaucoup plus sérieuse de posséder et d'assimiler une portion si importante de vos idées philosophiques pendant que l'impression de mon propre ouvrage sera encore dans ses commencements; je ne m'en prends qu'à la déplorable imperfection de notre organisation sociale, dont le principal tort, à l'égard des hommes du premier ordre est bien moins de leur refuser la considération et la dignité sociale qui leur est dûe, que de les contraindre à user leurs forces et à dépenser la principale partie d'une vie déjà si courte, en cherchant par des travaux tout à fait subalternes les moyens même les plus modestes de vivre.

J'ai délibéré s'il ne conviendrait pas d'ajourner indéfiniment l'impression et la publication de mon livre pour le revoir en entier après la complétion du vôtre. Voici ce qui m'en a surtout détourné. Les bases générales de mon travail avaient été jetées et les deux tiers environ de l'ouvrage étaient faits, du moins en brouillon, avant que j'eusse connaissance de votre Cours. Si j'avais pû le connaître antérieurement, sourtout en entier, j'aurais peut être traduit cet ouvrage au lieu d'en faire un nouveau, ou si je l'avais fait, j'aurais vraisemblablement donné à l'exposition de mes idées, même sans intention nette à cet égard, une tournure un peu différente, et en quelques parties, moins métaphysique par les formes. Toutefois en y réfléchissant je trouve que la tournure quasi-métaphysique des premiers chapitres est peut-être mieux faite pour attirer les penseurs les plus avancés de mon pays, en me mettant en contact direct avec les questions qui les occupent déjà, et en rattachant mes idées logiques aux traditions de l'école de Hobbes et de Locke, école, comme vous savez, beaucoup plus près de la positivité que l'école allemande qui règne aujourd'hui, et maintenant foulée aux pieds par cette école à cause surtout de ce qu'elle a de mieux, sa répugnance intime aux vaines discussions ontologiques. Je ne crois pas être trompé par l'amour-propre en croyant que si mon ouvrage est lû et accueilli (ce qui me parait toujours très douteux) ce sera le premier coup un peu rude que l'école ontologique aura reçu en angleterre, au moins de nos jours, et que tôt ou tard ce coup lui sera mortel: or c'était là chose la plus importante à faire, puisque cette école seule est essentiellement théologique, et puisque sa doctrine se présente aujourd'hui chez nous comme l'appui national de l'ancien ordre social et des idées non seulement chrétiennes, mais même anglicanes. Au reste je crois avoir tout fait pour ce qu'ence qui depend de moi, la positivité seule profite de cette victoire, si toutefois elle est remportée. Or je crains que si je refondais mon travail pour le rendre tout à fait conforme aux dispositions actuelles de mon esprit, je ne lui ôtasse une partie de ce qui le rend propre à la situation philosophique de mon pays. Ce livre est l'expression de dix années de ma vie philosophique, et il sera bon pour ceux qui sont encore dans les conditions intellectuelles où j'étais alors, ce qui malheureusement suppose déjà un public fort choisi. J'aurai donc moins de regret en le laissant essentiellement comme il est, en comptant pourtant ne pas livrer à l'impression la dernière partie, qui seule a des rapports directs avec la sociologie, avant d'avoir lu avec l'attention et la délibération nécessaires votre sixième volume.

Vous me connaissez sans doute assez aujourd'hui pour croire à la sincérité de la sympathie que j'ai ressentie en apprenant que les dégoûts inséparables d'une position si peu convenable à vos goûts et à votre portée intellectuelle se sont maintenant compliqués de douleurs morales. Je n'ose pas encore me permettre de vous demander, à cet égard, plus de renseignements que vous ne m'en donnez spontanément. Plus tard peut être, j'aurais conquis le droit de chercher à partager vos souffrances: quant à les soulager, quand elles sont réelles, il y a ordinairement de la fatuité à se croire capable de cela.

Pour parler maintenant de Gall, je crains de vous avoir donné une idée exagérée de mon éloignement actuel de sa doctrine. Je suis bien loin de ne pas la trouver digne d'être prise, selon votre propre expression, en sérieuse considération; bien au contraire, je crois qu'elle a irrévocablement ouvert la voie à un ordre de recherches vraiment positives, et de la première importance. Si je n'ai pas paru autant frappé que vous avez pû vous y attendre, de la polémique de Gall contre les psychologues, cela ne tient peut-être qu'à ce qu'essentiellement elle n'était pas nouvelle pour moi qui avais tant de fois lu et tant médité les parties correspondantes de votre Cours. Malheureusement je ne puis pas me flatter d'arriver de bonne heure à des idées beaucoup plus arrêtées sur la partie affirmative de la doctrine de Gall, puisque si lui-même il n'a pas, selon vous, suffisamment connu la zoologie et l'anatomie comparée, je saurais encore moins, moi qui n'ai de ces sciences qu'une connaissance très superficielle, apprécier la force réelle des preuves qu'elles fournissent à l'appui des résultats généraux de la physiologie phrénologique, à moins que quelque savant ne les recueille et ne les mette devant moi comme devant tout le monde, en fesent le travail important dont vous indiquez dans votre lettre la nature et la nécessité. Espérons qu'il se rencontrera quelqu'un doué des connaissances nécessaires pour entreprendre cette tâche du point de vue sociologique. En attendant, et par des considérations tirées seulement de l'observation ordinaire, je trouve comme vous vraisemblable qu'il n'existe pas moins de dix forces fondamentales, soit intellectuelles, soit affectives, sauf à en faire le dénombrement exact et à trouver pour chacune d'elles son organe propre. Malgré la profonde irrationalité, à certains égards, de la classification faite par Gall des facultés humaines et animales, je lui rends la justice de reconnaître qu'elle est, au moins dans sa conception générale, très au-dessus de la classification banale des métaphysiciens. Gall a du moins conçu comme facultés distinctes, des capacités ou des penchans visiblement indépendants l'un de l'autre dans leur activité normale, sauf leurs nombreuses sympathies et synergies, au lieu que les prétendues facultés de l'attention, de la perception, du jugement, &c. ou celles de la joie, de la crainte, de l'espérance, &c. s'accompagnent normalement dans leurs actions, se suivent dans leurs variations, et ne ressemblent qu'aux diverses fonctions ou aux différents modes de sensibilité d'un même organe. Vous accorderez probablement que ce qu'il a de vraiment important dans la critique que Gall a faite des théories psychologiques se porte surtout sur ce point capital.

Votre devoué

J. S. MILL.

363. TO JOHN MITCHELL KEMBLE[1]

India House
16th July 1842

MY DEAR SIR

Your note is a considerable disappointment to Mr. Potter,[2] as he had taken up the subject of his articles in no spirit of dilettantism but under the idea that it is specially applicable to the great questions of the present time & that "by cramming" as he writes "into the Religion of Socrates, the Mysticism of Plato, the Utilitarianism of Aristotle, & the Syncretism of Philo", all of which he regards as products of a social period in many respects similar to our own, he was likely to evolve principles eminently adapted to the solution of our present moral & social difficulties.

If you think the article does not sufficiently give evidence of this purpose you would, no doubt, be right in rejecting it. I fancied however when I read it that the object & spirit of the article would please you & suit your review though I could not judge whether the sentiments would.

Will you kindly inform me to what place I should send for the ms.?

Yours very truly

J. S. MILL

1. MS in the possession of Professor Ney MacMinn.
2. See Letter 352.

364. TO WILLIAM LOVETT[1]

India House,
27th July, 1842.

DEAR MR. LOVETT,

You will oblige me very much by letting me know when your Association[2] sets about the formation of the library which I had the pleasure of hearing mentioned in Mr. Hetherington's speech[3] as I may have it in my power to offer them a few books & should in particular be glad if they would accept from me one of the few sets which I have retained of the London review & the L & Westminster Review during the time of my connexion with those works, that is during the whole of the time they bore those names.

I have never yet met with any associated body of men whom I respect so much as I do your Association, or whom I am so desirous of aiding by every means & to every extent, consistent with my individual opinions. Those opinions, as you, at least, are aware, do not go with you to the full extent. The same horror which you yourself entertain of class legislation, makes me object, in the present state of civilization at least, if not on principle, to a legislature absolutely controlled by one class, even when that class numerically exceeds all others taken together. I would give you the choice of only a part, though a large & possibly progressively increasing part of the legislature but that part you should elect conformably to all the six points of the Charter[4] & I should object as much as any of you to surrendering one iota of any of them. For these reasons even if I were a public man, which I am not, I should not join either your movement or Sturge's,[5] while I would give any help I could to yours rather than to his,

1. MS in the Lovett Collection of the Municipal Reference Library, Birmingham. Copy supplied by Mr. Peter M. Jackson.
   William Lovett (1800–1877), one of the most influential leaders of the Chartist movement.
2. The National Association for Promoting the Political and Social Improvement of the People, founded in 1841 by Lovett and his Chartist associates. On July 25, 1842, two days before this letter, the Association opened its National Hall at 242A, High Holborn (the renovated Gate Street Chapel), with a public festival devoted to public meetings, lectures, concerts, and classes. John Temple Leader, MP, presided at the opening ceremonies. JSM was a subscriber to the Association during 1842–43, along with such liberals as Joseph Hume, George Grote, and Charles Buller (see Julius West, *A History of the Chartist Movement* [Boston, 1920], pp. 159–61).
3. Henry Hetherington (1792–1849), veteran publisher of unstamped workingmen's papers, including *The Poor Man's Guardian* (1832–35), and a leader in the Chartist movement. He was the first secretary of the National Association. JSM no doubt heard him at one of the meetings referred to in the preceding note.
4. The demands of the Chartists, formulated as early as 1837, comprised: (1) manhood suffrage; (2) vote by ballot; (3) abolition of the property qualification for membership in Parliament; (4) payment of members; (5) equal electoral districts; (6) annual parliaments.
5. Joseph Sturge (1793–1859), philanthropist and reformer, had founded the National Complete Suffrage Union on April 9, 1842.

because yours has a more comprehensive range of objects & is a far more powerful instrument of good.

I do not obtrude these opinions upon you from any notion that their being my opinions makes them particularly worthy of attention, still less do I wish to convert you or your friends to them. Even if I could, I should not desire it. If you were not Chartists in the full force of the term, you would have far less power either of promoting the just claims of the numerical majority or of regulating their efforts and elevating their moral & intellectual state. But as I am really anxious to come among you, & to know you better, & to find out what means I have of aiding you, I think it useful & even honest to make all the explanations necessary for establishing a complete confidence, grounded on a full knowledge of each other's views & purposes. When you know exactly how far I differ from you, & exactly why, you will be able to judge when & in what I can make myself useful to you. It is but little that I can do: I have no connexion with any party & none now with any portion whatever of the press: but I have access to it, & am personally acquainted with many of the most intelligent people in the country, over whom one can always hope to exercise more or less influence. Therefore I may at least be useful in giving you a good name, or in counteracting those who attempt to give you a bad one. If either in this or in any other way anything which I can honestly do for you is worth your acceptance, it would probably be worth your while that we should meet occasionally & discuss & understand each other's principles & views. I have just now only an empty house to ask you to, but some few weeks hence if yourself & one or two of your friends—any of those who spoke on Monday who would think it worth their while—could spare me an evening & would not mind coming so far, we might make a good deal of progress.

Yours very sincerely,

J. S. MILL

365. TO HENRY COLE[1]

I.H.
6th Aug. 1842

MY DEAR COLE

I cannot remember any other interesting plants, beyond the bounds of Surrey, than the few I have here noted down. I have botanized very little in other counties, near London at least.

1. Text supplied by Professor J. M. McCrimmon from original owned in 1944 by Mr. Edward C. Ames, 2904 Goddard Road, Toledo, Ohio. Photostat copy now at LSE.

If you have done with my Surrey Flora I should be obliged by your returning it.

ever yours

J. S. MILL

Plants found in the neighbourhood of London but not in Surrey

———

Sisymbrium sophia, near Lower Halliford, Middlesex—also between Crayford & Erith in Kent.

The following in the neighbourhood of Hayes & Keston in Kent:
Lathroea squammaria—lane near Keston church
Narcissus pseudonarcissus—in a wood & adjoining thickets between Keston church & West Wickham
Narthecium ossifragum ⎫
Drosera rotundifolia   ⎬
Hypericum elodes   ⎬ in marshy parts of Keston Heath
Eriphorum angustifulium ⎭
Hieracium sabaudum—Hayes common and neighbouring fields.
Potentille argentea—in dry gravelly parts of Keston Heath

———

Daphne laureola—in a wood near Chiselhurst
Hutchinsia petraea—wall of Eltham churchyard.

———

Sambucus ebulis, hedge between Loughton & Chigwell
Lactuca virosa, border of a field near Loughton on the east side of the high road.
Campanula hederacea—in different parts of the forest.

366. TO ALEXIS DE TOCQUEVILLE[1]

9th August 1842.

MY DEAR TOCQUEVILLE,

I am really ashamed of having allowed so long a time to elapse without writing to you. My excuses must be, a great deal to do, many letters to write which *could* not be postponed, & latterly (I mean during the last two months in which I have every day intended to write to you the day after)

1. Published in Mayer, pp. 336–38. MS in Tocqueville archives.

the languor of ill health. I am still far from well but I will not any longer defer writing to you. First, I have to thank you for your discourse to the Académie française[2] which I have read with great admiration, as to the most finished performance, both in point of style & in the elaboration of the ideas, which you have yet produced, at least to my knowledge, & sufficient in itself to justify your election to the body which represents or ought to represent the great writers of your country as you had already been deservedly placed in the still more illustrious body which represents its great thinkers.[3] I must at the same time add that I have read this stirring performance with an unusual share of the deep & melancholic interest with which I have long been affected by everything relating to the present state of France. I confess that the profound discouragement or at least the deeply rooted doubts & apprehensions respecting the destinies of France, which to me at least seemed to pervade the concluding portion of your discourse, have added greatly to the strength of the misgivings which I myself felt about that country, to which by tastes & predilections I am more attached than to my own, & on which the civilization of Continental Europe in so great a degree depends. I have often, of late, remembered the reason you gave in justification of the conduct of the liberal party in the late quarrel between England & France—that the feeling of orgueil national is the only feeling of a public-spirited & elevating kind which remains & that it ought not therefore to be permitted to go down. How true this is, every day makes painfully evident—one now sees that the love of liberty, of progress, even of material prosperity, are in France mere passing unsubstantial, superficial movements on the outside of the national mind & that the only appeal which really goes to the heart of France is one of defiance to l'étranger—& that whoever would offer to her satisfaction to that one want, would find the whole of her wealth, the blood of her citizens & every guarantee of liberty & social security flung down at his feet like worthless things. Most heartily do I agree with you that this one & only feeling of a public, & therefore, so far, of a disinterested character which remains in France must not be suffered to decay. The desire to shine in the eyes of foreigners & to be highly esteemed by them must be cultivated and encouraged in France, at all costs. But, in the name of France & civilization, posterity have a right to expect from such men as you, from the nobler & more enlightened spirits of the time, that you should teach to your countrymen better ideas of what it is which constitutes national glory & national importance, than the low & grovelling ones which they seem to have at present—lower & more

---

2. *Discours de M. de Tocqueville prononcé dans la séance publique du 21 avril 1842 en venant prendre séance à la place de M. Le Comte de Cessac* (Paris, 1842).
3. He had been elected a member of the Académie des Sciences Morales et Politiques in 1838.

grovelling than I believe exist in any country in Europe at present except perhaps Spain. Here, for instance, the most stupid & ignorant person knows perfectly well that the real importance of a country in the eyes of foreigners does not depend upon the loud & boisterous *assertion* of importance, the effect of which is an impression of angry weakness, not strength. It really depends upon the industry, instruction, morality, & good government of a country: by which alone it can make itself respected, or even feared, by its neighbours; & it is cruel to think & see as I do every day, to how sad an extent France has sunk in estimation on all these points (the three last at least) by the events of the last two or three years. Nothing can more destroy all impression of national strength, can more effectually prevent a nation from presenting an imposing aspect to its neighbours, than that determination neither to quarrel nor be friends—above all there is nothing which the English can less understand when they see France unwilling to come to an open breach & yet her ill humour breaking out on all petty second-rate occasions, the impression made upon them is one of simple puerility; it makes them feel the French to be a nation of sulky schoolboys. I myself make, I hope, all due allowances, certainly very great ones, for all this, but there are not, I fully believe, half a dozen other persons in England who do so, or in Germany either according to the best information I can obtain. If the French people did but know how much higher they would stand in the eyes of the world if they shewed only a great deal less solicitude about the *world's* opinion & less soreness about the consideration shewn them! for all the world knows that to be very uneasy about having one's importance recognized, shews that one has not much confidence in the grounds on which it rests.

I have not yet thanked you for your very kind reception of my young friend Lewes, who feels it as he ought to do & always speaks in the warmest manner of you and Madame de Tocqueville. He is very capable of appreciating the superiority of your philosophical ideas & was as much struck as it was natural he should be with the extreme rarity of impartiality such as yours: he found no other example of it among those he saw at Paris.

I hardly dare ask you to write to so bad a correspondent as I am, but a letter of yours has to me greater interest than that of a letter, it is like a new book, or a review article, giving materials for thought on great questions. I would rather have a monthly letter from you than read any monthly publication I ever knew—so pray think of me sometimes.

Yours ever affectionately

J. S. MILL.

India House.

367. TO AUGUSTE COMTE[1]

India House
le 12 août 1842

MON CHER MONSIEUR COMTE

Je commencerai ma lettre en répondant à la dernière partie de la vôtre du 22 juillet, à celle qui regarde la malheureuse famille dont vous me dépeignez d'une manière si intéressante la triste position.[2] Depuis que votre lettre m'est venue je n'ai pas cessé, et ne cesserai pas de faire pour le jeune homme dont il s'agit, la seule chose qui soit en mon pouvoir, c.à.d. de circuler parmi le petit nombre de banquiers et de négociants influents que je connais particulièrement et surtout parmi ceux qui connaissent votre nom, cette partie de votre lettre. La concurrence inouïe qui est le fléau de ce pays de mariages féconds, et l'engorgement perpétuel et en quelque sorte normal, de tous les canaux de l'industrie, rendent malheureusement fort incertain le succès de cette démarche, à laquelle du reste rien ne manquera de ma part. Quant à l'Inde il est inutile d'y penser. Vous avez très bien senti qu'on tient naturellement à ce que les places aux bureaux de la Compagnie soient remplies par des Anglais. Pour celles dans l'Inde, les plus considérables en sont destinées aux parens ou aux protégés des différents membres du corps dirigeant, et les emplois qu'on ne donne pas à des anglais sont réservés aux indigènes du pays. Restent les places au service des princes indiens. Mais d'abord on ne donne pas ces emplois en Europe: pour les avoir il faut aller les chercher dans le pays, et cela avec de très bonnes recommandations; encore a-t-on très peu de chances de les obtenir; sans compter que le gouvernement anglais, qui n'a pas perdu le souvenir des Bussy, des Deboigne et des Perron,[3] défendrait vraisemblablement aux princes qui sont dans leur dépendance, d'entretenir à leur service des étrangers Européens, et surtout peut être des français. Vous voyez ainsi combien peu je puis faire pour votre intéressant protégé. Au reste, la connaissance qu'il a des langues européennes me fait croire qu'il se trouverait mieux dans quelque maison de commerce où l'on aurait besoin de quelqu'un pour la correspondance étrangère. En fesant donc connaître sa position aux chefs de quelques maisons de commerce et de banque, je fais probablement pour lui ce qu'il y a de mieux à faire, au moins pour le moment.

Si le plaisir qu'une lettre a donné pouvait se reproduire tout entier dans la réponse, celle que je vous écris aujourd'hui serait certainement de toutes

1. MS at Johns Hopkins. Published in Lévy-Bruhl, pp. 90–94; in answer to Comte's of July 22, *ibid.*, pp. 81–90.
2. In his letter of July 22 Comte had asked JSM to help find a position for an unfortunate young friend of his.
3. Charles Joseph Patissier, marquis de Bussy-Castelnau (1718–1785); Benoît LeBorgne, comte de Boigne (1741–1830); Pierre Cuellier Perron (*ca.* 1755–1843); French military leaders in the Anglo-French wars in India.

les lettres que vous avez eues de moi jusqu'ici la plus agréable, car celle à laquelle je réponds a été pour moi une véritable fête: surtout par la nouvelle qu'elle m'annonçait de l'achèvement de votre 6ᵐᵉ volume et de sa publication toute prochaine, choses dont vos dernières lettres m'avaient presque fait désespérer. Il me tarde d'avoir ce volume et de le lire, et je me sens peu disposé en attendant, à entamer avec vous des discussions philosophiques quelconques, que la lecture de la portion finale de votre système pourra rendre sitôt superflues. Cependant, j'ai toujours beaucoup désiré qu'une véritable et franche comparaison, en quelque sorte systématique, de nos idées soit philosophiques soit sociologiques pût s'établir entre nous deux; en sentant toutefois que cela exigeait nécessairement comme condition préparatoire que j'eusse une connaissance complète de votre grand travail philosophique dans son ensemble, et même que vous prissiez connaissance jusqu'à un certain point de ce que j'ai moi-même écrit, afin de pouvoir apprécier mon point de départ et l'ordre de mon développement intellectuel, ainsi que de suppléer à beaucoup d'explications et de faire porter la discussion, dès le commencement, sur les points réels et fondamentaux de divergence si toutefois il s'en trouve finalement, ce dont je ne puis pas décider. Je sais que je me suis toujours de plus en plus rapproché de vos doctrines à mesure que je les ai connues davantage et mieux comprises, mais vous savez bien, en qualité de géomètre qu'un décroissement continu n'est pas toujours un décroissement sans limite.

Je vous remercie on ne peut pas plus des détails que vous me donnez si aimablement sur votre position personnelle, ce que je ne compte pas comme la moindre des marques d'amitié véritable auxquelles vous m'accoutumez toujours de plus en plus. En apprenant à quel point, par suite de l'absurde modicité des traitements en france, un homme comme vous est mal rétribué de ses pénibles et fatigants travaux, je me sens presque honteux en avouant que je retire d'une seule place, importante il est vrai mais bien moins laborieuse que ce cumul d'enseignements mathématiques qui vous est imposé par le système des petits traitements, à peu près le triple de votre rétribution: ce qui du reste, eu égard à la cherté plus grande des choses de consommation ordinaire et aux dépenses de position proportionnellement plus grandes, n'équivaut probablement qu'au double. Il y a maintenant six ans que ce traitement m'est échu par suite de ce que nous nommons une *promotion* au bureau:[4] avant cela j'avais fait pendant treize ans essentiellement le même travail moyennant une rétribution, qui en s'accroissant annuellement ne dépassait guère la moitié de mon traitement d'aujourd'hui.

4. Two promotions in 1836 had brought him to rank only behind David Hill and Thomas Love Peacock in the Examiner's office. His salary was £1,200 a year. When Peacock and Hill retired in 1856, JSM was promoted to the Examinership at a salary of £2,000.

J'espère avoir encore une lettre de vous avant votre départ pour l'Ouest. Je vous remercie de m'avoir indiqué le moyen de vous faire parvenir des lettres pendant que vous serez en tournée. J'en ferai certainement usage, car après la lecture du 6me volume je ne pourrai assurément pas attendre votre retour à Paris, pour vous exprimer ce que cette lecture m'aura fait éprouver: Je suivrai votre conseil en laissant quelque port à payer, afin de stimuler l'activité de Mm. de la poste. Puisque je suis sur ce chapitre je vous dirai par parenthèse que la compagnie des Indes me fait l'honêteté de payer pour moi le port des lettres qui me sont adressées à leur bureau. Ainsi je vous engage à ne plus affranchir les vôtres comme vous l'avez fait jusqu'ici, car je ne vois aucun inconvénient à ce que les habitans de l'Inde supportent une partie des frais d'une correspondance philosophique dont on peut se permettre d'espérer que l'avenir de l'humanité, là comme ailleurs, pourra retirer quelque fruit.

Je suis bien aisé d'apprendre que vous êtes natif de Montpellier; c'est encore une source de sympathie, car j'ai moi-même passé dans cette ville les six mois les plus heureux de ma jeunesse, ceux de l'hiver 1820/21. C'est même là que j'ai pour la première fois trouvé un ami, c'est-à-dire un ami de mon propre choix, à la différence de ceux qui me furent donnés par des rélations de famille. Cet ami, je ne l'ai pas revu depuis; nous avons longtemps entretenu une correspondance qui enfin a cessé un peu par la faute de tous deux, et je ne sais pas même s'il est en vie; s'il l'est, il doit être pharmacien à Montpellier, et vous pouvez en avoir quelque connaissance. Il se nomme Balard;[5] c'est celui à qui la chimie est redevable de la découverte intéressante du brome: je ne sais pas si ensuite il a fait autre chose.

votre tout dévoué

J. S. MILL.

368. TO WILLIAM TAIT[1]

India House
17th August
1842

MY DEAR SIR

Although in the inclosed note my friend Sterling speaks of his name as unknown to you, I have no doubt of its being known, & known very well.

5. Antoine Jérôme Balard (1802–1876), chemist, known for his discovery of bromine. Comte in his reply of Aug. 24 reported that Balard was now professor of chemistry in Paris. Several of Balard's early letters to JSM are at LSE.

* * * *

1. MS at LSE.

I should think the connexion he proposes a most desirable one for your Magazine.

In case you chuse to write to him direct, his address is

> Rev. John Sterling
> Falmouth

Very truly yours

J. S. MILL

"The Election"[2] which he speaks of is one of the cleverest semi-satirical poems published since Beppo & Don Juan.

369. TO SARAH AUSTIN[1]

India House
22d August 1842

I write to you today without having much to say, in order to tell you what I have done or tried to do respecting your commissions. Senior[2] never received your note, as he had set off before it reached me. He could not therefore have taken anything to you. I could have sent through Mr. Klingemann[3] but I found that Laing's book[4] was out of print & a bookseller whom I employed was not able to procure me a copy. There is to be another edition soon, & when it comes out I will send it you if you think fit. But I would rather recommend your making Napier get it,[5] as he certainly ought to do. I have no doubt a copy was sent to him.—I could not send any sheets of my Logic because I have not yet begun to print it. The delay is not with me but with Parker who talked of beginning to print in July but has given no notice of being ready, & as the thing really does not press & he has behaved very well I do not chuse to urge him on the subject. It is very satisfactory that Napier has consented to take an article on the book from Mr Austin & I am particularly glad to hear of two articles on the stocks. It is a sign at least that Napier is not displeased with the reception of the former article,[6] & he is likely to hear

---

2. See Letter 325.

•   •   •   •

1. MS in the possession of Mr. Gordon Waterfield.
2. Nassau Senior.
3. Unidentified.
4. Samuel Laing, *Notes of a Traveller on the social and political state of France, Prussia, Switzerland, Italy . . . during the present century* (London, 1842). The first edition was published in Jan.; a second, on Sept. 24, 1842.
5. Mrs. Austin was apparently planning to review the book for the *Edinburgh Review*.
6. See Letter 347, n. 5.

whatever complaints there are. As for dryness it is a fault belonging to the matter rather than the manner which was considerably more lively than I expected it to be though a little surcharged with classification in the first few pages. I *had* heard of that offer[7] & of Mr. Austin's refusal of it. Though I did not know the grounds of the refusal I felt that he was the best judge—& that no bystander can possibly judge for any person in such a case, especially for a person of his peculiarities & of his superiority of intellect. The expression of regret however at his determination, has been by no means confined to the persons whom you mention. I have not heard any *of them* speak of it but I have heard, & heard of several others of whose friendship for you & Mr Austin you have less doubt, & who expressed, not dissent, much less had they the presumption to express disapprobation, but rather seemed to feel discouragement, from an idea of its being very unlikely that anything should offer itself which would be liable to fewer objections than this Malta plan. Now however when I know his reasons I do not think so: & at all events if you are better as you are than with this, you are better as you are than with anything only as good as this.

I hope you will write other things like Steffens[8] both for Kemble & for Napier. I am sure they would be successful & profitable. I should have thought just the same of that article if it had been written by anybody else—it tells people with elegance & in an amusing garb & lively manner a number of the things which they most need to be told.

Thanks for your copious list of German books on Rome: I wish there was a chance of meeting with half of them, without buying *chat en poche,*— there are too many of them for such an experiment, nor is the occasion worth it. I shall read Wachsmuth[9] & one or two others if I can borrow them. I have already read to weariness about Rome for if one is particular about writing only what is true one has enough to do. I could have written a dashing article on the Romans such as Macaulay would write (though of course not so brilliantly) in a week, with the knowledge I had when I began to *read up* the subject. In the meantime I have been writing again for the old Westminster: Bailey of Sheffield has published a book to demolish Berkeley's theory of vision: & I have answered him,[10] feeling it

7. Austin had received an offer of an appointment to return to Malta. See letter of G. C. Lewis to George Grote, Sept. 6, 1842: "Austin had quite made up his mind as to the Malta project; his principal reason seemed to be that the salary was not sufficient to enable him to save anything, and he had enough to live upon in Germany. Moreover, he seemed quite uncertain about his health." (*Letters of Sir George Cornewall Lewis,* ed. Sir G. F. Lewis [London, 1870], p. 125.)

8. A review of the German philosopher Henrik Steffens' autobiography, *Was ich erlebte* (Breslau, 1840) in *BFR,* XIII (1842), 279–315.

9. Wilhelm Wachsmuth (1787–1866), German archaeologist and historian, author of *Die ältere Geschichte der Römer* . . . (Halle, 1819).

10. See Letter 373, n. 6.

my special vocation to stand up for the old orthodox faith of that school. I will send the article to Mr Austin for it will have a chance of interesting him, though few people else. It is the first fruits of my partial recovery from a three months illness, or rather out-of-health-ness, & it at least helps to pay my debt to Hickson who used to write for the review without pay when I had it.

It will be some comfort to get a real philosophical account of Prussia as the result of your winter in Berlin & I hope to hear from yourself somewhat more about the Berlinische Aufklärung from personal knowledge. From what you say I imagine it to be rather an un-German thing without the simplicity, cordiality, & above all the quietness, which are so agreeable in German life & ways to a person wearied with discontented, struggling (Benthamicè) devil-by-the-tail-pulling England. But my notion of it is quite vague & may be all wrong.

adieu

J. S. MILL.

370. TO ROBERT BARCLAY FOX[1]

India House
9th Sepr 1842

MY DEAR FRIEND

I can hardly justify myself for having left you so long without direct tidings of my existence, for I believe this is the first letter I write to you since we parted in London at the termination of your angel's visit. I was not very busy, either, in the earlier part of the time; but of late, that is from the beginning of July I have been both busy & unwell—the latter to a degree unusual with me, though without a vestige of danger. I am now so much better as to consider myself well, but am still busy, partly with revising my too big book, & making it still bigger by the introduction of additional examples & illustrations, partly by reading for an article on the Romans which I have promised to the Edinburgh. To this twofold drudgery, for it is really so I shall have to add presently the correcting of proofs, for part of the MS is already in the printer's hands.

I hardly know what subjects to write to you about unless I could know what are those about which you have been thinking: as for myself I have scarcely been thinking at all except on the two subjects I have just mentioned, Logic & the Romans. As for politics I have almost given up thinking on the subject. Passing events suggest no thoughts but what

1. *Addressed*: R. Barclay Fox Esq. / Falmouth. *Postmark*: FALMOUTH / SE 10 1842. Published in Pym, II, 334–36. MS in the possession of Mr. W. H. Browning.

they have been suggesting for many years past; & there is nothing for a person who is excluded from active participation in political life, to do, except to watch the signs which occur of real improvement in mankind's ideas on some of the smaller points, & the too slender indications of some approach to improvement in their feelings on the larger ones. I do believe that ever since the changes in the Constitution made by Catholic emancipation and the Reform Act,[2] a considerable portion of the ruling class in this country, especially of the younger men, have been having their minds gradually opened, & the progress of Chartism is I think creating an impression that rulers are bound both in duty & in prudence to take more charge, than they have lately been wont to do, of the interests both temporal & spiritual of the poor. This feeling one can see breaking out in all sort of stupid & frantic forms, as well as influencing silently the opinions & conduct of sensible people. But as to the means of curing or even alleviating great social evils people are as much at sea as they were before. All one can observe, and it is much, is a more solemn sense of their position, & a more conscientious consideration of the questions which come before them, but this is I fear as yet confined to a few. Still one need not feel discouraged. There never was a time when ideas went for more in human affairs than they do now—& one cannot help seeing that any one's honest endeavours must tell for something & may tell for very much, although, in comparison with the mountain of evil to be removed, I never felt disposed to estimate human capabilities at a lower rate than now.

On other subjects I have been doing very little except reading Maurice's "Kingdom of Christ"[3] &, for the second time, his "Moral Philosophy" in the Encyclopaedia Metropolitana.[4] The latter I like much the best, though both are productions of a very remarkable mind. In the former your Society has a special interest: did that or other considerations ever induce you to read it? He seems to me much more successful in showing that other people are wrong than that Churchmen or rather that an ideal Churchman is in the right. The Moral Philosophy is rather a history of ethical ideas. It is very interesting especially the analysis of Judaic life and society & of Plato & Aristotle & there seems to me much more truth in this book than in the other.

2. In 1829 and 1832 respectively.
3. Frederick Denison Maurice, *The Kingdom of Christ* (3 vols., London, 1837). A second, revised edition in 2 vols. appeared in 1842.
4. *Encyclopædia Metropolitana*, ed. Edward Smedley, Hugh James Rose, and Henry J. Rose, published in 59 parts (London, 1817–45). Maurice's article, published in 1840, was the basis of his later treatises on the history of philosophy which were eventually combined in his *Moral and Metaphysical Philosophy* (2 vols., London, 1871–72).

Our people[5] have been at Paris and are just returned. I suppose their or rather our friends will soon hear of them. They are full of the subject of what they have seen & enjoyed & altogether the thing has answered perfectly. Certainly however pleasant home may be there is great pleasure in occasionally leaving it. I wish some of *you* thought so and that *we* lived in some place where you wanted very much to come.—

Yours faithfully

J. S. MILL.

371. TO AUGUSTE COMTE[1]

India House
le 10 Septembre 1842

MON CHER MONSIEUR COMTE—

Vous me croirez à peine quand je vous dirai que même aujourd'hui je n'ai pas encore votre 6me volume. Personne ici ne l'a. Vous ne pouvez pas, sans en avoir fait l'expérience personnelle, vous faire une idée convenable des lenteurs et de l'indifférence de ce petit nombre de libraires qui entretiennent chez nous le commerce des livres entre la france et l'angleterre. Moi-même je ne croyais pas que ces lenteurs pussent se prolonger à tel point, d'autant moins que je n'en avais pas eu connaissance à l'occasion des autres volumes, n'ayant appris leur publication à Paris que par leur apparition ici. Aujourd'hui même pas un de ces libraires ne me donne une espérance certaine pour un jour donné. Si j'avais prévu de si longs retards, j'aurais fait venir l'ouvrage de Paris directement, au moyen de quelques personnes de ma famille qui s'y trouvaient alors: mais comme elles ne devaient revenir qu'au bout de quinze jours, je ne voulais pas attendre leur arrivée. Maintenant elles sont ici depuis huit jours, et moi, malgré ma faim, je suis encore à jeûn de votre livre. Jamais je n'ai trouvé plus difficile l'exercice de l'attribut essentiellement philosophique de la patience. Cependant c'est le seul remède, car je sais, par expérience, que si je m'adressais à quelqu'une des maisons de Paris qui font des expéditions à l'Angleterre, il faudrait peut-être attendre encore trois mois. On voit très bien que l'industrie n'est pas, au moins jusqu'à présent, du ressort des Français, car, bienque si éveillés à tant d'autres égards, ils font les affaires du commerce quasi en dormant. Leur défaut total de ce que nous

5. JSM's family.

* * * *

1. MS at Johns Hopkins. Published in Lévy-Bruhl, pp. 106–10; in reply to Comte's of Aug. 24, *ibid.*, pp. 95–105.

appelons ici ponctualité me paraît expliquer leur infériorité industrielle par rapport à plusieurs autres nations qui n'ont certainement sur eux aucune supériorité naturelle.

Aujourd'hui donc je n'ai à vous entretenir que d'affaires personnelles. Pour en commencer par celle de votre intéressant protégé,[2] je vous dis avec regret que par suite de l'immense concurrence dont l'accroissement progressif est à peine compensé par toutes les améliorations industrielles des temps modernes, mes efforts pour lui ont été jusqu'ici infructueux. Je vous envoie la réponse du banquier le plus important de Londres, homme recommandable à tous égards, et très distingué par son intelligence. C'est la plus favorable de celles qui j'ai reçues, et la seule qui donne une lueur d'espérance: vous verrez comme cette lueur est faible. Toutefois je ne relâcherai pas mes efforts, et si la chose est possible j'espère que j'y parviendrai.

Vous pouvez vous figurer, beaucoup mieux que je ne saurais l'exprimer, combien je dois sentir profondément l'honneur et la douceur de la preuve d'amitié réelle que vous me donnez en vous ouvrant à moi avec une si touchante confiance sur les chagrins de votre situation personnelle. Quant à l'événement important de la rupture probablement finale de vos liens domestiques,[3] je trouve très naturelles les souffrances morales qui ont accompagné chez vous cette crise de votre existence affective, mais en résultat je pense comme vous que cette séparation doit probablement exercer, sur votre avenir, une influence favorable. Lorsqu'une personne douée de l'élévation morale et intellectuelle qu'avec la noble impartialité qui vous distingue, vous accordez à Mme Comte—lorsque, dis-je, une personne pareille, et un homme de votre superiorité à tous égards se trouvent fatalement condamnés à ne pouvoir vivre ensemble qu'en état de lutte continué, je pense qu'ils doivent, dans l'intérêt bien entendu de l'un et de l'autre, surtout s'ils n'ont pas d'enfans, se résigner à vivre séparément. De pareilles incompatibilités, qui souvent existent sans aucun tort vraiment grave de l'une ou de l'autre part, ont rendu pour moi, jusqu'ici, la question du divorce une question indécise, comme plusieurs autres questions de morale particulière, depuis longtemps jugées et decidées pour vous. Je suis loin d'avoir sur ces matières, une opinion contraire à la vôtre; je n'ai pas, à vrai dire, une opinion arrêtée, et je suis même assez porté à croire[4] . . . car pour en décider irrévocablement il faudrait attendre une con-

---

2. See Letter 367, n. 2.

3. Comte had written in his letter of Aug. 24 (Lévy-Bruhl, pp. 102–4) of the "voluntary, and probably irrevocable, departure" on Aug. 2 of his wife, to whom he had been married for seventeen years. She had left him and been taken back several times before, but this time he refused. She continued to hope for a reunion and they corresponded for a number of years.

4. Here some words are missing in the MS.

naissance plus profonde de la nature humaine, soit en général, soit dans ses variétés. Peut être ma conversion, à cet égard, serait une œuvre réservée à votre Traité de Politique. En tout cas je sens profondément ce qu'il y a d'amer dans la position d'un homme fait comme vous pour le bonheur domestique, et dont les efforts pour y atteindre se terminent, après tant d'années, par un si triste dénouement. Cet isolement doit être surtout pénible à un homme qui par goût et par habitude se tient retiré du monde ordinaire et ne cherche que chez lui la satisfaction de ses besoins d'affection. Du moins ceux à qui vous faites l'honneur d'admettre en leur faveur des exceptions à votre règle ordinaire de vie, ne peuvent qu'éprouver le désir le plus vif de vous offrir des consolations sympathiques quelconques, tout en sentant l'insuffisance profonde de toute compensation pareille. Quant aux conditions accessoires de la séparation, vous avez agi dignement, et d'une manière convenable à l'élévation de votre caractère.

Je suis très sensible à votre désir, si honorable pour moi, d'employer les prémices du loisir comparatif dont vous allez jouir, à vous informer de mes divers écrits. Mais je serai charmé si Marrast n'a pas pu vous donner les renseignements que vous vous proposiez de lui demander à ce sujet. La plupart des articles que j'ai insérés dans des revues sont si intimement mêlés à des choses du moment, et presque tous se caractérisent, à plusieurs égards, par une si grande immaturité d'idées, que vous feriez mieux de vous borner, en ce qui les regarde, à la lecture d'un petit nombre d'entre eux, que je me propose de réimprimer avec des suppressions et des émendations considérables. Quand j'ai parlé de la lecture de ce que j'avais déjà écrit comme devant faciliter de votre côté la confrontation de nos idées philosophiques, j'avais principalement en vue l'ouvrage systématique dont l'impression vient de commencer, et qui avec toutes les imperfections que je lui reconnais, et toutes celles que je n'y reconnais pas, dépasse pourtant de beaucoup tout ce que j'avais fait antérieurement. Non seulement j'y ai traité des questions plus profondes, et en les approfondissant davantage, mais aussi les concessions que je suis forcé de faire aux opinions régnantes y sont bien moins étendues, en raison du public plus choisi auquel l'ouvrage est destiné.

Il ne me reste plus, pour le moment, qu'à vous faire les remerciements les plus sincères des renseignements si satisfaisants que vous m'avez donnés sur mon ancien ami M. Balard, que je croyais ne plus revoir. J'accepte avec reconnaissance votre proposition obligeante de me servir d'intermédiaire pour renouer mes relations avec lui, pourvu toutefois que cette aimable infraction en ma faveur d'une de vos régles d'hygiène mentale ne vous coûte réellement pas.

votre devoué

J. S. MILL.

372. TO ROBERT BARCLAY FOX[1]

I.H.
20 Sept. 1842

MY DEAR FRIEND

I write this line in haste to ask of you & your family an act of kindness for a destitute person, namely the little girl whose card, as a candidate for the Orphan Asylum, is enclosed. You know how these things are decided—by the majority of votes of an enormous number of subscribers: but the list, like all similar ones, swarms with the names of your friends the Friends & your interest with them would be equivalent to many promises of votes. I know nothing of the girl or her family personally, but one of the men I most respect is warmly interested for them, Joseph Mazzini, whom you have heard of (but whom I would not mention to everybody as his name, with some, would do more harm than good). Mrs Carlyle is also exerting herself for them.

I will send to you or cause to be sent as many cards as you can make use of, in case your interest is not preengaged for other candidates to the full number.

I am quite well again & everybody here is well, otherwise we have no particular news. Carlyle has been making a Cromwellian tour to Huntingdon, St. Ives, Hinchinbrook, &c. He will really, I think, write a Cromwellian book.[2]

ever yours,

J. S. MILL

373. TO MACVEY NAPIER[1]

India House
3d October
1842

MY DEAR SIR

I have been reading very much on the subject of the Romans, much more indeed than has turned out to be necessary or useful for the article I

1. *Addressed*: R. B. Fox, Esq. / Falmouth. *Postmarks*: B / PAID / SE 20 1842 and SE 21 / 1842. MS in the possession of Mr. W. H. Browning. Published by Pym, II, 337.
2. Carlyle's three-day "Cromwellian tour" had been made in the first week of Sept. See his letter to John Carlyle in J. A. Froude, *Thomas Carlyle: A History of His Life in London, 1834–1881* (2 vols., New York, 1884), I, 235. His "Cromwellian book" was published three years later: *Oliver Cromwell's Letters and Speeches* (2 vols., London, 1845).

* * * *

1. MS in Brit. Mus.

proposed to write. I am quite prepared to set about it if we could determine on what hook to suspend it. The following occur to me:

1. Michelet's Roman History which I mentioned to you formerly.[2]

2. Walter's excellent History of the Roman Constitution & Laws, published at Bonn in 1840.[3]

3. The Roman History in the Library of Useful Knowledge[4] the objection to which however is its being unfinished.

4. Arnold's Roman History.[5] Since reading this book again from the beginning it seems to me much more appropriate for my purpose than it did before. But as a posthumous third volume is expected this seems so far a reason for waiting until it comes out which I suppose will not be till the spring.

If this therefore be the book we determine upon, I cannot write my article just yet—& in the mean time if there is anything else which I could do for you I should like very much to do it. I would rather not write my review of Michelet's Hist. of France at present because another historical subject would be apt to drive my Roman history out of my head.

As I mentioned to your son, there is a metaphysical article of mine in the Westminster review just now published:[6] would that have suited the Edinburgh? I ask the question because it is convenient to know what sort of articles you would be willing to receive from me.

ever yours truly

J. S. MILL

374. TO ALEXANDER BAIN[1]

Oct. 3, 1842

I am quite well and strong, and now walk the whole way to and from Kensington[2] without the self-indulgence of omni*bi*.

2. See Letters 285, n. 3, and 296.

3. Ferdinand Walter, *Geschichte des römischen Rechts bis auf Justinian*.

4. *The History of Rome* published by the Society for the Diffusion of Useful Knowledge was in three parts: Division I [to 390 B.C.] by Henry Malden (London, 1830); Division II [390 B.C. to A.D. 31] by William Bodham Donne (London, 1841); *The History of Rome under the Emperors* by Charles Merivale (London, 1841–43).

5. Thomas Arnold, *History of Rome* (3 vols., London, 1838–43). The third volume, ed. J. C. Hare, appeared in 1843.

6. "Bailey on Berkeley's Theory of Vision," *WR*, XXXVIII (Oct., 1842), 318–36. A review of Samuel Bailey's *A Review of Berkeley's Theory of Vision* (London, 1842). Reprinted in *Dissertations*, II, 162–97.

* * * *

1. Excerpt published in Bain, *JSM*, p. 77. MS not located.

2. Where his home then was.

375. TO J[AMES?] WHITING[1]

India House

15th October 1842

S<small>IR</small>

I feel it highly complimentary to a person so little known to the public as myself, to have been thought of by you and recommended by the distinguished men whose names you mention, for so honorable an office as that of assisting to decide on the merits of remedies for the evils of the present social and economical condition of the country. After giving, however, my best consideration to the nature of the task to which I am solicited by your flattering invitation, I do not feel that I could undertake it with any prospect of a result satisfactory to you or to myself.

You have in view, if I understand your object rightly, something more than a mere dissertation upon the causes of commercial vicissitudes: No Essay would fulfil your intentions which did not include the whole subject of the condition of the labouring classes, and the means which might or should be adopted to alleviate the evils and improve the advantages incident to that condition. Now I will state to you candidly that I see little chance of the production of any essay which would appear to me adequate to so great a subject. It contains matter not for one essay, however able or comprehensive, but for many essays. The causes of existing evils, it seems to me, lie too deep, to be within reach of any one remedy, or set of remedies; nor would any remedial measure, which is at present practicable, amount to more than a slight palliative for those evils: their removal, I conceive, can only be accomplished by slow degrees, and through many successive efforts, each having its own particular end in view, and so various in their nature that a dissertation which attempted to embrace them all must be so general as to be very little available for the practical guidance of any. Although, then, I think it probable that many useful remarks and suggestions may be called forth by the competition which you propose to institute and shall watch its results with great interest, I have little expectation of its leading to the production of any paper to which, with the views I have stated, I could with any satisfaction join in awarding the prize, nor can I think that any person holding such views is one upon whom it would be agreeable to the competitors that the fate of their Essays should in any degree depend.

I have the honor to be

Sir

Your obedient Servant

J. Whiting Esq.

J. S. M<small>ILL</small>

1. MS owned by Frederick B. Adams, Jr., of New York.

The recipient has not been identified with certainty. He may have been James Whiting (*ca.* 1777–1871), founder of the *Atlas* newspaper in 1826 and a writer on social and economic questions.

376. TO MACVEY NAPIER[1]

India House
15th October
1842

MY DEAR SIR

Your letter received this morning is extremely satisfactory as to the article on the Romans & I shall probably make Michelet & Walter the text of it.[2] I could scarcely be ready by the January number, as when once one begins to read German books on historical subjects, the more one reads, the more one wants to read. I am rather glad that the Ed. Rev. should pay the tribute due from us all to the memory of Arnold,[3] before I have occasion to speak of his History. And if an early publication of the post-humous volume should be announced, I could still wait for it.

I do not know whether your approval of the article in the West[r],[4] especially as to the composition, may not have a bad effect upon me by encouraging me to write hastily as the article was written in three days & was never meant to be a thing of any pretension. I should hardly have thought it worthy of the Ed. but I should probably have given you the refusal of it, if I had not been committed to the West[r] before I contemplated anything more than one of the small-print notices which that review usually contains. I should never send there anything which you would take, if I were not under a sort of personal obligation to the present proprietor,[5] not only for saving me the mortification of letting the review drop while in my hands, but as one of my principal contributors (& a gratuitous one) while I managed it. My reason for asking whether you would have taken this particular article, was that I might know what subjects suit your review & are not preengaged. The historical articles which I have been thinking of for you are things of great labour & require a long time for the preparation, but there are many things which I could write offhand, & should often do so if I knew that they would suit you. I could easily have something ready for the January number without detriment to my progress with the Romans, if we could hit upon any subject which suited us both.

You have touched up Alison very well[6] & it was time. My fingers have often itched to be at him. The undeserved reputation into which that book

1. MS in Brit. Mus.
2. See Letter 373.
3. The tribute (written by Herman Merivale) appeared in the Jan., 1843, *Edinburgh*, "The Late Dr. Arnold," LXXVI, 357–81.
4. See Letter 373, n. 6.
5. W. E. Hickson.
6. Review of Archibald Alison, *History of Europe, from the Commencement of the French Revolution in 1789, to . . . 1815* (10 vols., Edinburgh and London, 1833–42) in *ER*, LXXVI (Oct., 1842), 1–60.

is getting, merely because it is the Tory history, & the only connected one of that important time, is very provoking.

Yours very truly

J. S. MILL.

377. TO AUGUSTE COMTE[1]

India House
le 23 octobre 1842.

MON CHER MONSIEUR COMTE—

Les incroyables retards que j'ai éprouvés à l'égard de votre 6me volume,[2] et ensuite son ampleur extraordinaire et l'abondance de ses matières, ne m'ont permis d'en achever la première lecture que la veille même du jour ou j'écris cette lettre. Ce volume a dignement complété un ouvrage nécessairement unique dans le développement de l'humanité, car en supposant même que vous n'eussiez pas posé les premières bases fondamentales de la doctrine sociologique positive, vous n'en resteriez pas moins le fondateur de la vraie méthode sociologique, dans tout ce qu'elle a de vraiment caractéristique et par suite celui de la systématisation définitive des connaissances humaines. Quant aux doctrines spéciales de ce précieux volume, j'étais, j'ose le dire, suffisamment préparé par l'ensemble des volumes précédents et par notre correspondance, pour ne sembler trouver même dans les parties les plus remarquables de cette élaboration finale, que la confirmation et le développement d'idées que je possédais déjà, sauf quelques dissidences d'opinion d'importance mineure, dont je m'étais déjà aperçu et que la lecture de ce volume a notablement diminuées. Une seule fois j'y ai ressenti cette sorte de secousse que vos travaux m'ont souvent fait éprouver, et qui résulte de la subite appréhension d'une grande idée lumineuse et nouvelle. C'est dans l'endroit où vous parlez des hautes qualités sociales qu'on finira par trouver dans la vie industrielle, malgré le mobile essentiellement égoïste qui la dirige presque exclusivement aujourd'hui. A ce sujet vous apprendrez peut être avec intérêt un rapprochement caractéristique qui a lieu entre vos idées et celles d'un de nos écrivains les plus remarquables, dont le nom ne vous est pas probablement resté inconnu, M. Carlyle, qui bien que doué de facultés plutôt esthétiques que scientifiques, et procédant par intuition beaucoup plus que par raisonnement, a souvent des éclairs de génie qui en font en quelque sort un prophète et précurseur du progrès social. Cet

1. MS at Johns Hopkins. Published in Lévy-Bruhl, pp. 119–24; in reply to Comte's of Sept. 30, *ibid.*, pp. 110–18.
2. *Cours de philosophie positive: Complément de la philosophie sociale, et conclusions générales* (Paris, 1842), Vol. 6.

homme recommandable avec qui je suis lié depuis onze ans, me disait dernièrement qu'il ne fallait pas désespérer de l'idéalisation poétique de l'industrie; car, disait-il, voyez quelle grande poésie on a su tirer de la vie militaire, quoiqu'il n'y ait rien de plus naturellement laid que l'acte de tuer, accompagné des diverses circonstances physiques qui s'y rapportent; mais cependant en fesant convenablement ressortir ce que cette opération brutale comportait ou suscitait de dignité et de noblesse morale, on est parvenu à trouver là dedans tout un monde de poésie et d'art. Cette réflexion m'a vivement frappé, mais je n'ai pas d'abord reconnu, pas plus que M. Carlyle, ce que vous avez si admirablement établi, c.à.d. que les éminentes qualités sociales de la vie militaire dérivent toutes entières de son organisation, et de son caractère de fonction sociale, l'instinct guerrier en lui-même étant un de nos plus ignobles penchants, tandis que la discipline intellectuelle et surtout morale qui a résulté de l'association d'hommes plus ou moins civilisés pour faire la guerre, même offensive, a été un moyen fécond, et dans une certaine époque le seule moyen possible, de développer la sociabilité humaine. Une fois donc qu'on sera parvenu à effectuer une véritable organisation de l'industrie, on lui imprimera par là même les qualités sociales qui lui ont semblé jusqu'ici les plus antipathiques, et dont la décroissance apparente dans notre époque de transition a motivé tant de craintes exagérées, que j'ai moi-même partagées, sur les tendances morales du type moderne de civilisation industrielle. Vous m'avez rendu le service immense de dissiper irrévocablement, en ce qui me concerne toute crainte pareille, et cette grande idée a eu tout de suite pour moi, comme il en arrive souvent à pareille occasion, un caractère d'évidence qui fait qu'on s'étonne de ne l'avoir pas rencontrée plus tôt et sans suggestion extérieure.

J'apprécie convenablement la sage réserve dont vous avez usé en écartant comme prématurée toute discussion immédiate sur la plupart des institutions politiques proprement dites, au moins dans l'ordre temporel. Vous avez très bien fait sentir que la régénération sociale dépend maintenant de l'essor spirituel, ce qui devient au reste de plus en plus évident aux esprits éclairés par l'impuissance aujourd'hui constatée de toutes les tentatives théoriques et pratiques qu'on fait depuis bientôt cent ans pour renouveler l'état de l'humanité par les seules institutions. Je crois même cette heureuse révolution spéculative plus avancée dans ce pays-ci que partout ailleurs, désenchantés comme nous sommes des institutions soi-disant libres à raison d'une plus intime familiarité pratique. Chez nous aujourd'hui les prolétaires croient presque seuls à l'efficacité réformative [*sic*] des institutions démocratiques, encore les chefs les plus considérés du mouvement politique prolétaire, parmi lesquels il y en a de très recommandables, mènent aujourd'hui habituellement de front avec leurs projets politiques, des idées de moralisation et de culture intellectuelle pour les masses populaires, dirigées à la vérité jusqu'ici, comme il n'en pouvait être autrement, par une philosophie métaphysique et négative. Vous avez donc très judicieusement employé vos efforts surtout à caractériser le nouveau pouvoir spirituel, dont la naissance même, et à plus forte raison son incorporation dans le système social, suffirait déjà, dans un gouvernement temporel quelconque, à dissiper en grande partie le désordre, même matériel, soit en rectifiant et en élargissant les idées des classes dirigeantes, soit en leur imposant, de gré ou de force, une moralité meilleure. Vous vous êtes donc sagement borné, quant à l'ordre temporel, à poser le principe incontestable, que la direction en doit désormais appartenir aux chefs industriels, en laissant indécises bien des questions, destinées à être progressivement résolues par les sociologistes positifs, et sur lesquelles je désirerais bien entamer déjà avec vous une discussion philosophique. Telles sont, par exemple, celle des moyens à prendre pour atténuer l'influence inévitable jusqu'à un certain point mais si exagérée aujourd'hui, que le hasard, celui de la naissance surtout, exerce en désidant du personnel de la haute industrie, indépendamment des conditions de la capacité industrielle. Vient ensuite la question de la part d'influence qu'il pourrait être convenable de réserver, dans l'ordre politique, aux classes industrielles inférieures, question qui renferme l'avenir des institutions représentatives, quant aux deux seules fonctions qu'on pourrait concevoir comme leur appartenant dans l'avenir, d'abord comme moyen d'enseignement politique pour les masses, et ensuite comme organe régulier pour constater ou refuser l'adhésion populaire aux réglemens généraux émanés des chefs.

Je me propose maintenant, après un court intervalle, de reprendre la lecture de votre élaboration sociologique depuis son commencement au 4^m volume, afin d'en mieux saisir l'ensemble et de m'en rendre en même temps plus familiers les principaux détails.

Je me suis réservé peu de place pour vous parler dans cette lettre, soit de la grande série de travaux futurs que vous annoncez à la fin du volume, soit de votre préface et de l'indigne conduite de votre éditeur et de son patron M. Arago.[3] Quant à ce dernier je me réjouis vraiment qu'il se soit

3. In his "Preface Personnelle" to the sixth volume Comte blamed his failure to secure tenure and an adequate compensation at the Ecole Polytechnique upon the antipathy of his colleagues to the positive philosophy. He singled out for particular attack Professor François Arago (1786–1853), one of the most distinguished scientists of the time. M. Bachelier, Comte's publisher, who was under obligations to Arago, demanded that Comte delete the attack on Arago. When Comte refused, Bachelier without permission printed before the Preface an "Avis de l'Editeur" in which he disavowed the attack on Arago. Comte later that year successfully brought suit against Bachelier in the Tribunal de Commerce, and the publisher was required to suppress the "Avis" in all the unsold copies.

For an account of the controversy which led to Comte's losing his position in 1844, see Emile Littré, *Auguste Comte et la philosophie positive* (2nd ed., Paris, 1864), chap. VII of Part II.

emporté tellement au delà des bornes que la prudence aurait imposées à tout homme moins aveuglé par la vanité et par l'instinct de la domination. S'il s'était contenté de dire qu'il reconnaissait à M. Sturm[4] des titres mathématiques supérieurs aux vôtres, on aurait pu croire à sa bonne foi, et sa réputation scientifique aurait donné à son opinion, ainsi exprimée, quelque poids auprès de la partie du public qui ne pouvait juger par lui-même. Heureusement il a manqué de cette prudence vulgaire et a donné à tous ceux qui ont lu même partiellement vos deux premiers volumes, ainsi qu'à une génération entière d'élèves polytechniques, le droit de lui dire avec pleine conviction qu'il en a menti: ce qui sera certes, beaucoup plus nuisible à la considération publique et européenne dont il se glorifie, que son mensonge ne le saurait être à la vôtre. Quant à votre préface, j'avoue qu'avant d'avoir lu le volume lui même je craignais que le défi ainsi jeté à ceux dont dépendaient vos moyens actuels de vie ne fût de nature à aggraver le danger qu'il signalait, mais dès que j'ai vu les dures vérités qu'avec votre franchise ordinaire vous avez dites dans le 57me chapitre sur l'incapacité et la bassesse morale de la plupart des savans actuels, j'ai trouvé profondément convenable une préface qui au fond ne contient rien de plus offensant pour eux que le livre lui même et qui en désignant personnellement les plus coupables est de nature à inspirer aux autres une salutaire crainte.

Votre dévoué

J. S. MILL.

378. TO JOHN STERLING[1]

I.H.
Saturday
[November 1842][2]

MY DEAR STERLING

I have at last got the enclosed paper for you from Henry Cole.

I have been reading your review of Tennyson[3] for the second time, after an interval of several weeks. I have found more difference than I expected in our judgments of particular poems, & I will not pretend that I think yours the more likely to be right, for I have faith in my own *feelings* of Art, but I have read & reflected so little on the subject compared with you, that I

---

4. Charles Sturm (1803–1855), French mathematician.

* * * *

1. All but first sentence published in Elliot, I, 121–22. MS at Leeds.
2. In pencil in another hand.
3. "Poems by Alfred Tennyson," *QR*, LXX (Sept., 1842), 385–416.

have no doubt you could give many more reasons for your opinions than I should be fully competent to appreciate. Still, I think I could justify my own feelings on grounds of my own, if I took time enough to meditate—but I doubt its being worth while—the thing is not in my *fach*.

The preliminary remarks are very delightful reading, & I think they do as much as can be done to render this age, what Carlyle says no age is, romantic to itself. But I think Tennyson, having taken up the same theory, has miserably misunderstood it. Because mechanical things may generate grand results he thinks that there is grandeur in the naked statement of their most mechanical details. Ebenezer Elliott has written a most fiery ode on the Press,[4] which is a mechanical thing like a railroad, but the mechanicality is kept studiously out of sight. Tennyson obtrudes it.

ever yours
J. S. MILL

379. TO JOHN STERLING[1]

I.H.
Wed^y
[Nov. 1842]

MY DEAR STERLING,

I am very glad indeed to hear that you are writing the sort of paper you mention. As to Tennyson, you were right in getting so much praise of him into the Quarterly[2] by no greater sacrifice than leaving some of the best of the earlier poems unmentioned. I do not differ from your principle that the highest forms of poetry cannot be built upon obsolete beliefs—although what you say of the Ancient Mariner & Christabel seems to me true of the Lady of Shalott, and the objection does not seem to me to lie strongly against the Lotos eaters or Œnone. But neither is the idyl one of the *highest* forms of poetry—neither Spenser, Tasso, nor Ovid could have been what they were by means of *that*. And greatly as I admire Michael & its compeers, that is not the crowning glory of Wordsworth. And how poor surely is Dora compared with some dozen of Wordsworth's poems of that kind.

---

4. "The Press; Written for the Printers of Sheffield on the Passing of the Reform Bill," in *The Splendid Village . . . and Other Poems* (3 vols., London, 1833–35), I, 121–22.

* * * *

1. Published in Elliot, I, 122–23. MS at Leeds.
2. See preceding letter.

My remark on mechanical details does not apply to Burleigh, which seems to me Tennyson's best in that stile—not much, if at all, to the Gardener's Daughter, a good deal to Dora which I do not like—a little to some parts of Locksley Hall: but in a most intense degree to such things as Audley Court, Walking to the Mail, the introduction to Morte d'Arthur; & the *type* of what I object to is the three lines of introduction to Godiva, which he has stuck in, as it were in defiance. But, mind, I do not give my opinion as worth anything, to you especially—& my feeling is only to be reckoned as that of one person, competent in so far as capable of almost any degree of *exalté* feeling from poetry.

Have you seen Macaulay's old-Roman ballads?[3] If you have not, do not judge of them from extracts, which give you the best passages without the previous preparation. They are in every way better, & nearer to what one might fancy Campbell[4] would have made them, than I thought Macaulay capable of. He has it not in him to be a great poet; there is no real genius in the thing, no revelation from the depths either of thought or feeling—but that being allowed for, there is real *verve*, & much more of the simplicity of ballad poetry than one would at all expect. The latter part of the Battle of the Lake Regillus, & the whole of Virginia, seem to me admirable.—

Yours ever,

J. S. MILL

380. TO GEORGE HENRY LEWES[1]

I.H.
Friday
[Nov. (25?) 1842]

MY DEAR LEWES,

I return Sand's letter which it was very pleasant to have an opportunity of reading. I have no right or claim to send any message to her but I should be very willing she should know that there [are] other warm admirers of her writings & of herself even in this canting land—among whom I am neither the only nor the best.

I think your article on Göthe[2] decidedly your highest flight, as yet.

---

3. *Lays of Ancient Rome* had been published on Oct. 27, 1842. JSM reviewed it favourably in *WR*, XXXIX (Feb., 1843), 105–13.
4. Thomas Campbell.

* * * *

1. Published in Kitchel, pp. 27 and 38. MS at Yale.
2. "Character and Works of Göthe," *BFR*, XIV (March, 1843), 78–135.

Without being the *dernièr mot* on such a man, it recommends itself to my knowledge of him as *truer* than any other writing on the subject which I have met with. There are also some striking thoughts in it & although there is considerable Carlylism in the opening pages, & something of the tranchant manner which makes people call you by various uncomplimentary names indicative of self-conceit, both these defects disappear as you go on & full two thirds of the article seem to me to be in a stile infinitely nearer to excellence than any of your other writings known to me: for being perfectly simple & apparently unconscious, it shews its good points to the best advantage and wherever feeling is shewn, it is, consequently, really eloquent. All that seemed to me unsuccessful in the beginning of the Spinosa,[3] because it looked artificial & studied, is here, for the contrary reason, completely successful.

Please to observe here that I am by no means biassed in favour of the article by its compliments to myself,[4] which rather tell the other way for I have a dislike to seeing my own ugly name in print.

Tell the lady, with my best wishes, that I am getting very hungry.[5]

Yours (in the dual number)

J. S. MILL

After receiving your tart note I reopen this to add my warmest congratulations.[6]

381. TO ALEXANDER BAIN[1]

Dec. 5, 1842

I have not been very well, but am a little better.

3. "Spinoza's Life and Works," *WR*, XXXIX (May, 1843), 372–407.
4. Lewes in the article on Goethe quoted a long passage from JSM's essay on Bentham (see *BFR*, XIV [March, 1843], 131: the passage beginning, "Every human action has three aspects,—its *moral* aspect, or that of its *right* and *wrong*; its *aesthetic* aspect, or that of its *beauty*; its *sympathetic* aspect or that of its *lovableness*," and ending "the error of moralists in general, and of Bentham, is to sink the two latter entirely," may be found in *Dissertations*, I, pp. 412–13).
5. In the original a line is drawn through the sentence, probably because of the postscript.
6. "The congratulations were, no doubt, on the birth of Lewes's eldest son, Charles Lee Lewes, born Nov. 24, 1842" (Kitchel, p. 39).

* * * *
1. Excerpt published by Bain, *JSM*, p. 77. MS not located.

382. TO GEORGE HENRY LEWES[1]

I.H.
Wedy
[Dec. 7, 1842]

MY DEAR LEWES,

I think your preface[2] excellent & likely to be of extremely great use. You have hit off the characteristics of the different authors admirably, & the style is uniformly good & quite free from any of the defects which have been complained of. I intend reading it again & making a remark or two but they are really of little importance.

Did you see the letter in the Times today in answer to your article on anonymous writing.[3]

Commend me to the respectable mère de famille.[4]

Yours

J. S. MILL

383. TO AUGUSTE COMTE[1]

India House
le 15 décembre
1842

MON CHER MONSIEUR COMTE

Depuis la venue de votre lettre du 5 novembre jusqu'à la réponse que j'y fais maintenant, il s'est écoulé un intervalle d'une longueur qui, je l'espère bien, se répétera rarement dans notre correspondance. Ce laps de temps a été fort rempli chez moi par des devoirs indispensables et par une santé momentanément dérangée, mais surtout par une lecture lente et approfondie de votre élaboration sociologique dans sa totalité, lecture dont le commencement a été retardé, bien malgré moi, et que j'ai voulu terminer avant de vous rien écrire, résolution dont je crois avoir à me féliciter.

1. Published in Kitchel, pp. 39–40, but undated. Now dated by reference in paragraph 2. MS at Yale.
2. Professor Kitchel thinks that this refers to an early draft of the Preface to his *Biographical History of Philosophy*, which was not published, however, until 1845.
3. A letter signed Z (*The Times*, Wednesday, Dec. 7, 1842, p. 5) objects to Lewes' attack (in "The Errors and Abuses of English Criticism," *WR*, XXXVIII [Oct., 1842], 466–86) on anonymous criticism. Z. calls Lewes a radical and takes issue with his contention that anonymous criticism harmed Keats, Shelley, Byron, and Coleridge.
4. See Letter 380, n. 6.

* * * *

1. MS at Johns Hopkins. Published in Lévy-Bruhl, pp. 134–40; in reply to Comte's of Nov. 5, *ibid.*, pp. 124–33.

Vous avez très bien senti qu'un travail comme celui de vos trois derniers volumes ne pouvait être pleinement jugeable que dans son ensemble, et même après une lecture plusieurs fois renouvelée. J'en ai fait moi-même l'épreuve la plus décisive. D'abord je n'avais jamais, malgré plusieurs lectures très attentives, convenablement senti la haute valeur scientifique du 4me volume, faute d'en avoir pu suffisamment assimiler les doctrines avant de les avoir vu compléter par vos derniers travaux: jusque-là je n'y voyais surtout que la préparation indispensable de l'élaboration historique du 5me volume, en sentant toutefois dignement la portée de votre grande conception de la statique sociale. Quant au 5me volume, je lui avais toujours rendu pleine justice, mais il me restait de m'en pénétrer encore plus profondément. En ce qui se rapporte spécialement au 6me volume, vous avez dû d'après ma lettre précédente, me croire moins capable que je ne l'étais réellement d'en apprécier la grandeur, qui dépasse peut-être à mes yeux, tout ce que vous aviez fait antérieurement. En effet, par un privilège réservé aux esprits pleinement systématiques et *compréhensifs*, (mot anglais dont je ne connais pas d'exact équivalent en français) vous aviez jeté dans les volumes précédents de si féconds germes de toutes les principales conceptions du volume final, que les choses les plus merveilleuses que j'y lisais me faisaient l'effet de les avoir toujours connues. C'est en relisant successivement, et à loisir, toutes les parties de l'élaboration, que j'ai éprouvé une impression finale et décisive, non seulement plus forte mais essentiellement nouvelle, en tant que celle-ci est surtout morale. Je crois que ce qui se passe à présent en moi est une première vérification spéciale de la grande conclusion générale de votre Traité, l'aptitude de la philosophie positive, une fois organisée dans son ensemble, à prendre pleine possession des hautes attributions sociales jusqu'ici très imparfaitement remplies par les seules religions. Ayant eu la destinée, très rare dans mon pays, de n'avoir jamais cru en Dieu, même dans mon enfance j'ai toujours vu dans la création d'une vraie philosophie sociale le seul fondement possible d'une régénération générale de la moralité humaine, et dans l'idée de l'Humanité la seule qui pût remplacer celle de Dieu. Mais il y a loin de cette croyance spéculative au sentiment que j'épreuve aujourd'hui de la pleine efficacité ainsi que de l'avènement prochain de cette inévitable substitution. Quelque bien préparé qu'on puisse être, comparativement à la plupart des esprits, à subir les conséquences mentales de cette conviction, il est impossible qu'elle ne détermine pas une sorte de crise dans l'existence de tout homme dont la nature morale n'est pas trop au dessous des devoirs qu'elle impose; soit en démontrant clairement que le travail direct de la régénération politique et surtout morale qu'on a toujours rêvée pour un avenir indéfini, est réellement devenu possible de nos jours et que le temps est venu où les dévouemens individuels peuvent vraiment réaliser un fruit appréciable pour une si grande cause, soit en déterminant, par une réaction nécessaire, un sentiment amer des diverses imperfections particulières qui tendent à nous rendre plus ou moins indignes d'une telle destinée. Il n'y a du reste, aucune raison de croire que cette crise doive se terminer chez moi autrement que d'une manière favorable soit à mon bonheur individuel, soit à l'utilité de mon action sociale.

Quant au désir si honorable pour moi, que vous me témoignez de savoir si, après une mûre appréciation, je regarde vos derniers chapitres et surtout le premier des trois comme propres à déterminer la constitution finale d'une nouvelle philosophie générale, c.à d. d'une pleine systématisation durable de l'ensemble de nos conceptions réelles vous devez sans doute sentir déjà, d'après tout ce que je viens de dire que je ressens très profondément cette conviction, et que j'adhère entièrement aux conclusions générales de votre ouvrage, sauf quelques notions secondaires qui ne me semblent pas suffisamment éclaircies, et qui en supposant même qu'elles ne le fussent jamais, n'altéreraient en rien le caractère essentiellement satisfaisant de cette immense systématisation. A cela j'ajoute que bien que j'aie longtemps pensé qu'un esprit pleinement conséquent ne peut exister que sous l'ascendant complet de la philosophie positive, je n'avais jamais cru qu'il pût exister déjà, et dès le premier pas, une réalisation si complète de cette éminente propriété de l'esprit positif. Vous me faites peur par l'unité et le complet de vos convictions, qui semblent par là ne pouvoir jamais avoir besoin de confirmation de la part d'aucune autre intelligence, et je sens que cette précieuse sympathie que vous me témoignez à un degré très au dessus de mon mérite réel et que vous avez proclamée avec une si noble confiance à tous les esprits philosophiques de l'Europe dans la note que vous m'avez consacrée, m'est bien nécessaire aujourd'hui pour ne pas trembler devant vous.

Avec cela il y a toujours des questions plus ou moins secondaires sur lesquelles je conserve encore, soit une opinion différente de la vôtre, soit des difficultés non encore résolues. Quoique les unes et les autres tendent problement à disparaître, je ne dois pas chercher à atténuer ce qu'il peut exister entre nous de différence réelle, d'autant moins que je sens aujourd'hui, à l'égard de toute opinion que vous avez sanctionnée, la nécessité de me défendre contre l'entraînement, toujours plus à craindre dans ma nature particulière qu'un esprit critique exagéré. J'ajourne toute indication plus précise de ces différences, jusqu'à l'époque très prochaine de la publication de mon livre, qui vous en indiquera, soit directement, soit plus souvent indirectement, quelques-unes. Je vous dirai, à propos de ce livre, dont les trois quarts sont maintenant imprimés, qu'il me paraît toujours, même dans les parties qui ont l'air le plus métaphysique, très propre à faciliter, pour mon pays la transition de l'esprit métaphysique à l'esprit positif. Quant à la valeur propre des conceptions positives qui s'y trouvent, je ne puis avoir là dessus d'opinion définitive que lorsqu'elles auront été connues et jugées par vous, jusqu'ici seul juge compétent à ce sujet.

J'ai appris, avec le plus vif intérêt tout ce que vous m'avez dit dans votre dernière lettre sur les choses qui vous sont personnelles, d'abord, l'effet favorable de votre préface, que j'ai besoin au reste de savoir confirmé par le résultat de la réélection annuelle; ensuite l'éclatante punition que vous vous disposez à faire subir à vos indignes ennemis, et finalement, le programme des travaux que vous destinez à votre année de *repos*, qui serait certes une année de très forte contention intellectuelle pour tout autre que vous. Je crois que votre volume sur la géométrie analytique[2] pourra avoir un grand succès ici, ainsi que le traité de philosophie mathématique que vous annoncez pour un temps plus éloigné. Il y a certainement aujourd'hui chez nos jeunes géomètres un commencement de tendances à chercher la régéneration scientifique des conceptions mathématiques, tendances dont la métaphysique allemande qui domine maintenant ici, commence à s'emparer, à sa manière, à peu près comme la métaphysique française a tâché de le faire par l'organe de Condillac. Je crois au reste d'après l'accueil que plusieurs de nos savans ont fait à vos deux premiers volumes, qu'ils sont réellement mieux préparés que les savans français à sentir la portée de vos grandes conceptions de philosophie mathématique qui même aussi peu développées qu'elles le sont dans le 1er volume ont été dès lors pour moi la première preuve décisive de la force et de la fécondité de votre génie philosophique.

Le M. Carlyle dont je vous parlai est tout autre que le célèbre athée (Carl*i*le)[3] qui n'avait réellement d'autre mérite éminent que celui de son courage et qui a fini, je crois, par une sorte de conversion christiano-déiste. M. Carlyle est un homme très supérieur a celui-là, quoique moins complètement émancipé. Il est connu par plusieurs ouvrages, entr'autres par une Histoire de la Révolution française, prise d'un point de vue imparfait mais progressif pour ce pays-ci, et remarquable par un véritable génie épique, autant que ce génie peut se développer sans autre doctrine générale que ce qu'on peut appeler la critique de la critique. Cet ouvrage représente l'esprit organique dans l'état vague, ou plutôt l'esprit du besoin d'organisation, et comme c'est là l'esprit qui règne ici dans la partie la plus avancée du public, l'ouvrage a eu, malgré le style le plus excentrique, un grand retentissement.

Je ne négligerai aucune occasion de m'informer plus particulièrement sur les deux traductions allemandes de votre Cours. Je crois les penseurs allemands très préparés à abandonner, dès qu'on leur donnera quelque chose de mieux, leur ténébreuse métaphysique, essentiellement épuisée

---

2. *Traité élémentaire de Géométrie analytiqe à deux et à trois dimensions* (Paris, 1843).

3. Richard Carlile (1790–1843), printer and author of freethought papers.

aujourd'hui dans son pays natal. Je vous suis toujours très obligé de vos démarches amicales auprès de M. Balard, et bien heureux qu'on se souvienne encore de moi à Montpellier. Je serais bien aise de savoir les noms de ceux de vos amis qui me font l'honneur inattendu de ne m'avoir pas oublié![4]

tout à vous et pour toujours

J. S. MILL.

384. TO ROBERT BARCLAY FOX[1]

I.H.
19th Dec^r
1842

MY DEAR FRIEND

Do not think because I did not answer your last most interesting letter, that I either failed to sympathise with you with all in it that demanded sympathy or to appreciate the friendship and confidence shewn by your writing on such things to me. But it is little that can be done by words of consolation in such cases, & that little, few perhaps are less qualified to do than I, while you have those near you who are more than sufficient to do all that can be done. I do not feel the less but the more for your disappointment from the proof which the verses you sent me gave of your determination to be one of those to rise stronger & nobler from such trials.

There are abundance of subjects on which I should like a little mental communion with you if I could get my thoughts together for the purpose. First, there is in public affairs, much in the wind. Your prediction about the Corn Laws seems in a way to be verified sooner than we either of us expected, & that is sure to lead to great changes in the condition & character of our rural population & above all in the relation of landlords & tenants which on its present footing is essentially an unwholesome relation & *cannot* last. Things have certainly come to a strange pass when the manufacturing majority must starve in order that the agricultural minority may —starve also. But these things, important as they are, do not occupy so much of my thoughts as they once did; it is becoming more & more clearly evident to me that the mental regeneration of Europe must precede its social regeneration & also that none of the ways in which that mental regeneration is sought, Bible Societies, Tract Societies, Puseyism, Socialism, Chartism, Benthamism &c. will *do*, though doubtless they have all some

---

4. See Letter 386.

* * * *

1. *Addressed*: R. Barclay Fox Esq. / Perran Cottage / near Truro. *Postmark*: 19 DE 1842. Except first paragraph, published in Pym, II, 338–39. MS in the possession of Mr. W. H. Browning.

elements of truth & good in them. I find quite enough to do in trying to make up my own mind as to the course which must be taken by the present great transitional movement of opinion & society. The little which I can dimly see, this country even less than several other European nations is as yet ripe for promulgating.

In the meantime I do not know that there was anything better for me to do than to write the book I have been writing, destined to do its little part towards straightening & strengthening the intellects which have this great work to do. The said book is printed as far as p. 160, vol 2, & will be published when Providence & the publisher see fit. I heard of you the other day from Philip Melvill[2] who I believe brought the first intelligence which had reached the India House of such a thing being on the anvil. A propos, there was some time ago a very pretty, but very unnecessary—what shall I call it? deprecation from your sister Caroline relative to this book & to something which occurred near the tombs of the old Templars.[3] I do not recollect any more of what passed than that she accused herself of having impliedly instigated a very natural announcement which I made, *certainly* not for the *first* time then, touching the superfluousness of her troubling any bookseller respecting the two volumes in question, since I should as soon have thought of my own brother *buying* any book of mine as of any of your family doing so. You will certainly receive in due time what has been from the first destined for you—I mean you in the plural number, for I never separate you in fact or in thought—& the one who reads most of it may keep it, if the others chuse.

George is quite well and vigorous, & promises much. I think he will do credit to his bringing up. My other pupil Mary[4] is doing well too. As for the others you know them & they can answer for themselves. We are thankful for the exertions of you all about the little orphan.[5] What her chances are I do not know. Such elections by universal suffrage are as you truly say a monstrous thing.

ever affectionately

J. S. MILL

2. Philip Melvill (1817–1854), in the East India service, became Secretary to the Chief Commissioner for Affairs in the Punjab, 1853.

3. Caroline Fox in her journal (Pym, I, 316) records that on June 16, 1842, the Mills joined the Foxes in a tour of the old Church of the Templars. "John Mill talked about his book on Logic, which he is going to give us; but he declares it will be more intelligible than interesting—how intelligible he will find out in two years. He forbids my reading it, though, except some chapters which he will point out. 'It would be like my reading a book on mining because you [the Foxes] live in Cornwall—it would be making Friendship a burden.'"

4. His sister, Mary Elizabeth Mill (1822–1913), later (1847) Mrs. Charles Frederick Colman.

5. See Letter 372.

· · · 1843 · · ·

385. TO HENRY COLE[1]

I.H.
Friday
[Jan. 6, 1843]

DEAR COLE,

I should like very much to make acquaintance both with the Michael Angelos & with Mr. Dilke,[2] but if the weather & a bad cold permit me to go out I am supposed to go early & walk with Carlyle.

Yours ever,

J. S. MILL.

386. TO AUGUSTE COMTE[1]

India House
28 janvier 184[3]

MON CHER MONSIEUR COMTE

Votre dernière lettre, que j'avais bien vivement désirée, m'a fait grand plaisir sous tous les rapports. D'abord elle m'a appris l'heureux résultat de votre procès avec Bachelier,[2] résultat qui fait honneur au tribunal de commerce et qui donnera sans doute une idée juste de l'affaire à ceux qui n'en ayant aucune vraie connaissance, auraient pu n'y voir qu'une question d'amour-propre entre vous et Arago. Quant à ce qui s'est passé dans la

---

1. From a copy in the possession of Professor J. M. McCrimmon. A note on the verso in a hand other than JSM's dates this letter Jan 7—43, but this is probably the date of receipt of the letter, since Friday of this week fell on Jan. 6.
2. Probably Charles Wentworth Dilke.

* * * *

1. MS at Johns Hopkins. Published in Lévy-Bruhl, pp. 150–55; in reply to Comte's of Dec. 30, 1842, *ibid.*, pp. 140–50.
2. The case had been tried on Dec. 15. See Letter 377, n. 3.

première audience, je le savais déjà par la Gazette des Tribunaux, qui en a rendu un compte sommaire, mais à peu près exact puisqu'il s'accordait essentiellement avec celui que vous m'avez donné. Il me manquait seulement de savoir quel effet cette discussion avait fait sur votre esprit, et si les indignes menaces qu'on avait osé vous adresser à l'égard de votre réélection pouvaient offrir un danger réel. J'ai appris avec joie, par votre lettre que ce danger n'est pas fort à craindre, et que les charlatans qui pour conserver leur propre considération croient avoir besoin de rabaisser la vôtre, nuiront probablement moins à vous qu'à eux-mêmes.

J'ai appris aussi avec beaucoup d'intérêt que l'insurrection des biologistes contre la domination oppressive et aujourd'hui irrationnelle des géomètres, commence déjà à se prononcer. Votre dernier volume ne peut manquer de donner une forte impulsion à cette tendance salutaire, qui à son tour doit beaucoup favoriser l'avènement de la nouvelle philosophie à laquelle les biologistes sont nécessairement mieux préparés que toute autre classe de savans, au moins en france. Je dis en france, car je crains que si nos géomètres valent mieux à certains égards que les vôtres, il n'en est pas de même quant à nos biologistes. Cela tient à plusieurs causes. D'abord, malgré les défauts de l'éducation scientifique en france, je la crois au fond beaucoup meilleure que chez nous. Soit par les tendances trop exclusivement pratiques de notre caractère national, soit par le fractionnement encore plus exagéré qu'ailleurs des diverses études positives, le véritable esprit scientifique est très rare chez nous, et si quelques-uns le possèdent jusqu'à un certain point, ils l'ont, le plus souvent, puisé dans les livres français; sauf peut-être les écossais, chez qui l'éducation publique a un caractère plus français qu'anglais, ce qui explique le mérite éminent des penseurs écossais depuis Kaimes[3] et Ferguson[4] jusqu'à mon père qui mort en 1836, fut le dernier survivant de cette grande école. Quant à la biologie, elle reste encore chez nous, plus que chez vous, dans cet état provisoire si bien caractérisé par vous et même par Bacon, celui dans lequel la science n'est pas encore séparée de l'art correspondent. Sauf l'histoire naturelle concrète, qui a pris ici depuis douze à quinze années un élan très vigoureux, les connaissances biologiques ne sont guère cultivées que par des médecins ou chirurgiens, qui, s'ils ont de la capacité, sont bientôt absorbés dans les travaux accablants d'un métier ici surtout terrible. Sans doute la séparation

3. Henry Home, Lord Kames (1696–1782), Scottish judge and writer. His *Essays on the Principles of Morality and Natural Religion* (Edinburgh, 1751), written to combat the doctrines of David Hume, resulted in his own orthodoxy being questioned; he was tried but acquitted by the Presbytery of Edinburgh.
4. Adam Ferguson (1723–1816), professor of pneumatics and moral philosophy at Edinburgh University.

des recherches biologiques d'avec l'art médical serait aujourd'hui pleinement opportune; elle est très bien préparée par l'état général du public scientifique, mais chez nous les prévisions sociales ne sont pas encore allées jusqu'à doter cette classe de savans du moyen de vivre comme tels, soit par la cultivation de leur science, soit par sa propagation. Cela est tellement vrai qu'un jeune biologiste de mes amis, le Dr Carpenter,[5] que je crois être sans contredit le plus philosophe de tous ceux qui chez nous étudient les lois des corps vivans, qui a écrit les meilleurs traités de physiologie générale et humaine que nous possédons dans notre langue, et qui s'il était français obtiendrait sans peine une des meilleures chaires de vos écoles de médecine, est encore à chercher ici le moyen de gagner la subsistance même la plus modeste en se consacrant à la science. Ajoutez à ceci que nos biologistes sont en général bien loin d'être émancipés sous le rapport réligieux, quoiqu'ils soient peut-être plus près de cette émancipation que les autres savans et vous verrez qu'il n'y a pas de quoi s'encourager beaucoup pour le progrès rapide de la nouvelle philosophie.

A tout prendre, le public anglais ne me paraît assez bien préparé qu'à la réception de vos principes de philosophie générale, en y superposant toutefois, par une transaction profondément irrationnelle, l'idée d'une providence agissant par des lois générales; notion préparée et même beaucoup travaillée par les demi-philosophes timides qui ont rempli chez nous pendant le 18me siècle la place de l'énergique école négative française. Mais je ne trouve pas à beaucoup près chez notre public le même degré de préparation à l'égard de votre philosophie sociale, attendu que l'un des fondements principaux de cette philosophie est la loi naturelle du décroissement spontané de l'esprit réligieux, doctrine qui effraie encore presque tous les esprits en Angleterre, au point que si moi-même je la proclamais ouvertement on n'oserait pas me lire. Je risque déjà quelque chose en déclarant hautement, partout dans mon livre, l'admiration que je ressens pour votre grand ouvrage, sans faire la moindre réserve théologique, qu'à ma place tout autre anglais, je crois, n'aurait pas manqué de faire.

La publication de mon livre, aujourd'hui très prochaine, a été un peu retardée par le remaniement complet que j'ai cru devoir faire à la dernière partie pour la mettre plus en harmonie avec ma manière actuelle de penser, depuis la lecture de votre 6me volume et l'étude plus approfondie que j'ai faite des deux volumes précédens. J'y ai fait maintenant beaucoup plus de place à la nouvelle doctrine, tout en la prenant du point de vue de mon propre travail, et je crois que, sous ce rapport, mon livre est maintenant

---

5. William Benjamin Carpenter, best known for his *Principles of General and Comparative Physiology* (London, 1839), the second edition of which JSM had reviewed briefly in *WR*, XXXVII (Jan., 1842), 254.

le plus avancé que mon pays soit encore susceptible de recevoir. J'ai d'ailleurs l'espoir bien fondé que tout ce qui chez nous est capable de comprendre votre ouvrage viendra apprendre chez moi où trouver quelque chose de mieux que moi.

Je vous demande pardon de n'avoir jusqu'ici rien dit en réponse au désir que vous avez plus d'une fois si aimablement témoigné de resserrer notre amitié par une entrevue personnelle prochaine. M. Lewes m'avait mal compris: malheureusement j'ai toujours eu la presque certitude que des circonstances qui tiennent à mes relations personnelles les plus intimes, me retiendraient cet hiver à Londres, mais dans le cas où ces circonstances se prolongeraient beaucoup plus longtemps je suis très décidé à courir à Paris, ne fût-ce que pour deux ou trois jours, et dans l'unique intention de vous voir.

Je suis bien aise de savoir les noms de ceux de vos amis à Montpellier qui conservent encore quelque souvenir de mon séjour dans cette ville[6] que je ne cesserai jamais d'aimer. Cela ne m'étonne pas beaucoup de la part de l'aimable Roméo Pouzin,[7] avec qui j'ai été plus lié qu'avec toute autre personne de Montpellier, à l'exception de Balard et de la famille Bérard.[8] Quant à M. Emile Guillaume,[9] il me fait un honneur qui me flatte d'autant plus que je dois l'avoir très peu connu, puisque j'ai oublié jusqu'a son nom.

J'attends avec un vif intérêt le résultat de la sorte d'expérience sociale que vous allez faire à l'ouverture de votre cours annuel d'astronomie et qui aura comme vous le sentez une grande importance par rapport à la propagation libre de la philosophie pleinement positive. Heureux si je croyais qu'on en vînt jusque-là dans ce pays-ci, de mon vivant! Cette liberté de discussion dont on jouit en france est la compensation de bien des misères. Nous en sommes bien loin encore, mais qui sait? dans un temps de transition morale les choses marchent plus vite qu'elles n'en ont l'air.

Votre tout dévoué

J. S. MILL

6. In the winter of 1820–21.

7. Comte had reported that Dr. Roméo Pouzin was now a professor in the school of pharmacy.

8. The family of Etienne Bérard, prominent chemist of Montpellier. His son, Jacques Etienne Bérard (1789–1869), achieved an even greater reputation as a chemist (see *John Mill's Boyhood Visit to France*, ed. Anna Jean Mill [Toronto, 1960], p. 38).

9. Not identified. Perhaps the M. Guillaume referred to in JSM's Notebook of 1820 (see *ibid.*, p. 76, n. 140 and 141).

387. TO ROBERT BARCLAY FOX[1]

India House
14 Feb. 1843

MY DEAR FRIEND—In a few days you will receive two ponderous volumes,[2] concerning which you have shewn an interest that I desire very much they may justify. I have not defaced them with any marks because after going finally through the whole as it passed through the press I have come to the conclusion that it will not bear to be read in any way except straight through, & it is probably worth *your* reading it that way, while I am certain it is not worth it to your sisters being a kind of book so entirely abstract that I am sure they would never think of reading it if it did not happen to be written by one whom they know—& to make that a reason for reading a book out of one's line, is to make friendship a burden. If I could fix on any part as capable of being read with any interest apart from the rest, it would be the fifth book, on Fallacies, & especially the chapter in the sixth book on Liberty & Necessity, which is short & in my judgment the best chapter in the two volumes. However as Sterling will have a copy and will certainly read it through, he will be able to tell your sisters if there is any part which he thinks would interest them—in case they require any opinion besides yours. You will not suspect me of the stupid coxcombry of thinking that they could not understand it, which would be my own condemnation, for if they could not, the book would be a failure. I only mean that whatever be the value of the book, it is (like a book of mathematics) *pure* & not *mixed* science, & never can be liked by any but *students* & I do not want them to spoil themselves by becoming that, on my account —They know that when I write anything on philosophy in the *concrete*, on politics or morals or religion or education or in short anything directly practical or in which feeling & character are concerned I desire very much to be read by them because *there* I can hope really to interest them—but any interest they could feel in this would be only like what I might feel in a treatise on mining.

The last news I have heard about Sterling was not quite so satisfactory as before in respect to rapidity of recovery: will you write a line to me on the matter? Does he think of going away this spring?

Our little girl did not carry her election,[3] but the proxies were not lost,

---

1. *Envelope addressed*: R. Barclay Fox Esq. / Perran Cottage / Truro. *Postmark*: LS 14 / FE 1843. MS in the possession of Mr. W. H. Browning. Published in Pym, II, 340–41.
2. JSM'S *Logic*.
3. See Letter 372.

but bartered for an equivalent number next June, when Mazzini tells me
she is sure of success, that is (I suppose) if those who gave their proxies
this time will be kind enough to do so again.

yours ever,

J. S. MILL.

388. TO ALEXIS DE TOCQUEVILLE[1]

le 20 février 1843.

Je vous envoie, mon cher Tocqueville, une letter que j'ai insérée dans
le *Morning Chronicle*[2] à votre intention. Je ne sais pas si on la lira, mais
je sais qu'elle était bien nécessaire, car ici on donne raison à Lord
Brougham contre vous. Les passions en sont aujourd'hui au point où l'on
ne regarde plus assez près pour faire des catégories parmi ses adversaires,
et l'on fait peser sur les plus modérés la responsabilité des choses les
plus folles qu'on croit avoir été faites ou dites par les plus écervelés. Il
en est souvent ainsi entre deux partis, à plus forte raison entre deux
nations, qui arrivent plus difficilement à s'entendre par des explications
mutuelles, et dont chacune lit encore plus exclusivement les organes de
son opinion. J'ai souffert de voir la manière dont on envisage ici votre
conduite sur ces malheureuses questions de politique extérieure. On ne
veut rien voir sinon que vous vous êtes rangé du côté du "war party", et
comme on s'attendait à autre chose de votre part, on se venge sur vous de
sa propre incapacité de comprendre les idées et les principes qui vous ont
inspiré. Cela ne m'étonne point; il est très naturel que les Anglais ne
comprennent pas la France, pas plus que les Français ne comprennent
l'Angleterre. Vous même n'avez vous pas dit, dans le discours en question,
que les Anglais ont trouvé le moyen de chasser la France de l'Espagne? Ne
dirait-on pas que comme la plupart de vos compatriotes vous croyez les
Anglais tout occupés d'étendre leur territoire et leur importance au dehors?
Je vous jure qu'il n'y a pas deux Anglais qui se soient assez occupés de
l'Espagne pour avoir un seul instant eu l'idée d'y rivaliser d'influence
avec la France. Tout ce que vous voyez à ce sujet dans nos journaux est
une affaire d'amour-propre entre Palmerston et Peel, à quoi le public

1. Published in Mayer, pp. 340–41; in reply to Tocqueville's of Feb. 9, *ibid.*,
pp. 339–40. MS in Tocqueville archives. Tocqueville protested vigorously against an
attack made upon him in the House of Lords on Feb. 2 in a debate on the right of
search. Brougham centred his attack on a speech made by Tocqueville in the Chamber
of Deputies on Jan. 28, reprinted from the *Moniteur* in his *Œuvres*, ed. Gustave
Beaumont (9 vols., Paris, 1864–66), IX, 389–406. Tocqueville's letter to Brougham is
in Mayer, pp. 341–42.
2. "Lord Brougham and M. de Tocqueville," Feb. 20, 1843, p. 3.

hausse les épaules. Heureusement notre public ne s'occupe jamais d'affaires étrangères. Sans cela l'Europe serait toujours en feu: voyez ce qui est advenu de ce que nous avons eu, un seul instant, un homme à caractère français à notre Foreign Office. Vous savez que j'aime la France, mais j'avoue qu'il en est assez d'une seule en Europe. Vous voyez que je vous dis franchement ce que je pense, sans craindre de vous offenser et je vous dirai avec la même sincérité que je trouve votre discours admirable et que je ne suis pas éloigné de votre opinion sur la question elle-même. Je crois que si le gouvernement français avait pris dans le commencement le ton que vous lui conseillez, cela aurait pu réussir, mais aujourd'hui ce serait impossible. L'Angleterre ne voudrait pas céder aux provocations et aux menaces des forcenés de la Chambre et du journalisme, soit libéral soit conservateur, la Presse ou le National. Je voudrais qu'on crucifiât le premier homme qui osât dire à la tribune d'un peuple des injures contre un autre peuple. Il faut des générations entières pour guérir le mal que cela peut faire dans un jour. Cela est bien méprisable dans un siècle qui a tant besoin du concours des hommes énergiques et éclairés de tous les pays avancés pour l'œuvre difficile de réorganiser la société européenne.

Je suis charmé que vous soyez content de M. Hickson:[3] sans être un homme de génie, il est d'un mérite rare et très précieux dans son genre, et je connais peu d'hommes d'un patriotisme et d'une philanthropie plus active et plus éclairée. On le retrouve dans tout ce qui se fait de plus avancé chez nous.

Votre devoué

J. S. Mill.

India House.

389. TO SARAH AUSTIN[1]

India House
28th Feb.
1843

Dear Mrs Austin

I should have answered your letter much sooner, if only on account of the proposal to Parker, but that he told me he would himself write & no doubt you have long since received an answer from him, more explicit as to

3. William Hickson, for whom he had provided a letter of introduction to Tocqueville.

* * * *

1. MS in the possession of Mr. Gordon Waterfield.

details than the answer he gave *me*. The History of the Reformation[2] he thought would not suit him, but the other book you mentioned, he thought would, & was quite willing to close with the project, but did not seem confident as to the sufficiency of such pecuniary terms as the state of the market in his opinion allowed him to offer. And as your doing the thing at all would of course depend upon his making it worth your while, it is for him to make his proposition. *Au reste*, everything I have seen of him is in his favour: pretending to no character but that of a tradesman, he has in every respect in which I have had to do with him acted like a gentleman, while Murray who sets up for a gentleman & a patron of letters seems to be in reality a mere tradesman & not a good one. I believe however this is not the same with the Oxford Parker,[3] so that there may be a chance there if this fails. This one[4] is bookseller to the University of Cambridge.—In the meanwhile I am glad you are going on writing for the Edinburgh which I suspect is more lucrative work than even *your* translating & which you are so well qualified for. I liked your article on Mad. Schopenhauer[5] very much, both as pleasant reading & for the tone of its remarks, which are of a kind very much wanted here, & *now* likely as far as I can judge to be well received, for the eyes of a great number of English people are decidedly opening to much of what is wrong in their own country & comparatively right elsewhere. I hear your article underwent much excision from Napier, & that he wants more painting of manners & less general reflection. I think him wrong, &, as he always is, *arrière*, for the Edinburgh review & the Holland-house set[6] who preside over it are the last refuge of the ideas & tastes of a generation ago; but I suppose his mandates must be complied with, & he has left quite as much of valuable remark in this article as it needed & *more* than is in all the other articles taken together which he published along with it in his exceedingly poor extra number.

What you tell me about Grote does not surprise me though I am sorry for it both on his account & yours. As for Mrs Grote, you know her, & would not expect either good feeling or good taste from her. But Grote has always seemed rather a sensitive person—however he is a disappointed man, & has come to the time of life at which people generally fold their wings & take to their *comforts*. At that stage very few men, in my experience, retain their sympathies at all strongly towards those with whom they are

2. Mrs. Austin's translation of Leopold von Ranke's *History of the Reformation in Germany* was published by Longman in 1844.

3. John Henry Parker (1806–1884), bookseller and writer on architecture.

4. John William Parker, JSM's publisher.

5. See Letter 358, n. 3. The article was a review of books by two German novelists, Johanna Schopenhauer and Caroline Pichler.

6. Holland House, the London home of Henry Fox, Lord Holland, was for forty years the most famous of the Whig salons. For an account of the visitors who came there, see Princess Marie Liechtenstein, *Holland House* (London, 1875), chap. IV.

not in habits of daily intercourse. Perhaps too, half of the evil in Grote is shyness; & not knowing how to *express* sympathy: especially being perhaps in some degree concious of having already shewn less of it than you had reason to expect.—As to the calamity itself,[7] I could have told you months before, all that he *can* have had to tell, but I thought you would know it quite soon enough. The concern has declared itself insolvent & is in the hands of trustees, but from what I hear I do not believe it to be hopeless that something may be saved for the shareholders, though in any such case the probabilities are of course against it. Grote, as you know, habitually looks at the gloomiest side of things. The Mississippi matter[8] however is of much more importance really, as you were deriving no income from the money in the company before, so that in regard to *present* exigencies & interests the loss of the principal is only nominal. The Mississippi bonds I feel satisfied *must* ultimately be paid though I fear not quite so soon as I once thought. In the mean time I cannot help reverting to the idea I once threw out in a letter to you & which you promised to take into consideration at a proper time, & there seems none so proper as now. I really believe something might be done, though it is not very easy to hit upon the exact shape which would be best.

I have sent the remaining sheets of my book, addressed to Mr Austin, in the parcel from Asher's correspondent here (Nutt of Fleet Street) which was made up yesterday. The book is to be published tomorrow. But do not let Mr Austin suppose because the sheets are sent that he is under any engagement to make the use of them which he so kindly proposed. I should of course have sent the book to him in any case & though he would be the best of all reviewers for it he must not plague himself about it. It must take its chance.

I inclose a line from my sister Clara. I have neither encouraged nor opposed her project,[9] of the feasibility of which nobody can so well judge as you. If it be otherwise feasible of course the "cannot" in her note is not to be taken literally, as long as there are others who "can".

Yours affectionately

J. S. MILL.

---

7. The bankruptcy of an unidentified company in which both the Austins and the Grotes had investments must have been a much harder blow for the Austins than for the Grotes, who were comparatively well to do. The portion of George Grote's letter of Feb., 1843, to John Austin published in Janet Ross, *Three Generations of English-women* (London, 1892), p. 191, throws no light on the matter. Even the Grotes, however, found their losses serious enough as to oblige them to make some retrenchments; Mrs. Grote in a letter to her sister in June, 1843, reported that they had lost £11,000 "by American failures" (see *The Lewin Letters*, ed. T. H. Lewin [2 vols., London, 1909], II, 24).

8. See Letter 331, no. 2.   9. To go to Germany (see Letter 408, postscript).

390. TO AUGUSTE COMTE[1]

India House
le 13 mars 1843

Mon cher Monsieur Comte

Avant de recevoir cette lettre vous aurez sans doute reçu de ma part un exemplaire du livre en faveur duquel vous voulez bien admettre une exception à votre régime cérébral habituel.[2] Je souhaite qu'il mérite une distinction si honorable, et je me félicite toujours davantage de notre heureux rapprochement personnel, sans lequel je n'eusse pas pû espérer d'obtenir, sur mes spéculations philosophiques le seul jugement qui ait pour moi une importance réelle. C'est encore une bonne fortune pour moi que mon livre soit tombé précisément dans ce que vous nommez votre année de repos, et que vous puissiez en prendre connaissance sans déranger aucunement le cours de vos travaux. En sollicitant pour cet ouvrage toute votre indulgence j'ai besoin de vous indiquer que le premier livre date essentiellement de 1829, que le deuxième est un simple *rifaccimento* d'un travail fait en 1832, sauf la polémique contre le représentant de la métaphysique allemande, qui seule est récente; et que le troisième lui-même, où j'entre enfin franchement dans la méthode positive, a été fait, dans tout ce qu'il a de plus essentiel, avant que j'eusse pris connaissance de votre grand travail, même quant à ses premiers volumes. C'est peut-être une chose favorable à l'originalité de mon point de vue philosophique que d'avoir si tard connu ce qui devait exercer sur mon esprit une si grande influence, mais il est bien certain que mon livre en vaut moins, quoique peutêtre il n'en devienne que mieux convenable aux lecteurs qu'il aura. Quant à ses chances de succès vous apprendrez avec plaisir qu'elles se déclarent déjà d'une manière pleinement satisfaisante, en égard à l'apathie spéculative de notre public et à l'opposition tranchée qui existe entre l'esprit de ce livre et celui de la philosophie à la mode. Je commence à espérer que ce livre pourra devenir un vrai point de ralliement philosophique pour cette partie de la jeunesse scientifique anglaise qui ne tient pas beaucoup aux idées religieuses; et je crois cette émancipation essentielle moins rare, même chez nous, qu'elle ne le paraît. Surtout ce livre me semble propre à servir de digne pour arrêter le dangereux progrès de la philosophie allemande. Jusqu'ici cette philosophie nous a été plus utile que nuisible; elle a déterminé chez nous une véritable tendance aux généralités scientifiques et à la systématisation de l'ensemble des connaissances humaines; cela nous manquait presque entièrement, et ne pouvait guère nous arriver par une autre route:

1. MS at Johns Hopkins. Published in Lévy-Bruhl, pp. 165–70; in reply to Comte's of Feb. 27, *ibid.*, pp. 155–65.
2. Comte's practice of not reading other writers' books.

Mais socialement parlant cette philosophie est aujourd'hui chez nous pleinement rétrograde, quelle que soit la tendance sceptique qu'on lui ait reproché
d'exercer dans son pays natal, où en effet elle a rempli puissamment une
fonction dissolvante envers les anciennes croyances, tandis qu'ici on s'en
sert pour retremper philosophiquement ces croyances, contradiction qui ne
répugne en rien au caractère vague et arbitraire des prémisses logiques
d'une pareille philosophie. Depuis la chute irrévocable de la métaphysique
négative, cette philosophie allemande a pû se vanter d'offrir seule à l'esprit
humain une coordination systématique de la pensée; elle se prétend supérieure à ses prédécesseurs surtout en ce qu'elle constate tous les phénomènes
de la sensibilité et de l'activité humaine, et qu'elle en rend compte à sa
manière, tandis que les autres systémes nient tout ce qu'il ne savent pas
expliquer selon leurs principes propres: et jusqu'ici, personne n'est venu se
planter en face de cet ennemi, en remplissant convenablement les mêmes
conditions. Désormais on pourra choisir; on ne sera plus rejeté vers le
camp allemand faute de trouver ailleurs un système philosophique nettement formulé. Chez nous aussi le positivisme a déployé son drapeau.

J'attends maintenant avec un vif intérêt les discussions philosophiques
qui s'engageront probablement avant peu entre nous deux et qui auront une
grande influence sur mes travaux à venir. Il est vrai que très souvent dans
mon livre je n'ai fait qu'effleurer les questions où ma manière de penser ne
se recontrait pas encore précisément avec la vôtre, et il y en a même que
la nature du livre ne m'a pas permis d'aborder. Cependant ce livre vous
donnera le moyen de pénétrer assez à fond dans mon esprit, pour que les
discussions partielles deviennent beaucoup plus faciles et plus commodes.
J'ajourne jusqu'après ces discussions tout projet sérieux de travail nouveau.
L'essentiel pour moi, quant à présent, c'est de continuer ma propre éducation philosophique, et je n'écrirai probablement, d'ici à quelque temps, rien
de plus important que quelques études historiques d'un ordre secondaire.
J'espère du reste recueillir de vos conseils amicaux un grand avantage en
ce qui tien à la direction de mon activité intellectuelle, surtout lorsque
vous serez mieux en état de juger mon genre de capacité caractéristique.
Cette espérance donne un nouvel attrait à mon projet d'aller passer quelques
jours auprès de vous, et il ne tiendra pas à moi que ce projet ne s'accom-
plisse avant la fin du printemps. En ce cas, votre aimable proposition de me
recevoir chez vous serait trop agréable pour pouvoir être refusée, d'autant
plus que ce serait le moyen de ne perdre, pour le but presque unique de
mon voyage, que le moins possible d'un temps nécessairement très
raccourci.

Je vous félicite bien cordialement de la terminaison de votre travail
classique, qui devait être effectivement pour vous d'autant plus ennuyeux
qu'il a été moins fatigant; et je me réjouis avec vous de la reprise de vos

promenades habituelles, dont j'apprécie la douceur par ma propre expérience. Comme vous j'ai toujours eu l'habitude de beaucoup marcher, et je prépare toujours les méditations un peu difficiles en me promenant: je trouve cet acte physique tellement favorable à la pensée que même dans mon bureau je marche toujours, ne restant assis que strictement le temps qu'il faut pour écrire des choses déjà préparées debout. Votre traité de géométrie analytique me sera encore plus précieux parce que je le tiendrai de vous-même. Ce trait est vivement attendu non seulement par moi mais encore par un jeune frère[3] dont l'éducation m'a été léguée par mon père et qui par les dispositions scientifiques qu'il montre, jointes à un heureux caractère, m'aide à supporter la perte irréparable d'un autre frère[4] plus âgé, mort en 1840 avant l'âge de vingt ans, noble jeune homme qui a fait le charme des dernières années de mon père et sur l'amitié duquel je comptais pour ma vie tout entière.

Je suis bien sensible à l'honneur que vous me faites en demandant mon avis sur votre project de prendre une connaissance spéciale de la philosophie allemande. Je ne suis pas peutêtre en droit de donner là-dessus une opinion très décidée, n'ayant moi-même lu ni Kant ni Hegel ni aucun autre des chefs de cette école, que je n'ai d'abord connue que par ses interprètes anglais et français. Cette philosophie m'a été, à moi, fort utile; elle a corrigé ce qu'il y avait de trop exclusivement analytique dans mon esprit nourri par Bentham et par les philosophes français du 18me siècle: ajoutez à cela sa critique de l'école négative, et surtout un sens réel quoique trop incomplet des lois historiques et de la filiation des divers états de l'homme et de la société, sens qui est, je crois, le plus développé chez Hegel. Moi j'avais encore besoin de tout cela, et vous ne l'avez pas. Plus tard lorsque j'ai essayé de lire quelques ouvrages philosophiques allemands, il s'est trouvé que je possédais déjà tout ce qu'ils avaient d'utile pour moi, et le reste m'a été fastidieux au point de ne pouvoir pas en continuer la lecture. En me mettant donc à votre place, je doute si cette étude peut vous offrir un avantage suffisant pour décider en sa faveur une infraction à votre hygiène cérébrale, et je ne sache pas qu'une connaissance plus exacte des points de rapport entre cette doctrine et la vôtre puisse vous servir de grand chose dans vos travaux. Je crois que pour être lu et goûté en Allemagne, ce qu'il faut est surtout l'esprit systématique; cet esprit vous le possédez au suprême degré: et votre véritable point de contact avec les philosophes allemands est dans les faits concrets que vous expliquez bien tandis qu'ils les expliquent mal. Cependant j'approuve beaucoup votre dessein d'apprendre la langue allemande afin de lire les grands poètes de ce peuple. Les poésies lyriques de Goethe surtout me semblent dignes des plus beaux temps de l'antiquité

3. George Mill.
4. Henry Mill.

par la perfection de la forme, et souvent bien supérieures par le fond, comme la matière esthétique moderne l'est à l'ancienne.

Je n'ai pas besoin de dire que je verrai avec grand plaisir Mazhar Effendi,[5] et que tout ce que je puis faire pour lui pendant son séjour ici lui est d'avance assuré.

tout à vous

J. S. MILL

391. TO GEORGE BENTHAM[1]

India House
14th March
1843

DEAR MR BENTHAM

I was very glad to see your handwriting again, though the mere fact of sending my book[2] did not require or merit any acknowledgment from you. My object in writing to you now is to ask whether you are making or likely to make an *English* herbarium or whether you care about having English specimens because if you do I am likely to be thinking a little of botany this year & being in a different part of England from that in which you are now fixed,[3] I should be much pleased by being permitted to collect specimens for you. Any that I already have I need hardly say I should be most happy to send but they amount to so little compared with what I should like & might hope to do that I hardly like to offer them. If however you would give me what lawyers call a roving commission, I would do my best.

You probably have abundance of the Edinburgh Catalogues. However I enclose one in case you should be willing to take the trouble of returning it to me after marking any plants of which you might wish to have other *English* specimens from the south east parts of England. I could also send you a catalogue of Surrey plants & their habitats, tolerably large though very incomplete, being derived solely from my own individual observations —it would shew you what the plants are that I could most readily procure from this neighbourhood.

ever truly yours

J. S. MILL

5. Comte in his letter of Feb. 27 bespoke JSM's help for him as a former pupil who has become an official in charge of public works in Egypt and who plans to visit England to gain technical information.

* * * *

1. MS at Kew.   2. The *Logic*.
3. George Bentham in 1841 had moved to Pontrilas House, Hereford. Previously, from 1834, he had lived in the house in Queen Square which he had inherited from his uncle Jeremy.

392. TO GEORGE BENTHAM[1]

India House
24th March
1843

DEAR MR BENTHAM—I am sorry you troubled yourself to send back the Catalogue, not having marked it. I will keep on the lookout for the rare Orchidiae &c. I fear none of those I have from Surrey &c. are decidedly rare ones. I collected a few rather rare species in Italy, the orchis romana, papilionacea provincalis, & a few other plants almost peculiar to the Roman Campagna—the rarest, I believe, being the Vicia tricolor. Nothing but the persuasion that you must certainly have all these has prevented me from long since offering you them or any others I have. If any of the two or three I have mentioned would be of the least value to you I should feel really obliged by your saying so, as I should try anything else however trifling which you would put it in my power to do for you or yours.

I am very glad you are occupied in aiding the completion of the Prodromus as you have already done so essentially by your settlement of the Labiatae & Scrophulariacea.[2] I am always to be seen or heard of here at 18 Kensington Square & though I am not often at the Athenaeum without some special cause, your being to be met with there would be cause sufficient.

ever truly yours

J. S. MILL

393. TO SIR EDWARD LYTTON BULWER[1]

India House
27th March
1843

MY DEAR SIR LYTTON

You very much overpraise my rather ambitious attempt, but I am very glad that you find enough in the book[2] to repay the trouble of reading and I shall be amply satisfied if it is found to deserve half the good you say of it. I hope you may have time to give me the benefit of the doubts & suggestions you speak of. I can say quite sincerely & I believe from sufficient

1. MS at Kew.

2. In his *Labiatarum Genera et Species* . . . (London, 1832–36) and other publications. See the bibliography of his scientific publications in B. Daydon Jackson, *George Bentham* (London, 1906), pp. 269–84.

* * * *

1. MS in the possession of Lady Hermione Cobbold. Collated by Dr. Eileen Curran. Published in Elliot, I, 123–24.

2. The *Logic*.

self-knowledge that I value the pointing out of an error more highly than any amount of praise.

I am afraid the proposition that Morality is an Art, not a Science, will hardly be found on closer examination to have so much in it as you seem to have thought was intended. It follows as a necessary corollary from my particular mode of using the word Art, but at bottom I fancy it is merely what everybody thinks, expressed in new language.

You would find Comte exceedingly well worth your better knowledge. I do not always agree in his opinions but so far as I know he seems to me by far the first speculative thinker of the age.

Yours very truly

J.S . MILL

394. TO JOHN AUSTIN[1]

I.H.
Saturday
[Spring, 1843?]

MY DEAR AUSTIN

Your opinion of my Logic is very gratifying to me.

I have read the little tract which you sent me from Mr Ramsay.[2] There is much good in it; evidence of many right opinions & feelings & of some sound knowledge. The chief fault seems to me that of entire unpracticalness.

I cannot surmise from it of what character Mr Ramsay's ethical book[3] may be, but if it falls in my way I will certainly make myself acquainted with it.

Yours ever truly

J. S. MILL

395. TO AUGUSTE COMTE[1]

India House
le 20 avril 1843.

MON CHER MONSIEUR COMTE

Aussitôt que j'ai appris par votre lettre du 25 mars que mon livre ne vous était pas encore parvenu, j'ai pris des informations chez l'éditeur, et j'ai trouvé que par un retard du libraire Dulau qui s'en était chargé, le paquet ne

1. MS at LSE.
2. Probably George (later Sir George) Ramsay (1800–1871), philosophical writer. The tract in question has not been identified.
3. *An Enquiry into the Principles of Human Happiness and Human Duty* (London, 1843).   * * * *
1. MS at Johns Hopkins. Published in Lévy-Bruhl, pp. 178–83; in reply to Comte's of March 25, *ibid.*, pp. 171–78.

devait partir que le 30. Je me suis depuis assuré qu'en effet il est parti ce jour-là, et j'espère que l'exemplaire est entre vos mains depuis 15 jours. Dans le cas contraire c'est Bossange, du quai Voltaire, qui vous en répondra. Ces sortes de délais, auxquelles je suis fort habitué, indiquent, ainsi que le port monstrueux qu'on vous a demandé, un état de véritable barbarie dans l'organisation matérielle du commerce intellectuel entre nos deux pays. Quant aux difficultés fiscales je crois que la faute est du côté de notre gouvernement, qui, suivant l'esprit national, n'a jamais vu dans la propagation de la pensée autre chose qu'une industrie particulière, et n'a pas plus songé à faciliter l'envoi des livres par la poste, que celui des draps; pas plus dans l'intérieur qu'avec l'étranger. Toutefois, puisque nous sommes entrés depuis quelques ans dans la voie des réformes postales, je crois que nous adopterons bientôt dans cette matière spéciale un régime plus civilisé. La disposition d'esprit qui permet de pareilles mesquineries change tous les jours: nous sommes à cet égard en plein progrès; et la préoccupation absolue des intérêts industriels que naguère on pouvait encore regarder comme nationale, est déjà très généralement flétrie comme indice d'un esprit étroit et d'une éducation inférieure. La génération actuelle vaut mieux, à mille égards, que celle qui l'a précédée. On respire un air bien plus libre et plus pur que dans ma première jeunesse.

Je vous remercie mille fois de l'envoie de votre ouvrage classique.[2] J'aurais volontiers commencé, selon vos conseils, par une première lecture très rapide, mais je n'avais pas d'abord assez de loisir continu pour cela, et je tenais à commencer sans délai; ensuite, j'ai perdu depuis si longtemps l'habitude des lectures mathématiques ou du moins algébriques, que j'eusse craint de ne pas saisir réellement l'esprit du livre si je ne m'attachais pas à y suivre, avec connaissance de cause, tous les calculs. Ainsi que beaucoup de ceux qui s'occupent habituellement de méditations générales, j'ai la mémoire très mauvaise pour toute sorte de détails, même scientifiques; et quoique je retrouve toujours avec une grande facilité tout ce que j'ai une fois appris, je ne puis jamais présumer avec sûreté de la suffisance de mes connaissances actuelles d'un sujet quelconque lorsqu'elles ne sont pas d'acquisition récente. Je me suis donc mis à travailler comme un écolier à votre ouvrage, et je me flatte que je serai bientôt capable de subir passablement un examen assez approfondi à son sujet. Malgré la lenteur inévitable de cette manière de lire, je n'ai pas manqué d'apercevoir dans l'ouvrage cette sorte de symétrie qui fait d'un traité scientifique parfait, en quelque façon un ouvrage d'art, et je ne doute point d'éprouver encore davantage ce sentiment à une seconde lecture exclusivement dirigée à l'appréciation de l'ensemble. Sous le rapport logique, je connaissais assez votre merveilleuse puissance de généralisation philosophique pour ne m'étonner nulle-

2. See Letter 383, n. 2.

ment à trouver dans votre manière de traiter ce sujet spécial un vrai modèle de ce que sera un jour l'enseignement mathématique comme moyen d'éducation des facultés spéculatives de l'homme. Mais j'avoue que malgré la profonde impression faite sur moi par le premier volume de votre grand ouvrage, je n'avais pas senti aussi profondément que je la sens maintenant, l'aptitude éminent de l'analyse mathématique, convenablement étudiée, pour développer l'esprit scientifique. Il est bien fâcheux que jusqu'ici cette heureuse qualité soit non seulement neutralisée mais vraiment tournée en sens contraire par la routine irrationnelle qui préside partout à l'éducation mathématique. Votre ouvrage aura ici un lecture diligent dans la personne de Sir William Molesworth, que vous connaissez peutêtre de nom comme ayant fait les frais intellectuels et pécuniaires de la belle édition des œuvres de Hobbes,[3] dont vous avez fait une mention honorable dans une note de votre 5me volume. Sir William Molesworth, d'ailleurs admirateur éclairé de votre grand ouvrage, a fait de fortes études scientifiques. Il s'occupe beaucoup à présent de philosophie mathématique, et comme il a une véritable capacité scientifique, malgré une certaine raideur intellectuelle qui gêne un peu la marche de son intelligence, je m'efforce de le décider à faire un livre à ce sujet, en attendant celui que vous avez annoncé et que vous avez dû ajourner à un avenir un peu lointain. J'espère qu'il se trouvera bientôt parmi la jeunesse scientifique française des penseurs capable de régénérer, sous l'inspiration de vos ouvrages et de votre conversation, les diverses branches de l'enseignement mathématique, travail si important que bien qu'il ne puisse pas vous appartenir, voué comme vous l'êtes à des travaux encore plus élevés, le temps que vous avez consacré à en fournir un premier exemple décisif n'est certainement pas mal employé. Votre projet primitif d'écrire votre cours populaire d'astronomie offrait une utilité analogue, et j'aurais regretté que ce projet fût abandonné si je ne craignais, pour une santé si précieuse l'effet d'un nouveau travail sédentaire pendant l'année naturellement destinée à raffermir vos forces physiques pour la noble tâche qui vous attend. Ne se pourrait-il pas que, dans l'impossibilité où vous vous trouvez d'écrire vos divers cours, quelqu'un de ceux qui ont l'avantage de les suivre le fit à votre place, comme on l'a fait quelquefois pour d'autres professeurs? Une simple révision par vous-même pourrait alors suffire, et le succès pécuniaire ne manquerait guère de récompenser suffisamment le travail du rédacteur.

Je trouve que vous avez sagement fait en renonçant à votre velléité passagère de vous occuper de la philosophie des allemands et en vous bornant

---

3. *The English Works of Thomas Hobbes of Malmesbury*, ed. Sir William Molesworth (11 vols., London, 1839–45). Also, *Thomae Hobbes Malmesburiensis Opera philosophica quae Latine scripsit omnia . . .* , ed. Sir William Molesworth (5 vols., London, 1839–45).

à leur poésie, dans laquelle Goethe est comme vous le sentez déjà, sans rival. Je crois pourtant que le jugement sévère que vous portez sur Schiller[4] n'est pleinement mérité que pour la première moitié de ses écrits, très hautement condamnés par lui-même à un âge plus mûr. Vous trouveriez peut être dans son Wallenstein, dans sa Jeanne d'Arc, dans son Guillaume Tell, et dans ses poésies lyriques une capacité poétique réele quoique de second ordre, et une ombre même du génie créateur de Goethe, avec une élévation morale que généralement on ne reconnaît pas dans ce dernier, ou qui du moins est loin d'y être aussi saillante. Il y a de très belles choses dans Richter,[5] dans Tieck,[6] etc. mais le plus souvent sous la forme du roman en prose. Les romans de Goethe sont au contraire, à mon avis, ce qu'il a fait de moins bon, soit par la forme, soit même par le fond, quoiqu'il y ait semé une foule de pensées justes et profondes et qu'on y trouve un grand nombre de tableaux d'une poésie admirable.

Je me promets d'écrire incessamment à M. Balard que j'espère aussi voir si, comme je le désire, ma visite domiciliaire chez vous s'accomplit avant la fin du printemps. Il se peut toutefois que je sois forcé de l'ajourner jusqu'au mois d'octobre, aussitôt après la terminaison de votre tournée officielle. Dans ce cas-là je crains que M. Balard ne soit plus à Paris quand j'y serai.

Je n'ai pas encore vu Mazhar Effendi, qui probablement n'est pas arrivé. Je l'attends avec un grand intérêt.

Votre dévoué

J. S. MILL.

J'allais oublier de vous dire qu'en lisant votre ouvrage j'ai trouvé dans les formules un assez grand nombre d'erreurs typographiques dont je vous donnerai si vous voulez la liste.

396. TO JOHN STERLING[1]

I.H.

26 April [1843]

I do not write to you, my dear Sterling, with any such vain notion as of attempting to offer you any comfort under the double blow[2] which has

4. Comte in his letter of March 23, 1843 (Lévy-Bruhl, p. 175), had written: "le fameux Schiller ne m'a jamais paru, d'après les traductions, qu'une sorte de gauche imitateur du grand Shakespeare, bien plutôt qu'un vrai poète; sa niaise sentimentalité métaphysique, réchauffée par l'influence de Rousseau, m'est d'ailleurs insupportable."
5. Johann Paul Friedrich Richter (1763–1825), German novelist and humorist.
6. Johann Ludwig Tieck (1773–1853), German poet, dramatist, and novelist.

* * * *

1. MS at Leeds. Published in Elliot, I, 124–25. The year has been pencilled in in another hand.
2. Sterling's mother had died on April 16; his wife, two days later.

fallen upon you—the first so hard, the last so much harder—though I hardly know among possible things any which I would not do or which it would not be the truest joy to me to do if it could help to lighten your burden either of grief or of care. But it is a kind of mockery to talk of the great things one will never have the power of doing—it is only little things one has the opportunity to be useful in, & little enough in *them*. Heaven knows there are few things which we, here, can do for you, & we have little claim to be preferred to others in regard to even those few; but I know how oppressive small cares are when they come on the back of great sufferings, & if any here could assist in relieving you from even the smallest of those, I do not believe you know, or can know, how pleasant it would be to do and how pleasant to think of when done. And with so many young creatures in your charge and your own health requiring so much care, even we might sometimes and in some ways be able to give useful help without intruding into the place of any who might be equally desirous & more capable. If it should be so, it will be real friendship & kindness in you to give us the opportunity. Do not think of writing in answer to this unless it be to tell us of something that can be done—but by & by, when you are better able, we shall wish very much to hear what your plans are both for yourself & the children & if possible, to be in some, if even the smallest degree, included in them.

Ever most affectionately,

J. S. MILL.

397. TO SIR JOHN F. W. HERSCHEL[1]

India House,
1st May 1843

MY DEAR SIR,

Permit me to acknowledge with much pleasure your kind note, which deserves much more of thanks than my sending you the book, since that was due to the very great help I derived from your speculations in writing it. You will find that the most important chapter of the book,[2] that on the four Experimental Methods, is little more than an expansion & a more scientific statement of what you had previously stated in the more popular manner suited to the purpose of your "Introduction."[3] Besides, you were,

1. MS in the possession of the Royal Society and published with its permission.
2. The *Logic*.
3. Herschel's *A Preliminary Discourse on the Study of Natural Philosophy* (London, 1831), which constituted "The Introduction or Preface to the Cabinet of Natural Philosophy" in Dionysius Lardner's *Cabinet Cyclopædia* (133 vols., London, 1830–49). JSM had reviewed it favourably in the *Examiner*, March 20, 1831, pp. 179–80.

perhaps, of all living Englishmen, the one by whom I was most desirous that my book should be judged, since most of those who would be competent judges of the metaphysical part are not thoroughly competent in the physical, and conversely.

Mr. Beneke's book[4] I have heard of & intend to read. I feel little doubt of your finding Comte's book worthy your better knowledge. It is a book very likely to be undervalued on a partial inspection, especially as those of his opinions which are most objectionable to most Englishmen (& now I believe even to Frenchmen) lie on the surface.

I am so conscious of superficiality in many of the departments of knowledge from which I have been forced to gather materials for attempting to methodize the process of investigating truth, that I should be very grateful if you could, without encroaching on time which is more valuably employed, note down some of the many errors I must have committed as well as of the important ideas I must have missed. It is very uncertain if I shall ever have an opportunity of improving the book by any such memoranda but for my own instruction I should value them much and could make them useful in other ways.

Believe me
Yours with great respect
J. S. MILL.

398. TO AUGUSTE COMTE[1]

India House
le 15 juin 1843

MON CHER MONSIEUR COMTE—

Je me reproche un peu d'avoir tant retardé ma réponse à vos deux lettres si pleines d'intérêt, lettres qui avaient droit à la réponse la plus prompte, et qui l'auraient sans doute obtenue de moi dans l'état normal de mes facultés mentales; mais j'éprouve, pour toute communication avec vous, le besoin, ou du moins le désir, de me sentir dans la plénitude de mes forces, et je suis tombé au contraire depuis quelque temps dans une sorte de langueur intellectuelle, pour ne pas dire morale, qui tient, à ce que je crois, surtout à des causes physiques. Sans aucune maladie bien définie, j'éprouve une faiblesse nerveuse et une affection quasi-fébrile chronique

---

4. Probably Friedrich Eduard Beneke's *System der Logik als Kunstlehre des Denkens* (2 vols., Berlin, 1842).

* * * *

1. *Addressed*: Monsieur / Auguste Comte / 10 Rue M. le Prince / près l'Odéon / à Paris. *Postmark*: 15 JU 15 / 1843. MS at Johns Hopkins. Published in Lévy-Bruhl, pp. 204–10; in reply to Comte's of May 16 and May 28, *ibid.*, pp. 183–204.

que j'ai, du reste, ressentie à diverses époques antérieures de ma vie, et que je connais assez familièrement pour savoir qu'elle ne durera pas longtemps. Le meilleur moyen de me rétablir entièrement serait, je crois, un voyage de quelques mois, mais à dèfaut d'un pareil remède, qui en effet me serait à peu près impossible, je suis sûr de retrouver peu à peu ma santé ordinaire si rien ne m'arrive de nature à l'affaiblir davantage. Les médecins me conseillent en attendant de ne travailler que le moins possible, mais je ne suivrai leur conseil qu'autant que ma propre expérience peut m'en faire reconnaître la nécessité, la médecine ne me paraissant pas être parvenue à un état de positivité assez parfaite pour que la liberté de conscience ait encore cessé dans cet ordre d'idées.

Pour en venir à des choses plus importantes, je vous remercie bien vivement de m'avoir donné de si amples détails sur un sujet que vous avez cru avec raison devoir être pour moi du plus vif intérêt, celui de la lutte que vous avez eu à subir lors de votre réélection.[2] Dans l'intervalle de vos deux lettres j'ai beaucoup réfléchi sur l'issue possible de cette lutte et sur la manière dont il y aurait lieu d'organiser la transition que peutêtre il vous faudra opérer de votre position présente à une autre qui ne serait plus pénible qu'en ce qu'elle serait d'abord plus précaire. L'heureuse terminaison, au moins momentanée, de cette crise, me dispense de vous entretenir aujourd'hui des diverses choses qui me sont passées par la tête, au sujet surtout de la conduite à tenir par vos amis dans le cas où l'affaire aurait tourné autrement. J'ai besoin pourtant de vous dire une chose qui est de celles qu'on peut dire hardiment lorsqu'on s'adresse à un caractère aussi supérieur à toute fausse délicatesse qu'incapable de manquer à la vraie: C'est que, quelque avenir qui vous soit réservé, toute pensée de détresse matérielle réelle vous est interdite, aussi longtemps que je vivrai et que j'aurai un sou à partager avec vous. Je crois même qu'après votre première lettre j'aurais osé vous faire en ce sens une proposition spéciale, sans certains éventualités personnelles, qui seront sans doute décidées avant l'époque de la réélection de l'an prochain et dont l'issue influera nécessairement beaucoup sur la proposition à faire. Comme ces éventualités se décideront probablement en peu de temps j'aime mieux en ajourner l'explication jusqu'à ce que je puisse vous en annoncer en même temps le résultat, qui au reste ne saurait, quel qu'il soit, m'ôter la faculté de servir d'abri temporaire, s'il y a lieu, à celui qui de tous les hommes vivants, honorerait le plus une pareille offre en l'acceptant.

Quant à ce qui dans votre lettre me regarde personnellement, il est presque superflu de vous dire avec quelle satisfaction profonde j'ai appris l'accueil que vous avez donné à mon travail philosophique, et la haute approbation que vous en témoignez, approbation propre à remplir mes

2. The renewal of his annual appointment at the Ecole Polytechnique.

désirs les plus ambitieux, et qui dépasse de beaucoup mes espérances. Vous devez bien sentir que votre opinion, sur la valeur de cet écrit, est la seule qui pouvait notablement influer sur la mienne propre, tandis que celle-ci n'était, et ne pouvait être que provisoire, tant que la partie vraiment positive et dogmatique de l'ouvrage n'avait pas reçu la sanction du juge le plus compétent, et même jusqu'ici le seul compétent, dans les questions quelconques de méthodologie systématique. Maintenant que cette sanction si précieuse lui est acquise, il m'est permis de me féliciter de l'assurance désormais inébranlable que je possède, d'être pour quelque chose non seulement dans la propagation initiale mais même dans la fondation de la philosophie finale, quelque modeste que soit la part qui m'appartienne dans cette noble œuvre. Nous pouvons aussi nous réjouir ensemble de l'heureux augure à retirer pour cette philosophie d'un tel accord spontané entre deux esprits qui seuls jusqu'ici se sont sérieusement occupés d'organiser la méthode positive, après une préparation convenable ou même passable, et qui partant de points très éloignés l'un de l'autre et ne se réunissant qu'à deux tiers du chemin, se trouvent pourtant en harmonie sur tous les points essentiels. Un pareil accord serait à lui seul une preuve presque suffisante de la vérité et même de l'opportunité de la nouvelle philosophie, en fesant juger qu'elle est propre à déterminer de vraies convictions dans tout esprit qui réunira les conditions nécessaires de connaissances positives et de capacité intellectuelle primitive.

Rassuré dorénavant quant aux questions de méthode, où je ne crains plus aucune divergence sérieuse, soit sur la théorie générale de la positivité, soit sur son application spéciale aux études sociales, je n'ai plus qu'à souhaiter un accord également parfait à l'égard des doctrines sociales. Jusqu'ici cet accord existe surtout par rapport à la partie de vos doctrines qui plus que toute autre vous appartient en propre. Je parle des lois générales de la dynamique sociale et du développement historique de l'humanité, en y comprenant les corollaires pratiques si importants qui en dérivent, et dont le plus essentiel est à mes yeux le grand principe de la séparation des deux pouvoirs. A l'égard des doctrines de la sociologie statique, que vous n'avez pas inventées mais bien acceptées des anciennes théories sociales, quoique vous les ayez soutenues avec votre énergie accoutumée de conviction philosophique, il y a encore entre nous des dissentiments réels. Ces dissentiments ne tiennent, sans doute, à plusieurs égards, qu'à ce que je n'ai pas encore atteint un état de conviction complète sur des choses qui sont à vos yeux démontrées. Tout en reconnaissant pleinement, par exemple, la nécessité sociale des institutions fondamentales de la propriété et du mariage, et en n'admettant aucune utopie sur l'un ou sur l'autre sujet, je suis cependant très porté à croire que ces deux institutions peuvent être destinées à subir de plus graves modifications que vous ne le semblez penser, bien que je me sente totalement inhabile à prévoir ce qu'elles seront.

Je vous ai déjà dit que la question du divorce est pour moi indécise, malgré la puissante argumentation de votre 4me volume, et je suis atteint d'une hérésie plus fondamentale encore, puisque je n'admets pas en principe la subordination nécessaire d'un sexe à l'autre. Vous voyez qu'il nous reste encore des questions d'importance majeure à discuter entre nous, discussion qu'il serait au reste fort oiseux d'entamer à la fin d'une lettre. Ces matières tombent précisément dans la partie de votre grande entreprise philosophique qui va vous occuper le plus prochainement, et dans laquelle cet ordre de questions obtiendra naturellement une discussion plus approfondie que dans votre grand ouvrage.

Je suis bien heureux que mon livre vous paraisse capable d'être utile aussi en France, pourvu qu'il soit convenablement traduit en français, et je suis forcé à croire que je pourrais moi-même exécuter cette traduction, puisque vous ne m'en jugez pas incapable. Ce serait cependant pour moi un travail très pénible et très ennuyeux, car si j'écris passablement la langue française, je suis loin de l'écrire avec facilité: j'ai d'ailleurs lieu de croire que la chose sera faite sans que je m'en mêle. Avant l'impression du livre, notre ami Marrast a exprimé, avec une persistance amicale à laquelle j'ai dû céder, le désir de le traduire en français, et quoique, suivant ma prévision, il n'a pas trouvé le loisir nécessaire pour une pareille occupation, il vient de me mander que le livre est entre les mains d'un des professeurs de Paris les plus distingués "qui," dit-il, "profitera de ses premiers loisirs pour le traduire." M. Marrast ne m'a pas encore dit le nom de ce professeur, mais il vous le dira sans doute, et l'intérêt que vous voulez bien porter à cette entreprise aura peut-être sur son exécution une heureuse influence.[3]

Veuillez dire à M. de Blainville[4] combien je me sens flatté de l'attention dont cet illustre savant veut bien honorer mon ouvrage. Quel que puisse être son jugement éventuel sur ce livre, je mettrai toujours un grand prix à avoir été lu par un homme que j'ai appris de vous à estimer si profondément. Je me réjouis avec vous de l'honorable conduite de M. Poinsot[5] dans la crise que vous avez subie. J'ai rempli votre commission auprès de Sir William Molesworth qui aura, j'espère, un jour l'avantage de vous connaître plus directement.

Votre dévoué

J. S. MILL.

3. Comte replied that he now saw little of Marrast and did not know who the professor was; he further warned JSM against blindly entrusting the translation of the *Logic* to someone who might be hostile to positivism (Lévy-Bruhl, p. 215). On Dec. 23 Comte reported that the professor in question was a M. Mallet, professor of philosophy at the Collège de Saint-Louis (*ibid.*, p. 293) [Charles Auguste Mallet (1807–1876)]. Mallet did not translate the *Logic*.

4. Henri Marie Ducrotay de Blainville (1777–1850), eminent naturalist.

5. Louis Poinsot (1777–1859), mathematician, secretary of the Academy of Science.

399. TO ROBERT BARCLAY FOX[1]

I.H.
Thursday
[Probably June or July 1843][2]

MY DEAR BARCLAY—

Could you not manage on your way to Cornwall (which will be I suppose by the Great Western Railway) to halt for a day & see my sisters, who are at Marlow, only 5 or 6 miles from the Maidenhead Station? It would be a great pleasure to them & would not detain you long.

I wish we could prevail on Mr & Mrs Charles Fox[3] to do the same—& I wish I could see them. How long do they remain in town?

ever yours
J. S. MILL.

400. TO AUGUSTE COMTE[1]

India House
le 13 juillet 1843

MON CHER MONSIEUR COMTE—

J'espère que cette lettre vous atteindra avant le commencement de votre tournée officielle, qui du reste ne suspendra pas sans doute notre correspondance, et je ne doute pas qu'à quelque temps d'ici je serai plus en état de vous écrire convenablement. Le dérangement passager que je vous ai annoncé dans ma dernière lettre, de ma santé morale et physique, ne s'est pas encore terminé, tandis que le remède que vous jugez avec raison être le mieux assorti à cette situation, celui d'un voyage de quelques mois, me semble plus éloigné que jamais. Il ne s'ensuit point cependant que je ne puisse pas me permettre une absence de quelques jours, et si mes espérances, à cet égard, ne sont pas trompées, je compte toujours passer auprès de vous un court intervalle vers la fin d'octobre. Quant au conseil amical que vous me donnez, de me distraire autant que possible, ce conseil est un peu difficile à suivre, par la raison que j'ai le malheur, si c'en est un, d'être très peu amusable. Je ne suis guère capable de goûter

1. MS in the possession of Mr. W. H. Browning.
2. The only evidence for dating this letter is that in his letter of Oct. 23 (Letter 408) JSM refers to a visit of Barclay Fox to London earlier in the year, and that Barclay appears to have been absent from Falmouth in June and July.
3. Barclay Fox's uncle and aunt, of Trebah, near Falmouth.

* * * *

1. MS at Johns Hopkins. Published in Lèvy-Bruhl, pp. 219–25; in reply to Comte's of June 29, *ibid.*, pp. 210–19.

longtemps aucun délassement, à moins qu'il ne se rattache, et même assez directement, à un grave intérêt quelconque, et surtout à l'ensemble de mes occupations sérieuses: j'ajouterai même que le demi-travail intellectuel qui a toujours été mon principal amusement, n'a le pouvoir de m'intéresser longtemps qu'à la condition d'une alternation rapide avec le travail complet. Dans un état de faiblesse chronique qui m'empêche de sérieusement travailler, ma nature et mes habitudes ne comportent guère d'autre remède efficace qu'un voyage, et celui-là n'est pas à ma portée. Cependant il n'y a pas là de quoi vous inquiéter sur ma santé à venir car dans le cas où ce mal chronique viendrait à s'empirer beaucoup, les obstacles cesseraient probablement, et je pourrais m'éloigner pour un temps plus ou moins prolongé. A présent même, tout irait mieux si je me trouvais dans l'état normal de mes occupations intellectuelles, c.à.d. occupé à suivre un travail commencé, ou même une série de travaux homogènes; mais je ne me sens pas momentanément la vigueur d'esprit et de volonté nécessaire pour entrer dans un nouvel ordre quelconque de travaux.

Cette même raison me défend aussi d'entamer dès à présent, comme je l'aurais désiré, la discussion sérieuse des graves questions sociales sur lesquelles nos opinions ne s'accordent pas encore. La confiance que vous m'exprimez que cette divergence d'opinion ne sera que passagère est pour moi un nouveau témoignage de la haute estime que j'ai eu le bonheur d'obtenir de vous et dont il me serait très pénible de voir la moindre diminution. En effet, nous qui sommes si pleinement d'accord sur l'ensemble de la méthode scientifique et qui sommes, j'ose le dire, également émancipés à l'égard des préjugés quelconques, soit révolutionnaires, soit conservateurs; si nous ne devions pas nous accorder finalement sur les questions dont il s'agit, notre dissentiment serait presque une preuve que les principes biologiques dont dépend en dernier ressort la solution de ces questions, ne sont pas encore suffisamment mûris, ce qui assurément ne serait pas fort étonnant, vû la positivité si récente et si imparfaite des hautes études biologiques. Je crains pourtant que notre dissidence n'ait des racines plus profondes que celles que vous me signalez dans votre lettre. Je partage complètement votre manière de penser sur la tendance de notre époque à régler par les lois ce qui ne devrait dépendre que des mœurs, aberration fort naturelle dans une époque de transition sociale, où l'on respecte si peu les institutions qu'on les crée ou les détruit avec la même légèreté, tandis que le défaut de croyances communes prive l'opinion générale de sa force normale de répression morale. Je ne crois pas être atteint, dans le cas dont il s'agit, de cette tendance irrationnelle, et je ne prétends nullement à décider quelles devraient être les lois sur l'association domestique, ni que ces lois doivent être autres qu'elles ne sont. Ce que nous aurions à vider entre nous serait précisément la question de mœurs: si nous pouvions nous accorder là dessus, je crois que nous nous rencontrerions bien facilement à l'égard des institutions. En attendant, ce que j'aurais à dire à l'appui de mon hérésie principale serait tiré tout entier de principes biologiques, très imparfaits sans doute, ce qui peut tenir à l'insuffisance de mes connaissances en biologie, mais peut être aussi à l'insuffisance actuelle de la théorie biologique elle même, dans sa partie la plus directement applicable aux spéculations sociologiques. Il se peut même que je mérite d'être rangé parmi ceux que vous avez caractérisés par une phrase de votre lettre, celle où vous parlez de ceux dont le cœur est complice des déviations intellectuelles. Quant à cela, vous en jugerez; toujours est-il que, tout en repoussant, de toutes les forces de mon esprit, l'anarchique doctrine des temps révolutionnaires, hautement contradictoire à l'ensemble de l'expérience humaine, que l'attachement, même passionné, exige l'absence d'autorité, et croyant comme je le crois fermement que dans l'état normal des relations humaines une sympathie réelle et réciproque peut et doit exister entre le protecteur et le protégé, et peut exister même entre l'esclave et le maître, je ne trouve pourtant pas que toutes les sympathies doivent être d'inégalité: je ne crois pas que ce soit là leur dernier mot et je crois qu'il y a place aussi pour l'égalité dans les affections humaines. Je ne la crois incompatible avec l'harmonie que chez les natures inférieures, les plus livrées aux penchants égoïstes, ou au moins lorsque l'une des deux natures est de cette espèce. Sans aucune vaine sentimentalité, je trouve que l'affection qu'une personne d'une nature un peu élevée peut éprouver pour un être réellement subordonné à son autorité, a toujours quelque chose d'imparfait, dont on ne se contente qu'à désespoir de pouvoir placer ailleurs une sympathie plus complète. Il est très possible qu'en ceci je juge trop la nature humaine d'après la mienne propre, qui, à plusieurs égards, est peut-être exceptionnelle. Mais voici en quoi je ne crois pas que je puisse me tromper: c'est que pour décider cet ordre de questions la philosophie a besoin de l'expérience des femmes autant que de celle des hommes, et cette expérience elle ne l'a pas encore. Ce n'est guère que d'avant-hier que les femmes pensent, ce n'est que d'hier qu'elles disent leurs pensées, et, ce qui est plus important encore, leur expérience de la vie: le plupart de celles qui écrivent, écrivent pour les hommes, ou du moins ont peur de leur désapprobation, et on ne peut pas plus se fier au témoignage de celles-là qu'à celui du très petit nombre de celles qui sont en état de rébellion ouverte. Or il me semble que l'influence sur la vie intime et morale, d'une relation quelconque de dépendance ne peut pas se décider uniquement sur les idées et sur l'expérience des supérieurs. Ceci ressemble, je le sais, à une idée émise par les saint-simoniens, à qui, en effet, je reproche surtout qu'après avoir proclamé leur propre incompétence à décider les grandes questions sociales qu'ils ont soulevées, ils ont eu la folie ou la charlatanerie d'en offrir une prétendue solution, dont ils avaient ainsi eux mêmes reconnu d'avance l'absurdité. Je n'avais pas, en commençant cette lettre, l'intention d'y tant dire sur ce sujet, mais je compte vous soumettre petit à petit tout ce que je trouve à dire là dessus, comme à mon frère aîné, pour ne rien dire de plus, en philosophie.

Je me félicite de la manière fraternelle dont vous avez accueilli une offre qui ne méritait pas la qualification que vous lui avez donnée de généreuse, puisque je me serais senti avili à mes propres yeux en ne la fesant point. En effet, pensant ce que je pense de vous, et du rôle que vous remplissez dans notre époque et même en ne comptant pour rien notre amitié, si je vous savais dans la détresse ou même en danger d'y tomber, et qu'ayant les moyens de vous en retirer je n'en usais point pour quel usage les réserverais-je? Je sens comme vous que ce devoir appartiendrait normalement à d'autres que moi, et je ne prétends pas à leur dérober l'honneur de son accomplissement, mais il m'importait beaucoup d'avoir l'assurance que si, le cas arrivant, ceux-là ne vous tendaient pas la main, vous accepteriez la mienne, pendant la durée du besoin que vous en auriez.

Quant au projet de traduction de mon livre, j'aurai les yeux là dessus, et si ce projet s'exécute, je tâcherai d'empêcher toute suppression importante, surtout si elle était de nature à atténuer les expressions destinées à vous rendre une justice philosophique que je tiens encore plus à vous rendre en france qu'en angleterre. Si malgré mes efforts le traducteur se permettait un pareil acte d'infidélité, je n'hésiterais certes pas à le dénoncer en France par une réclamation publique.

Mon jeune ami Lewes, qui se range de plus en plus à notre doctrine commune, vient d'insérer dans une revue anglaise, le *British & Foreign Review*, un article sur les diverses écoles philosophiques,[2] ou prétendues telles qui existent actuellement en France, dans lequel après une critique assez sévère de toutes les autres, il finit par une appréciation sommaire et assez intelligente de votre système, dont il fait un éloge franc et vigoureux, accompagné de la haute expression d'admiration de votre éminente supériorité intellectuelle. Je compte que cet article fera aussi sa part pour attirer sur votre grand ouvrage l'attention des lecteurs anglais.

Je ne manquerai pas de faire un emploi convenable des exemplaires que vous m'avez addressés de l'arrêt du tribunal de commerce, qui me semble aussi satisfaisant dans ses termes que dans ses conclusions.

votre tout dévoué

J. S. MILL

2. "The Modern Metaphysics and Moral Philosophy of France," *BFR*, XV (1843), 353–406.

India House
le 30 août 1843

MON CHER MONSIEUR COMTE

Au moment d'écrire cette lettre, c.à d. après en avoir fait le brouillon, travail indispensable chez moi lorsque j'écris en français quelque chose d'un peu important, je reçois la lettre que vous a inspirée votre aimable inquiétude sur ma santé. Je suis heureux de pouvoir dissiper cette sollicitude. Si mon état physique ne s'est pas beaucoup amélioré, il n'a certainement pas empiré, et je commence à rentrer, sous le rapport moral, dans mon état ordinaire. Je me promets bien de répondre dorénavant à vos lettres avec plus de promptitude et je me reproche les alarmes que mon silence a fait naître chez vous. Ce retard inusité tient effectivement un peu à Mazhar Effendi, mais non pas de la manière que vous pensiez. Je désirais seulement pouvoir vous parler un peu de lui. Il est venu à mon bureau avec le Docteur Bowring,[2] et m'a donné votre lettre peu de jours après sa date: depuis cela il n'est plus revenu, et comme il n'a pas non plus répondu à un billet que je lui ai écrit, je crois qu'il doit être parti pour l'intérieur du pays, où en effet il trouverait, en fait d'établissements industriels et de travaux publics, des choses bien plus intéressantes qu'à Londres. Dans ce cas-là j'espère le voir davantage lorsqu'il sera de retour, d'autant plus que la première fois il n'est pas resté assez longtemps pour que j'aie pu faire vraiment connaissance avec lui. Lorsqu'il est venu, ma famille était à la campagne et ma maison encombrée d'ouvriers, mais à son retour j'aurai la faculté de lui donner un accueil plus satisfaisant.

Pour reprendre notre importante discussion sociologique, je crois comprendre ce que vous voulez dire en comparant la constitution organique du sexe féminin à un état d'enfance prolongée. Je n'ignore pas ce qu'ont dit à ce sujet beaucoup de physiologistes, et je sais que non seulement par les systèmes musculaire et cellulaire mais encore par le système nerveux, et très probablement par la structure cérébrale, les femmes sont moins éloignées que ne le sont les hommes, du caractère organique des enfants. Cela pourtant est bien loin d'être décisif pour moi. Afin qu'il le fût, il faudrait prouver que l'infériorité des enfants par rapport aux hommes dépendît de la différence anatomique de leur cerveau, tandis qu'elle dépend évidemment en majeure partie, sinon entièrement, au seul défaut d'exercice. Si l'on pouvait garder toujours son cerveau d'enfant, pendant qu'on en dévelop-

1. MS at Johns Hopkins. Published in Lévy-Bruhl, pp. 236–42; in reply to Comte's of July 16 and Aug. 28, *ibid.*, pp. 225–35.
2. John Bowring.

perait les fonctions par l'éducation et par un exercice soigné et réglé, on ne resterait certainement pas enfant, on serait homme, et on pourrait devenir homme très supérieur, tout en offrant, sans doute, des déviations notables du type ordinaire de l'humanité. De même je ne nie pas que le type moral féminin ne présente, en terms moyen, des divergences considérables du type masculin. Je ne prétends pas définir au juste en quoi consistent ces divergences naturelles et je ne sais pas si le temps est encore venu pour cela, mais je sais que des physiologistes très éminents prétendent que le cerveau des femmes est moins grand, moins fort par conséquent, mais plus actif que celui des hommes. D'après cela les femmes devraient être moins capable de travail intellectuel continu et prolongé, mais propres à plus faire en peu de temps que les hommes, et à faire mieux qu'eux tout ce qui exige une grande promptitude d'esprit. Elles seraient donc moins propres à la science, et plus propres au moins par leur organisation, à la poésie et à la vie pratique. Ceci me semble s'accorder assez bien avec ce qui s'observe dans la vie. Cependant on risquerait d'exagérer beaucoup le degré de diversité réelle, si on ne tenait pas compte de la différence d'éducation et de position sociale: car, que les femmes soient ou ne soient pas naturellement inférieures en capacité d'effort intellectuel prolongé, il n'est pas douteux que rien dans leur éducation n'est arrangé de manière à développer en elles cette capacité, tandis que chez les hommes l'étude des sciences, et même celle des langues mortes, a certainement cette tendance. D'ailleurs chez un grand nombre d'hommes, surtout dans les classes supérieures des travailleurs, leurs occupations journalières exigent, ou du moins permettent, un travail suivi de la pensée, tandis que chez la grande majorité des femmes l'obsession perpétuelle des soins minutieux de la vie domestique, chose qui distrait l'esprit sans l'occuper, ne permet aucun travail intellectuel qui ait besoin soit d'isolement physique, soit même d'attention suivie. Parmi les hommes eux-mêmes on ne reconnaît certainement pas une grande aptitude pour le travail de l'intelligence chez ceux dont l'enfance a été étrangère à toute étude tandis que les nécessités de leur vie postérieure n'ont pas remplacé à cet égard ce qui avait manqué à leur éducation primitive. Je trouve aussi que dans les choses ordinaires de la vie, sur lesquelles l'intelligence des femmes s'exerce autant ou plus que celle des hommes, les femmes, même médiocres, montrent ordinairement plus de capacité que les hommes médiocres. Un homme ordinaire n'a guère d'intelligence, que dans sa spécialité propre, au lieu qu'une femme en a pour des intérêts plus généraux. Vous me direz que la vie affective prédomine plus chez les femmes sur la vie intellectuelle: mais vous avouerez vous-même que ceci ne doit s'entendre que de la vie sympathique: l'égoïsme pur prédomine beaucoup plus chez les hommes: et si la sympathie devient le plus souvent chez les femmes un égoïsme à plusieurs personnes, elle le devient de même chez tous les hommes, sauf ceux qui une éducation, justqu'ici très rare, a développé à un haut degré le point de vue d'ensemble et l'habitude d'envisager les effets les plus généraux d'une conduite quelconque. Vous savez que c'est là précisément ce qui manque plus que tout le reste à l'éducation des femmes, au point qu'on ne compte même pas comme vertu à leur sexe de donner la préférence à l'intérêt général sur celui de leur famille ou de leurs amis. Je ne veux pas pour cela nier que les femmes, comme tous ceux dont l'excitabilité nerveuse dépasse le degré ordinaire, ne doivent naturellement ressembler plus pour le caractère aux hommes jeunes qu'aux hommes âgés, ni qu'elles n'aient naturellement plus de difficulté que les hommes du premier ordre à faire abstraction des intérêts présents et individuels; mais je crois que ce défaut-là trouve une compensation spontanée dans l'absence d'un autre défaut particulier aux philosophes, qui souvent font abstraction non pas seulement d'intérêts immédiats mais de tout intérêt réel; au lieu que les femmes, toujours placées au point de vue pratique deviennent très rarement des rêveurs spéculatifs, et n'oublient guère qu'il s'agit d'êtres réels, de leur bonheur ou de leurs souffrances. N'oublions pas qu'il n'est nullement question de faire gouverner la société par les femmes mais bien de savoir si elle ne serait pas mieux gouvernée par les hommes et par les femmes que par les hommes seuls. Au reste il est peutêtre très naturel qu'à cet égard vous et moi soyons d'opinion différente. Vous êtes français, et l'on a remarqué de tout temps que le caractère français tient déjà un peu des défauts, ainsi que des qualités, propres aux jeunes gens et aux femmes; vous pouvez donc penser qu'en fesant aux femmes une part plus large, on donnerait plus de force à ce qui déjà en a trop; au lieu que les défauts du caractère anglais sont plutôt en sens contraire. Sans entrer plus loin dans cette discussion subordonnée, je vous ferai observer cette seule circonstance qu'on a toujours reconnu dans les français, jusqu'à un certain point, l'organisation qu'on regarde comme féminine, et cependant quel peuple a produit de plus grands philosophes et des hommes d'Etat plus distingués?

En voilà assez pour le moment sur cette grande question biologique et sociologique. Je vous dirai maintenant une bonne nouvelle. Nous avons fait pour notre philosophie commune une conquête de premier ordre: c'est celui [*sic*] du jeune Bain, dont j'ai fait une mention honorable dans mon livre, que je lui avais communiqué avant sa publication, et qu'il a enrichi de beaucoup d'exemples et même de quelques idées utiles. Quoique âgé seulement de 26 ans il occupe depuis deux ans provisoirement en Ecosse une chaire de philosophie morale qu'il espère obtenir définitivement. C'est de tous les hommes de sa génération à moi connus, celui qui a posé le plus solidement les bases de l'éducation positive, par l'étude approfondie des cinq premières sciences fondamentales dans leur ordre hiérarchique: il a ensuite étudié mon livre, et cet été, le jugeant assez bien préparé, je lui ai fait lire le vôtre, qu'il a tout de suite compris et apprécié, et auquel il vient de consacrer trois mois d'étude vigoureuse. Il avait reçu de son éducation écossaise de fortes impressions religieuses, qui bien que déjà un peu affaiblies, n'ont réellement cédé qu'à l'influence directe de vos spéculations. Par une exception rare de nos jours, il ne s'était pas beaucoup occupé de politique et de questions sociales: il avait vaguement l'esprit progressif de notre siècle, et voilà tout. Sous l'influence de la méthode positive qu'il a parfaitement comprise et dont ses antécédents intellectuels lui avaient donné l'habitude, l'esprit de généralisation scientifique qu'il possède à un haut degré ne risque pas de s'égarer dans le vague. C'est un penseur véritable, qui devait entrer sans effort dans la bonne voie dès qu'elle lui serait indiquée, et qui, soit par l'universalité, soit par l'originalité de son esprit, doit servir non seulement à répandre puissamment mais aussi à perfectionner la sociologie positive. Sa position dans l'enseignement public lui donne sous le premier rapport de grands avantages, d'autant plus que je luis crois un talent didactique très supérieur.

Je vous félicite cordialement de l'accomplissement de votre pénible corvée de l'hôtel de ville. Vous me ferez grand plaisir en disant à M. Roméo Pouzin combien je suis sensible au souvenir si durable qu'il a gardé de relations si courtes, souvenir aussi doux que flatteur pour moi. Je voudrais qu'il dépendit de moi d'aller le revoir avec vous à Montpellier, où j'espère bien retourner un jour. Si vous voyez M. Balard à Montpellier, je serai charmé d'avoir de ses nouvelles. Je lui ai écrit il y a, je crois trois mois. A moins de quelque chose d'imprévu, je ne doute pas de l'accomplissement de la visite fraternelle que j'ai si longtemps désirée. Au revoir donc dans les derniers jours d'octobre.

Votre tout dévoué

J. S. MILL.

402. TO ALEXANDER BAIN[1]

[Sept., 1843]

I am now vigorously at work reviewing Michelet's *History of France* for the *Edinburgh*. I hope to *do* Napier, and get him to insert it before he finds out what a fatal thing he is doing.

1. Excerpt published in Bain, *JSM*, p. 78. MS not located.

403. TO JULES MICHELET[1]

India House
le 12 septembre
1843

MONSIEUR

Il y a longtemps que notre correspondance est suspendue, et en effet j'ai eu honte de vous écrire à cause de la longue interruption de mon projet de donner dans la revue d'Edinbourg une analyse de vos principaux ouvrages. Une santé faible et des occupations encore plus urgentes ont causé ce délai inattendu, mais aujourd'hui je m'occupe sérieusement d'un article sur votre Histoire de France, où j'ai fait déjà beaucoup de progrès, et je prends la liberté de vous écrire pour vous demander s'il y a des explications quelconques que vous désireriez qu'on donnât au public anglais et dont la revue d'edinbourg serait susceptible de servir d'organe.

Vous savez probablement qu'une revue anglaise, le *British and Foreign Review*, a fait, l'année passée, une assez vive sortie contre vous au sujet de Boniface VIII.[2] Le critique prétend que vous avez fait un récit fort peu exact de la vie de ce pape. Cette revue vous a fait depuis reparation jusqu'à un certain point en citant et en louant votre ouvrage,[3] mais comme l'attaque peut avoir laissé des traces dans quelques esprits, je serais bien aise de faire dire quelque chose là dessus dans l'Edinburgh review si vous m'en fournissez les moyens.

Agréez, Monsieur, l'assurance de ma plus haute estime.

J. S. MILL.

1. *Addressed*: Monsieur / le Professeur Michelet / aux archives du royaume / à Paris. *Postmarks*: LONDON / 12 / SEP / 1843 and [...] ANGL. / 14 / SEPT / 43. MS at Bibliothèque Historique de la Ville de Paris, rue de Sevigné, Paris. Transcript provided by Professor Cecil Lang.
2. "Boniface VIII," *BFR*, XIII (1842), 415–41. Michelet was attacked for misstatements, inadequate use of sources, groundless assertions, important omissions, and "stupid" mistakes.
3. In "Histories of the Reformation" (a review of works by Leopold Ranke and J. H. Merle d'Aubigné), *BFR*, XV (1843), 101–51. At one point, after citing Michelet, this reviewer, in a footnote (p. 119), remarks: "We must not pass by this opportunity of noticing this most singular and original writer; the most attractive of recent historians, with all his faults, of which the vulgar Anti-Anglicism of his last volumes seems to us not the least."

404. TO AUGUSTE COMTE[1]

India House
le 13 octobre
1843

MON CHER MONSIEUR COMTE

Je vous écris à la hâte pour vous annoncer que notre entrevue si long-temps attendue est destinée, cette fois encore, à subir un empêchement. Des circonstances, dont j'ai entrevu la possibilité mais que depuis quelque temps j'avais cessé de croire probables, ont fini par devenir un obstacle décisif à mon voyage.[2] Je suis, par plusieurs raisons, très peu à même de pouvoir faire d'avance avec certitude des projets d'absence, ce qui fait que j'évite toujours soigneusement de faire à cet égard des engagements absolus. Toutefois je croyais, presqu'avec assurance, que celui-ci s'accomplirait. Je regrette beaucoup que je n'aie pas pu vous avertir plustôt, mais les circonstances ne se sont décidées qu'hier au soir après l'heure de la poste. Je désire infiniment que ceci vous parvienne avant le jour fixé pour votre départ de Montpellier.

En répondant à la lettre que vous m'avez écrite de Bordeaux, je reprendrai la discussion sociologique que nous avons entamée et que je regarde avec vous comme une des plus graves que la science puisse comporter. Mais je ne veux pas tarder à vous exprimer dès à présent la félicitation la plus cordiale sur la perspective d'une amélioration important dans votre position à l'école polytechnique.

L'influence naturelle de ce changement, non seulement sur votre propre bonheur, si essentiellement lié à la sécurité de votre avenir matériel, mais encore sur votre autorité intellectuelle et même à certains égards sur la liberté de vos travaux, doit faire accueillir par vos amis toute espérance semblable avec la plus vive satisfaction.

votre dévoué

J. S. MILL.

---

1. *Addressed*: A Monsieur / Auguste Comte / Examinateur pour l'Ecole Polytechnique / en tournée à / Montpellier / département de l'Hérault. *Postmark*: LONDON / 13 / OCT / 1843. MS at Johns Hopkins. Published in Lévy-Bruhl, pp. 254–55; in reply to Comte's of Oct. 5; *ibid.*, pp. 242–53.
2. The probable reasons were the very poor health of Mrs. Taylor at this time and the financial losses he had suffered in the repudiation of some American bonds.

405. TO MACVEY NAPIER[1]

India House
14th Oct. 1843

MY DEAR SIR

I have been a good deal surprised & even pained by some passages relating to my father, in the article on Bentham just published in the Edinburgh Review.[2] Several of the statements made on the authority of Bowring are incorrect in point of fact, but what I chiefly complain of is the insertion of some things reported to have been said by Bentham, calculated to give a most unfavorable, & as every one who really knew my father must be aware, an utterly false impression of the character & temper of his mind. Mr Bentham's best friends well knew—I have heard some of those who were most attached to him lament—his entire incapacity to estimate the characters even of those with whom he associated intimately. The opinions he expressed of people depended very much upon their personal relations to himself: & as in the last few years of his life there was some coolness on his part towards my father, it is not unlikely that he may at times have said unpleasant things of him; but it is surely very blamable in a biographer to publish to the world every casual expression which such a man, or indeed any man, may have let fall to the disparagement of others. The additional publicity which your reviewer has given to the reflection on my father, was entirely unnecessary & uncalled for, in the place where it is introduced, (unless, indeed, lowering my father's character was his express object): & you will, I know, excuse me for saying that I should not have expected, from so old a friend of my father & one who respected him so much as yourself, that you would have been a party to the needless publication of an attack upon him of the most personal kind, from a quarter so suspicious, & yet from the connexion of the reporter with Bentham (which is not commonly known to have been confined to the period of his extreme old age) so likely to be generally credited & circulated.

I feel that something on my part to counteract the impression has now become indispensable. While the mischief was confined to the readers of Bowring's book, I thought it better to take no notice, but publication in the Edinburgh review is another matter. The silence of my father's friends, & of his natural representative, would now amount to acquiescence, & an illhumoured remark, very probably misreported by Bowring, would go down to posterity as a true judgment of my father's character—On such wretched trifles depends the remembrance that mankind retain of those

1. MS in Brit. Mus. Published, with one omission, in *Napier Corresp.*, pp. 441–42.
2. A review [by William Empson] of John Bowring's *Memoirs of Jeremy Bentham* (Edinburgh, 1843) in *ER*, LXXVIII (Oct., 1843), 460–516.

whose whole lives have been devoted to their service. I know I am asking an unusual thing, & though not I believe an unprecedented one, yet one with which I can hardly hope for your compliance—but would it be quite impossible for you to print, with the next number of the review, a short letter from me, containing my protest on the subject?[3] If such a thing is ever admissible, I think this case gives a claim to it, & you are aware how difficult it will otherwise be to find a channel for communicating the truth as extensively & as efficaciously as your review will circulate the calumny.

Believe me my dear Sir
yours very truly
J. S. MILL

406. TO AUGUSTE COMTE[1]

India House
le 17 octobre 1843

MON CHER MONSIEUR COMTE

Je désire vivement que vous ayez reçu, avant de quitter Montpellier, une lettre que je me suis trouvé dans la fâcheuse nécessité de vous écrire pour vous avertir que notre projet d'entrevue avait de nouveau échoué. Quoique je susse toujours que dans certaines éventualités, cette visit amicale pouvait devenir impossible, de manière à me défendre nécessairement toute promesse absolue, cependant depuis quelque temps je croyais ces éventualités assez peu probables pour ne conserver plus aucun doute sérieux sur la réalisation de notre projet. Cette attente a été trompée et j'ai, de plus, le regret de n'avoir pû vous annoncer cette nouvelle que, pour ainsi dire, au dernier moment.

Je ne vous écris aujourd'hui qu'à cause de l'incertitude si ma lettre antérieure vous est parvenue. Je me réserve de répondre, au premier jour de loisir, à votre discussion sur l'importante question sociologique qui nous divise. Je n'ai dans ce moment-ci que le temps d'écrire quelques mots de plus, et je les emploierai à vous parler d'un ancien ami de mon père et de moi-même, M. Austin,[2] qui va passer l'hiver actuel à Paris et qui m'a témoigné un vif désir de vous connaître. C'est un homme d'une haute intelligence et d'une grande élévation de caractère, et je ne pourrais vous

3. The request was granted. See Letter 407.

* * * *

1. *Addressed*: Monsieur / M. Auguste Comte / 10 Rue M. le Prince / près l'Odéon / à Paris. *Postmark*: 17 OCT 17 / 1843. MS at Johns Hopkins. Published in Lévy-Bruhl, pp. 255–56.
2. John Austin.

citer aucun homme dont l'amitié me soit plus précieuse. Par suite d'une mauvaise santé et de son peu de goût pour la société ordinaire, il évite, comme vous, plutôt qu'il ne recherche, toute liaison personnelle nouvelle. Cependant, malgré la superficialité de ses connaissances mathématiques, et nonobstant plusieurs graves dissentimens d'opinion d'avec vos théories sociales, votre ouvrage l'a tellement frappé qu'il regretterait beaucoup de demeurer à Paris sans vous connaître personnellement. Sa femme,[3] beaucoup plus connue que lui, a une certaine réputation de femme supérieure, réputation méritée à quelques égards; elle a d'ailleurs une sociabilité presque française. Je crois vraiment que vous auriez quelque plaisir à les connaître tous deux.

tout à vous

J. S. MILL.

407. TO MACVEY NAPIER[1]

I.H.
21st October 1843

MY DEAR SIR

I am truly sorry that what seems to me a most natural feeling on the subject of the reflections on my father[2] should appear to you unreasonable, & I am proportionally obliged to you for your friendly compliance with a request which you think uncalled for.[3] I shall adhere to your conditions, as indeed I should have done if you had said nothing about them. No review can be expected to insert a controversy with itself—I have no claim upon you for more than an opportunity of correcting false statements or false impressions of fact.

After the most honest self examination I cannot charge myself with any oversusceptibility in the matter. If I had been really chargeable with any, I should have found much more to complain of than I did; for there are other things in the article quite as injurious to my father as the passage which I wrote to you about. There are misstatements of fact, as well as true facts presented in a false light, respecting my father's connexion with Bentham, sufficient to make any one believe that Bentham had conferred upon my father the most sacred obligations, for which he had shewn himself ungrateful. To this however I did not feel that I had any right to object since the

3. Sarah Austin.

* * * *

1. MS in Brit. Mus. Published, with omissions, in *Napier Corresp.*, pp. 442–44.
2. See Letter 405.
3. JSM's vindication of his father appeared under the title, "Letter from John S. Mill, Esq., to the Editor" in *ER*, LXXIX (Jan., 1844), 267–71.

statements were taken from Bowring's book, & had not, as you truly say, been contradicted—indeed I did not know of their existence till I read them in the review. But I did feel hurt, when instead of reprobating the practice of publishing the idle words which one man may say of another in a moment of ill humour, your reviewer repeated & circulated, on no better foundation, general imputations against my father of a selfish, malignant disposition, which I thought you could have told him, from your own knowledge, were grossly unfounded. If he did not give his direct sanction to them, the impression on every reader must be nearly if not quite the same as if he had. Besides, in such a case not to defend is to attack, & the attack was more painful as coming from a friendly quarter.

Neither can I agree with you that the needlessness of the citation is not a thing to be considered. Everybody must judge for himself whether it was needless or not, but whoever judges that it was, will draw his presumptions accordingly respecting the animus of the writer.

The reason why I took no notice of Bowring's book was literally that I had not read it. I never attached sufficient value to anything Bowring could say about Bentham, to feel any curiosity on the subject. I was not then aware that the book contained any misstatement respecting my father's private affairs. This particular passage I certainly was aware of, & intended to notice when I had again occasion to write anything either about Bentham or my father. But my experience of the literary estimation in which Bowring is held, & of his reputation for judgment & accuracy, was not such as to make me believe that the loose talk of Bentham, reported by him, would excite general attention, or pass for more than it is worth. The case is very much altered when that loose talk has received the imprimatur of the Edinburgh Review.

I feel sure that you acted as you thought right, & that you did not know my father sufficiently to feel, in the way I thought you would, the injustice of the accusation. This is no small disappointment to me, but I cannot justly blame you for it, & I can sincerely say that I shall not retain, respecting yourself, any feeling of soreness whatever.

Believe me

my dear Sir

very truly yours

J. S. MILL

My review of Michelet[4] is finished, & I shall probably send it in next week's parcel from Longmans'. I am keeping it a few days for revision.

4. See Letters 285, n. 3, and 333.

India House
23[d] October 1843

MY DEAR FRIEND

I am ashamed when I think that I have not once written to you since you called upon me in your way home—but you would excuse me if you knew in how many ways my time and thoughts have been occupied. It is not, however, so much my work, in the proper sense, as by other things, for I have written little or nothing, extraofficially, except an article on the recent French historians, & especially on Michelet's History of France,[2] which I have just finished & which has brought my hand in again for work. You will see it in the Edin. Review unless Napier takes fright at some of the very heterodox things, in the eyes of an Edinburgh reviewer, still at the point of view of the 18th century, which the article contains. There is in particular some arrant Hildebrandism[3] which I suspect will shock him especially after the Scotch kirk controversy.[4]

By the by you will perhaps see in the same number another communication[5] from me, with my name signed to it, occasioned by a shabby, trumpery article on Bentham which has just appeared in the review. The writer's object seems to be to bring down as much as he can the character both of Bentham and of every one whose name has ever been connected with his— & he states facts & opinions respecting my father against which I have thought it imperative on me to protest publicly & have asked Napier to let me do it by a letter in his review, which he has consented to. I am sure if you have seen the article you will say it was high time.

I went down for a day to Sterling at Ventnor[6] a few weeks ago, & found him as cheerful & as well as could be hoped for after what he has gone through. He had got into his house, & what remained to be done by work-

1. *Addressed*: R. Barclay Fox / Perran Cottage / near Truro. *Postmark*: TRURO / OC 24 / 1843. MS in the possession of Mr. W. H. Browning. Published in part in Pym, II, 341–42.
2. See preceding letter, n. 4.
3. In the review JSM praised the mediaeval Catholic Church as "the authorized champion of intelligence and self-control" and as at that time "the great improver and civilizer of Europe" (*Dissertations*, II, 231). He also praised Hildebrand, Pope Gregory VII (*ca.* 1025–1085), for strengthening the power of the papacy against the state and for his reforms within the church itself (*ibid.*, pp. 236–37).
4. Earlier in 1843 a long-threatened schism in the Church of Scotland on the question of its Assembly's power over local presbyteries had resulted in the withdrawal of about one-third of its ministers and members to form the Free Church of Scotland.
5. See preceding letter, n. 3.
6. After the death of his mother and his wife in April, Sterling had bought a house at Ventnor, Isle of Wight, and moved his family there in June, 1843.

people would soon be finished. Ventnor is a little cocknified place which has grown up on the site of a very small country village, but Sterling's is the most desirable situation in it, being the *highest*—it looks over the village to the sea, & itself abuts upon the almost precipitous side of a walk down where the sheep bells tinkle close to his windows. Moreover there are just trees enough about the house to cover it up when you look at it from below. He is much pleased at the thought of having at last a fixed home & it is much in favour of his health & spirits that he is now, for the first time quite free from all anxiety about pecuniary matters. But here have I been describing the place to you as if you had not seen it. I have probably, indeed, a stronger *impression* about it than you, as I have *lived in* the house for 24 hours.—Sterling is now in town, on business, for a few days. I have seen him—he continues well. His father though still appearing much broken, certainly seems a good deal better.

Thanks for the votes which *your* (*plural*) persevering kindness has got for the little girl.[7] With regards & remembrances to all

Yours

J. S. MILL.

Clara continues well & prosperous—she is still at Frankfort.

409. TO CAROLINE AND ANNA MARIA FOX[1]

[Oct. 23, 1843][2]

I just slip in this little bit of paper for the sake of remembrance & to say—no, to say that I do not know what to say to such a flaming panegyric as that bestowed on my unworthiness by a young lady who has done me the honour to learn fallacies under my tuition. In spite of so much encouragement I cannot in conscience take off my injunction against reading the remainder of the book (which however is, I assure you, quite as clever) so whoever does read any of it must know that she does it at her own risk & responsibility.

The only as lofty panegyric that I have yet met with is from the Puseyite review the British Critic,[3] which almost exhausts language in admiration of me & my book, & then adds that notwithstanding I shall certainly go

7. See Letter 387.

* * * *

1. MS in the possession of Mr. W. H. Browning.
2. As the article referred to in the body of the letter appeared in Oct., this letter is probably of the same date as the preceding one to R. B. Fox, with which it was presumably enclosed.
3. *British Critic*, XXXIV (Oct., 1843), 349–427, by W. G. Ward.

to ———. I trust there was no such mental reservation in the praise of my other eulogist.

I wish heartily I could walk to Falmouth (or Rome) one of these fine mornings. I want extremely to look upon the blue Cornish sea or the Mediterranean for one half hour, not to speak of the Ariadne in the Vatican, & the two young Cornish women whose names you will find somewhere on the envelope.

J.S.M.

410. TO AUGUSTE COMTE[1]

India House
le 30 octobre 1843

MON CHER MONSIEUR COMTE,

Notre dissidence sur la question que vous caractérisez avec raison comme la plus fondamentale que puissent présenter les spéculations sociales ne doit certainement faire naître aucune inquiétude sur la possibilité finale d'une suffisante convergence d'opinion parmi les gens instruits, sur des bases purement rationnelles. Mais cette dissidence, et la manière de penser que la discussion dévoile de part et d'autre, me confirme dans l'opinion que les bases intellectuelles de la sociologie statique ne sont pas encore suffisamment préparées. Les fondements de la dynamique sociale sont aujourd'hui, à mon gré, pleinement constitués: mais, quant à la statique, l'histoire n'y tenant plus la première place, et n'y pouvant servir qu'à titre d'éclaircissement en quelque sorte accessoire, quoique je ne me dissimule pas l'importance de ce rôle secondaire; le passage de la statique sociale à l'état vraiment positif exige par conséquent, comparativement à la dynamique, une bien plus grande perfection de la science de l'homme individuel. Il suppose surtout un état très avancé de la science secondaire que j'ai nommée Ethologie,[2] c.à.d. de la théorie de l'influence des diverses circonstances extérieures, soit individuelles, soit sociales, sur la formation du caractère moral et intellectuel. Cette théorie, base nécessaire de l'éducation rationnelle, me paraît aujourd'hui la moins avancée de toutes les spéculations scientifiques un peu importantes. Une certaine connaissance réelle, même empirique, de cet ordre de rapports naturels, me semble on ne peut plus rare, et les saines observations ne le sont pas moins, soit par la difficulté du

---

1. *Addressed*: Monsieur / Auguste Comte / 10 Rue M. le Prince / près l'Odéon / à Paris. *Postmark*: 30 OCT 30 / 1843. MS at Johns Hopkins. Published in Lévy-Bruhl, pp. 259–72; in reply to Comte's of Oct. 5 and 22, *ibid.*, pp. 242–53, 257–59.
2. JSM's projected book on ethology, the science of the formation of character, had been outlined in Book VI, chap. 5 of the *Logic*, but it was never completed. See also Letters 416, 417, and 482.

sujet, soit par la tendance qui prévaut le plus souvent dans cet ordre de recherches, à regarder comme inexplicable tout ce qu'on n'est point parvenu à expliquer. Le genre d'étude biologique commencé, quoique avec une grande exagération, par Helvétius, n'a trouvé personne pour le poursuivre; et je ne puis pas m'empêcher de croire que la réaction du 19ᵐᵉ siècle contre la philosophie du 18ᵐᵉ a déterminé aujourd'hui une exagération en sens contraire, tendant à faire aux diversités primitives une part trop large, et à dissimuler, sous plusieurs rapports, leur vrai caractère. Je trouve très naturel que vous expliquiez chez moi cette opinion par mon insuffisante connaissance de la théorie physique de la vie animale, et surtout de la physiologie cérébrale. Je fais, et je continuerai à faire mon possible pour faire disparaître toute objection semblable. J'ai fait des études consciencieuses sur ce sujet; j'ai même lu avec une attention scrupuleuse les six volumes de Gall. J'ai trouvé fort juste une grande partie de sa polémique contre la psychologie de ses devanciers, dont au reste j'avais dès longtemps dépassé le point de vue: mais vous savez déjà que les principes généraux qui seuls selon vous sont jusqu'ici constatés dans la science phrénologique, ne me paraissent nullement prouvés par son livre, qui, au contraire, s'il prouvait quelque chose, tendrait plutôt, il me semble, conformément à l'intention de l'auteur, à déterminer l'organe cérébral de certains instincts spéciaux, soit animaux, soit particulièrement mentaux. J'admets la nécessité de prendre en sérieuse considération tous les rapports qu'on peut espérer d'établir entre la structure anatomique et les fonctions intellectuelles ou morales: je saisirai avec empressement tout moyen de m'éclairer davantage sur ce sujet; si vous m'indiquez dans ce but quelques nouvelles lectures à faire, je les ferai: mais tout ce que j'ai lu ou pensé jusqu'ici me porte à croire que rien n'est vraiment établi—que tout est encore vague et incertain dans cet ordre de spéculations. Il me semble même très difficile qu'elles sortent de cet état, tant que l'analyse éthologique de l'influence des circonstances extérieures, même générales, est aussi peu avancée qu'elle l'est; les diversités anatomiques ne devant répondre qu'à des *résidus* (pour me servir ici de ma terminologie logique),[3] après qu'on a soustrait du phénomène total, tout ce qui comporte une autre explication quelconque. Si, dans notre discussion sur les tendances caractéristiques des deux sexes, j'ai cité une opinion que je savais être celle de plusieurs physiologistes éminens, et qui ferait croire les femmes moins propres que les hommes aux travaux cérébraux de longue haleine, partant aux sciences et à la philosophie, ce n'est pas que ce soit là mon opinion propre; je la donnais comme la seule parmi les théories de ce genre qui ne me semblait pas en contradiction flagrante avec les faits: encore si on l'admettait, elle n'indiquerait de la part des

---

3. See his discussion of the method of residues in his *Logic*, Book III, chap. VIII, sec. 5.

femmes, aucune inaptitude pour la science, mais seulement une moindre vocation spéciale pour elle. Maintenant, que cette théorie physiologique soit vraie ou non, c'est ce que je ne prétends pas décider; les progrès scientifiques le décideront probablement un jour. J'écarterai donc, dans la suite de notre discussion, les considérations anatomiques en me tenant disposé à accueillir tout renseignement nouveau que vous puissiez m'indiquer ou qui se présente de toute autre part. Vous pensez d'ailleurs qu'indépendamment de ces considérations, une analyse exacte de l'expérience générale, tant usuelle qu'historique, suffit pour établir vos conclusions.

Quant à l'expérience usuelle, j'avoue que la mienne ne s'accorde pas, en ce qui est en question, avec la vôtre. Ne croyez pas que je me flatte aucunement de bien connaître les femmes; il est très difficile de connaître intimement qui que ce soit; et la difficulté pour tout être mâle de connaître réellement, je ne dis pas les femmes, mais une femme quelconque, est le plus souvent insupérable [*sic*]. Celui qui les connaît le mieux à certains égards, ne les connaît pas du tout à d'autres. Cependant je crois le milieu anglais plus favorable, à tout prendre, pour les connaître, que le français. D'après tout ce que j'ai pu apprendre, soit par les livres, soit par ma propre observation ou par celle des autres, l'éducation des jeunes filles est beaucoup plus sexuelle, pour ainsi dire, en france, qu'elle ne l'est en angleterre. Je ne dis pas ceci dans le sens physique, quoique à cet égard aussi ce soit vrai: je veux dire que l'effet à produire sur l'autre sexe leur est habituellement présent, pour ne pas dire habituellement proposé, comme but principal de leur conduite, et même dès l'enfance. Cela est beaucoup moins vrai ici, cela n'est même pas vrai du tout, en thèse générale, et cette différence a des résultats immenses, non seulement sur le développement propre de leurs facultés mais sur la possibilité aux hommes de les bien connaître, puisqu'en france elles sont constituées en état permanent de simulation: ici, au contraire, il y a seulement, en général, de la dissimulation, effet de la compression sociale, encore celle-là même est essentiellement involontaire, les femmes, le plus souvent, n'en ayant, elles-mêmes presque pas conscience. Elles se regardent certainement chez nous, et les hommes les regardent aussi, moins comme femmes, et beaucoup plus comme des êtres humains en général. Leur éducation leur impose bien, en leur qualité de femmes, quelques règles spéciales de bienséance, mais comme préceptes généraux, et sans qu'elles les rapportent à leur position envers les hommes, ou envers un homme quelconque. Leur dépendance sociale gêne beaucoup leur développement mais ne l'altère pas autant qu'en france.

Quoi qu'il en soit de cela, mes propres observations ne m'indiquent rien qui puisse justifier le jugement absolu que vous portez sur les femmes, d'incapacité pour toute direction des affaires quelconques. D'abord à l'égard du gouvernement domestique, il est, je crois, généralement reconnu que les ménages sont mieux gouvernés en angleterre que partout ailleurs, du moins en ce qui regarde la discipline et l'obéissance, tant à l'égard des enfants qu'à celui des domestiques. Ces derniers ont en général (si on excepte l'Ecosse) moins d'intelligence qu'en France ou en Italie, mais ils font leur tâche avec beaucoup plus d'exactitude et de perfection matérielle, qui pourtant ne s'obtiennent qu'au prix d'une surveillance intelligente et continue. Or le gouvernement domestique appartient ici exclusivement à la femme: le mari se croirait ridicule s'il s'en mêlait: il est très souvent d'une ignorance et d'une incapacité souveraine dans tout ce genre de détails. Pour la direction industrielle, les femmes ne l'ont jamais exercée jusqu'ici qu'en des établissements d'une étendue très modérée, où pourtant on n'a pas remarqué quelles s'en soient plus mal acquittées que les hommes, ni que l'esprit de suite leur ait manqué: effectivement quand on veut s'entendre sur le sens des mots, je ne trouve pas que ce soit du tout ce qui leur manque. L'esprit de suite qui vous paraît avec raison la principale condition du succès prolongé dans les entreprises industrielles de premier ordre, ne peut pas être la capacité de soutenir une forte contention intellectuelle pendant huit ou dix heures par jour: s'il en était ainsi, fort peu d'hommes s'en tireraient avec succès. Ce qui fait l'esprit de suite, c'est sans doute la persévérance dans un dessein arrêté ou dans un plan donné, jusqu'à ce que l'essai en soit suffisamment fait. Or je ne crois pas qu'on puisse contester cela aux femmes, comparativement aux hommes. Je ne crois pas que le caprice, que la mobilité, dont on les accuse (quoiqu'on soit bien loin de les en accuser en angleterre) s'exercent dans les choses qui regardent leurs intérêts permanents; je crois qu'on ne trouve nulle part, dans les desseins importants, plus de patience et de longanimité que chez elles: d'ailleurs je trouve leur caprice, même dans les cas les plus caractérisés, beaucoup plus apparent que réel, quoiqu'elles sachent quelquefois très bien s'en servir comme moyen d'agir sur ceux parmi les hommes qui les envisagent, pour citer vos paroles, comme de charmans jouets. Vous les jugez moins aptes que les hommes à la prépondérance de la raison sur la passion, c'est-à-dire, plus portées à suivre l'impulsion présente de tout désir énergique. Je pourrais dire au contraire qu'elles le sont beaucoup moins, si je voulais juger cette question d'après l'expérience journalière; car le renoncement aux choses qu'elles désirent est chez elles l'ordre usuel de la vie, au lieu que chez les chefs de famille mâles ces sacrifices n'arrivent guère que dans les grandes occasions, et que ces chefs se montrent ordinairement très peu patients à les supporter dans les choses où ils ne s'en sont pas fait une habitude. Mais je ne veux rien fonder là dessus, parce que je reconnais dans la patience des femmes ainsi que dans l'impatience des hommes en ce qui froisse leurs inclinations, l'effet naturel de la puissance d'une part et de la dépendance de l'autre. Il faut donc décider cette question par des considérations *à priori*. Or il me semble que la prépondérance de la raison sur l'inclination est proportionnée à l'habitude qu'on a de s'examiner soi-même, et de se rendre compte de son caractère et de ses défauts. Celui qui n'est point parvenu à avoir la conscience exacte de son propre caractère, ne saura pas diriger sa conduite d'après sa raison. Il continuera d'obéir à ses habitudes, soit d'action, soit de sentiment ou de pensée. Je crois que cet examen de soi-même, malheureusement trop rare partout, l'est pour le moins autant chez le sexe mâle que chez les femmes. Une conscience intime de soi-même, et l'empire sur soi qui en résulte, sont des faits très exceptionnels chez les uns et les autres: mais si vous demandiez à la plupart des anglais leur jugement sur ce point, vous trouverez chez eux, quelle que soit d'ailleurs leur opinion sur le compte des femmes, un préjugé tout contraire à la doctrine que vous soutenez; beaucoup d'entre eux seraient portés à croire les mâles incapables d'exercer sur eux-mêmes une force de répression morale égale à celle qu'ils regardent comme le propre des femmes. Sans partager cette idée exagérée, je l'admets au moins comme indice que le témoignage de l'expérience n'est pas exclusivement de l'autre côté. D'ailleurs, l'opinion générale accorde aux femmes une conscience ordinairement plus scrupuleuse que celle des hommes: or qu'est-ce que la conscience, si ce n'est pas la soumission des passions à la raison?

Je viens maintenant à l'argument fondé sur la persistance, jusqu'à notre temps, de la subalternité sociale des femmes, comparée à l'émancipation graduelle des classes inférieures dans les nations les plus avancées, quoique ces classes aient partout commencé par être esclaves. Cette différence historique ne vous paraît explicable que par une infériorité organique de la part des femmes. Je crois pourtant voir à cet argument une réponse suffisante. Il est vrai que les esclaves sont parvenus, dans les populations d'élite, à s'élever jusqu'à la liberté, et même quelquefois à l'égalite sociale. Mais je ne crois pas que cela ait jamais eu lieu à l'égard des esclaves domestiques. Ceux-là ne se sont, je crois, jamais émancipés eux-mêmes: ils y sont parvenus à la suite des autres esclaves, sans y avoir contribué par leurs propres efforts. C'est qu'il y a dans la dépendance continue, dans celle de tous les instants, quelque chose qui énerve l'âme, et qui arrête dès le commencement tout essor vers l'indépendance. Le serf est dans une tout autre position: il a des devoirs plus ou moins fixes à remplir envers son maître; ces devoirs remplis, il est à peu près libre: il a de la propriété à lui; il est forcé à la prévoyance; il ne reçoit pas le pain d'autrui, il est chargé du soin de sa propre subsistance: il a même du pouvoir sur les autres; il est maître chez lui; il a femme et enfants, il est responsable pour eux, il s'exerce dans le commandement, il apprend à se croire quelque chose. Tout cela était déjà vrai, jusqu'à un certain point, chez les esclaves agricoles des anciens; et pourtant, le premier pas dans leur émancipation, celui de leur transformation en serfs, n'a pas, je crois, résulté de leurs propres efforts, mais de l'intérêt des maîtres, secondés par l'autorité morale de l'église. C'est seulement depuis l'état de servage que leur élévation sociale a été essentiellement duê à eux-mêmes. Or il faut reconnaître que la position spéciale des femmes, quoique sans doute très supérieure en Europe à ce que furent jamais les serfs, est dépourvue de cette demi-indépendance, de cette habitude de diriger, entre certaines limites, leurs propres intérêts, sans aucune intervention supérieure, qui a toujours appartenu aux serfs, et qui a été, ce me semble, la principale source de l'essor par lequel ils se sont peu à peu élevés à la liberté. La servitude des femmes, quoique bien plus douce, est une servitude sans intermission, et qui s'étend à tous les actes, et qui les décharge, bien plus complètement que les serfs de toute haute prévoyance et de toute vraie direction de leur propre conduite, soit envers la société, soit même dans le sens de l'intérêt individuel. Cela étant, la douceur comparative de cette servitude est une raison de plus pour qu'elle se prolonge. Je ne crois pas qu'il y ait un homme sur cent mille, qui, n'ayant jamais joui de la liberté, soit capable de la préférer à l'état d'esclave caressé, état si conforme à la paresse qui est universelle et à la lâcheté qui est très générale dans notre espèce. Jamais d'ailleurs des esclaves quelconques n'ont été si soigneusement élevés, dès la première enfance, dans la ferme croyance qu'ils doivent toujours être assujettis à d'autres hommes, et que les affaires réelles de la vie ne sont pas du tout de leur ressort, que le sont et l'ont toujours été les femmes. Tous les ressorts sympathiques de leur nature particulière sont employés à leur faire chercher le bonheur non pas dans leur vie propre, mais exclusivement dans la faveur et dans l'affection de l'autre sexe, ce qui ne leur est accordé qu'à condition de dépendance: peu importe alors qu'un grand nombre d'entr'elles vivent et meurent sans se lier à aucun homme, puisque la direction exclusive de leur esprit et de leur ambition dans ce sens pendant leur jeunesse doit empêcher plus tard, si ce n'est dans des cas tout à fait exceptionnels, tout élan réel dans une autre direction, même en supposant une suffisante indépendance pécuniaire, et le milieu social le plus favorable. Il est inutile de vous parler de l'influence que doit exercer l'intimité toute particulière de cette classe de dépendants avec leurs maîtres, intimité si au-delà de celle qui peut exister dans tout autre cas; je ne parle pas non plus de l'influence morale de l'infériorité en force physique, qui, même en ne supposant, du côté des mâles, aucun abus direct de leur puissance musculaire, doit nécessairement amener un certain respect involontaire, et une certaine habitude de dépendance, qui finit même souvent par s'établir entre deux mâles dont l'un est plus faible que l'autre, s'ils sont très liés ensemble.

Ces considérations me paraissent plus que suffisantes pour expliquer un retard presqu'indéfini de l'émancipation sociale des femmes, sans qu'on puisse induire delà qu'elle ne doive jamais arriver. Au moins vous avouerez qu'elle ne pouvait avoir lieu que longtemps après celle des serfs, qui n'est pas elle-même un fait très ancien. Il me semble, au reste, que l'élévation des femmes est déjà aussi avancée, et qu'elle s'avance aussi vite, qu'on pourrait s'y attendre, d'après la théorie de l'égalité naturelle. Elles ne peuvent pas faire comme les serfs, qui ne se sont affranchis qu'en formant des sociétés à part, c'est-à-dire les villes, où même, le plus souvent, ils ont eu à soutenir une longue lutte militaire avec leurs seigneurs: lutte dans laquelle leur supériorité en nombre, accompagnée d'égalité en forces physiques, fut une compensation puissante de leur infériorité en éducation militaire. Les femmes, au contraire, ne pouvaient s'élever socialement qu'en prouvant de plus en plus, par des efforts individuels, dans toutes les carrières qui ne leur sont pas interdites, qu'elles sont capables de plus grandes choses qu'on ne leur accordait auparavant. Il me semble qu'à cet égard elles font de rapides progrès, et que par ce moyen, le seul possible, leur affranchissement s'opérera par elles-mêmes. Depuis un siècle chaque génération a dépasse la précédente quant au nombre et au mérite de leurs écrits: ce mouvement progressif est surtout devenu très accéléré en France et en Angleterre depuis 50 ans. Plusieurs femmes se sont même élevées, dans leurs écrits, jusqu'au génie créateur; quoique les facultés qui le con-stituent ne dussent servir le plus souvent, chez le sexe qui ne fait pas d'ordinaire des études sérieuses et qui n'a pas à vivre de son travail, qu'à titre d'ornement, ou tout au plus au bonheur de la vie intérieure. Ce qui leur a principalement manqué jusqu'ici en littérature comme dans les beaux-arts, c'est une forte originalité; mais il est très naturel que cela manque, surtout dans les commencemens, à ceux qui viennent les derniers: ce sont les romains qui viennent après les grecs. La littérature féminine a nécessairement commencé par imiter la masculine; elle s'est conformée aux types et aux idées reçues, et ce n'est que d'aujourd'hui qu'on voit des femmes qui écrivent comme femmes, avec leurs sentimens et leur expérience féminine. Elles feront cela, je crois, de plus en plus, et je ne doute pas qu'alors on ne voie cesser le reproche qu'on leur a fait de n'avoir rien su créer de premier ordre, car toute grande création suppose nécessairement une conception originale.

Je ne dirai qu'une chose de plus. Dans la haute direction des affaires humaines, le rôle de reine est le seul qui ne soit pas fermé aux femmes. Ce rôle seul, par une anomalie accidentelle que vous qualifiez de ridicule, et qui l'est en effet par son contraste bizarre avec l'ensemble de leur position sociale, leur est resté ouvert dans la plupart des pays européens. Or, à partir du tems où la royauté a cessé d'exiger surtout la capacité militaire, jusqu'à celle [*sic*] où elle a commencé à ne plus exiger, ni même en quelque sorte comporter, aucune capacité quelconque; dans cet intervalle d'à peu près deux siècles, les reines n'ont-elles pas honorablement rempli leur fonction sociale? et l'histoire ne montre-t-elle pas dans ce temps tout autant de grandes reines, proportion gardée, que de grands rois? Je le crois du moins, et cette expérience, faite en des circonstances qui sont très loin d'être favorables, ne doit pas avoir peu de poids, à ce qui m'en semble, dans la question de leur capacité gouvernementale. Je vous envoie, comme vous voyez, mon cher Monsieur Comte, un traité au lieu d'une lettre.[4] Je ne m'en excuse pas, car sans doute vous pensez comme moi qu'une question si fondamentale mérite qu'on la retourne de tous les côtés, et qu'on ne perd pas son temps à la discuter longuement. Je tiens d'ailleurs beaucoup à ce que vous ne croyiez pas que ce soit ici de ma part une idée légèrement adoptée: il y a peu de questions que j'aie plus méditées, et bien qu'en général je sois connu pour ne pas tenir à des opinions une fois admises, dès qu'on me prouve qu'elles sont mal fondées, celle-ci a résisté chez moi à tout ce qu'on lui a opposé jusqu'ici. Comme vous avez aussi de votre part une opinion très arrêtée, il n'est guère probable qu'une discussion épisto-laire, ou même orale, fasse disparaître notre dissentiment, mais elle peut, sans cela, nous être, de plus d'une manière, très utile.

Il me reste peu de place pour vous parler d'autre chose. J'ai fait part à M. Austin de votre aimable intention de faire en sa faveur une exception à votre règle d'éviter les nouvelles connaissances. Il y est très sensible et se propose d'aller vous voir. Je pense que vous vous en trouverez bien: c'est un homme très digne de votre sympathie, et dont la conversation est pleine d'idées justes et profondes. Je ne connais personne qui juge plus sainement l'angleterre, et aussi, autant que je puis prononcer là dessus, l'allemagne, où il a longtemps séjourné.

Mon jeune ami Bain est digne de tout votre intérêt, et tout annonce qu'il ne trompera pas nos espérances. Il m'écrit souvent de l'Ecosse des lettres admirables de bon sens et de profondeur. Il trouve les esprits, même dans ce pays si religieux en apparence, merveilleusement bien préparés pour l'avènement final du positivisme. "At a distance," dit-il, "one can hardly believe, how very few points of every day human life are touched by theologic views. Theology is descending rapidly to the mere Esthetic & to a bond of social agglomeration, the desire of which last is its greatest hold."

votre dévoué

J. S. MILL.

---

4. JSM's discussion here of the role and education of women should be compared with his final treatment of the topic in *The Subjection of Women* (London, 1869).

411. TO ALEXANDER BAIN[1]

Nov. 3, 1843

My review of Michelet is in Napier's hands. If he prints it, he will make some of his readers stare.

412. TO ALEXIS DE TOCQUEVILLE[1]

Le 3 novembre 1843.

Vous savez, mon cher Tocqueville, combien tout ce qui vient de vous m'est agréable et vous ne pouvez douter du plaisir que m'a donné l'opinion si flatteuse que vous venez de me témoigner à l'égard de ma *Logique*, et qui est d'autant plus précieuse qu'elle vient d'une lecture lente et consciencieuse. C'est un grand bonheur d'écrire pour des intelligences et pour des caractères comme la vôtre, quand on est assez heureux pour obtenir leur approbation. Je vous suis d'ailleurs redevable de tant d'instruction et de plaisir intellectuel que j'ai toujours très vivement désiré de pouvoir un jour payer *in kind*, comme nous disons, et de mériter auprès de vous l'honneur d'être regardé comme un collaborateur réel dans la cause du progrès intellectuel et social. J'éprouve un grand plaisir en apprenant que vous partagez mes idées sur la méthode propre à perfectionner la science sociale: les suffrages qu'on doit le plus ambitionner en pareille matière sont ceux du très petit nombre des penseurs qui, comme vous, ont rendu des services vraiment importants à cette science. Votre approbation du point de vue d'où j'ai envisagé la question de la liberté humaine m'est aussi très précieuse. Je regarde moi-même ce chapitre-là[2] comme le plus important du livre : il est l'expression fidèle des idées où j'étais arrivé depuis bientôt quinze ans, que je n'avais jamais écrites, mais dans lesquelles je puis dire que j'avais trouvé la paix, puisqu'elles seules avaient satisfait pleinement chez moi au besoin de mettre en harmonie l'intelligence et la conscience, en posant sur des bases intellectuelles solides le sentiment de la responsabilité humaine. Je ne crois pas qu'aucun penseur un peu sérieux puisse jouir d'une vraie tranquillité d'esprit et d'âme, jusqu'à ce qu'il ait accompli quelque solution satisfaisante de ce grand problème. Je ne desire pas imposer ma propre solution à ceux qui sont satisfaits de la leur, mais je crois qu'il y a beaucoup d'hommes pour qui elle sera, comme elle a été pour moi, une véritable ancre de salut.

Je compte bien, suivant vos aimables conseils, ne pas en rester à ce

1. Excerpt published in Bain, *JSM*, p. 78. MS not located.

* * * *

1. Published in Mayer, pp. 346–47; in reply to Tocqueville's of Oct. 27, *ibid.*, pp. 344–46. MS in Tocqueville archives.
2. Book VI, chap. 2, "Of Liberty and Necessity."

seul ouvrage, quoique je ne me trouve pas de force à traiter systématiquement une science aussi difficile et aussi peu avancée que celle de la politique.
J'ai l'espoir d'y contribuer quelque chose par des travaux partiels quoique
je n'aie pas encore décidé ce qu'ils seront. En attendant je m'occupe un
peu de faire connaître en Angleterre les bons écrivains français: je viens
de faire un article sur les historiens et notamment sur Michelet.[3] Et vous,
que ferez-vous? Vous consacrerez-vous maintenant uniquement à la
politique? Je le regretterais beaucoup, car tout en appréciant très hautement
la valeur de la chaire politique (si cette expression est permise), je crois
qu'il y a plus d'hommes capables de faire le peu qu'on puisse faire à présent
dans la vie publique qu'il y en a qui peuvent écrire des livres tels que vous
pourriez les faire. Ne traiterez-vous jamais la France comme vous avez
traité l'Amérique? Vous l'avez bien commencé dans ce petit écrit dont
vous parlez dans votre lettre et qui déjà jette une lumière importante sur
plusieurs questions sociales et historiques généralement très mal comprises.

Merci mille et mille fois de votre invitation amicale. Il n'y en a point
à laquelle je me rendrais avec plus de plaisir mais je n'ose rien promettre,
à cause de la rareté et de la courte durée de mes vacances qui, par conséquent, sont presque toujours remplies par des obligations indispensables.

Ne viendrez-vous jamais ici?

Votre tout dévoué

J. S. MILL.

India House.

413. TO ALEXANDER BAIN[1]

[Autumn, 1843]

There is no chance, for Social Statics[2] at least, until the laws of human
character are better treated.

414. TO HENRY COLE[1]

I. H. Tuesday
[Nov. 14, 1843]

MY DEAR COLE

A year or two ago when you said something to me about paying the
£100 which I had the pleasure of accommodating you with formerly, I

---

3. See Letters 285, n. 3, and 333.

* * * *

1. Excerpt published in Bain, *JSM*, p. 78. MS not located.
2. See Letters 410 and 416.

* * * *

1. MS in the possession of the Rt. Rev. Charles Larrabee Street, as is also Cole's
reply of Nov. 15, 1843.

said to you "pay me *last*". Now however I have certain reasons for wishing to call in all money due to me[2] & I therefore write to retract what I then said.

I have always considered the help I then gave you as a just & proper support to the honorable & public spirited course you took at that time.[3] If you had been thrown out of office and emolument permanently by your conduct at that time I should never have asked you for payment nor regretted the loss. Nor have I ever said a word to you about it until now. Now however I should really be very glad if you would make the earliest arrangements for the payment, either at once or by instalments, as would not interfere with you & your family's comfort & convenience, and I only mention this because, though I always knew you would pay me if you lived & had the means, you might suppose that the time of payment still continued to be altogether unimportant to me, which however is no longer the case.

Very truly yours,

J. S. MILL

415. TO HENRY COLE[1]

I.H. Thursday
[Nov. 16, 1843]

MY DEAR COLE

Your letter is all that is right & honorable, & kind also. No explanation was requisite of your not having paid the money, as I always ascribed it to the causes you mention—except that I did not know how you had acted about the Guide,[2] which does you great honour.

The reasons which induce me to wish for the money are not so urgent

2. JSM and his family had lost heavily by the repudiation of debts by some of the American states. See Letter 331, n. 2.

3. Cole had been employed by a newly established Record Commission in 1831, under the secretaryship of Charles Purton Cooper (1793–1873). In 1836, at the risk of losing his position, Cole had memorialized the Record Commission about the arbitrary conduct of Cooper. Cole's appeal to his friend Charles Buller led to Buller's bringing the subject of the mismanagement of the Record Commission before the House of Commons on Feb. 18, 1836. A subsequent investigation led to the vindication of Cole and the establishment of the Public Record Office in 1838, at which time Cole was appointed one of the four senior assistant-keepers (see Sir Henry Cole, *Fifty Years of Public Work* [2 vols., London, 1884], I, 1–33).

* * * *

1. MS in the possession of the Rt. Rev. Charles Larrabee Street. Endorsed in another hand: "J. Mill 1843. Agreeing to proposed time of payment of loan—H.C."

2. The *Guide* was a weekly newspaper established by Molesworth, J. T. Leader, Cole and others, with Cole as editor; it ran from April 22, 1837, to April 1, 1838. Cole, in his answer to JSM's letter of Nov. 14, 1843, explained that he had discharged debts of the *Guide* of £150 more than need to have been ascribed to him.

as to time, as to require that you should put yourself at all out of the way to pay me in a shorter time than that you mention. Nor even, if it should prove more inconvenient than you expect, would I have you make a point of doing it even in that time unless my need of it should grow stronger than I can at present foresee. All I intended to ask of you was exactly what you say—that it should be put in train as among the first things to be settled.

Ever yours
with sincere regard
J. S. Mill

416. TO AUGUSTE COMTE[1]

India House
le 8 décembre 1843

Mon cher Monsieur Comte,

Puisque vous jugez que la discussion qui a tenu dernièrement une si grande place dans notre correspondance, est maintenant parvenue au point au delà duquel elle ne peut plus être portée avec avantage, je m'abstiendrai de la prolonger en y ajoutant des observations quelconques sur votre dernière lettre. Cette lettre n'a nullement ébranlé ma conviction, comme, en effet, elle n'y était pas destinée, mais seulement à mieux constater les points de divergence entre nos deux manières de penser. Je dois dire pourtant que plus je médite cette question, et plus je me raffermis dans mon opinion, qui, de très ancienne date chez moi, ne s'est pas trouvée démentie mais certainement confirmée par les faits qui se sont présentés à mon observation dans la vie; en quoi elle diffère de beaucoup d'autres opinions que j'avais seulement acceptées de la philosophie négative de mon temps et que j'ai depuis modifiées ou abandonnées. Permettez-moi de dire aussi que notre discussion, par cela même qu'elle n'a pas changé mon opinion, a nécessairement tendu à la fortifier; car malgré l'élaboration plus complette que vous vous proposez de donner à cette question dans le Traité dont vous allez commencer la préparation, je suis bien persuadé que vous possédez parfaitement tout ce qu'on peut dire de mieux à l'appui d'une doctrine à laquelle vous tenez si fortement, et je crois que ce qui vous reste à dire ne pourra plus être que le commentaire, en quelque sorte, de ce que vous m'avez déjà indiqué.

Cette discussion a laissé chez moi, à d'autres égards, des traces permanentes, et je pense qu'elle aura un certain effet sur la direction de mes travaux à venir. Je vois de plus en plus que c'est la statique sociale qui maintenant appelle surtout les esprits convenablement préparés. Vous avez

---

1. MS at Johns Hopkins. Published in Lévy-Bruhl, pp. 283–87; in reply to Comte's of Nov. 14, *ibid.*, pp. 273–83.

fondé définitivement la sociologie dynamique, et nul esprit émancipé, suffisamment pourvu de connaissances positives, ne peut manquer à reconnaître dans votre grande loi du développement humain et dans ses divers corollaires, une explication vraie de l'ensemble du passé social, et la prophétie d'un avenir indéfini. Il importe à présent que la statique sociale soit maintenue au niveau de la dynamique, qui sans elle, ne peut pas être, comme vous le dites très bien, suffisamment rationnelle, ni surtout servir nullement à contrôler l'anarchie actuelle des doctrines sociales. Pour cela je crois qu'il faut surtout travailler à perfectionner, ou plutôt, on peut presque dire, à créer l'Ethologie; en appréciant convenablement la nature et le degré des effets éthologiques produits soit par l'organisation, soit par les diverses circonstances extérieures. Je conviens avec vous que dans ces spéculations, où la méthode des résidus doit nécessairement devenir d'un usage très étendu, l'ordre des soustractions partielles n'est rien moins qu'indifférent. On doit, ce me semble, commencer par soustraire les influences dont l'effet comporte, avec le plus de facilité et de précision, l'appréciation directe: ce seront, le plus souvent, celles qui ont le plus d'importance réelle; mais peut être pas toujours. Au reste, on devra probablement procéder tantôt du dehors en dedans, tantôt en sens inverse, suivant les moyens qu'on a d'apprécier directement les effets dûs soit à une position extérieure quelconque, soit à un type quelconque d'organisation. Je me promets, à ce propos, de lire le cours de M. de Blainville, ou du moins la partie qu'il en a livrée au public: je regrette beaucoup que ce travail ne soit pas publié intégralement. J'ai commencé à lire les œuvres anglaises de M. Spurzheim, et je ne négligerai pas les ouvrages que vous m'avez indiqués de cet auteur. Je voudrais essayer de me rendre propre à faire quelque chose pour l'Ethologie, qui sera probablement, quoique je ne sache pas encore sous quelle forme, le sujet du premier livre que j'écrirai.

Je compte sur la lecture très prochaine de votre petite brochure sur l'école polytechnique, qui, d'après votre indication, doit être à peu près terminée, et qui, si elle n'influe pas immédiatement sur la constitution à donner à cette importante école, attirera du moins, sans doute, l'attention publique par l'opportunité de sa publication. Je désire vivement que les mutations à faire dans le personnel polytechnique s'opèrent de manière à vous rendre enfin la justice qu'on vous refusa si indignement à la dernière occasion, et j'attends avec impatience le dénouement de cette sorte de crise.

Quant à mon traducteur, dont Marrast ne m'a jamais dit le nom, je ne sais rien à son égard, que ce que je vous ai déjà annoncé. J'écrivis à Marrast, il y a plusieurs mois, une lettre un peu chaleureuse pour le déterminer à veiller sur la fidélité de la traduction, notamment en ce qui regarde le juste hommage que j'ai rendu à votre ouvrage et à vous-même.

Je n'ai pas reçu de réponse, ce qui tient peut-être de la part de Marrast, à son étourdissante occupation de journaliste, qui lui permet rarement de m'écrire. Au reste je ne compte pas beaucoup sur cette traduction, et je ne serai nullement étonné si elle n'a jamais lieu, ce qui vaudrait beaucoup mieux que des suppressions quelconques.

Je suis bien flatté de l'honneur que M. de Blainville a rendu à mon livre par une lecture soigneuse et par la haute approbation qu'un esprit si supérieur a bien voulu lui témoigner. Dans mon propre pays cet ouvrage a un succès bien au-delà de ce que j'avais espéré: la plupart des esprits compétents soit à juger, soit seulement à profiter de ce genre de spéculations, ont pris, ou se préparent à prendre, connaissance de ce livre, et les opinions qu'ils expriment lui sont jusqu'ici très favorables. Ce qui vous étonnera peut être, l'école Anglo-Catholique, sur laquelle je vous donnai autrefois quelques renseignements et qui a pris une importance très considérable, quoique seulement passagère dans notre public spéculatif, a trouvé bon d'afficher une haute protection de mon ouvrage: leurs divers organes lui ont consacré des articles[2] quelquefois assez remarquables, et on me dit qu'à Oxford où ils sont très puissants, tout le monde me lit. C'est à peu près comme si De Maistre préconisait votre grande ouvrage. Vous comptez bien qu'ils font ceci avec de nombreuses réserves, surtout sous le rapport religieux, mais cela vaut mieux à tous égards que s'ils me louaient sans restriction. D'un autre côté, on me lit à Cambridge pour se préparer aux examens de l'université, car M. Whewell y interroge les élèves sur son propre ouvrage, et comme on pense qu'il dirigera volontiers des questions dans le sens des doctrines que j'ai combattues, on lit mon livre afin de savoir ce qu'elles sont.

Je n'ai pas revu Mazhar Effendi. Je suis parvenu à savoir qu'il a quitté Londres, où probablement il n'est pas encore revenu. Quand il sera de retour il trouvera mon dernier billet, et j'aurai fait à son égard tout ce qui dépendait de moi.

Votre dévoué,

J. S. Mill

417. TO ALEXANDER BAIN[1]

[Late 1843]

I do not know when I shall be ripe for beginning "Ethology".[2] The scheme has not assumed any definite shape with me yet.

2. The most notable was W. G. Ward's in the *British Critic* (see Letter 409, n. 3).

* * * *

1. Excerpt published in Bain, *JSM*, p. 78. MS not located.
2. See Letters 410 and 416.

1844

418. TO ALEXANDER BAIN[1]

Jan. 8, 1844

I am reading a German professor's book on Logic—Beneke[2] is his name—which he has sent to me after reading mine, and which had previously been recommended to me by Austin and by Herschel as in accordance with the spirit of my doctrines. It is so in some degree, though far more psychological than entered into my plans. Though I think much of his psychology unsound for want of his having properly grasped the principle of association (he comes very close to it now and then), there is much of it of a suggestive kind.

419. TO MACVEY NAPIER[1]

India House
10th Jan[y]
1844

My dear Sir

Your note of the 6th arrived safe, & permit me to thank you for the very handsome remittance inclosed in it.

I do not feel *confident* of having the Guizot[2] ready for your next number, even if you should have room for it. When I can speak more positively on the subject I will inform you.

The insertion of the words "my father" required no apology. I should very willingly have inserted them myself, if you had asked me: although *of* myself I should not have used them—the ground on which I begged you to insert my letter[3] not being filial feeling but the desire to correct an injustice. However, considerations which affect only manner, are always, in my eyes, of quite subordinate importance to matter.

1. Excerpt published in Bain, *JSM*, p. 79. MS not located.
2. See Letter 397, n. 4.

* * * *

1. MS in Brit. Mus.
2. "M. Guizot's Essays and Lectures on History," *ER*, LXXXII (Oct., 1845), 381–421; reprinted in *Dissertations*, II, 297–362.
3. See Letters 405 and 407.

Senior's article[4] is full of excellent matter, though I think he is too hard upon O'Connell & the Repealers.

With cordial return of your kind wishes on the occasion of the new year, believe me

yours very truly,

J. S. MILL

420. TO AUGUSTE COMTE[1]

India House
le 17 Janvier 1844

MON CHER MONSIEUR COMTE

Je suis comme vous voyez un peu en retard pour ma réponse à votre dernière lettre, ce qui tient surtout à un nouveau dérangement chronique de ma santé qui gêne considérablement ma faculté de penser. Je crains que ma lettre actuelle ne se ressente un peu de cet affaiblissement, d'autant plus que la paresse d'esprit qui en est la suite, me décide pour la première fois depuis le commencement de notre correspondance à vous écrire sans faire de brouillon. Je vous préviendrai à ce propos, que malgré mon habitude à cet égard je ne suis pas, par rapport à la conservation de notre correspondance, en meilleur état que vous: je garde soigneusement toutes vos lettres, mais je n'ai pas conservé les miennes, pas même en brouillon, excepté toutefois les parties qui se rapportent à notre grande discussion récente que j'ai transcrite en entier sur vos lettres et sur les miennes et recueillie dans un livre.

Il est fort peu probable que je me trouve naturellement amené à imprimer quelque chose d'un peu important sur la question dont il s'agit, avant d'avoir eu l'occasion de lire votre traité de sociologie, malgré le retard nécessairement produit par votre intention de ne le faire paraître qu'intégralement. Quant à cette résolution elle-même, bien que j'en doive nécessairement retirer un vrai désappointement, en ne lisant pendant plusieurs années rien de vous et en ne pouvant suivre comme je l'ai fait jusqu'ici le progrès de votre grande entreprise philosophique, je dois pourtant applaudir à votre décision. Cette élaboration, en effet, ne me paraît pas susceptible d'être appréciée ou même étudiée avec fruit, si ce n'est dans

4. [Nassau Senior], "Ireland," *ER*, LXXIX (Jan., 1844), 189–266.

* * * *

1. MS at Johns Hopkins. Published in Lévy-Bruhl, pp. 295–98; in reply to Comte's of Dec. 23, 1843, *ibid.*, pp. 288–95.

son ensemble. Vous avez déjà donné toutes les idées de philosophie sociologique qui soient à mon sens, vraiment propres à être accueillies à titre de préparation: il reste à présent à établir systématiquement, dans leur connexité, les principales doctrines de la science sociale; et une publication partielle serait aussi peu propre à remplir ce but-là, qu'elle l'eût été dans le cas par exemple, de mon propre livre.

Je croyais avoir donné dans l'avant-dernier chapitre de mon ouvrage,[2] une adhésion publique complette à votre loi fondamentale de l'évolution humaine. J'en avais certainement l'intention bien arrêtée. Je n'ai pas le moindre doute, ni sur la vérité et l'universalité de cette grande loi, ni sur sa susceptibilité de servir de fondement à l'explication des principaux faits secondaires du développement humain ce que je n'aurais jamais cru possible, à un degré si complette, avant les preuves nombreuses que vous en avez données dans votre grand ouvrage, en réalisant, à tant d'égards importans, cette explication. C'est parce que le travail dynamique se trouve par là dans un état déjà assez avancé que je regarde l'établissement des principes de la statique comme devant occuper la place la plus importante dans la phase prochaine de notre entreprise.

Je serai vraiment heureux si la traduction de mon libre vient enfin à dépendre du jeune Bernard[3] que je préférais de beaucoup à un professeur quelconque ignoré, non seulement par ce que vous m'en dites, mais encore plus parce que vous exerceriez naturellement sur lui une autorité morale qui empêcherait toute atteinte grave à l'exactitude soigneuse qu'exige une pareille tâche.

Je suis très content de l'impression qu'ont faite sur vous M. et Mme Austin.[4] Le premier mérite bien tout ce que vous dites à sa louange, soit sous le rapport de son intelligence, soit par élévation de son caractère et par la noblesse de ses sentimens. C'est d'ailleurs l'homme le plus dénué de préjugés, conservatoires [*sic*] ou révolutionnaires, religieux ou anti-religieux, qu'on puisse trouver peut-être dans toute l'angleterre. Sa femme est non seulement très aimable mais vraiment supérieure, quoique je connaisse des femmes qui la dépassent infiniment. C'est par le bon sens

2. The *Logic* (first edition) Book VI, chap. x, "Of the Inverse Deductive, or Historical Method." Professor John M. Robson has called to the editor's attention the fact that late editions have twelve chapters; chap. xi was added in the fifth edition.

3. Otherwise unidentified than as Comte's unfortunate protégé (see Lévy-Bruhl, p. 293), for whom Comte had sought JSM's help (see Letter 367, and Comte's letter of July 22, 1842, Lévy-Bruhl, p. 88). Apparently nothing ever came of the proposal to have Bernard translate the *Logic*. A translation was eventually published by Louis Peisse: *Système de logique déductive et inductive, exposé des principes de la preuve et des méthodes de recherche scientifique, par John Stuart Mill. Traduit sur la 6e édition anglaise* . . . (2 vols., Paris, 1866).

4. See Comte's letter of Dec. 23, 1843, Lévy-Bruhl, p. 294.

des idées et par la clarté et l'élégance de l'expression qu'elle excelle le plus, soit dans la conversation, soit dans le peu qu'elle a écrit. Quant à la tendance *blue* je crois qu'elle s'en défendrait très vigoureusement: Son genre de vanité me semble tout autre, c'est du reste, un reproche qui atteint tout naturellement toute femme qui se mêle de littérature.

Mon ami Bain me mande qu'à sa recommandation un libraire d'Aberdeen y a fait venir deux exemplaires de votre grand ouvrage. Il ajoute: "The Bookseller who ordered them found it impossible to procure them in London, which he ascribed, I know not with what truth, to a great and sudden demand for the book through the country." Il est certain que votre nom se rencontre aujourd'hui beaucoup plus souvent dans les feuilles périodiques. Je ne vois pas encore beaucoup de citations une peu considérables, si ce n'est dans les articles de notre ami Lewes.[5]

Les tentatives des meneurs jésuitiques auprès de vous m'amusent beaucoup. Je crois nos chefs anglo-catholiques beaucoup plus consciencieux. Il y a meme parmi eux quelques esprits supérieurs.

tout à vous

J. S. MILL

421. TO WILLIAM TAIT[1]

I.H.
5th Feb.
1844

MY DEAR SIR

It will not be in my power at present for reasons connected with my other engagements & with my health, to furnish you with the paper you wish for, nor am I sure that if I could furnish one, it would be of the kind you wish— so much new light having been thrown on banking questions by the discussions of the last few years that my former opinions require much reconsideration.

I should be glad to hear anything you can tell me about Professor Nichol, as he has written to me very seldom of late years.

Very truly yours

J. S. MILL.

5. See Letter 400, n. 2.   * * * *

1. MS at LSE.

422. TO SARAH AUSTIN[1]

India House
26th February
1844

DEAR MRS. AUSTIN—I had heard a favourable account of Mr Austin from Lewis[2] before I received your letter, & I am very glad to have it confirmed —the experiment of whether Paris agrees with his health & whether he likes it as a place to live in, which is one great element of health, was well worth trying & I congratulate him on its having succeeded thus far. I hope he is well enough to go on with what he had begun to write. It seems to me of more importance than ever that the public should have his account of Prussia & the Prussian government since I have read Laing's.[3] I want to see *his* view of *that* view of Prussian affairs. There is a real faculty of observation & original remark about Laing which is likely to give his book considerable influence here, whenever his prejudices coincide with the common English ones, which in spite of many appearances to the contrary, they generally do. It is strange to find a man recognizing as he does that the Norwegian, & German, & French state of society are much better for the happiness of all concerned than the struggling, go-ahead English & American state, & yet always measuring the merit of all things by their tendency to increase the number of steam engines, & to make human beings as good machines & therefore as mere machines as those. His attacks on the peculiarities of the German governments are likely to have the more influence because they are in all probability exaggerations of truths.

Comte's taking to you is what I should have expected. I do not find that his profession of avoiding society stands good at all towards those who seek, or whom he thinks likely to value, him. He is at war with most of his cotemporaries, & is disposed to like those who give him the appreciation he thinks unjustly withheld by others: reste à savoir whether his liking would hold unless kept up by homage or services to himself.

Thanks for your invitation—but there is nothing in the state of my health to require change, that being much the same as it was when I saw you last —& I do not wish to leave London or apply for any holiday at present. I am looking forward to a real holiday in summer which will set me up for some time—

yours ever

J. S. MILL

1. MS at King's.   2. George Cornewall Lewis.
3. Samuel Laing, *Notes of a Traveller on the Social and Political State of France, Prussia, Switzerland, Italy, and other parts of Europe, during the present century* (London, 1842).

423. TO ROBERT BARCLAY FOX[1]

India House
22d March
1844

MY DEAR FRIEND

Many thanks for your writing to tell me of your present & prospective happiness.[2] I had heard of it through your sisters & mine, but it was pleasant to receive the intelligence from yourself.

If this important event in your life turns out as favourably as you have apparently the best reasons to expect, there are as I often think, few persons whose lot in life is more favourable than yours or who have more reason to look forward to a happy existence. In any case you have my sympathy & good wishes in the fullest measure.

I am sorry for what you tell me about Sterling. I had not heard of or from him for some time, nor indeed had I written to him lately, having been rather unsocial & neglectful of such duties for the last few months. I have the most agreeable remembrance of a visit to him last October.[3] The brightness of that sea & air have often "flashed upon the inward eye" between that time & this.

yours most truly

J. S. MILL

424. TO WILLIAM TAIT[1]

India House
22ᵈ March
1844

MY DEAR SIR

The opinion you expressed the other day that those Pol. Economy papers[2] of mine if printed would have a good chance of selling enough to pay their expenses, induces me to ask you whether you would be inclined, on that chance, to take the risk of publishing them. I have never hitherto offered them to any publisher, but if you were really inclined to it I should think

1. MS in the possession of Mr. W. H. Browning.
2. His engagement to Miss Jane Backhouse of Darlington had been announced.
3. See Letter 408.

* * * *

1. MS at LSE. Page 3 of letter bears note in another hand [Tait's]: "Agreed to this, by letter 25 March 1844."
2. Later that year published by J. W. Parker: *Essays on Some Unsettled Questions of Political Economy* (London, 1844). See Letter 43, n. 14.

seriously of the matter. I should probably think it right to offer them first to Parker, but I have no idea that he would publish them.

Yours very truly

W. Tait Esq.   J. S. MILL.

425. TO JOHN WILLIAM PARKER[1]

India House
30th March
1844

MY DEAR SIR

I have been urged by various people to publish certain Political Economy essays[2] which I wrote some years ago & have kept by me in manuscript, in which form several of my friends have read them. They are of too abstract a character for popularity, but the most important of them has a direct bearing upon the question of Reciprocity which has been raised by Col. Torrens in his "Budget"[3] & so much discussed of late & therefore, among political economists, they would doubtless excite some attention though not, I am afraid, among the general public.

I should not have thought of proposing to any publisher to take the risk of printing them, if I had not lately had an offer to that effect—but having had such an offer I should at once close with it if I did not wish first to ascertain whether you would undertake the publication. I should prefer you as publisher to any one else, though I do not feel at all confident that it will suit you.

The Essays will I think make an octavo volume of some 250 pages.

Very truly yours,

J. S. MILL

426. TO AUGUSTE COMTE[1]

India House
le 3 avril 1844

MON CHER MONSIEUR COMTE

Depuis plusieurs jours deux exemplaires de votre Discours[2] me sont parvenus par l'intermédiaire de Madame Austin, qui m'en promet encore

1. MS at Goldsmiths' Library, University of London.   2. See preceding letter.
3. Robert Torrens, *The Budget. On Commercial and Colonial Policy, with an introduction, in which the deductive method, as presented in Mr. Mill's System of Logic is applied to the solution of some controverted questions in political economy* (London, 1844).

* * * *

1. MS at Johns Hopkins. Published in Lévy-Bruhl, pp. 306–9; in reply to Comte's of Feb. 6, *ibid.*, pp. 299–305.
2. *Discours sur l'Esprit positif* (Paris, 1844). See Lévy-Bruhl, p. 301.

trois par la première occasion et je viens d'en recevoir cinq directement. Je commence à les placer le plus convenablement que je le puis, en évitant d'en donner à ceux sur qui on peut compter pour en acheter et qui le peuvent sans aucun inconvénient. Ce petit sommaire m'est parvenu au moment où je faisais une nouvelle lecture sérieuse de votre sixième volume, qui en raison de sa publication plus récente, et aussi parce que je l'avais laissé emporter en Ecosse par mon ami Bain, était celui de tous que j'avais lu le moins souvent. J'ai trouvé dans le Discours un résumé admirable des conclusions générales de votre Système, avec quelques éclaircissements accessoires. Mais plus j'y réfléchis, plus il me semble merveilleux que vos artisans parisiens puissent comprendre cela. Sans doute puisqu'ils y portent un intérêt soutenu ils doivent en recueillir un certain fruit, et je suis bien persuadé que ce qu'ils en retirent doit nécessairement leur profiter beaucoup. Mais il me semble très difficile, même pour les intelligences très cultivées, de se placer au point de vue philosophique de ce petit Traité sans s'y être élevé graduellement par la préparation des six volumes de votre grand Traité. Je trouve, de même, qu'il ne pourrait résulter qu'un avantage très problématique de la traduction actuelle de votre Discours en anglais. Les principes logiques énoncés dans ce Discours dans une forme nécessairement abstraite feraient ici peu d'effet, sans avoir été précédés de l'exposition concrète; ceux même à qui ces principes ne répugneraient pas n'en sentiraient probablement pas assez la valeur et la portée, tandis que des lecteurs mal préparés, qui craignent le travail lent et fatigant d'une étude suivie de votre Cours, se croiraient le droit de juger définitivement votre philosophie d'après une appréciation rapide d'un petit écrit qui leur semblerait à tort destiné à en présenter les titres, ainsi que les principaux résultats. Le seul attribut caractéristique de la nouvelle philosophie, dont on aurait par cet écrit une suffisante connaissance réelle, ce serait son incompatibilité radicale avec toute théologie quelconque, et c'est précisément ce qu'il importe beaucoup qu'on ne reconnaisse pas encore, parce que cette idée, généralement répandue, détournerait de cette étude un grand nombre d'esprits, surtout jeunes, qui, si on ne les effrayait pas dans le commencement, finiraient par s'accoutumer à toutes les conséquences, même anti-religieuses, du positivisme. Le temps n'est pas venu où sans compromettre notre cause, nous pourrons en angleterre diriger des attaques ouvertes contre la théologie, même chrétienne. Nous pouvons seulement l'éluder, en l'éliminant tranquillement de toutes les discussions philosophiques et sociales et en passant à l'ordre du jour sur toutes les questions qui lui sont propres. Par conséquent il me paraît que le propagandisme que vos ouvrages ne manqueront pas d'exercer en angleterre comme ailleurs, aura lieu par leur lecture directe. Ceux qui ajoutent une certaine culture scientifique à une émancipation ou même à une demi-émancipation religieuse, sont presque toujours capables de lire votre livre en français et la traduction ne leur en serait d'aucune utilité.

J'attends avec beaucoup d'intérêt votre Cours populaire d'astronomie. Je désire vivement apprendre la manière dont vous présentez cette science à des esprits sans aucune préparation mathématique sérieuse. Nous avons chez nous des traités populaires d'astronomie, assez bien faits au reste, mais qui se contentent, comme à l'ordinaire, d'en faire connaître empiriquement les résultats, sans donner, comme vous avez dû le faire, une idée nette et juste, quoique générale, de la méthode par laquelle la raison humaine est parvenue à découvrir et à démontrer les lois des phénomènes soustraits en apparence à ses principaux moyens d'exploration.

J'ai reçu dernièrement une nouvelle preuve de l'impression générale produite par le succès de ma Logique. Un libraire m'a fait la proposition d'imprimer un petit recueil de discussions en économie politique,[3] que j'ai écrites il y a longtemps et que ce même libraire avait autrefois refusé de publier. Il y a là des choses qui peuvent encore être utiles et je me suis décidé d'accepter la proposition en ajoutant à ce petit livre la réimpression d'un article de revue[4] dans lequel j'avais autrefois expliqué, à propos de l'économie politique, les principes de la méthode déductive. J'ai même encore l'idée, puisque mes méditations éthologiques ne seront pas mûres de longtemps, de faire en attendant ce qui ne serait pour moi qu'un travail de quelques mois, c'est-à-dire un traité spécial d'économie politique,[5] analogue à celui d'Adam Smith qui n'est certainement plus au niveau de ce temps-ci, tandis que sa place n'est pas encore convenablement remplie. Je sais ce que vous pensez de l'économie politique actuelle: j'en ai une meilleure opinion que vous, mais si j'écris quelque chose là dessus ce sera en ne perdant jamais de vue le caractère purement provisoire de toutes ses conclusions concrètes, et je m'attacherais surtout à séparer les lois générales de la production, nécessairement communes à toutes les sociétés industrielles, des principes de la distribution et de l'échange des richesses, principes qui supposent nécessairement un état de société déterminé, sans préjuger que cet état doive ou même qu'il puisse durer indéfiniment, quoiqu'en revanche il soit impossible de juger les divers états de la société sans prendre en considération les lois économiques qui leur sont propres. Je crois qu'un pareil traité peut avoir, surtout ici, une grande utilité provisoire et qu'il servira puissamment à faire pénétrer l'esprit positif dans les discussions politiques.

tout à vous

J. S. MILL

3. See next letter.
4. See Letter 43, n. 14.
5. Eventually published as *Principles of Political Economy, with Some of their Applications to Social Philosophy* (2 vols., London, 1848).

427. TO WILLIAM TAIT[1]

India House
8th April
1844

MY DEAR SIR

After receiving your note I determined to publish the Essays & accordingly made a tender of them in the first instance, as I felt bound to do, to Parker, who after a few days consideration contrary to my expectation consented to publish them.

I am therefore precluded from closing, as I should otherwise have done, with your proposition. But I consider you as completely the primary cause of their being published, as I should not probably have thought of offering them to any publisher if you had not mentioned the subject to me.

You certainly do not lose much profit by not being the publisher.

Very truly yours

J. S. MILL

428. TO JOHN MITCHELL KEMBLE[1]

I.H.
Saturday [May (?) 1844]

MY DEAR SIR

I have commenced an article on Duveyrier's Lettres Politiques[2] & expect to have finished it in a fortnight or three weeks when if you are inclined to take such an article I will send it to you.

Very truly yours

J. S. MILL

429. TO JOHN WILLIAM PARKER[1]

India House
10 May
1844

MY DEAR SIR

This will introduce to you my friend Mr. G. H. Lewes who wishes to converse with you on the subject of a literary work projected by him.[2]

1. MS at LSE.   * * * *

1. MS in 1944 in the possession of Dr. Adrian Ver Brugghen, Evanston, Ill. See Letter 433.

2. Eventually published as "Duveyrier's Political Views of French Affairs," *ER*, LXXXIII (April, 1846), 453–74.

* * * *

1. *Addressed*: J. W. Parker Esq. / West Strand. MS at LSE.

2. Presumably Lewes' *A Biographical History of Philosophy*, which Parker published in four volumes, 1845–46.

Of course I cannot judge how far such a work would suit you as a publisher but I have a very high opinion of Mr Lewes' qualifications for undertaking it.

Very truly yours

J. S. MILL

430. TO JOHN MITCHELL KEMBLE[1]

India House
28th May 1844

MY DEAR SIR

My friend Mr David Masson,[2] of Aberdeen, has requested me to give him a line of introduction to accompany an article on Wallace[3] which he proposes offering to your review. I think you will find that he has treated the subject in a way by no means commonplace or trite & I consider him likely to be a valuable contributor to any review. If I were still an editor myself I should certainly print the article.

Believe me
very truly yours
J. S. MILL

431. TO JOHN STERLING[1]

India House
29th May 1844

MY DEAR STERLING

For some time after I heard of your last dreadful attack I was afraid to write to you, your father having given me what seemed strong reasons against doing so—but as these do not seem any longer to exist, I venture to write. I do most earnestly hope that you will not give way to discouragement about your state, although I know by painful experience how natural it is to do so & what mere idle words everything must appear that can be said to you by persons who have so much less means of judging than yourself. But there is a surprising elasticity in your constitution which has

1. MS in the possession of Professor Ney MacMinn.
2. David Masson (1822–1907), Scottish man of letters, best known for his *The Life of John Milton* (6 vols., Cambridge and London, 1858–80). Bain had introduced him to JSM in the summer of 1843 (see David Masson, *Memories of London in the "forties"* [Edinburgh, 1908]).
3. No such article appeared in the *BFR*.

* * * *

1. Published in Elliot, I, 125–27. MS at Leeds.

carried you through shocks which would have been fatal to many a stronger person, & that is what we have to rest hope upon. And there is one thing which cannot be said to you too often, because I have seen before that there was real need of saying it. If there should be but little chance of your recovering anything like solid or perfect health, or even of your possessing permanently & safely such a degree of it as you have sometimes had for considerable periods together, in the last few years, I am afraid you will think that anything short of this is not worth having or worth wishing for—that you will be useless & helpless & that it is better to be dead. I enter most perfectly into such a feeling & should very likely feel the very same if I were as I have several times thought I might be, in your circumstances—but I cannot conceive anything more completely mistaken than in your case such a feeling would be. If you were never able to go through any active exertion, or to write a single line, except an occasional letter, or to exercise any influence over mankind except the influence of your thoughts & feelings upon your children & upon those by whom you are personally known and valued, you would still be, I sincerely think, the most useful man I know. It is very little that any of us can do, except doing good to those nearest to us—& of what we *can* do the smallest part, in general, is that which we calculate upon & to which we can attach our name. There are certainly few persons living who are capable of doing so much good by their indirect & unconscious influence as you are & I do not believe you have ever had an adequate conception of the extent of influence you possess & the quantity of good which you produce by it. Even by your mere existence you do more good than many by their laborious exertions. I do not speak of what the loss of you would be, or the blank it would make in life even to those who like me have except for short periods had little of you except the knowledge of your existence & of your affection. None of us could hope in our lives to meet with your like again—& if we did, it would be no compensation. And when I think how many of the best people living are at this moment feeling this, I am sure that you have much to live for.

All connected with me whom you know are feeling deeply interested about you, including Clara,[2] who has repeatedly written most anxiously wishing to know all that can be known about your health & intentions. She is now at Dresden & has been much interested & excited by the change of scene & manner of life; her ἀποδημια[3] has been a completely successful experiment & she does not seem at all disposed to return soon. George is now working under me in the India House to which he has been appointed by the Directors in a way very kind & agreeable to me. He is learning his business very successfully & is in other respects of great promise. I myself

2. JSM's sister.
3. "being away from home."

have been writing several review articles, one on Guizot's essays[4] & lectures, at the request of Napier though I do not know when he will print it, & one on the Currency,[5] which is just coming out in the *Westminster*. I have also been able to get published some Political Economy essays,[6] written fourteen years ago. This is one effect of the success of the Logic. I think my next book will be a systematic treatise on Political Economy, for none of the existing ones are at all up to the present state of speculation.

Ever my dear Sterling yours most affectionately

J. S. MILL

432. TO AUGUSTE COMTE[1]

India House
le 6 juin 1844

MON CHER MONSIEUR COMTE

Vous devez recevoir bientôt, si vous ne l'avez pas encore reçu, un exemplaire d'un petit volume de moi[2] que je vous ai fait adresser par l'éditeur, quoique je ne puisse pas espérer qu'il vous intéresse beaucoup ni que fous fassiez en sa faveur une nouvelle exception à votre règle d'hygiène cérébrale, à laquelle vous avez dérogé d'une manière si honorable pour moi, en faveur d'un ouvrage plus important. Je ne le vous ai envoyé que pour mémoire, et parce que je ne voudrais pas qu'il parût quelque chose en mon nom, sans que vous en eussiez connaissance. Je n'y mets pas au reste beaucoup d'importance; c'est un recueil de discussions d'économie politique, écrites il y a 14 ou 15 ans et restées depuis lors en manuscrit, à l'exception d'une seule qui se rapportant principalement à la méthode, comportait un intérêt plus général et qui a paru dans une revue en 1836.[3] Puisque je les avais écrites et qu'on m'a proposé de les publier j'ai cru qu'elles valaient la peine de les imprimer mais non celle de les refaire, sauf des corrections verbales et quelques suppressions motivées par le progrès postérieur de mes conceptions logiques, progrès essentiellement dû à votre grand ouvrage.

Je me félicite de l'approbation que vous voulez bien donner à mon projet de faire sur l'économie industrielle des sociétés un traité un peu plus systématique. Je ne me sentais pas auparavant suffisamment assuré de votre adhésion à ce projet, qui pouvait vous paraître essentiellement anti-scienti-

4. See Letter 419, n. 2.
5. "The Currency Question," *WR*, XLI (June, 1844), 579–98.
6. See Letter 427.

* * * *

1. MS at Johns Hopkins. Published in Lévy-Bruhl, pp. 321–25; in answer to Comte's of May 1, *ibid.*, pp. 310–20.
2. *Essays on Some Unsettled Questions of Political Economy*.
3. See Letter 86, n. 3.

fique, et qui le serait en effet si je n'avais le plus grand soin de bien établir le caractère purement provisoire de toute doctrine sur les phénomènes industriels qui fasse abstraction du mouvement général de l'humanité. Je crois que ce dessein, s'il pouvait être convenablement exécuté, aurait l'avantage de préparer l'éducation positive de beaucoup d'esprits qui s'occupent plus ou moins sérieusement des questions sociales, et il me semble aussi qu'en prenant pour modèle général le grand et le beau travail d'Adam Smith, j'aurais des occasions importants de répandre directement quelques-uns des principes de la nouvelle philosophie, comme Adam Smith a fait pour la plupart de ceux de la métaphysique négative dans ses applications sociales sans éveiller les défiances ombrageuses en déployant aucun drapeau. Je crois d'ailleurs qu'un tel ouvrage a aujourd'hui des chances favorables pour s'emparer de son terrain spécial, en écartant les traités existants, tous essentiellement surannés même par rapport à l'état actuel de l'opinion publique, qui si elle ne trouve pas bientôt quelque chose d'un peu mieux, se détournerait certainement de cet ordre d'études, sans que ce dégoût puisse encore profiter à autre chose qu'à l'empirisme systématique qui nie toute doctrine générale en matière sociologique.

Je vous remercie vivement de vos remarques philosophiques sur la discussion pendante en France sur la liberté d'enseignement. Sans avoir suivi les différentes phases de cette discussion j'avais saisi ce qu'il y a d'anormal et de contradictoire dans les positions respectives des théologiens et des métaphysiciens à l'égard de cette lutte, où leurs rôles sont comme vous l'avez si bien dit, essentiellement renversés: ce qui du reste a lieu aujourd'hui dans presque toutes les grandes discussions politiques, non seulement en france mais même ici, où les situations, malgré des différences superficielles, sont les mêmes au fond. Le parti des anciennes idées a cessé, ici comme ailleurs, de gouverner: quel que soit le parti dominant, il n'y a des différences réelles de doctrine que chez ceux qui suivent: les chefs se conduisent toujours dans des intentions de juste milieu; ils n'ont que les prémisses convenues de leur parti politique, en renonçant à toutes les conséquences. C'est seulement depuis quelques ans, et surtout depuis le dernier avènement du parti tory,[4] que cette situation commence à être généralement comprise; et c'est surtout aujourd'hui qu'elle se dessine très fortement par les attaques systématiques qu'une partie des Torys,[5] dirigée par quelques jeunes gens assez remarquables, a entreprisés au nom des anciens principes, contre la politique actuelle du parti conservateur. C'est là encore une phase indispensable de notre mouvement social et intellectuel. Les doctrines négatives étant tombées en discrédit avant d'avoir accompli leur œuvre, il est indispensable que les anciennes doctrines sociales reprennent un peu de leur

4. In 1841.
5. The Young England party, which included Benjamin Disraeli.

influence antérieure afin qu'elles aussi puissent de nouveau démontrer expérimentalement leur impuissance actuelle. C'est ce qu'elles ne tarderont pas à faire. En attendant tout cela sert à ranimer les spéculations sociales. Dans les temps modernes la pensée n'est jamais, au fond, ennemie de la pensée: tous les penseurs sont tellement en danger d'être opprimés par les médiocrités de leur propre parti que leur sympathie mutuelle est à peu près assurée, sauf des rivalités personnelles directes.

Je regrette beaucoup, quoique je n'en sois nullement surpris, que vous ayez éprouvé un dérangement physique auquel il est très difficile d'échapper quand on travaille comme vous, à peu près sans intermission. La cessation totale de travail cérébral soutenu, pendant quelques mois, que vous me recommandez avec un intérêt si amical, vous serait probablement encore plus avantageux qu'à moi. Je ne manquerais pas de profiter de votre conseil si une pareille relâche me devenait réellement importante, et dans ce cas-là je n'aurais aucune difficulté à obtenir un congé de la longueur suffisante. Il n'y a lieu aujourd'hui à aucune démarche pareille, puisque je me porte mieux que je ne me suis porté depuis deux ans, et je me sens aussi propre qu'à l'ordinaire à toute espèce de travail intellectuel. J'espère m'y livrer beaucoup cette année.

Ne vous mettez pas en peine à l'égard de la traduction de mon livre; il en sera comme il pourra. Si, comme je l'espère, le professeur de Marrast ne la fait pas, il sera toujours libre au jeune Bernard[6] de l'entreprendre, pourvu toutefois qu'il y ait un éditeur qui veuille s'en charger, ce qui peut-être ne se trouvera pas, par des raisons que vous sentirez très facilement, car les doctrines de mon livre sont tout aussi opposées à celles de toutes les écoles régnantes en France, que celles du vôtre, et si de mon côté je n'ai attaqué personne, au moins je vous ai loué, en m'abstenant de louer aucun chef de coterie. Si par ces raisons le livre n'est pas traduit, nous l'avons bien merité.

tout à vous

J. S. MILL

433. TO JOHN MITCHELL KEMBLE[1]

I.H.
6th June 1844

MY DEAR SIR

I have been disappointed by not finding time to finish my article on Duveyrier.[2] Part of it is completed & the first draught made of the rest but I have been so taken off by things of more immediate emergency &

6. See Letter 420, n. 3.

* * * *

1. MS in the possession of Professor Ney MacMinn.
2. See Letter 428, n. 2.

especially by official work that I have not been able to get it completed &
now I am about to go out of town for some weeks during which it must be
suspended. I have no doubt however of being able to let you have it before
the end of August, which I suppose will be in time for your autumn number.

Very truly yours

J. S. MILL

434. TO AUGUSTE COMTE[1]

India House
le 12 août
1844

Il fallait, mon cher Monsieur Comte, que la première de vos lettres qui
ne me fût pas venue promptement fût précisément celle dont la prompte
arrivée importait le plus. J'arrive aujourd'hui d'un congé court et dont la
destination était depuis longtemps rigoureusement fixée et je viens seulement de lire cette lettre et d'apprendre tout ce qu'elle contient. Vous me
connaissez, j'espère, assez pour croire que je m'associe on ne peut pas plus
à votre indignation et que je me réjouis cordialement que les indignes
menées de ceux que vous avez avec votre franchise philosophique si justement dénoncés vous aient moins nui qu'il n'y avait d'abord lieu de craindre.
Quoique le rétard de ma réponse vous ait probablement décidé à vous
adresser directement à M. Grote, je n'ai pas perdu un moment à lui faire
part de votre lettre; il est à la campagne et je n'ai pas pu encore avoir de
réponse. Je connais assez son caractère et je suis assez sûr de l'estime
profonde qu'il a pour vous pour que je n'eusse pas hésité, même si vous n'y
aviez pas pensé, à demander ses conseils dans un pareil cas, en lui offrant
l'occasion de participer par lui-même et de provoquer la participation de ses
amis riches à une œuvre qui ne peut manquer de faire honneur à ceux qui
y prennent part. Comme vous le désirez, par des raisons dont je reconnais
la justesse, je réserverai mes propres ressources pour le cas où leur emploi
serait indispensable ce dont je pourrai mieux juger en quelques jours d'ici.
Je vous écris, mon cher ami, au milieu des embarras de toutes sortes dont
on est entouré quand on arrive. Je vous écrirai au long le plustôt possible.

tout à vous

J. S. MILL

1. MS at Johns Hopkins. Published in Lévy-Bruhl, pp. 340–41; in reply to Comte's
of July 22, *ibid.*, 325–39.

Comte had written that in May his enemies had defeated him for re-election to his
examinership at the Ecole Polytechnique, thereby depriving him of much of his
income. He asked JSM to help raise 6,000 francs among his English friends for his
support. Grote and Molesworth subsequently provided the money (see Letters 435,
438, and 439).

435. TO AUGUSTE COMTE[1]

India House
14 août 1844

MON CHER AMI

M. Grote prend sur lui la moitié de la somme nécessaire. Demain j'espère pouvoir vous dire définitivement d'où viendra l'autre moitié. En tout cas les six mille francs sont assurés.

votre dévoué

J. S. MILL

436. TO JOHN MITCHELL KEMBLE[1]

I.H.
14th Aug. 1844

MY DEAR SIR

How much time can you give me to finish Duveyrier[2] for your next number. I have just returned & find myself loaded with occupation.

Very truly yours

J. S. MILL

437. TO JOHN STERLING[1]

I.H.
16 Aug. 1844

MY DEAR STERLING—The trifling thing you ask might have been done without asking—& if there is anything in which I can ever be useful or

1. MS at Johns Hopkins. Published in Lévy-Bruhl, p. 341.

* * * *

1. MS in the possession of Professor Ney MacMinn.
2. See Letters 428 and 433.

* * * *

1. Published in Elliot, I, 127. MS at Leeds. In reply to a letter from Sterling reporting that he was at the point of death. He died Sept. 18, 1844.

Sterling's last letter to JSM, dated Hillside, Sept. 8, 1844, is at Yale University:
My dear Mill—We neither of us can need assurances of what we are to each other but your letters have a tone in them that I would fain reply to fittingly if I could. But I am so weak that I dare not in the least give way to any strong feeling or it leaves me completely broken & helpless. I have been looking at old letters of my own (yours you shall have again) & how much I find if that were wanted to put me in mind of you. How many many scores of times have I been thinking how we sat together on the Baths of Caligula. Let us hope to meet upon some other height with a still nobler prospect. Heaven bless you. Always & entirely yours

JOHN STERLING

On the verso in JSM's hand:
"Sterling
8 September 1844
nine days before his death"

helpful to you or yours, you cannot do me a greater kindness than by telling me of it.

I have never so much wished for another life as I do for the sake of meeting you in it. The chief reason for desiring it has always seemed to me to be that the curtain may not drop altogether on those one loves & honours. Every analogy which favours the idea of a future life leads one to expect that if such a life there be, death will no further change our character than as it is liable to be changed by any other important event in our existence—and I feel most acutely what it would be to have a firm faith that the world to which one is in progress was enriching itself with those by the loss of whom this world is impoverished.

If we lose you, the remembrance of your friendship will be a precious possession to me as long as I remain here, & the thought of you will be often an incitement to me when in time of need & sometimes a restraint. I shall never think of you but as one of the noblest, & quite the most loveable of all men I have known or ever look to know.

J.S.M.

438. TO AUGUSTE COMTE[1]

India House
le 20 août
1844

MON CHER AMI

Nous tenons une partie de la seconde moitié du déficit, et je suis assuré d'obtenir le reste sans recourir à mes propres fonds. La chose a traîné un peu, seulement à cause de l'absence de tous ceux à qui on devait s'adresser de préférence et qui ne sont pas à Londres dans ce tems-ci. D'un jour à l'autre je puis être à même de vous annoncer le résultat définitif de mes démarches.

Je ne tarderai pas à faire parvenir à M. Whewell de votre part un exemplaire de votre Discours.[2] Il m'en reste encore, puisque je ne le donne qu'à ceux que je juge capables d'en profiter, et pas assez riches pour devoir l'acheter. Comme mon libraire-éditeur est aussi celui de M. Whewell, il m'est facile de me servir de son intermédiaire dans le cas dont il s'agit.

Je désire beaucoup savoir de vous la nature de cette nouvelle crise polytechnique. Il me semble qu'elle offre à l'autorité un puissant moyen de changer tout ce qu'il y a de nuisible dans le règlement de l'école.

tout à vous

J. S. MILL

1. MS at Johns Hopkins. Published in Lévy-Bruhl, pp. 344–45; in reply to Comte's of Aug. 15, *ibid.*, pp. 342–44.
2. *Discours sur l'Esprit positif*, which Comte had asked JSM to send.

439. TO AUGUSTE COMTE[1]

India House
le 23 août
1844

MON CHER AMI

Il est ouvert en votre faveur chez MM. Delamarre Martin Didier et C°
banquiers, Rue des Jeuneurs, à Paris un crédit de 3000 francs et le 1er
février prochain une autre somme pareille sera à votre disposition chez les
mêmes banquiers. La somme provient tout entière de M. Grote et de sir
William Molesworth, M. Grote s'étant opposé formellement à ce qu'on
essayât d'y associer d'autres. Il a trouvé plus convenable de ne s'adresser
qu'à des esprits complètement émancipés sous le rapport religieux, jugeant
que nul autre n'était capable de vous apprécier suffisamment. Sans cela
je n'eusse pas craint de m'adresser à deux d'entre les chefs de banque les
plus distingués, qui admirent beaucoup vos ouvrages: chez l'un d'eux
surtout j'ai pu m'assurer personnellement qu'il avait pour vous une admiration *sentie*, malgré ses opinions religieuses assez prononcées. Cependant
je trouve avec M. Grote que la chose est mieux comme elle est. Lui et Sir
William Molesworth sont tous deux assez riches pour que vous ne puissiez
pas vous croire obligé en conscience de les rembourser jamais, et je sais
que vous leur feriez plus de plaisir en ne les remboursant pas. Ainsi tout
est arrangé pour le mieux, et vous pourrez ainsi jouir sans inquiétude de
votre loisir inaccoutumé, et vous occuper en tems opportun du commencement de votre second grand ouvrage.

votre dévoué

J. S. MILL

440. TO AUGUSTE COMTE[1]

India House
le 5 october 1844

MON CHER MONSIEUR COMTE

Mon absence de Londres, quoique courte, a laissé aux affaires du bureau
le temps de s'accumuler de manière à m'avoir laissé jusqu'ici peu de loisir
pour m'occuper d'autre chose que de mes devoirs officiels et d'affaires
domestiques. Après deux mois de travail et de préoccupation qui ne m'ont

1. MS at Johns Hopkins. Published in Lévy-Bruhl, pp. 345–46.

* * * *

1. MS at Johns Hopkins. Published in Lévy-Bruhl, pp. 354–59; in reply to Comte's
of Aug. 23 and 28, *ibid.*, pp. 347–53.

permis ni aucune étude ni le très peu de distractions dont j'ai l'habitude, ce n'est vraiment que depuis hier que je me suis trouvé assez libre d'occupation et de pensée pour pouvoir songer à vous écrire. Je n'ai, par conséquent, rien de bien intéressant à vous apprendre sur mon propre compte, sauf l'état de ma santé, qui sans être forte, est maintenant à peu près bonne et capable de supporter tout ce que je serai probablement en lieu d'exiger d'elle. A cet égard le congé que j'ai obtenu m'a rendu un service véritable. Puisse le loisir inusité qui vous est échu cette année vous avoir pareillement servi, en dissipant le dérangement exceptionnel que votre santé semblait avoir subi sur les commencemens de l'année, que la crise que vous avez traversée était de nature à empirer, mais qui était apparemment de la sorte de dérangement qui lorsqu'ils ne sont pas de trop longue date, n'ont guère besoin pour la guérison, que d'un changement suffisant d'habitudes, et surtout d'une intermission de travail. Si, en outre, cette intermission vous a permis de commencer votre seconde grande élaboration philosophique, je n'ai assurément pas besoin de vous dire que je m'en réjouirai profondément. Plus on s'avance dans la vie, et mieux on sent le prix du temps. J'ai souvent besoin de me rappeler avec une émotion pénible, combien l'incertitude de la vie fait un devoir à chacun de mettre le plutôt possible à l'abri de tout hasard les choses utiles qu'il peut faire mieux que les autres ou que les autres ne peuvent ou ne veulent pas faire. Peu d'années s'écoulent sans que cette réflexion soit douloureusement fortifiée par quelque perte irréparable. Je viens d'en subir une, par la mort prématurée d'un du très petit nombre de ceux pour qui j'éprouvais une amitié vive et une estime parfaite.[2] Il réunissait à l'un des plus nobles caractères qui puissent exister, une profondeur de sympathie qui tient de l'idéal féminin et qu'on ne trouve que fort rarement en angleterre si ce n'est dans les femmes et encore très exceptionnellement. Avec une grande étendue de connaissances et une forte intelligence, il n'avait pas le véritable esprit positif; il était pourtant très au delà de nos écoles métaphysiques les plus avancées. Ecclésiastique anglican, il avait depuis longtemps cessé d'appartenir par ses opinions à une église quelconque, et à en juger par ce qu'il avait fait et par les progrès de son intelligence pendant dix ans d'une santé faible et fragile, il eût rendu de très grands services au progrès moral et intellectuel par l'influence qu'il aurait exercée sur des esprits auxquels le positivisme pur ne peut pas encore avoir accès. Il est mort de phtisie pulmonaire à l'âge de 38 ans. M. et Mme Austin l'ont connu et aimé, sans avoir été, je crois, autant que moi en état d'apprécier sa valeur.

Je trouve toujours que le positivisme marche ici, mais il y a encore très peu d'hommes qui par la force primitive de leur esprit et par le degré

2. John Sterling. See Letter 437, n. 1.

de leur préparation, soient capables de s'approprier complètement la méthode et de faire faire des progrès à la doctrine. Je ne vois que Bain en qui, si je mourais demain, je serais sûr de laisser un successeur. Vous avez pu juger notre digne ami M. Grote. Il a bien dépassé son Benthamisme primitif, mais la métaphysique négative fait toujours le fond de sa culture intellectuelle. Molesworth, avec les mêmes tendances générales, a l'esprit plus libre; il est, aussi plus jeune mais son intelligence est plus déductive qu'inductive; sa nature est géomètre: il est par nature ce que j'étais il y a quinze ans par mon éducation. Austin s'est élevé très lentement et très péniblement au-dessus de ce niveau, mais sa déplorable santé, l'imperfection de son éducation scientifique, et son incapacité maladive de rien terminer, empêchent malheureusement de pouvoir compter sur lui pour des choses du premier ordre, qu'il est, à tout autre égard, fait pour dignement accomplir. Restent donc les jeunes gens, et parmi ceux de ma connaissance je ne vois que chez Bain l'étoffe d'un esprit du premier ordre, avec des habitudes intellectuelles parfaitement bonnes. Et nous pouvons nous vanter, vous et moi, d'avoir décidé de sa direction. S'il vit, et il a heureusement une organisation forte, il fera de grandes choses, et il soutiendra dignement la cause du positivisme chez nous. Je compte sur lui pour former beaucoup d'élèves à Aberdeen, où il enseigne publiquement avec un succès remarquable. Je crois d'ailleurs que la philosophie positive trouvera plus d'apôtres actuels en écosse qu'en angleterre, non seulement à cause de l'influence des antécédents philosophiques de ce pays, qui sont, comme vous savez plus voisins de l'esprit positif, mais encore par plusieurs autres raisons. D'abord, l'instruction supérieure y est beaucoup plus répandue qu'ici: les écoles supérieures et les universités sont de nature à mettre cette instruction à portée de la classe moyenne, et même de quelques fils de paysans, classe qui a fourni noblement son contingent à la gloire intellectuelle de l'Ecosse. Ensuite cette instruction elle même est moins exclusivement littéraire et plus scientifique qu'en angleterre. En troisième lieu, bien que les croyances religieuses soient restées plus fortes chez le peuple écossais, l'influence ecclésiastique y est beaucoup plus faible, ce qui est aujourd'hui plus qu'équivalent. Enfin, je trouve qu'il y a une analogie réelle dans la tournure de l'esprit écossais et de l'esprit français. Vous n'avez certainement pu méconnaître à quel point les Hume, les Ferguson, les Adam Smith, les Millar,[3] les Brown, les Reid,[4] même les Chalmers ressemblent intellectuellement à des français, tandis que nos philosophes anglais, en exceptant peut

3. John Millar (1735–1801), professor of law at Glasgow, author of *Observations concerning the distinctions of Ranks in Society* (London, 1771) and *An Historical View of the English Government* . . . (London, 1787, and later enlarged editions), works which James Mill had greatly admired.
4. Thomas Reid (1710–1796), exponent of the "common sense" school of philosophy.

être Hobbes, appartiennent à une type différent: chez Locke, chez Berkeley, chez Hartley, chez Coleridge, ches Bentham même, c'est un ordre d'idées et de tendances intellectuelles profondément disparates, et je pense qu'un esprit vraiment anglais, sorti de notre éducation publique, et étranger à toute culture continentale, est, à beaucoup d'égards, plus éloigné du véritable esprit positif qu'aucun autre homme instruit. Vous vous plaignez avec raison de l'état du public français, dont l'incapacité positive tient aujourd'hui, ce me semble, à des causes plutôt morales qu'intellectuelles. Ici nous avons encore beaucoup de chemin à faire pour nous placer au niveau intellectuel de Guizot, et ce sont déjà des hommes très supérieurs au vulgaire qui ont accompli ce progrès, quelque minime qu'il doive paraître au point de vue de la vraie positivité.

Je ne sais si je vous ai dit que j'avais exécuté votre commission auprès de M. Whewell, en lui faisant parvenir un exemplaire de votre Discours. J'avais, comme vous, reçu son petit opuscule.[5] Je conçois que ne connaissant probablement pas ses autres ouvrages, vous ayez vu avec une juste indulgence ce qu'il y avait de bon dans cette brochure. Pour moi je l'ai trouvée très faible: tout ce qu'il a dit, il l'avait beaucoup mieux dit ailleurs, et ce qui m'y a le plus frappé c'est qu'en reproduisant, très imparfaitement, les objections de son critique, il en a montré si peu d'intelligence qu'il oppose à ses objections les mêmes choses qu'il avait dites auparavant sans tenir aucun compte des réponses. Le critique auquel il répond, et que moi-même j'ai cité dans l'avant-dernier chapitre de mon 2ᵐᵉ livre, est l'illustre physicien sir John Herschel, que je trouve très supérieur à M. Whewell. Je ne sais (par parenthèse) si je vous ai dit qu'il m'a mandé que mon livre l'avait décidé à étudier le vôtre: je ne sais s'il l'a fait avec fruit. On me dit que M. Whewell se propose de me réfuter aussi, dans le premier ouvrage qu'il publiera.[6] J'ai toujours comté un peu sur son goût polémique, pour engager une discussion utile. D'ailleurs il mérite toute notre reconnaissance par les améliorations importantes qu'il a faites dans le système d'enseignement de Cambridge et par l'attention qu'il a attirée sur les grandes questions philosophiques. Il a trouvé l'esprit philosophique assoupi: il est un de ceux qui ont le plus fait pour le réveiller.

tout à vous

J. S. Mill

5. Whewell had printed and circulated privately a reply to Sir John Herschel's review of his *History of the Inductive Sciences* and his *Philosophy of the Inductive Sciences* in the QR for June, 1841. Whewell subsequently published the reply in the second edition of *The Philosophy of the Inductive Sciences* (London, 1847), II, 669–79.

6. *Of Induction, with especial reference to Mr. J. Stuart Mill's System of Logic* (Cambridge, 1849). Professor J. M. Robson has pointed out that JSM took note of Whewell's arguments in the third (1851) edition of the *Logic*.

441. TO WILLIAM TAIT[1]

India House
4th November
1844

MY DEAR SIR

Are you provided with an article on Johnstone's [*sic*] "Travels in Southern Abyssinia"?[2] & if you are not, should you be disposed to insert one in the Magazine if on seeing it you find it suitable?

Very truly yours
J. S. MILL

442. TO HENRY S. CHAPMAN[1]

India House
8th November, 1844

MY DEAR CHAPMAN,

I am afraid you must by this time think that I have forgotten my promise to write to you, but I have never ceased to bear it in mind, although in the matter of letter writing there is usually a long interval with me, between purpose and performance. I have not much personal news to tell you. My own life goes on just as it did, and I see very few people, Roebuck, Graham, and our other friends, as seldom as anybody else.

You will rather, I suppose, expect to hear from me about public matters; but even these I have scarcely anything prominent or prononcé to relate, in the way of events. It is rather the state of the public mind which is curious and interesting. There is a prodigious current setting in every day more strongly, of superficial philanthropy. English benevolence can no longer be accused of confining itself to niggers and other distant folks; on the contrary everybody is all agog to do something for the poor. A great many things have conduced to this, some good, some bad. The anti-poor-law cry; the state of the houses of the poor, and their sanitary condition, as made

1. MS at LSE.
2. Charles Johnston, *Travels in Southern Abyssinia* (2 vols., London, 1844).

* * * *

1. MS in the possession of Mrs. W. Rosenberg, Wellington, N.Z. Copy supplied by Professor J. M. McCrimmon. Copy bears date of 8th November, 1846, but internal evidence (see notes 5 and 9, below) clearly indicates 1844 as the correct date.

Henry S. Chapman had left England in June, 1843, for New Zealand to take up his duties as the newly appointed Judge of the Supreme Court for the Southern Division.

known by Chadwick's official investigations; the conditions of large masses of people as shown by the enquiries of Commissions about factories, mines, etc., then in another way the speculations of Carlyle,[2] the Puseyites,[3] and others, about the impossibility of any social stability or security if there is not a habitual bond of good offices and sympathy between the ruling classes and the ruled, especially the poor—which speculations would have had no effect whatever if there were no chartism and socialism to frighten the rich. One sees plainly that while the noise is made up by a few sincere people, the bulk of the following has for its motive the desire of preventing revolution, and perhaps still more, the desire of taking the *popularis aura* out of the sails of the Anti-Corn-law league.[4] In both these things they will fail. The Corn Law *must* go, and very soon,[5] and as for revolution, there has been nothing in our day so calculated to produce it as the talk now in vogue, none of which is lost upon the working class, who do not thank them for it one jot, but whom it greatly strengthens in the faith that it is other people's business to take care of them, that all of the rich have more than they is a wrong to them, and that the rich themselves are partly ashamed of this wrong, and partly afraid of its consequences and desiring to buy them off at the expense of those who are better off, is always asserted; and I never remember a time when any suggestion of anti-population doctrine[6] or of forethought and self-command on the part of the poor was so contemptuously scouted as it is now. The "Times" is at the head of this movement, and has contributed very much to set it going. Strange to say, I believe it is sincere. There has been a great change of late years in the "Times", owing it is said, to young Walter,[7] who is a sort of Puseyite, and the "Times" falls in with everything which Puseyism has set going. There is a great appearance of honesty now about all it does. You are not to suppose, however, that all is bad and stupid about this philanthropy-movement—on the contrary there is very much good in it, and it will lead to many very good things being done. Among other things I have no doubt it will lead in time to a considerable move in favour of colonization, and to shew what other things it leads to, the "Times" already talks occasionally

2. Notably in his *Past and Present* (1843).

3. See Letter 270 and JSM's letters, "Puseyism," in the *Morning Chronicle* for Jan. 1, 1842 (p. 1) and Jan. 13, 1842 (p. 3) for his views on the Oxford Movement.

4. The League, which had been founded in 1839, led the agitation for the repeal of the Corn Laws.

5. The repeal did not take place until June, 1846.

6. Doctrine based on the theories of T. R. Malthus.

7. John Walter III (1818–1894), soon (1847) to become the third bearer of the name to be proprietor of *The Times*. The younger Walter's adherence to the Oxford Movement was a source of serious friction with his father and led to estrangement between them (see *The History of the Times, 1841–1884* [New York, 1939], pp. 10–11).

of the great benefits of the labourers being proprietors of land! Things never seemed to tend so rapidly to a complete bouleversement of our social system, though whether peaceably or violently, none can tell. I am thinking of saying out my say on all these things in a treatise on political economy, not in the abstract manner of Ricardo and my father, but in the practical and popular manner of Adam Smith. The whole science requires extremely to be recast, incorporating, of course, Wakefield's and all the other new doctrines and shewing how they do not contradict but *fit into* the others, and such a book if one were able to do it well would at once supersede all the existing treatises, which are, one and all, effete and useless except as matter of history, and would give a right direction to the revived interest which begins to be felt in the study, and which languishes for want of a book at once free from gross error and teaching the applications along with the principles, which it is the beauty of Adam Smith's book that he did. A propos, I published, last spring, the political economy essays which you know of. The success of my Logic brought an offer from Tait to publish them,[8] whereupon I made an offer of them to my own publisher, Parker,[9] which he accepted, and to my surprise the trade subscription was nearly 100. I have not heard anything about the sale; I should fear it is but small. However, Parker has no reason to complain, as it was his own choice, and he has made money by me. On the 25th March we had already divided profit on the Logic, and I expect it will soon be out of print. It has had a degree of success I never expected, and has got into the hands of almost everybody who could be supposed to read such a book.

There is no probability of any change of Ministry here; the Whigs are in as much discredit as ever, Peel is much greater than ever, but nobody wants him turned out, because his hinges are so well oiled and he yields to pressure. I fully expect every session to shew concessions to liberalism, and every year certainly helps to disorganise all the old order. I only wish for personal changes, because I wish that ill-conditioned fellow Stanley[10] to be out of his post of mischief. The Governor[11] he has sent you seems to be hardly better than the last, although so much better was expected from him.

I hope to hear from you soon, as I am very much interested both in the

8. See Letter 424.

9. Letters 425 and 427.

10. Edward George Geoffrey Smith Stanley, then Lord Stanley of Bickerstaffe, later the fourteenth Earl of Derby, at this time Colonial Secretary. For an account of Stanley's conduct of New Zealand affairs, see W. D. Jones, *Lord Derby and Victorian Conservatism* (Oxford, 1956), pp. 94–101.

11. Robert Fitzroy (1805–1865), from 1843 to Nov., 1845, Governor of New Zealand. He had commanded the *Beagle* during Charles Darwin's famous voyage. As Governor he was in frequent conflict with the New Zealand Company and was accused of favouring the natives over the white settlers.

prospects of the Colony and in your own. I fancy that I can figure to myself the position of a New Zealand settler better than I can that of most distant objects, sufficiently well to make it really interesting to me. I hear a little about Nelson[12] by means of Bell's circulars,[13] but I am more curious about Wellington, though I have no land there. Give my kind regards to Revans,[14] and will you kindly ask him if he was out of pocket in any way by my rascal of a relation John Burrow.[15] His draft of £10 was paid. If there is anything more I will repay it.

Ever yours truly,

J. S. MILL.

443. TO MACVEY NAPIER[1]

India House
9th November
1844

MY DEAR SIR

I have been feeling lately a very great inclination to write something on the doctrines & projects which are so rife just at present on the fashionable subject of the "Claims of Labour"[2]—& the little book so called, would furnish an appropriate text, if you are inclined to the subject, & would not prefer seeing it in other hands. It appears to me that along with much of good intention, & something even of sound doctrine, the speculations now afloat are sadly deficient, on the whole, in sobriety & wisdom—forgetful, in general, of the lessons of universal experience, & of some of those fundamental principles which one did think had been put for ever out of the reach of controversy by Adam Smith, Malthus, & others. The general tendency is to rivet firmly in the minds of the labouring people the persuasion that it is the business of others to take care of their condition, with-

---

12. The towns of Nelson and Wellington were both in the Southern Division over which Chapman had jurisdiction as Judge.

13. Probably information circulated by the New Zealand Company which it had obtained from Francis (later Sir Francis) Dillon Bell (1821–1898), a relative of E. G. Wakefield. Bell, who had been in the service of the Company in London since 1838, had gone to New Zealand in 1843 to select lands on behalf of the Company.

14. Samuel Revans (1808–1888) in the 1830's had founded with Chapman the *Daily Advertiser* in Montreal. He left Canada in 1837 and joined Wakefield in the New Zealand colonization; he published the first newspaper there, the *New Zealand Gazette*.

15. Presumably a cousin of JSM on his mother's side.

* * * *

1. Published in *Napier Corresp.*, pp. 477–78. MS in Brit. Mus.

2. JSM's review of Arthur Helps' *The Claims of Labour: an Essay on the Duties of the Employers to the Employed* (London, 1844) appeared in *ER*, LXXXI (April, 1845), 498–525.

out any self control on their own part—& that whatever is possessed by other people, more than they possess, is a wrong to them, or at least a kind of stewardship, of which an account is to be rendered to them. I am sure you will agree with me in thinking it very necessary to make a stand against this sort of spirit while it is at the same time highly necessary as well as right, to shew sympathy in all that is good of the new tendencies, & to avoid the hard, abstract mode of treating such questions which has brought discredit upon political economists & has enabled those who are in the wrong to claim, & generally to receive, exclusive credit for high & benevolent feeling.

I do not know of anything so important at the present time as to attempt to place these subjects in their right position before the public—& it can nowhere be done so well as in the Edinburgh review—where I hope it will be done even if it should not suit you that I should do it—although I know no reason for thinking that the manner in which I should treat the subject would be unsuitable to you.

Very truly yours

J. S. MILL

444. TO WILLIAM TAIT[1]

India House
12ᵗʰ Novʳ 1844

MY DEAR SIR

I send you the article on Johnston,[2] which as you will see, is not mine. It is a light amusing article, chiefly of extracts, & I think it will be pleasant reading for the readers of the Magazine. The few words said about Harris's book[3] are, I should hope, not sufficient to come into unpleasant collision with anything you have said before. Johnstone [*sic*] & his book are, I think, worthy of better treatment than they have received—the book seems to me both more amusing & more interesting than Harris's.

I have ordered a copy of the Essays[4] to be sent to you. I ought to have done so before, as you had certainly a good claim to a copy. I have given away scarcely any. As for Parker it is not his way to give copies, either to the press or to any one else. But I ought myself to have looked to your receiving one.

Very truly yours

J. S. MILL

W. Tait Esq.

1. MS at LSE.
2. See Letter 441, n. 2. The article seems not to have been published.
3. Sir William Cornwallis Harris, *The Highlands of Æthiopia* (3 vols., London, 1844). It had been reviewed in *Tait's* in March and April, 1844.
4. *Essays on Some Unsettled Questions of Political Economy.* See Letter 427.

445. TO MACVEY NAPIER[1]

India House
20th Novr 1844

MY DEAR SIR

The article[2] which I have in view would, according to my present conception of it, be rather one of principles than of details; & would, so far, admit the more easily of being brought within the space to which you consider it necessary to confine it. My object would be to examine & controvert what appears to me an erroneous theory of the condition of the labouring classes. The practical consequences of the theory break out in all sorts of propositions of things to be done for the poor either by the Government, the millowners, the landowners, or the rich in general; some of which propositions have more or less of utility & good sense in them, others are quite chimerical & absurd, but *all* are absurd when looked to as things of great or permanent efficacy. The discussion of the theory will naturally involve a consideration of the real nature of the duties both of Government & of the various classes of society towards the poor; tending mainly to the conclusion, that the greater part of the good they can do is indirect, & consists in stimulating & guiding the energy & prudence of the people themselves: in all which I should wish to use details copiously for purposes of example & illustration, but without laying any particular stress upon them, & still less undertaking to specify with any minuteness what particular things either the Government, or the employers of labour, ought to do or attempt.

According to this idea of what the article would be, it does not seem to be of any special importance that it should precede in its appearance any particular discussion in the House of Commons; but of very considerable importance that it should appear soon: the question being, as you justly remark, the greatest of the day, & moreover most emphatically the question of *the* day: & although the interest of it with thinkers is not likely to abate, anything written on the subject would both be more useful, & much more successful, if it appeared before the subject has been overlaid by the wearisome longwinded discussions of all the periodicals & all the speakers in parliament.

The Times gives us little else from day to day—& the other newspapers are beginning to be full of it. For a time, this works in favour of the interest of the subject—but after a time it will work the contrary way, by exhausting the freshness of the ideas.

We seem quite to agree in our general view of the subject & if you think favorably of the sketch I have now given you of the mode in which

1. Published in *Napier Corresp.*, pp. 478–79. MS in Brit. Mus.
2. See Letter 443.

it should be treated, I will set about it & write the article while my mind is full of the subject.

ever yours truly

J. S. MILL

Guizot of course can wait indefinitely.[3]

446. TO AUGUSTE COMTE[1]

India House

le 25 novembre 1844

MON CHER MONSIEUR COMTE

Vous ne vous trompiez pas en jugeant que votre volume astronomique[2] ne m'était pas encore parvenue lorsque j'écrivais ma dernière lettre. Il ne m'est arrivé, comme de coutume, que très tard, ce qui a depuis longtemps cessé de me surprendre. C'est seulement depuis une huitaine de jours que j'ai pu achever la lecture de ce travail intéressant, dont la valeur a dépassé mes espérances. Il est vraiment heureux que vous vous soyez décidé à écrire ce Traité: quoique d'une importance secondaire en rapport à votre grande entreprise philosophique, il n'en est pas moins fait pour exercer une notable influence en hâtant la formation d'une véritable école positive, et il me semble que vous même vous n'appréciez pas encore suffisamment sa valeur à cet égard. Nous reconnaissons l'un et l'autre de plus en plus combien on doit peu compter pour la cause du positivisme sur ceux qui en possèdent déjà les bases scientifiques. Il importe donc infiniment, sous tous les rapports de mettre le plus tôt possible à la portée des intelligences convenables, non fournies d'instruction scientifique spéciale, ce qu'il faut de connaissances positives pour s'approprier les idées fondamentales de la méthode scientifique, sans les assujettir préalablement à de longues et pénibles études techniques, qui leur répugneraient le plus souvent au point d'empêcher tout développement ultérieur de leur capacité scientifique, attendu que pour sentir réellement l'importance de cette préparation positive, il faudrait posséder déjà l'esprit positif. Pour sortir donc de ce cercle vicieux, il n'y a rien de plus urgent que d'avoir un Cours de *science* positive, préliminaire naturel de votre Cours de philosophie positive. Or ce petit ouvrage en remplit admirablement les conditions, autant que le comportent son étendue et son caractère de spécialité. Depuis quelque temps les traités scientifiques à l'usage du public paraissent chez nous en grande abondance;

3. See Letter 419, n. 2.

* * * *

1. MS at Johns Hopkins. Published in Lévy-Bruhl, pp. 369–73; in reply to Comte's of Oct. 21, *ibid.*, pp. 359–69.
2. *Traité philosophique d'astronomie populaire* (Paris, 1844).

il y en a d'assez bien faits; J. Herschel lui-même a fait un traité populaire d'astronomie.[3] Mais dans ces traités on n'essaie pas même de faire servir de si mémorables conquêtes de l'intelligence humaine à constater la manière dont elle doit procéder pour en faire de nouvelles. Il est même, je crois, heureux que ces écrivains n'aient pas tenté d'enseigner la méthode, mais seulement la doctrine, vu l'insuffisance de leurs propres notions logiques; insuffisance tellement prononcée qu'il n'y a presque pas un seul traité de science positive, soit classique, soit populaire, qui ne tende sous quelques égards notables à fausser le véritable esprit de la marche scientifique. Or il me paraît que vous avez comblé, d'une manière admirable, cette déplorable lacune. Je ne croyais guère qu'il fût possible de donner à des lecteurs à qui on supposaerit si peu de préparation mathématique une connaissance si pleinement satisfaisante du vrai caractère de la science astronomique, et des procédés scientifiques qui l'ont créée. Après un pareil exemple, nous pouvons nous flatter de voir prochainement des ouvrages au moins passables du même genre, par rapport aux autres sciences fondamentales. Ce sera je crois le fruit que nous recueillerons de la première extension notable de la philosophie positive parmi les intelligences du second ordre. Aujourd'hui même je sens que les difficultés du propagandisme positif commencent à s'aplanir par suite de ce que vous avez fait. Le défaut d'instruction scientifique préalable n'est plus un obstacle pour faire comprendre ce que c'est que le positivisme à ceux qu'on pourrait décider à lire votre petit Traité. On peut même dire qu'après cette seule lecture une intelligence bien organisée se trouverait mieux préparée aux spéculations sociales que la presque totalité des savans actuels, sans parler des métaphysiciens.

J'ai appris avec une joie véritable que la méprisable taciturnité de la presse française à votre égard allait enfin être rompue, et je suis bien aise que ce soit par M. Littré,[4] à qui depuis longtemps j'ai voué une haute estime. Je le connais très bien de réputation; je l'ai même vu, en 1836, à Paris, où sa figure de savant solitaire et son maintien calme et modeste m'on beaucoup frappé. Probablement, il ne se souvient guère de notre entrevue. Je ne savais pas qu'il fût en sympathie avec la nouvelle philosophie, et je m'en réjouis vivement: son accession, quelqu'incomplète qu'elle puisse être, est du plus heureux augure, et j'attends avec impatience son appréciation de votre grand ouvrage. Si cette publication s'effectue dans le National, ou même dans un journal quelconque, elle attirera sur la philosophie positive l'attention de beaucoup de lecteurs qui n'en tenaient

3. Herschel's treatise on astronomy published in Lardner's *Cabinet Cyclopædia* in 1833 and translated into French by M. Peyrot in 1834 was the basis of his much expanded *Outlines of Astronomy* (London, 1849, and later editions).

4. Emile Littré (1801–1881), scholar, philosopher, and lexicographer; one of Comte's most ardent disciples, though he rejected Comte's later theories; author of *Auguste Comte et la philosophie positive* (Paris, 1863).

auparavant aucun compte, qui n'en avaient peut-être pas même entendu le nom, et parmi eux il doit s'en trouver de bien préparés pour sa réception complète. Si vous pouviez m'envoyer les numéros du journal qui contiendront ces articles ce serait me faire un très grand plaisir: ceux-là on peut les confier à la poste. Dans tout cas je compte sur vous pour m'en indiquer les dates.

J'espère que vous êtes depuis longtemps parfaitement rétabli des suites du trouble physique que vous avez subi le mois dernier. Une maladie éruptive par suite d'une surexcitation nerveuse est certainement un exemple très remarquable, quoique d'un genre aujourd'hui très familier, du *consensus* biologique, et surtout de cette complication des phénomènes de la vie animale avec ceux de la vie organique qui a rendu si difficile et si tardive leur séparation logique, sans laquelle pourtant la biologie ne pouvait nullement devenir positive. J'ai appris avec un vif intérêt le résultat de vos observations spontanées sur les effets intellectuels du jeûne, et je vous félicite d'avoir surmonté la plus sérieuse difficulté de votre nouvelle élaboration philosophique. Je juge essentiellement comme vous le genre d'esprit de M. Herschel, et je ne fonde aucun espoir sérieux sur sa lecture de votre Cours, qui, je crois, aura peu d'influence, ici comme ailleurs, sur les hommes dont la réputation est faite. Je trouve toutefois dans la critique qu'il a faite de la philosophie de Whewell, des marques d'une certaine capacité philosophique: au moins il a échappé aux influences germaniques, ce qui chez nous n'est pas peu de chose. Je n'ai jamais lu Vico[5] mais autant que j'en puis juger je crois votre opinion de lui très bien fondée.

Tout à vous,

J. S. MILL

447. TO ADOLPHE D'EICHTHAL[1]

India House
10th December
1844

MY DEAR ADOLPHE

I was truly disappointed the other day when I found that you had been here & that I had missed you. Wednesday is a day on which I am usually

5. Giovanni Battista Vico (1668–1744), Italian jurist and philosopher, often regarded as the founder of the philosophy of history, and mentioned by JSM in the *Logic*, Book VI, chap. x, sec. 3.

* * * *

1. MS at Arsenal.

engaged with the Court of Directors, as it is the day of their meeting. I should have enjoyed greatly seeing you once again & comparing notes with you (as we say) on a great many subjects.

I have read with very great interest the papers you sent me, the report on the *caisse de retraite*, & the four numbers of the Moniteur Grec.[2] The first is very important, & all the views & propositions seem to me extremely well-considered & reasonable: what is the probability of their being adopted? The Greek paper is well written & seems candid. I have always been inclined to think well of Coletti[3] because I knew him to be a friend of yours & of your brother's & I knew Gustave's high opinion of him, & I was not inclined to think the worse of him for being attacked by our newspapers with which I am as thoroughly disgusted as I am with yours. But I do not know how to get over the gross illegalities which his party seem to be committing in the exclusion of the partisans of the former ministry from the chamber on any or on no pretext—a thing which the Moniteur Grec in its fourth number seems to admit, or at least to be unable to deny. It is impossible for me to think otherwise than ill of any minister to whom a constitution & laws are a dead letter which they think nothing of violating— & the infamous conduct of your government in the affairs of Spain inclines every one here to put the worst construction on whatever is done in any constitutional country by the party which is supposed to have the support of the French diplomatic agent.—I doubt if I could induce any English newspaper of influence to insert the correspondence which you propose— but I could perhaps succeed either with the Times or the Morning Chronicle, both of which however would probably combat in their leading articles the views of their correspondent. Still, if you think it worth while, I will try—& I should for my own part have much pleasure in doing so.

I owe a letter to Gustave in return for one he wrote to me communicating the interesting fact of the birth of his son, on which I beg you to offer to him my sincere congratulations. Although I have not been a very frequent correspondent lately, either with him or my other friends at Paris, I have not lost any of my regard for them & there is no one I shall be more glad to see again than him.

ever & most truly yours

J. S. MILL

2. *Moniteur grec*, a tri-monthly ministerial journal in French sponsored by M. Coletti; it began publication in Athens in Oct., 1844 (see *Moniteur universel*, Oct. 30, 1844, p. 2809, and Nov. 11, 1844, p. 2857).
3. John Kolettis [Jean Coletti] (1788–1847), Greek general and statesman, ambassador to France, 1835–44.

448. TO AUGUSTE COMTE[1]

India House
le 31 décembre
1844

MON CHER MONSIEUR COMTE

C'est avec une peine extrême que j'ai appris le déplorable résultat, en ce qui vous regarde, de cette tentative avortée de réorganisation dans l'école polytechnique,[2] qui devait au contraire, suivant toute apparence, consolider votre position de manière à vous mettre à l'abri de toute attaque future de la part de ceux que votre franchise philosophique a soulevés contre vous. Malheureusement il y a lieu de s'attendre à une inimitié plus forcenée de leur part, en raison directe de l'importance croissante de la nouvelle école. On peut croire que les savans, ainsi que les prêtres, auraient pu se soumettre à vous laisser tranquille dans la position modeste qui vous était échue, s'ils avaient pu compter que par un silence calculé ils pourraient vous ensevelir dans l'obscurité: mais, lorsqu'ils s'aperçoivent que votre nom commence à percer, et que partout où l'on vous fait une place quelconque, on vous en fait une très élevée, dès lors, ce n'est plus seulement la vanité blessée qui est en jeu, c'est toute l'importance sociale d'une classe puissante qui se trouverait compromise si on ne parvenait à étouffer une voix qu'on sait bien ne pouvoir réduire au silence qu'en vous ôtant tout moyen de vivre ou du moins de loisir. Vous aurez donc des ennemis de plus en plus acharnés, et plus ils vous auront nui, plus ils chercheront à vous nuire. Il est certes bien digne de vous, de voir dans cet ensemble de circonstances, si fâcheuses en ce qui vous regarde personnellement, des motifs de consolation fondés sur le retentissement social auquel ce duel à mort doit donner lieu et qui sans doute, comme vous en faites l'observation, serait resté dans des proportions minimes si nulle existence sociale ne se trouvait compromise dans la lutte. Il faut espérer du moins que si vous subissez les peines du martyre vous en aurez aussi les honneurs, et que l'humanité en recueillera le fruit. Il n'y a d'esperi réel que dans l'opinion, et ce sera une importante expérience sociologique qui décidera si aujourd'hui une classe sociale peut persécuter un philosophe isolé sans avoir même le concours du gouvernement. Il est très malheureux que la fermeté du maréchal Soult[3] ne se soutienne pas: je craindrais bien que l'influence

1. MS at Johns Hopkins. Published in Lévy-Bruhl, pp. 384–87; in reply to Comte's of Dec. 25, *ibid.*, pp. 373–83.
2. A reorganization of the council of the Ecole Polytechnique, which Comte had hoped would lead to a vote favourable to his reinstatement as examiner, had proved disappointing; by a vote of ten to nine the new council had confirmed the action of the former council in displacing Comte (see his letter of Dec. 25).
3. Nicolas Jean de Dieu Soult, Duke of Dalmatia (1769–1851), Marshal of France, at this time Minister of War. The administration of the Ecole Polytechnique lay within the jurisdiction of his department.

auguste dont on vous a parlé n'y soit pour quelque chose. Le devoir du gouvernement serait, s'il répugne à casser l'arrêt du nouveau conseil polytechnique sitôt après l'avoir organisé, de vous enlever à cette carrière, en vous en faisant une autre, plus importante, en vous nommant, par exemple, à quelque chaire du premier ordre, qui conviendrait à quelque partie du cercle immense de vos connaissances scientifiques et historiques. Ce serait pour M. Guizot une belle occasion de montrer de la magnanimité, s'il en a, suivant le noble exemple de M. Poinsot, et j'ai appris avec un vrai plaisir que dans la question immédiate au moins, un homme de sa capacité, auquel je n'ai jamais pu refuser une certaine estime, s'est montré disposé à bien agir. Il est fâcheux que cette affaire doit probablement traîner en longueur, et que vous ne pouvez pas savoir au plus tôt, à quoi vous en tenir. Si malheureusement vous êtes réduit de nouveau à la ressource de l'enseignement privé, comptez sur tous mes efforts et sur ceux de tous mes amis qui vous connaissent ou sur lesquels je puis exercer quelque influence. Je ne connais actuellement aucun anglais riche qui habite Paris, mais il doit sans doute y en avoir que je pourrais mettre en mouvement, du moins indirectement. Vous m'indiquerez le moment où il conviendrait de commencer cette tentative, si malheureusement il y a lieu.

Les articles de Littré[4] sont excellents. Je ne m'attendais nullement à une si pleine adhésion, et je la trouve du plus heureux augure. Quel que soit le génie de l'auteur d'une théorie quelconque le public n'y prend pas beaucoup d'intérêt tant qu'il reste seul de son avis, trouvant fort naturel qu'un homme tienne à ses propres idées: mais dès que ces idées sont solennellement adoptées par un second penseur d'une supériorité reconnue, la bataille est presque gagnée; les esprits supérieurs ne tardent plus à y affluer en foule. C'est une véritable époque dans la nouvelle crise sociale, que cette importante adhésion, qui me rappelle celle de Berthollet aux doctrines de Lavoisier.[5] La mienne n'était pas, à beaucoup près, aussi importante, ne pouvant guère agir sur la France, seul pays vraiment préparé aujourd'hui pour la régénération philosophique. Je voudrais bien savoir quelle réception l'Allemagne donne à votre grand ouvrage. J'ai lieu de croire que le mien y est mieux accueilli que je ne pouvais m'y attendre, si je puis me fier aux rapports d'un allemand que je vis il y a huit jours et qui me raconta entr'autres choses qu'il avait lu un article très favorable à ce sujet dans un journal publié dans la petite ville de Hohenzollern——quelque chose (j'ai oublié le reste du mot) ce qui équivaudrait au plus à un simple chef lieu de département au centre de la France et qu'on y disait que c'était le

4. On Comte and positivism, in the *National*.
5. Antoine Laurent Lavoisier (1743–1794), chemist famous for overthrowing the hypothesis of phlogiston and thereby reorganizing the science of chemistry. Claude Louis Berthollet (1748–1822) readily accepted and extended Lavoisier's theories.

meilleur ouvrage philosophique que l'angleterre a produit de nos jours, en y ajoutant que ce n'était certainement pas de la philosophie allemande. Je pense qu'il y a en allemagne un commencement très décidé de réaction contre la philosophie qu'on appelle allemande et que la méthode positive y trouvera de l'appui plus tôt qu'on ne pouvait le croire. Il doit y avoir parmi les physiciens et physiologistes et même parmi la jeunesse active qui désire s'occuper de politique, une sincère aversion, d'un côté pour le vague et d'un autre côté pour les tendances quiétistes de la métaphysique de Schelling et de Hegel.

Tout à vous

J. S. MILL

449. TO SARAH AUSTIN[1]

India House
January 18, 1845

. . . About poor Comte's affairs, he has himself written to me very fully,[2] and informed me of the final close of the whole matter, so far as his restoration to the examinership is concerned. I am glad on every account that you interested yourself with Guizot for him, and that you mentioned my name in the manner you did,[3] although it would hardly have been warrantable in me to take any direct measure of the same kind, as my acquaintance with Guizot is so very slight. It may be useful to Comte on future occasions to have given evidence to Guizot of our interest in him. He himself seems to bear up bravely against his misfortune. I perceive he has considerable hope that when a vacancy occurs in any one of the several other Polytechnic offices, the opportunity may be taken of repairing the injustice done him; and I hope the occasion may occur soon, as I have much doubt about the success of his other plans. The private lessons in mathematics may answer, notwithstanding their high price, but not, I fear, if he relies at all upon the rich English. What do you think of his Review project?[4] To me it seems a very doubtful one; and I fear, too, he will be disappointed by the very little help I shall be able to give him in writing for it, although I will do all I can. About Comte himself I have formed very much the same opinion that you have,[5] both as to his good and bad points

1. Published in Janet Ross, *Three Generations of English Women* (revised ed., London, 1893), pp. 208–10. MS not located. Though addressed to Sarah Austin this is also an answer to an as yet unpublished letter (MS at Yale) by John Austin, dated Dec. 25, 1844.

2. Comte's letters of Dec. 25, 1834, and Jan. 10, 1845, Lévy-Bruhl, pp. 373–83 and 388–400.

3. Austin had reported in his letter of Dec. 25 that he had called on Guizot on Dec. 23 and told him that if he could help Comte he would thereby "confer a great personal favour upon Mr. John Mill & myself."

4. In his letter of Jan. 10, 1845, Comte outlined at length a proposal initiated by Emile Littré for the establishment of a Positive Review. See also JSM's letter of Jan. 27, 1845 (the next letter).

5. Austin had written: "I fear, from what M. Dunoyer told me, that there is a good deal of prejudice against Comte, as being a mere man of speculation, more intent upon impressing his own theories upon the students, than upon exactly performing the duties of his office. It is probable, too, that the fit of insanity under which he has

of character. He is evidently (either from character or the tendencies of a solitary thinker, little appreciated by the world), most obstinately bent upon following his own course, regardless not only of giving offence (which might be a virtue), but of compromising his means of livelihood.[6] He piques himself exceedingly upon being the only Frenchman who speaks out his opinions without any compromises or reserves, and he has gone so far in that course that I think he would do himself more harm than good now by swerving from it. At all events, I am certain he will not abate one jot of his "franchise philosophique," and therefore there is not much use in advising him to do so. He is a man one can only serve in his own way.

What you say about Guizot and his family interests me exceedingly.[7] A man in such a position as his, acts under so many difficulties, and is mixed up in so many questionable transactions that one's favourable opinion is continually liable to receive shocks, and I have for many years been oscillating in Guizot's case between great esteem and considerable misgivings. Nothing I ever heard of him tells so much in his favour as the feeling you express about him after familiar intercourse. If he was an angel he would be sure to be misunderstood in the place he is in. I do not know whether to wish or to deprecate his being thrown out of it, which seems now so likely to happen.

I have been chiefly occupied lately in writing an article for the *Edinburgh Review* on the "claims of labour."[8] I never knew a time when so much nonsense, and mischievous nonsense, too, was afloat on that subject, and

---

suffered, coupled with the hostility of the men of science whom he has provoked, may have led to a general belief that he is half mad. . . .

"From all that I have seen of Comte, I believe that he is a man of great sincerity and uprightness (which appears, indeed, to be generally admitted); and (what, perhaps, you would not think) that he is a man of a generous and affectionate temper. But of all the men I ever saw (excepting Mr. Bentham) he is the most confident in his own capacity and views, and the least inclined to attend to the suggestions of others. It is, therefore, nearly impossible to get him to act with ordinary prudence.

"I have rarely seen a man so interesting, and who so well supported, on personal acquaintance, the favourable impression made by him at a distance. . . ."

6. Austin had written: "I wish you could persuade Comte to be more reserved about religion. He sets it aside with a cool contempt, which even in impious France, does harm to his worldly condition; not to mention, that his peremptory rejection of that, and of all philosophy concerned with the insoluble and transcendent, raises a presumption against his scientific capacities in many of the best minds not acquainted with his book. But, like Mr. Bentham (of whom he constantly reminds me), he is so wedded to his own devices and so full of presumptuous contempt for all which has been done by others, that I fear he would not be moved even by your insinuations."

7. "Nothing can exceed the kindness of M. Guizot, and of his noble-hearted mother, to Mrs. Austin and myself. Though his talents are great, various & imposing, I am far more struck by the elevated moral character which seems to break out spontaneously in his conversation & manners. . . . Neither he nor his children (so far as I can see) are at all spoiled by his extraordinary rise in the world. . . ."

8. See Letters 443 and 445.

I thought it a most useful thing to enter a protest against the intolerable mass of pseudo-philanthropy now getting into vogue, and to commit the *Edinburgh Review* at the same time (if possible) to strong things in favour of good popular education and just laws. I am afraid, however, that some of the strong things I have said on both sides will frighten so timid a man as Napier, and that he will not dare to print them unmodified. He always, of himself, seems to like my articles, and evidently always hears so much said against them afterwards, by the octogenarian clique, Rogers,[9] Sidney Smith,[10] etc., whom he looks up to, that he has now, I think, a constant terror lest I should get him into a scrape.

Is there any chance of the article on Prussia soon, or of a book rather than an article, or of a reprint of your husband's former book,[11] with the second volume which he projected? I feel certain that a book with his name would be read by numbers of people to whom it would do good, and nothing but books seems to do good now. The time for writing books seems to have come again, though unhappily not for living by doing it.

Ever affectionately yours,

J. S. MILL

450. TO AUGUSTE COMTE[1]

India House
le 27 janvier 1845

MON CHER MONSIEUR COMTE

Comme vous me l'avez demandé dans votre dernière lettre, j'ai mûrement réfléchi sur le projet de revue qui vous a été proposé par M. Littré, et j'ai consulté ceux de mes amis les plus compétens en pareille matière, qui se trouvaient à portée de communication. Avant de vous en donner le résultat général, je dois m'expliquer pleinement en ce qui regarde ma coopération personnelle. Je trouve des obstacles insurmontables à ce qu'elle soit aussi étendue que vous le désirez, ou même assez étendue pour que vous puissiez beaucoup compter là-dessus. Le degré de coopération que vous me demandez me prendrait à peu près tout le temps dont je puis habituellement disposer pour écrire, même en renonçant à toute publication ultérieure en mon propre nom. Ensuite quand cette difficulté n'existerait

9. Samuel Rogers.
10. Sydney Smith (1771–1845), canon of St. Paul's, writer and wit; one of the founders of the *Edinburgh Review*.
11. *The Province of Jurisprudence Determined* (London, 1832).

* * * *

1. MS at Johns Hopkins. Published in Lévy-Bruhl, pp. 400–404; in reply to Comte's of Jan. 10, *ibid.*, pp. 388–400.

pas, je ne comprends pas assez ce que serait la revue, ni même ce qu'elle pourrait être, pour que je puisse aujourd'hui prendre un engagement absolu de collaboration. Tant qu'il s'agit de méthodes philosophiques, de doctrines historiques, des lois du développement social passé et présent, je sais à quoi m'en tenir: je ne crois pas qu'il y ait entre nous deux aucune divergence d'opinion très sérieuse. Mais en fondant une revue, et surtout en la fondant au nom d'un système de philosophie, on prend l'engagement de se jeter dans toutes les questions, d'une certaine importance, qui se discutent aujourd'hui: et sur ce terrain-là il n'y a pas à présumer qu'il y aurait une harmonie suffisante dans nos opinions. Je pense que si vous étiez appelé à vous prononcer sur toutes les questions et à dire toutes vos idées, nous nous trouverions en désaccord plus souvent et plus sérieusement que vous ne semblez le croire, et que moi-même je ne l'avais d'abord espéré. Ce n'est qu'après avoir vu au moins un ou deux numéros de la revue que je pourrais décider avec connaissance de cause jusqu'à quel point je pourrais utilement y prendre part.

En m'expliquant ainsi sur ce qui me regarde, je vous indique déjà les doutes que j'éprouve sur l'opportunité du projet en lui-même. En effet, le positivisme ne me paraît pas encore bien en état de se produire avec avantage comme école. Pour en faire une aux yeux du public il faudrait un corps commun de doctrine, et il n'y a encore qu'une méthode et quelques principes très généraux, qui même ne sont pas encore reconnus par la majorité de ceux qui acceptent le principe essentiel du positivisme, celui de rejeter absolument toute spéculation sur les causes premières, en se bornant à la recherche des lois effectives des phénomènes. Dans l'intérêt donc du développement spéculatif, cet essai de propagande me paraîtrait prématuré: voilà du moins quel serait mon avis, si l'on pouvait faire abstraction de la légitime influence des circonstances personnelles. Sous ce dernier rapport, tout dépend des chances du succès, dont je ne suis pas, comme observateur éloigné, en position de juger; mais l'opinion d'un homme tel que Littré, fortifiée par celle de M. de Blainville et des autres amis que vous m'indiquez, doit avoir un grand poids. Quant à l'Angleterre, tout m'avertit qu'il y a peu à espérer. Je vous dirai ce que me mande, à ce sujet, M. Grote. Il dit qu'il ne connaît, outre lui-même, que deux individus qui probablement s'abonneraient à la revue. Ce sont Molesworth et le docteur Arnott,[2] médecin très estimé, auteur d'un traité de physique populaire, et qui a connu même avant moi les premiers volumes de votre Cours. Il peut tout au plus se trouver, selon M. Grote, quelques savans qui liraient la revue avec plaisir pour y recueillir des idées philosophiques sur les sciences physiques: encore serait-ce de rares exceptions, vu la tendance aujourd'hui si prononcée à transiger avec la théologie par des concessions générales, en se réservant la liberté tacite des détails, qui seuls importent à des esprits

2. Neil Arnott.

emprisonnés pour la plupart dans leur étroite spécialité. Comme le dit M. Grote, nous sommes à présent dans un temps où le philosophe se prosterne avec affectation devant le prêtre. Je serais plein d'espoir si je croyais l'époque venue où l'on pourrait, avec succès, arborer un drapeau franchement positif, en secouant ouvertement tout lambeau des doctrines du passé (sauf leur valeur historique) et refusant toute concession, même tacite, envers les théories surnaturelles. Je ne crois pas cette époque aussi éloignée qu'elle paraît à bien d'autres: il n'y faudrait peut être qu'un peu de hardiesse, et je ne serais pas très éloigné d'en faire moi-même l'essai. Mais alors ce serait dans un livre. Comme en toute révolution spéculative, il faut que les livres précèdent les revues. Je pense bien que votre grand ouvrage fait du chemin ici; on en parle peu, mais on y fait de tems en tems des allusions, et Bain, qui fréquente plus que moi le monde savant, me dit qu'il en voit des preuves croissantes. Quoique je craigne que ceci ne regarde principalement les premiers volumes, ces volumes mêmes doivent tendre à accoutumer ceux qui les lisent à l'élimination totale de l'élément théologique, comme ils l'ont décidée chez Bain lui-même. Mais cette action sur les penseurs isolés serait plus gênée que hâtée par une tentative quelconque de constituer publiquement une école anti-religieuse, qui en effrayant le public et en entamant des discussions prématurées du moins en angleterre, donnerait probablement ici une nouvelle force à la réaction religieuse. Au reste M. Grote m'a témoigné son intention de se faire inscrire comme actionnaire. De mon côté je vous engage à m'inscrire pour cinq actions et à m'indiquer l'époque où j'aurai à verser la première souscription. Si je fais des articles on pourra me les compter jusqu'à concurrence des versements ultérieurs, mais je ne veux pas accepter d'autre rétribution pécuniaire.

Quant à l'avis que vous me demandez sur le choix d'un titre, l'un ou l'autre de ceux que vous me désignez me semble admissible mais il me paraîtrait plus simple de dire tout court, *revue positive*, en vous désignant ensuite comme directeur. Quant aux autres questions, nous avons le temps d'y songer.

tout à vous

J. S. MILL

451. TO DR. WILLIAM BENJAMIN CARPENTER[1]

31 Jan. 1845

I had heard the "Vestiges"[2] several times attributed to you, but I have always said I was certain you were not the author.

1. Excerpt published in Maggs Bros. Catalogue No. 641, 1937, item 144. MS not located.
2. [Robert Chambers], *Vestiges of the Natural History of Creation* (London, 1844).

I do not think I ever told you that I heard from Comte that M. Littré, the very distinguished editor & translator of Hippocrates,[3] values very highly your "General Physiology"[4] & that Comte saw the book at Littré's house & from a hasty inspection of it thought very favourably both of the plan & execution.

452. TO HENRY COLE[1]

I.H.
5 Feb. 1845

MY DEAR COLE

Many thanks for the cheque, which I did not expect to receive so soon.[2] I hope your sending it is a good sign of the success of the Hist. Register.[3] Above all I hope you have not sent it at any inconvenience. If you have, pray tell me so & I will refund it. The remaining £45 can wait your perfect convenience.

Most truly yours

J. S. MILL

453. TO HENRY C. CAREY[1]

East India House
London
15th February 1845

SIR—I have to acknowledge, with thanks, the letter which you did me the honour to address to me on the occasion of my sending you a small volume of Political Economy Essays. I have also to repair my omission to acknowledge the receipt of the systematic Treatise[2] which you were so good as to send to me some time before.

3. Hippocrate, *Œuvres complètes* . . . ed. Emile Littré (10 vols., Paris, 1839–61).
4. See Letter 386, n. 5.

* * * *

1. MS in the possession of Professor J. M. McCrimmon.
2. See Letters 414, 415.
3. *Historical Register, with the sanction and assistance of various government departments*. This short-lived paper (Jan. 10–Mar. 8, 1845—10 nos.) was described as "a stamped newspaper and register of family events, national and private biography, life and health."

* * * *

1. *Addressed*: Henry C. Carey Esq. / care of Messrs Carey, Lea, and Blanchard / Philadelphia / United States. *Postmarks*: 1 / PAID / 15FE15 / 1845 and L/FE 16. MS in Princeton University Library.
   Henry Charles Carey (1793–1879), publisher and economist.
2. *Principles of Political Economy* (3 vols., Philadelphia, 1837–40).

I was fully prepared to find that you would differ widely from many of the opinions I had expressed, as I do from many of those contained in your more elaborate work. Those differences do not surprise me, on a subject so imperfectly understood, a subject too, which independently of all defects in the manner of studying it, is, I cannot but think, in its own nature much more complicated than you appear to believe. It is fortunate that political economists do not differ so radically in their conclusions, as the diversity of their premises might lead any one to expect, & that your doctrines point as directly as those of any follower of Adam Smith or Ricardo, to the gradual abandonment of the restrictive, or as it is improperly called, the protective policy—to which I am not the less rootedly hostile because I differ from you in thinking that in certain exceptional cases, the conditional maintenance of some part of the system may be justified or even required by self-protection.

I thank you very sincerely for having taken the trouble to express your sentiments so fully & freely on those parts of my little book which you disagree with. I could give what would appear to me sufficient answers to your objections, but it will perhaps be preferable to state in few words what I conceive to be the principal difference between your scheme of Political Economy, as very clearly set forth in your book, & my own. Most of what appears to me erroneous in your opinions, flows by direct consequence from your refusing to admit (as of any influence in practice) any other source of exchangeable value than labour.

In the case of all useful articles which admit of indefinite increase by means of labour, the labour required for producing them is, no doubt, the regulator & measure of their value; & I look upon it as one of the chief merits of Ricardo to have established in its full generality this law, which is still far from being admitted by the common herd of political economists. It therefore gave me pleasure to see so fundamental a principle thoroughly recognized & enforced by an American political economist; but it seems to me that you overlook half the truth when you deny that a different law governs all cases of either natural or artificial monopoly, & that cases partaking more or less of that character are so far from being exceptions, that they constitute a full half of all the cases which arise; land & its produce being the most conspicuous, but very far from the sole, example.

In the case of land, this principle of value would indeed be of no practical importance if you were right in your doctrine that the effect of an increase of capital & population is to enable the increased agricultural produce thereby required, to be obtained at a smaller instead of a greater cost. This is true up to the point of density in population, which is indispensable to the use of costly machinery & to the adequate combination & division of labour. The limit cannot be fixed precisely. But, that there is a limit, it is hardly possible, I think, for any one living in an old country, to doubt; & that when this point is attained, the natural law by which (in any given state of knowledge) a double expenditure on land yields less than a double return, prevails, on the average, over the antagonist influence of new inventions & discoveries. I cannot help attributing the contrary opinion which you entertain on this subject, to your living in a country where population does not yet press upon the productive powers of the soil, & where, consequently, the value of land does not yet much exceed a compensation for the capital expended in clearing & bringing it into cultivation.

The nature & tendencies of our difference of opinion need not be further explained to one who has shewn so correct a comprehension as you have, of the doctrines which he contends against; & I need only further add my congratulations upon the increasing cultivation of these speculations in so important a portion of the civilized world as the United States, & my unfeigned acknowledgment of the spirit of complete fairness, so rare in controversial writers, with which you have throughout treated the opinions & writers that you controvert.

Believe me with sincere respect
yours

J. S. MILL

454. TO MACVEY NAPIER[1]

India House
17th Feb[y] 1845

MY DEAR SIR

I did not know, or had forgotten, that the review was or considered itself committed on Wakefield's[2] principle & on small holdings, otherwise I should not have written on them as I have, nor have written on them at all without communicating with you. I am sorry that the great power of the Edinburgh Review is engaged on what appears to me the wrong side of two of the most important questions which political economists or statesmen have to do with, & I am sorry too on account of the article, which will suffer very much by the excision of those two discussions—I cannot consider them excursions from the subject of the article,[3] which I take to be, not solely the things which cannot, but also those which can, be done for the labouring classes. The grand defect of the subject, both in itself & with a view to effect, was, that almost everything to be said was negative—that there was so little positive to propose—& even of that little the article now loses the

---

1. MS in Brit. Mus.   2. Edward Gibbon Wakefield, the colonizer.
3. "The Claims of Labour," *ER*, LXXXI (April, 1845), 498–525.

greater part, & that to which I chiefly trusted for gratifying the disagreeableness & unpopularity of the other branch of the argument & shewing that the doctrines called Malthusian do not as is vulgarly supposed, imply that in one's opinions on social arrangements one looks only to amount of production & not to the producers. However since it is as you tell me, there is no more to be said. I have struck out all that I had written on colonization, expressly reserving that question to be discussed separately, & merely expressing an opinion that something *is* to be done in that way—from which opinion I hope the review does not dissent. I cannot think it even *possible* to pass over the subject of allotments.[4] If that were left out, in addition to colonization & the short time question, it would be leaving out not the part of Hamlet merely, but all the principal characters, those three being the only projects now afloat, for improving the condition of the poor, to which any one really attaches any serious importance. In treating of this I have attempted, without expressing my opinion in favour of small holdings, to retain, for the sake of the general argument, as much of what I originally said on that subject, as may serve to shew that the allotment question as it now presents itself is quite independent of that larger question, & that one may be in favour of small holdings, under some institutions & in some circumstances, & yet disapprove of allotments. This is quite necessary to the strength of our case against allotments & unless it can be managed I do not see how I could make a satisfactory thing of the article.

Since the whole is actually in type as I originally wrote it, I should be very much obliged if you would have struck off for me one copy (two or three would be still better) before the alterations in the last half sheet are made; that in case of the republication which I meditate, my opinions may be represented fairly,[5] which in the present case unfortunately they cannot be in the review. In the hope that you will thus oblige me I have corrected the printing of the passages which are to be cancelled.

In the various minor matters you will see that I have endeavoured as far as possible to comply with your wishes—except in one instance, that of the word *ideas* in page 7, which I cannot admit to be not English as there used; it is used in the ordinary sense in which we speak of "men of ideas" or of a book as being "wanting in ideas" or say that a writer's "ideas are better than his mode of expressing them" &c &c. I should not wish to retain the word if I could find any other that would replace it, but I have tried every cognate word that I could think of, & for different reasons all are objectionable. If that were altered the whole of the first part of the paragraph must

4. The practice of allotting garden plots to labourers. In the article JSM expressed approval of the practice when it was adopted to increase the happiness of workers but not when it was designed simply to supplement low wages.

5. The article was reprinted in *Dissertations*, II, 260–96, with omissions but without substantial additions.

be recast & I am sure I could not express the meaning as well in any totally different arrangement & phraseology.

As for a heading, would there be any objection to "The Claims of Labour"? It gives at once a complete notion of what the article is about, & as it happens also to be the title of the book reviewed, the review will be relieved from the responsibility of any little tinge of affectation that there may appear to be in the phrase.

I have made a few alterations of my own in different parts of the article, all tending towards curtailment.

Very truly yours,

J. S. MILL.

455. TO ALEXANDER BAIN[1]

[March, 1845]

Have you seen Ward's book, *The Ideal, &c.?*[2] It is a remarkable book in every way, and not the least so because it quotes and puffs me in every chapter, and Comte occasionally, though with deep lamentations over our irreligion.

456. TO MACVEY NAPIER[1]

India House
21 April
1845

MY DEAR SIR

I have this morning received your remittance, which, as on former occasions, is extremely liberal in its amount.

I hope you will be much benefitted by quiet & country air & that the next accounts will report a great improvement in your health.

It could scarcely be expected that the review would be much noticed by the press in the thick of the Maynooth discussions,[2] but the effect of the Ed. Rev. is not dependent on newspaper notices.

1. Excerpt published in Bain, *JSM*, p. 80. MS not located.
2. William George Ward, *The Ideal of a Christian Church Considered in Comparison with Existing Practice* (London, 1844).

* * * *

1. MS in Brit. Mus.
2. Sir Robert Peel, Prime Minister, had proposed on April 3 a measure increasing from £9,000 to £26,000 the parliamentary grant to Maynooth College in Ireland. Since Maynooth educated Roman Catholic priests, Protestant fury in both England and Ireland rose to extravagant heights. The Maynooth grant became the great political controversy of the year. The measure finally became law on June 16.

The great majority[3] makes the victory over religious bigotry a most valuable triumph. Since so much opposition to a reasonable Irish policy still exists we may rejoice that it has collected itself in such force to be so completely beaten. Peel's & Graham's speeches[4] are of most favourable augury, though one is glad that they received personally their deserts from Macaulay[5] & others.

yours ever truly

J. S. MILL

457. TO AUGUSTE COMTE[1]

India House
le 26 avril 1845

Mon cher Monsieur Comte

Depuis le jour où j'appris que la crise polytechnique s'était terminée, au moins pour le moment, à votre désavantage, je n'ai perdu aucune des occasions, malheureusement assez rares, qui se sont présentées pour faire connaître votre nouvelle position à ceux qui pourraient avoir des relations quelconques avec des anglais riches demeurant à Paris. Je ne sais pas si ce que j'ai pû faire produira quelque fruit, mais jusqu'ici ce fruit ne s'est pas encore montré. Je crains qu'il n'y ait besoin d'une grande persévérance pour en obtenir. Les riches anglais, même lorsqu'ils ne demeurent pas en angleterre ont l'habitude bien établie d'envoyer leurs fils à Oxford ou à Cambridge. Pour être admis à ces établissemens-là on exige à peine les premiers éléments de la géometrie et de l'algèbre; et l'on désire si peu chez nous les connaissances mathématiques en elles-mêmes, que naguère encore il ne se trouvait presque pas un seul bon professeur ou maître de mathématiques à Londres. Il n'y en avait guére qu'à Cambridge. Aujourd'hui cet état de choses s'est un peu amélioré. Toutefois on peut encore dire que ce qu'il a de goût pour les études mathématiques chez nous s'est concentré à Cambridge, et que le peu d'hommes riches, qui désirent que leurs fils s'en occupent, les y envoient, le plus souvent sans aucun enseignement préparatoire digne du nom. Il est donc fort douteux s'il se trouve à Paris un seul anglais qui serait disposé à profiter de vos leçons quand

3. For the bill on its second reading in the Commons.
4. Peel spoke on April 18; Sir John Graham (1792–1861), Home Secretary at the time, on April 17.
5. Macaulay in his speech on April 14, though he supported the Maynooth grant, castigated the Tories for their inconsistencies on Irish policy.

* * * *

1. MS at Johns Hopkins. Published in Lévy-Bruhl, pp. 412–16; in reply to Comte's of Feb. 28, *ibid.*, 404-12.

même on serait parvenu à lui faire croire sur parole votre éminente capacité scientifique que certainement très peu de mes compatriotes sont en état d'apprécier directement. Voilà les difficultés qu'on m'a faites, et dont je reconnais la gravité. M. Grote s'accorde là dessus avec moi, et comme moi il s'efforce de les vaincre. De mon côté je ne me découragerai pas et peutêtre le hasard nous favorisera.

Je m'occupe à présent principalement de lectures préparatoires au traité populaire d'économie politique dont je vous entretenais dernièrement. Entre autres livres plus ou moins intéressans je n'ai pas manqué de lire celui de M. Dunoyer,[2] dont le nom ne m'était déjà pas inconnu: je l'avais même vu autrefois chez J. B. Say et ses travaux dans le Censeur avec votre homonyme,[3] m'étaient connus depuis longtemps. Son ouvrage actuel me paraît, à plusieurs égards, très digne d'éloge. Il est certainement beaucoup trop absolu dans ses idées négatives: cependant, on ne peut guère regretter une opposition, même exagérée, à la tendance qui porte à faire par les lois ce qui ne devrait dépendre que des mœurs. Je lui reproche davantage de n'avoir pas même entrevu la nécessité, si prononcée pourtant dans son système, d'un pouvoir spirituel. Il est bien étonnant aujourd'hui qu'un homme éclairé puisse faire un système social, dans lequel nécessairement il suppose la réception générale de ses propres opinions morales et politiques, sans cependant s'occuper le moins du monde des conditions que suppose essentiellement l'existence d'un système d'opinions communes faisant autorité. Il est vraiment trop naïf de croire aujourd'hui que la simple liberté de discussion suffise pour cela. Cependant, puisque dans votre avis la négation totale de toute organisation spirituelle est préférable à la mauvaise ébauche d'organisation qui existe à présent, il serait probablement à désirer qu'on essayât d'appliquer les idées de M. Dunoyer dans leur simple nudité. Ce serait une grande expérience sociologique. Je sais beaucoup de gré à M. Dunoyer pour la mention honorable qu'il a faite de votre Cours, tout en se reconnaissant incompétent pour le juger définitivement.

A propos de cela, nous avons obtenu, vous et moi, les honneurs d'une publicité assez éclatante par l'intermédiaire d'une des chefs de l'école anglo-catholique, M. Ward, qui fit paraître, il y a une année ou davantage, un assez gros volume[4] dans lequel il peignit en de très noires couleurs l'état actuel de l'église anglicane, et de la société anglaise, se déclara très nettement contre la réformation de Luther et appela l'église anglicane à

2. Charles Barthélemy Dunoyer (1786–1862), economist and statesman. Comte had recommended to JSM a new book by Dunoyer: *De la liberté du travail* (3 vols., Paris, 1845).

3. Dunoyer had edited with Charles Comte, son-in-law of J. B. Say the economist, the journal *Le Censeur* from 1820 to 1825, to which Auguste Comte had also contributed.

4. See Letter 455.

rentrer dans le giron du catholicisme romain. Cet ouvrage fit grand scandale ici, et l'Université d'Oxford vient de priver l'auteur de ses grades universitaires comme ne faisant plus partie, au moins en droit, de l'église anglicane. Ce n'est que dernièrement que j'ai lu son ouvrage, bien que j'eusse entendu qu'il y était question de moi. Je m'y suis trouvé cité dans chaque chapitre et plus souvent encore, avec d'immenses éloges, entremêlés de plaintes sur mon incrédulité et sur la tendance athéistique de mes écrits: il disait, de plus, avoir lu la plus grande partie de votre Cours, sur la foi de ce que j'en disais; il va sans dire qu'il vous tance encore plus vertement que moi sur votre irréligion; cependant il cite plusieurs passages, il fait l'éloge de votre capacité, et même de vos intentions; il dit que vous reconnaissez avoir pris bien des choses chez de Maistre, mais qu'il vous trouve très supérieur en profondeur à ce penseur. Suivant lui, il faut en venir à notre irréligion à nous, si on ne revient pas à la philosophie catholique car il prône la philosophie du catholicisme tout autant que la foi. C'est une chose assez amusante que nous trouvions un appui si décidé dans ce camp-là et que M. Ward soit accusé par ses adversaires dans la Quarterly Review,[5] d'avoir tiré plus d'enseignements de mon école que de celle des théologiens anglicans.

Mon ami Bain vient de se servir de votre traité d'astronomie pour son enseignement universitaire. Il a fait cette année-ci un cours de physique, au lieu du cours de philosophie morale qu'il avait fait trois années de suite. Il n'était malheureusement que suppléant, dans la dépendance absolue du professeur,[6] vieux radoteur qui ne voulait plus de lui cette année, malgré le vœu général de ses collègues. Bain a été recommandé au gouvernement par six professeurs pour la chaire de physique, mais on y a nommé un autre, très inférieur probablement à lui. Il n'y a été nommé que par interim. Je ne sais par conséquent ce qu'il fera dorénavant.[7] Il est décidé à se présenter comme candidat à la chaire de philosophie morale quand elle viendra à vaquer, ce qui probablement aura lieu bientôt, mais n'ayant que son mérite et l'appui des professeurs, il peut se voir de nouveau mis de côté. Il dit sur votre cours d'astronomie "I never saw a finer specimen of philosophical or scientific arrangement. There is almost a startling propriety in the places alloted to each point. Herschel's book is a mere chaos in comparison."

tout à vous

J. S. MILL.

5. "Ward's *Ideal of a Christian Church*," *QR*, LXXV (Dec., 1844), 149–200.
6. The Rev. George Glennie (d. Nov. 9, 1845), professor of moral philosophy at Marischal College.
7. Later that year Bain was appointed professor of mathematics and natural philosophy in the Andersonian University of Glasgow, a position which he resigned after one year.

458. TO JOHN HAMILTON THOM[1]

India House
9th May 1845

MY DEAR SIR,

I have purposely delayed thanking you for your present of the Memoirs and Portrait of our friend Mr Blanco White, until I had time to read the book regularly through. It is a book of very solemn and painful interest. If, as Carlyle says, there is the fifth act of a tragedy in every peasant's death-bed,[2] we may say that the tragedy of Mr Blanco White's life is both of a deeply pathetic and of a truly heroic character.

I feel something almost amounting to remorse when I consider that, having had the privilege of knowing such a man, I have so few of the recollections which I so envy you the possession of—recollections of having contributed by sympathy and service to soothe the sufferings of his last few years. But though I always respected him highly, I never knew a tenth part either of his nobleness or of his sufferings, and still less that yearning for sympathy which seems to have been his characteristic through life, and which so greatly enhances the honour due to his repeated sacrifices of all earthly ties and friendship to the love of truth and of duty. It is always so. Men's worth is only known when they are dead and we can do nothing more for them.

But, to change from the elegiac to the epic—the third volume appears to me of great intrinsic worth, and likely to serve the cause for which he suffered so much in an eminent degree, by the clear, strong, earnest manner in which it declares things which when spoken are almost too obvious not to be admitted, but which hardly any one dares to speak.

Believe me, with great respect, yours sincerely,

J. S. MILL

459. TO AUGUSTE COMTE[1]

India House
le 21 juin 1845

MON CHER MONSIEUR COMTE

C'est avec bien de la peine que j'ai appris l'insuccès des démarches que vous aviez prises jusqu'à la date de votre dernière lettre, pour reprendre l'enseignement privé. M. Grote a vivement partagé mon regret, et mal-

1. Published by J. H. Thom in "Archbishop Whately and the Life of Blanco White," *Theological Review*, IV (Jan., 1867), 112–13. MS not located.
2. In his essay on Burns, *ER*, XLVIII (Dec., 1828), 278.

* * * *

1. MS at Johns Hopkins. Published in Lévy-Bruhl, pp. 426–29; in reply to Comte's of May 15, *ibid.*, 417–26.

heureusement nous n'avons eu ni l'un ni l'autre un meilleur succès dans tout ce que nous avons tenté ici en votre faveur. Il y a parmi les anglais en général une indifférence profonde envers l'éducation scientifique. On regarde la science comme une spécialité qui n'est l'affaire que des savans par état, ou qui touche tout au plus certaines fonctions industrielles, comme celle d'ingénieur, encore dans ce métier même on se contente presque toujours de connaissances empiriques. Nous sommes à cet égard très en arrière de la France, malgré le fâcheux effet qui résulte à certains égards chez vous, de l'organisation prématurée d'une classe savante qui n'est pas au niveau de sa destinée à venir. En France le cas qu'on fait de la science est prouvé par l'abus même que les savans peuvent faire de leur influence, et dont vous avez été malheureusement mais très naturellement la victime, précisément parce que la grande réforme que vous vous efforcez d'accomplir dans les choses humaines s'annonce comme devant commencer par la classe savante elle-même.

En retournant dans ma pensée votre position actuelle et les moyens d'y remédier, j'ai eu l'idée de vous proposer de faire l'essai de notre milieu anglais d'une nouvelle manière. Quoique, dans mon opinion, le temps ne soit pas venu où une revue franchement positive aurait ainsi la moindre chance de succès, il n'en est pas de même lorsqu'il ne s'agit que de faire pénétrer l'esprit positif dans l'intelligence publique d'une manière plus graduelle, au moyen des revues existantes. L'accueil qu'on a fait ici à ma Logique est une preuve entre plusieurs qu'il existe chez nous un public capable de goûter des discussions, même très élevées, dans l'ordre positif, sauf quelques réserves indispensables mais faciles: ces discussions serviraient même à donner de la réputation à la revue qui les ferait paraître, quoique ne pouvant pas en faire le fond. A cet égard, l'Angleterre est peutêtre en ce moment-ci mieux préparée que la France. Je conçois très bien que même en ne supposant pas les obstacles qu'y opposerait l'esprit de coterie de la presse française, il pourrait vous répugner d'entrer en relation avec des ouvrages périodiques quelconques en France: mais il me semble que la chose serait plus practicable ici, d'autant plus que les rapports pourraient n'être qu'indirects, par mon intermédiaire. Je vous engage donc à réfléchir s'il n'y a pas telle ou telle question secondaire que vous pourriez traiter, ou tel ou tel travail scientifique ou historique par exemple, dont vous pourriez faire la critique, d'une manière qui conviendrait à quelque revue anglaise. Je ferais moi-même la traduction, ou la ferais faire sous mes yeux, et d'ailleurs à mon défaut il n'est pas douteux que Bain ou Lewes tiendraient à honneur de la faire. Il est vrai que cette sorte de travail accessoire dérangerait nécessairement jusqu'à un certain point votre régime cérébral habituel; mais à tout prendre, le pénible métier de l'enseignement privé exigerait peut être des frais d'énergie cérébale encore plus considérable, sans laisser espérer une aussi grande utilité secondaire. Ce dont je vous parle, je l'ai toujours fait moi-même. Pendant l'élaboration de mon ouvrage scientifique, et même quelquefois depuis, j'ai publié dans des revues de petits opuscules que je pouvais faire avec facilité, mais que je savais bien n'avoir qu'une valeur transitoire ou même momentanée, et qui n'étaient guère pour moi, en effet, qu'une sorte de délassement intellectuel. Cela n'a pas laissé d'être utile au succès de mes travaux plus sérieux; j'y dois très probablement la majorité de mes lecteurs, sans compter que je leur fais un peu, par ce moyen, une sorte d'éducation préparatoire. Je crois qu'il y a sous ce rapport, quelque chose à faire, que cela pourrait être utile aussi bien que lucratif, et si ce projet vous semble exécutable je vous offre tout ce que je puis faire pour en surmonter les diverses difficultés.

Bain est très flatté de ce que son jugement favorable de votre traité astronomique vous a fait plaisir, et il dit "His remarks of sympathy with my disappointment and difficult position, I received with sincere delight." Il est ici depuis quelques jours. En ce moment-ci il est sans position, et sans aucune perspective certaine d'en avoir; mais il a plusieurs chances plus ou moins prochaines: il est jeune et d'heureux caractère, et il ne manquera pas d'obtenir tôt ou tard une digne réparation. Au reste ses tribulations sont bien loin d'être aussi graves ni aussi injustes que les vôtres. Il est maltraité parce que sa supériorité n'est pas encore assez connue, et non pas à cause de sa supériorité même.

votre tout dévoué

J. S. MILL

460. TO AUGUSTE COMTE[1]

India House
le 24 juin
1845

MON CHER MONSIEUR COMTE

Depuis samedi, jour où je vous écrivis ma dernière lettre, voici ce qui est arrivé. Je viens de voir un anglais ou plutôt un écossais de ma connaissance nommé Williamson[2] dont le fils,[3] âgé d'à peu près 21 ans, s'est beaucoup occupé d'études positives. Il désire placer son fils en pension à Paris chez quelque professeur ou savant, pendant l'hiver prochain, et peut être plus longtemps encore, pour y profiter des avantages scientifiques de cette capitale du monde savant. J'ai pensé que cela pourrait vous con-

1. *Addressed*: Monsieur / Auguste Comte / Rue M. le Prince / près l'Odeon / à Paris. *Postmark*: PAID / 24 JU 24 / 1845 / and BOULOGNE. MS as Johns Hopkins. Published in Lévy-Bruhl, pp. 429–31.
2. Alexander Williamson, long a clerk at the East India Co., in 1830 had moved to Wright's Lane, Kensington, near the home of his fellow employee, James Mill.
3. Alexander William Williamson (1824–1904), later professor of chemistry at the University of London. JSM's recommendation led to his studying for three years with Comte.

venir. Je ne connais le fils que par ce que m'en dit le père. D'après celui-ci, le jeune homme a fait de bonnes études mathématiques et biologiques mais il s'est appliqué encore davantage à la chimie et à l'électrologie. Il a étudié à Giessen en Hesse sous le célèbre Liebig,[4] qui en a, selon le père, la plus haute opinion, et qui en parle comme d'un homme destiné à faire des choses importantes dans la chimie. Il paraît s'être attaché avec zèle aux recherches originales et au perfectionnement des généralites scientifiques. Le père désirerait en faire un professeur. Le père, ex-employé de la compagnie des Indes, n'est pas, je crois, un homme très intelligent, mais il a longtemps demeuré en France et en allemagne, il s'est désappris de tout préjugé insulaire, il aime beaucoup les Français, et, chose importante, il n'a, pas plus que son fils, aucune croyance religieuse, au contraire, il y répugne profondément. C'est au reste un homme d'un caractère irréprochable. Sans être riche il jouit d'une certaine aisance. Je lui ai parlé de vous, en lui disant que je ne savais pas s'il vous conviendrait de prendre son fils en pension, mais que je vous en parlerais. Il aurait préféré à quelques égards, pour son fils, une vie de famille, mais, d'après ce que je lui ai dit de vous, il ne regarde pas votre vie de célibataire[5] comme un obstacle insurmontable; et je crois que vous pourriez vous entendre avec lui, soit pour des leçons spéciales de haute science, soit pour la direction générale des études scientifiques du jeune homme, même dans le cas où il ne vous conviendrait pas de le prendre en pension, ou ne vous conviendrait qu'à des conditions que le père regarderait comme inacceptables. En attendant j'ai conseillé au père de faire lire au fils votre grand ouvrage, et j'ai pris sur moi de dire que vous lui donneriez volontiers des conseils d'ami, si même vous ne pouviez pas accueillir l'affaire d'une autre manière. Le père part en quelques jours pour la Saxe, par conséquent si la chose vous semble digne de considération ce ne serait pas mal de me le faire savoir au plus tôt.

tout à vous,

J. S. MILL

461. TO AUGUSTE COMTE[1]

[June, 1845]

MON CHER MONSIEUR COMTE

Ce petit mot est destiné à servir d'introduction auprès de vous pour MM. Williamson, père et fils, qui vous sont déjà assez connus par mes

4. Baron Justus von Liebig (1803–1873), German chemist.
5. Comte's wife had left him in 1842; see Letter 371, n. 3.

* * * *

1. MS at Johns Hopkins. Published in Lévy-Bruhl, pp. 450–51. Undated, but JSM in his letter of July 8, 1845 (Letter 463), mentions having written this note of introduction.

lettres. Je n'ai pas besoin de les recommander de nouveau aux bons offices et conseils que vous m'avez déjà permis de leur promettre en votre nom.

Votre tout dévoué

J. S. MILL

462. TO THOMAS CARLYLE[1]

I.H.
Monday
[July 7, 1845]

MY DEAR CARLYLE

I have no pretium affectionis nor any other kind of pretium attached to the Whitelocke[2] & I should think it money wasted on your part to provide me with another, for which I shall probably never have any use. "The tools to him who can use them" & it would be a real pleasure to me if you will keep the Whitelocke, with your annotations & come to me some evening *without*, instead of *with*, another to replace it.

Yours ever

J. S. MILL

463. TO AUGUSTE COMTE[1]

India House
le 8 juillet 1845

MON CHER MONSIEUR COMTE

Votre lettre à Mme de V.[2] est sans doute fort propre à adoucir les préventions de ceux ou de celles qui, déjà à moitié détachés des anciennes

---

1. *Postmark*: 7 JULY 1845. MS at NLS.
2. Probably Sir Bulstrode Whitelocke's *Memorials of the English Affairs . . . from the Beginning of the Reign of King Charles the First, to King Charles the Second his happy restauration*, first published in London, 1682. Carlyle had no doubt borrowed the book in preparing his edition of *Oliver Cromwell's Letters and Speeches* (2 vols., London, 1845).

* * * *

1. MS at Johns Hopkins. Published in Lévy-Bruhl, pp. 447–50; in reply to Comte's of June 27 and 30, *ibid.*, pp. 431–46.
2. In his letter of June 30 Comte had asked JSM's advice about publishing in an English periodical a letter he had written to Mme de Vaux (Clotilde de Vaux, sister of one of his students, whom he had met that year and for whom he developed a passionate devotion that survived her death in 1846). In his letter of July 14 to JSM, Comte refers to the composition as *Sainte Clotilde*.

idées, tiennent fortement par l'imagination et par les affections à la satisfaction que l'ancien système, en tant que système organique, offrait et
devrait offrir à la partie morale et sympathique de notre nature. Par ces
raisons mêmes je la crois impropre au public anglais. Poser le positivisme
en contradiction ouverte avec toute religion quelconque est peut être la
seule manière de le présenter dont il serait à mon avis très inopportun de
faire usage aujourd'hui en angleterre. Un temps viendra où ce sera peut
être très utile de donner ici de la publicité à cet opuscule: ce sera le temps,
peut être prochain, où vous serez publiquement attaqué et dénoncé ici
comme athée. Alors il conviendra peut être de faire voir et comprendre au
public l'intervalle immense qui sépare votre athéisme de celui, seul connu
ici, de l'école de Diderot et d'Holbach.[3] Aujourd'hui je pense qu'il faudrait,
en écrivant pour l'angleterre, se taire absolument sur la question religieuse,
sauf à porter indirectement aux croyances religieuses tel coup qu'on voudra.
Cette réserve serait surtout nécessaire de la part d'un écrivain déjà connu
pour avoir professé ouvertement des opinions anti-religieuses parce que
les directeurs des revues y regarderont de plus près que dans tout autre cas.
C'est au reste la seule réserve dont vous auriez besoin. A tout autre égard
il n'y a rien dans vos écrits qui puisse servir d'obstacle à ce qu'on les
accueille ici. Je conçois au reste l'impossibilité de laisser à côté la question
religieuse dans un ouvrage systématique, ou même en traitant une seule
question sociale du premier ordre: mais, tant qu'il ne s'agit que de critique
ou des questions secondaires, on pourrait, ce me semble, se contenter de
traiter le sujet comme si la religion n'existait pas. Mais aujourd'hui la
publication, en anglais, d'un opuscule en votre nom, où toute croyance
religieuse serait ouvertement repoussée, vous fermerait très probablement
toutes les revues de ce pays-ci. On craint et on repousse ici les *mots* anti-
religieux bien plus que la chose.

Je trouve au contraire très convenable à l'Angleterre votre idée d'écrire
sur la situation des sciences et des savans en france et en angleterre: seulement je conseillerais que ce ne fût pas en forme de lettres: les revues chez
nous ne voudraient pas de cette forme, et les magazines, outre qu'ils rétribuent moins leurs collaborateurs, ont beaucoup moins d'importance intellectuelle et sociale. Je conseillerais d'écrire, en tête de l'article, le nom de
quelque ouvrage récent, ayant un rapport plus ou moins direct au sujet
traité: sauf à n'en dire que deux mots, si l'ouvrage ne mérite pas davantage:
vous pourrez, après cela, n'en plus tenir compte.

Quant à la question pécuniaire immédiate, je compte, de manière ou
d'autre, à entamer auprès de M. Grote la question d'un subside supplé-
mentaire, de façon à sonder sa disposition à y coopérer: malheureusement

3. The French *philosophes* and Encyclopedists, Denis Diderot (1713–1784) and
Paul Henri Dietrich, baron d'Holbach (1723–1789).

le jour même où je devais le voir, et où je comptais discuter avec lui votre proposition, il s'est trouvé dans la nécessité de partir subitement pour les eaux de Kissingen à cause de la santé de Mme Grote. Il compte être de retour avant le milieu d'août. Quant à Molesworth, une plus grande délicatesse m'est commandée par diverses raisons. D'abord j'ai été, en partie, la cause pour lui d'une perte pécuniaire considérable par une revue qu'il fonda sous ma direction;[4] ensuite, il n'y a pas un an qu'il s'est marié, et qu'il a fait plusieurs dépenses considérables qui l'ont empêché de fournir au subside de l'année passée une aussi forte part qu'il en avait je crois, très sincèrement le désir. Je l'ai peu vu depuis son mariage, et c'est surtout M. Grote qui est intervenu auprès de lui et s'il s'agissait d'une seconde intervention je crois qu'elle se ferait le plus avantageusement par le même moyen. Je ne sais pas si M. Grote vous a averti dans le temps (je pense que c'était surtout à lui de le faire) que par suite de gêne momentanée de Molesworth, il (M. Grote) avait admis contrairement à son intention première, et pour la somme de 50 livres sterling, un troisième coadjuteur, M. Raikes Currie, banquier et député.[5] Au reste, voici probablement ce que se diraient ces messieurs. S'ils croyaient certain que, dans un temps défini et pas trop prolongé, vous obtiendriez soit une réparation officielle, soit d'autres ressources équivalentes, je ne doute nullement que ceux qui vous ont aidé jusqu'ici, seraient disposés à prolonger leur secours, pour vous épargner soit la nécessité de déranger vos habitudes permanentes par un motif temporaire, soit l'ennui et la perte de temps qui résulteraient d'une tentative pour obtenir des ressources auxiliaires dont bientôt vous n'auriez plus besoin. C'est la question de temps, et de l'indéfini, qui seule pourrait les faire hésiter. Je trouve donc qu'il serait utile que sans faire aucune démarche auprès d'eux vous m'adressiez une lettre destinée à leur être montrée, où vous exposeriez simplement, et comme avertissement général à vos amis d'ici, ce que vous pensez sur votre avenir pécuniaire en France. Par suite de l'absence de Mr. Grote, on ne pourra rien faire qu'à une époque qui approchera très près du terme fatal du 1er septembre, mais s'il vous arrive par là quelque inconvénient, vous savez qu'en cas d'urgence je suis là.

M. Williamson[6] est reparti pour la Saxe. Je lui ai donné pour lui et pour son fils, une lettre d'introduction adressée à vous. Il sera à Paris en octobre et c'est alors qu'il pourra être question de leçons à donner au jeune homme.

votre dévoué

J. S. MILL

---

4. The *London Review* in 1835.
5. Raikes Currie (1801–1881), banker; MP for Northampton, 1837–57.
6. See Letter 460.

464. TO SIR JOHN F. W. HERSCHEL[1]

India House
9th July 1845.

MY DEAR SIR

The correspondence which took place between us, two years ago,[2] must be my warrant, if the object I have in view requires any, for taking the liberty of writing to you respecting a passage in the Address which you delivered to the British Association for the Advancement of Science at its first evening meeting on the 19th of last month.[3]

In that discourse you spoke of a recent publication of mine in so handsome a manner as would have more than satisfied a much greater degree of vanity than I possess. But my purpose in writing to you is not to make acknowledgments for your politeness nor to express my gratification at your favourable opinion, but to call your attention to an act of injustice which you have, I am sure unintentionally, committed against the scientific reputation of a distinguished man. You have publicly imputed to M. Auguste Comte, not only a gross blunder in reasoning, but one inconsistent with the most elementary knowledge of the principles of astronomical dynamics. If M. Comte had been capable of such a blunder, he would have been quite incapable of writing any one chapter of the Cours de Philosophie Positive, & I am sure nothing is necessary but a more careful reference to that work, to convince you that he never was guilty of it.

You say that for the purpose of giving a numerical verification to the hypothesis of the nebular origin of the solar system, M. Comte computes the time of rotation which the sun must have had about its axis so that a planet situated on its surface should not press upon that surface. That as the basis of this calculation M. Comte employs "the elementary Huyghenian theorems for the evaluation of centrifugal forces, in combination with the law of gravitation—a combination which, I need not explain to those who have read the first book of Newton, leads direct to Kepler's law," and then you accuse him of "gravely turning round upon us and addressing the coincidence of the resulting periods compared with the distances of the planets with this law of Kepler, as *being* the numerical verification in question." Well may you add "where is there a student to be found who has graduated as a Senior Optime in this University, who will not at once lay his finger on the fallacy of such an argument, & declare it a vicious circle." But, that Mr. Comte has fallen into this vicious circle is a statement

1. MS in the possession of the Royal Society, as is also Herschel's reply of July 10. A further letter of Herschel's of July 13 is at Yale.
2. See Letter 397.
3. Herschel's presidential address at the fifteenth meeting of the Association, at Cambridge, published in the *Athenæum* for June 21, 1845, pp. 612–17.

only to be accounted for by supposing that you have not read the astronomical portion of M. Comte's work, but only referred, & that cursorily, to a single passage of it.

It would be difficult for even the shallowest person to have attempted to give a philosophical outline of astronomy without being aware that the evidence by which Newton proved the law of gravitation was the fact of its leading demonstratively to Kepler's laws; & that Kepler's law of the relation between the distances & the periodic times, was deduced from the law of gravitation combined with the Huyghenian measure of the centrifugal force. Accordingly if you refer to an earlier chapter in the same volume of M. Comte, being that in which he unfolds the evidence of the law of gravitation, you will find (pp. 227–231) that all which you so contemptuously bring forward in condemnation of M. Comte, is brought forward *by* him. You will find the same exposition repeated in the corresponding chapter of his very striking "Traité Philosophique d'Astronomie Populaire." It was impossible that the accordance of Kepler's law with the premises from which he knew & said that it demonstratively followed, could appear to him to be a "numerical verification," not of those premises, but of something quite unconnected with them, viz. the nebular hypothesis.

And if you only refer again to the very passage, to which I venture to think that your former reference must have been a very hasty one, I am confident that you will see how completely you have mistaken its import. It was not the coincidence of the resulting periods of the planets "with this law of Kepler" that M. Comte considered as a numerical verification of their nebulous origin; it was the coincidence (within certain limits of error) between the periods, as resulting from the calculation, & *the actual periodic times of the planets, as known by observation.* The reference to Kepler's law is only incidental, & the sole use made of it is to dispense with the necessity of performing the calculation separately for each planet, since, when it has been made for any one, Kepler's law gives the correlative result for every other.

I speak without any knowledge of the Memoir or Memoirs on the subject, which M. Comte read before the Academy of Science, and with which you appear to be equally unacquainted. A reference to them would doubtless shew both "the steps" & "the data of his calculations," which could not have been given with any propriety in the Cours. I also write without communication with M. Comte, who is probably quite unaware of the attack made upon him. But on the face of the Cours itself & of the very passage from which you quote, it is evident to me that the attack has been made under a misapprehension, & I cannot doubt that your love of justice will induce you to reexamine the subject.

A judgment from you, delivered with preparation, & on an occasion of so much publicity, must have a serious effect upon the scientific reputation of any author: and you cannot be unaware how little chance anyone, who may dispute its justice, would have of obtaining, from the scientific or from the general public of this country, even a hearing, against your authority. So great a power involves a proportional responsibility; and when it has been inadvertently exercised to the injury of anyone, I cannot doubt your being most desirous that the error should be pointed out.

I remain,

Yours very truly

J. S. MILL

Sir J. F. W. Herschel, Bart.

465. TO SIR JOHN F. W. HERSCHEL[1]

India House
14th July
1845

MY DEAR SIR

I beg to acknowledge your letters of the 10th & 13th. If you will permit me I should like to send the Athenaeum[2] to M. Comte as from yourself, *with a copy of your last note*,[3] which I think would be more agreeable to him, or to any man, than the direct communication of your animadversions could be disagreeable.

The question raised by your criticism of M. Comte appears to me, I confess, to be one which a mere reference to his book would decide. In saying (as he does) that a theorem compounded of Huyghens and Newton's laws leads directly to the law of Kepler, does he represent *this* as a verification of the nebular hypothesis? In your address you say he does. I continue to think, that if you refer again to his book, you will see that he does not; & moreover that he does, elsewhere, represent that same logical sequence as a verification not of the nebular hypothesis, but of the law of gravitation.

1. *Addressed*: Sir J. F. W. Herschel Bart. / Collingwood / Hawkhurst / Kent. *Postmarks*: W / PAID / 14 JY 14 / 1845, and STA . . . HURST / JY 15 / 1845. MS in the possession of the Royal Society, as is also Herschel's reply of July 16.
2. See preceding letter, n. 3.
3. Of July 13, in which Herschel had asked JSM to avoid mentioning his name in sending the *Athenæum* to Comte: "In all such cases I consider it highly unjust to remark on the writings of an author unfavorably without putting him in possession of the *ipsissima verba* of the remarks, but then it should be so done as to give no unnecessary offence of a personal nature."

What may be the value of what he *does* bring forward as a numerical verification I cannot pretend to say; I am not acquainted with what he has written expressly on the subject; & if I were, it would become me to express myself much more modestly on *that* question. The verification would of course consist in the agreement of the periodic time of each planet, with what would be the period of the sun's revolution if it were suddenly expanded so as to touch the planet. For computing that period the elements would be, the present period of the sun's rotation, the sun's equatorial radius, the mean distance of the planet from the sun, and—Kepler's law. I therefore presume that M. Comte *must* either prove or assume (as stated in your letter) that Kepler's law applies to the successive states of the sun itself, & not merely to the planets when detached from it. On what grounds he does so, his own dissertation must shew.

Admitting, however, the impossibility of proving the proposition stated in your letter, still it cannot be considered a mere arbitrary assumption; & if it can be shewn that the present rotation of the sun takes place in the same time in which it ought to take place supposing that proposition & the nebular hypothesis to be true, would not that be of considerable weight as an additional argument in favour of the nebular hypothesis? A proof, it would not be; but M. Comte, you will observe, distinctly disclaims the pretension of having *proved* the hypothesis.

And now, without troubling you further on this subject, permit me to say, that I thankfully accept your offer[4] with respect to my own book. I am well aware that any one, not a mathematician by profession, is likely in going over such a field as I have done, to have committed many such errors as those you propose pointing out; & for myself, though I formerly went quite through the usual course of mathematics & its applications & have occasionally revived my recollection by recurring to parts of it, I do not pretend to have retained any accurate memory of more than the outline. I have therefore always hoped that if my book had any success, some of those who possess the requisite knowledge would take the trouble to free it from errors of this description, & I shall endeavour to profit to the utmost by every indication you may give.

> I remain
> Very truly yours
> J. S. MILL.

4. In his letter of July 10 Herschel in speaking of JSM's *Logic* noted "the general high opinion I have formed and expressed of it in a philosophical point of view" but thought "the least felicitous portions of it, those in which points of physical science and mathematics are touched upon. I should have no objection if you desired it, to specify some particular instances which have occurred to me inter legendum to which this remark applies. . . ."

466. TO SIR JOHN F. W. HERSCHEL[1]

India House
17th July 1845

MY DEAR SIR,

I have now nothing more to do than to thank you for the fullness and explicitness of your letter[2] received this morning, & to say that I will immediately send a copy of it to M. Comte.[3]

Very truly yours

J. S. MILL.

467. TO AUGUSTE COMTE[1]

18 juillet 1845

MON CHER MONSIEUR COMTE—

Dans une lettre très récente vous vous êtes félicité du ton bienveillant et amical dont vous aviez été traité jusque là par vos critiques anglais. Il était impossible que cela durât très longtemps, et déjà cela ne dure plus. Comme, par la nature de votre grand ouvrage il ne devait guère être connu encore que des savans, c'est de leur part qu'est venue la première attaque, et elle porte sur une question isolée, celle de votre vérification numérique de l'hypothèse cosmogonique de Laplace. A la réunion annuelle des savans anglais qui eut lieu cette année à Cambridge, sir John Herschel a prononcé un discours d'ouverture dont vous trouverez dans le journal *The Athenæum*[2] une copie corrigée par l'auteur, que je vous envoie de sa part. Quoique je fusse nommé avec éloge dans ce discours, je n'en ai pas eu une connaissance immédiate. L'ayant enfin lu, je me sentis blessé de l'injustice qu'il me semblait montrer à votre égard, et encore plus par le ton de supériorité qu'il s'était permis envers vous et je lui adressai la première lettre de la correspondance ci-jointe. Les lettres suivantes[3] s'expliquent toutes seules. J'y ajoute (numéro 6) une autre attaque d'une main différente, qui a paru dans la revue d'Edimbourg.[4] L'année passée un ouvrage anonyme a paru

1. MS in the possession of the Royal Society, as is also Herschel's reply of July 18.
2. Herschel's letter of July 16 criticizing in detail Comte's astronomical theories.
3. In his note of July 18 Herschel expressed some reluctance to JSM's sending a copy to Comte.

＊　＊　＊　＊

1. MS at Johns Hopkins. Published in Lévy-Bruhl, pp. 465–68; in reply to Comte's two letters of July 14, *ibid.*, pp. 451–65.
2. See Letter 464.
3. Letters 464, 465, and copies of Herschel's replies.
4. [Adam Sedgwick], "The Vestiges of the Natural History of Creation," *ER*, LXXXII (July, 1845), 1–85.

ici, ouvrage très superficiel, mais dont l'auteur inconnu mérite, au moins par ses intentions, beaucoup d'éloges. Sous le titre de "Vestiges of the Natural History of Creation" il tâche de *deviner* une sorte de cosmogonie positive, en y ajoutant, sous une forme différente et moins absurde, l'hypothèse de Lamarck sur la transformation des espèces, &c. &c. Quoique d'une valeur purement négative, cet ouvrage n'a pas laissé de faire ici une sensation assez prononcée, et je crois qu'il tend à préparer un peu les esprits pour le positivisme. Son succès a été un grand scandale pour les gens religieux et pour beaucoup de savans, et la revue d'Edimbourg vient de publier un long article plein de rancunes savantes et sacerdotales, que je sais de bonne part être d'un nommé Sedgwick, professeur de géologie à Cambridge, avec lequel j'eus des démêlés autrefois.[5] Or, l'auteur des "Vestiges" cita votre vérification de l'hypothèse de Laplace. C'est, je crois, ce qui détermina l'attaque de Herschel, et Sedgwick vous attaque de même dans le passage ci-joint. Vous verrez que celui-ci parle un peu plus en connaissance de cause, puisqu'il paraît avoir lu votre mémoire original, tandis que Herschel ne parle que d'après le Cours de Ph. Positive. Vous verrez que j'ai pris bien garde de ne pas vous compromettre dans ce que j'ai osé dire, de ma propre part, en votre défense. C'est maintenant à vous de juger s'il vous convient ou non de repousser ces attaques, d'une manière publique ou privée.

J'ai appris avec le plus grand intérêt ce que vous me mandez sur la maladie nerveuse dont vous venez de sortir, et dont vous avez si heureusement profité pour déterminer par des méditations décisives, le caractère distinctif de vos travaux sociologiques à venir. J'ai envoyé de suite votre billet à M. Raikes Currie. Je tombe d'accord sur l'ineptie de notre usage de donner à tous les articles de revue la forme d'un compte rendu: malheureusement, cela est de rigueur dans toutes nos grandes revues, qui outre leur importance plus grande, sont aussi les seules qui rétribuent convenablement leurs rédacteurs. Mais cette obligation n'est que de forme; vous pouvez y mettre le titre de l'édition la plus récente de quelque ouvrage bien connu: il arrive quelquefois que, sauf le titre mis à l'article, il n'y est pas une seule fois question de l'écrit dont on prétend rendre compte.

Ayant obtenu un congé, beaucoup plus court pourtant que celui de l'année passée, je vais partir pour une tournée dans laquelle mon adresse sera trop incertaine pour qu'on puisse m'envoyer des lettres. Ce temps ne sera pourtant pas perdu pour vos affaires. Comme M. Grote sera peut être de retour avant moi, je lui adresserai la lettre que vous m'avez écrite à ma demande,[6] et je l'accompagnerai des observations qui me paraîtront con-

---

5. JSM's "Professor Sedgwick's Discourse [*On the Studies of the University*]— State of Philosophy in England," *London Review*, I (April, 1835), 94–135. Reprinted in *Dissertations*, I, 121–85.

6. Comte's second letter of July 14, Lévy-Bruhl, pp. 460–65. See Letter 463.

venables, de manière à ce qu'il les reçoive dès son arrivée. Il en arrivera alors ce qu'il pourra. Le succès me paraît le résultat le plus probable.

tout à vous

J. S. MILL

468. TO GEORGE GROTE[1]

[July, 1845]

DEAR MR. GROTE,—A short time ago Comte, finding that his attempts to replace by private teaching the deficit in his income did not promise any immediate success, asked my opinion as to the possibility of a prolongation, for a short time, of the aid so generously afforded to him last year. I thereupon advised him to write me a letter[2] containing an exact statement of the grounds of his expectations of a change for the better in his position, after which I would have a consultation with you on the subject. This letter, as you will probably be in London again before I shall, I enclose.

In Comte's position I think my conduct would have been different: in the first place, I should have endeavoured by saving to provide a fund for such emergencies, and if this failed I should have preferred living as I could upon my reduced income so long as it was physically possible. But it is to be said for him, on the first point, that he had every reason to believe his income a permanent one, and on the second, that it is harder to be advised to break up all his arrangements and to alter his confirmed habits from a cause which he firmly believes to be not only temporary, but of very short duration. If, therefore, you think that it would be possible and advisable to raise another subscription for him I should be happy, in case of need, to contribute my part towards it. At the same time, as he certainly does not mean to be understood as asking for such a favour, so, if the answer be negative, it need not have the character of a refusal.

469. TO AUGUSTE COMTE[1]

India House
le 22 septembre
1845

MON CHER MONSIEUR COMTE

Je suis de retour ici depuis longtemps, mais M. Grote ne l'est que depuis quelques jours, et votre lettre est restée chez lui pendant son absence.

1. Published in Elliot, I, 139–40. MS not located. Dated by Elliot as of Dec. 22, 1848, but evidence from this and from the Mill-Comte correspondence indicates that it should be dated as of the summer of 1845.
2. See preceding letter, n. 6.

* * * *

1. MS at Johns Hopkins. Published in Lévy-Bruhl, pp. 475–76; in reply to Comte's of Aug. 8, *ibid.*, pp. 468–74.

Aussitôt après son retour nous nous sommes vus, et nous avons causé sur votre position. Il a dû lui-même vous annoncer le résultat, qui ne paraît pas devoir être de nature à remédier à vos embarras.

Quant à Molesworth, dont je n'ai eu que plus tard la réponse, tout en témoignant un regret sincère que la gêne de vos affaires se soit encore prolongée il ne paraît nullement disposé à renouveler son subside à moins d'une nécessité absolue qu'il ne juge pas être arrivée.

Je ne connais aucune autre personne à laquelle je puisse convenablement m'adresser dans un cas pareil.

Je ne veux pas mêler des causeries ordinaires à l'annonce d'une chose sérieuse, et je me bornerai par conséquent à vous dire que je n'ai cru devoir mettre aucune suite à ma correspondance avec Herschel. Si je lui avais dit que vous n'aviez pas l'intention de lui répondre, il n'aurait certainement pas apprécié les raisons que vous avez pour cela: il n'y aurait vu qu'un aveu indirect de l'irréfutabilité de son raisonnement, surtout si de mon côté je m'abstenais également de le réfuter; ce que je ne pourrais certainement faire sans avoir connaissance de votre mémoire en manuscrit, à moins de recevoir de vous-même des renseignements équivalents.

Mandez-moi bientôt ce que vous comptez faire.

tout à vous

J. S. MILL

470. TO HENRY REEVE[1]

India House
23rd Sept. 1845

MY DEAR SIR,

You can hardly feel more interested in preventing the removal of Captain Meadows Taylor from Shorapur[2] than I do myself, because (to say nothing of personal considerations), I have a very high opinion of the merits of his administration of Shorapur. I may say, indeed, that his being at Shorapur now is owing to me, for some expressions of approval and praise in a dispatch written by me was what induced the Indian Government to suspend their intention of replacing him by a civil servant of the company, and to refer the matter home. I have endeavoured to induce the Court of

1. Excerpt published in the Preface by Henry Reeve to Meadows Taylor's *The Story of My Life* (Edinburgh, 1877). New edition, with Introduction and Notes by Henry Bruce (London, 1920). MS not located.
2. Philip Meadows Taylor (1808–1876), military officer in India and novelist; carried out the pacification of the State of Shorapore in 1841 and remained there as resident until 1853. Early in 1845 a move had been made to supplant Captain Taylor with a civil servant of the East India Co. (see *The Story of My Life* [1920 ed.], pp. 204–9). Taylor was a second cousin of Reeve.

Directors to negative the proposition. I do not, however, expect to obtain anything so decided, as they do not think it right to fetter the Indian Government in its choice of instruments. But as the Court will certainly give no encouragement to the project, I think it will blow over, and Captain Taylor will remain.[3]—Very truly yours,

J. S. MILL

471. TO HENRY REEVE[1]

[Late Sept., 1845]

Whatever may be the cause that is working against Captain Taylor, I am convinced that Fraser[2] has nothing to do with it. Fraser, as far as I know, has always written to Government very much in his favour. Captain Taylor is quite in error if he supposes that the Nazarana[3] business has done him any harm. Fraser did not agree with him on the subject, but the home authorities and Sir H. Hardinge[4] did, and do most strenuously.

472. TO AUGUSTE COMTE[1]

India House
le 3 octobre 1845

MON CHER MONSIEUR COMTE

J'espère que vous ne trouverez pas mauvais que je regarde toute nouvelle intervention auprès de sir W. Molesworth comme peu convenable de ma part. Pour l'autoriser il faudrait être beaucoup plus lié que je ne le suis avec lui. Il n'y a jamais eu d'intimité entre nous; et depuis longtemps nous ne nous voyons presque pas, si ce n'est une ou deux fois par an peut être, chose assez fréquente à Londres, comme vous savez sans doute, même entre de très anciennes connaissances. Il y a plusieurs ans que je ne suis pas entré une seule fois dans sa maison. Vous voyez donc que je ne suis guère en droit de faire un appel quelconque, surtout réitéré, à sa liberalité, lorsqu'il n'y a pas lieu de compter d'avance sur un accueil favorable. Ensuite, quant

3. JSM's prediction was fulfilled.

* * * *

1. Excerpt published, like the preceding letter, in Henry Reeve's Preface to Meadows Taylor's *The Story of My Life*. MS not located.
2. General James Stuart Fraser (1783–1869), the Resident in Hyderabad.
3. Occasional dues exacted from the State of Shorapore by the ruler of Hyderabad. Taylor had sought to lessen the tribute levied on the weaker State, Shorapore.
4. Sir Henry Hardinge, later first Viscount Hardinge of Lahore (1785–1856), Governor General of India, 1844–47.

* * * *

1. MS at Johns Hopkins. Published in Lévy-Bruhl, pp. 480–82; in reply to Comte's of Sept. 24, *ibid.*, pp. 476–79.

à la sorte de communication indiquée dans votre lettre, vous me pardonnerez, j'espère, si je ne trouve pas que dans le cas actuel, elle soit justifiée
par sa réponse antérieure. Il n'y a, en effet, rien de nouveau à lui annoncer.
Il sait déjà quelle est votre position, ou à peu près. Je conçois bien combien
il est dur de se voir privé de la moitié d'un revenu qu'on croyait assuré, et
sur lequel on avait réglé ses habitudes; je sens combien est minime, pour
un homme comme vous, la rétribution de cinq mille francs qui vous reste.
Mais enfin, puisque vous avez encore cette somme, Sir W. Molesworth a
sans doute jugé que votre gêne, quelque regrettable qu'elle soit, ne fait pas
un cas de nécessité absolue. Voilà les raisons qui me détourneraient personnellement de faire auprès de lui une nouvelle démarche quelconque.
Mais ces raisons, vous êtes vous-même en état d'en juger; et si vous êtes
disposé à lui écrire directement en votre nom, son adresse est Sir William
Molesworth Bart, M.P. I Lowndes Square, Knightsbridge, London.

Je regrette vivement que ce que je puis avoir dit sur les chances d'un
nouveau subside vous ait donné une confiance que j'étais loin de vouloir
vous inspirer, et qui a abouti à un désappointement. Quelles que puissent
être ces chances, j'ai pensé et même dit qu'elles devaient dépendre de
l'opinion qu'auraient MM. Grote et Molesworth sur l'extrême probabilité
d'une prompte terminaison de votre crise actuelle: or c'est apparemment
cette opinion qui s'est trouvée en défaut: la perspective qu'offrait votre
lettre leur aura paru trop indéfinie, et ils auront pensé qu'un secours
modique ne ferait que retarder le moment de sacrifices pénibles sans remédier à leur nécessité.

Il est heureux que les mutations déterminées par le choix qu'on fera au
poste de directeur des études vont fournir un moyen de voir plus clair dans
les chances d'une réintégration officielle. Si les nominations à faire dépendent, comme celle d'examinateur, du conseil polytechnique, vous aurez
probablement lieu de juger, par l'allure que prendra le conseil à l'occasion
de votre candidature, s'il est vraiment disposé à changer de conduite envers
vous. Si, d'un autre côté, les nominations dépendent du gouvernement, vous
pourrez également juger de sa bonne volonté. Je désire beaucoup que de
manière ou d'autre, l'occasion puisse amener, sinon une réparation, au
moins l'indication sûre d'une disposition à l'accorder prochainement.

Je n'ai pas encore commencé, sauf quelques lectures préliminaires, le
travail d'économie politique qui doit m'occuper pendant l'hiver. Le plan de
l'ouvrage est tout fait, et je suis assez familiarisé avec la plupart des
matériaux pour pouvoir espérer que lorsque j'aurai commencé à écrire,
j'avancerai vite, et que le livre sera terminé avant l'été.

tout à vous

J. S. MILL.

473. TO MACVEY NAPIER[1]

India House
20th October
1845

MY DEAR SIR

Your liberal remittance reached me duly, & I thank you for it, and also for the separate copies which you were so considerate as to think of although I neglected to ask for them at the proper time.

The omission of the concluding paragraph[2] I do not regret: it could be well spared, & though I am fully convinced of the truth of all it contained, I was not satisfied with the manner in which it was expressed. You are of course quite right in not printing what you think would expose you to attack, when you do not yourself agree in it. At the same time, I do not know how a public writer can be more usefully employed than in telling his countrymen their faults, & if that is considered anti-national I am not at all desirous to avoid the charge. Neither do I think that the English, with all their national self-conceit, are now much inclined to resent having their faults pointed out—they will bear a good deal in that respect.

I am glad you find the reception of the article satisfactory. I am not acquainted with Gilbert Stuart's writings:[3] those of Millar[4] I have long known, & there is as you say, a considerable similarity between some of his historical speculations & Guizot's.

With regard to a review of the Logic, I am not disappointed by your having had to give up the attempt. As far as the compliment is concerned, the wish is equivalent to the deed—& for the interests of the book itself, which is the main point, the notice of the Ed. Rev. might have been of essential importance to it, but as things have luckily turned out the book has reached nearly everybody who could be expected to buy or read a book of the kind. By the bye, it has narrowly missed being reviewed in the Quarterly by Herschel but he also has abandoned the intention.[5] Believe me

Very truly yours

J. S. MILL

1. Published in *Napier Corresp.*, pp. 510–11. MS in Brit. Mus.
2. Of his review of Guizot (see Letter 419, n. 2).
3. Gilbert Stuart (1742–1786), historian and reviewer; Napier may have referred to Stuart's *A View of Society in Europe* (Edinburgh, 1778), a study of the early and mediaeval period influenced by the principles of Montesquieu.
4. John Millar. See Letter 440, n. 3.
5. Herschel had so informed JSM in his letter of July 10, 1845.

474. TO MACVEY NAPIER[1]

India House
27th October
1845

MY DEAR SIR

I have just finished an article which I am desirous of offering to the Edin. Rev. It is a review[2] of a book which I had occasion to mention in a note to the article on the "Claims of Labour," Duveyrier's Lettres Politiques. But as the title of the book gives little or no indication of the contents of the article, I have taken the liberty of sending it at once through Longman. It is the last I mean to write, for the present on any French topic—& its subject is, not French history or literature, but present French politics, introducing, however, remarks & speculations of a more general character. I cannot of course judge whether it will suit you, but I have put nothing into it which seemed inconsistent with its admission into the Edin. Rev. If you take it, pray let it wait your own time for insertion—& the more so, as it may be some little time before I have leisure to write another article on any subject.

Whewell's book,[3] which you kindly suggest, I have not yet read, but from turning over the pages I do not think it is a book on which I should be at all desirous of writing.

Believe me
yours ever truly

J. S. MILL

475. TO HENRY S. CHAPMAN[1]

India House
12th November, 1845.

MY DEAR CHAPMAN,—

Thank you exceedingly for your long and interesting letter. Since it was written the troubles of the Colony are, I hope, nearly blown over, the fool Fitzroy[2] being recalled, and matters made up between the Company and the Government. As the revenue cannot get up again immediately, and as there

1. MS in Brit. Mus.
2. See Letter 428, n. 2.
3. Presumably William Whewell's *The Elements of Morality, including Polity* (2 vols., London, 1845). JSM eventually wrote on "Whewell's Moral Philosophy" in *WR*, LVIII (Oct., 1852), 349–85 (reprinted in *Dissertations*, III, 132–92).

* * * *

1. MS in the possession of Mrs. W. Rosenberg. Copy supplied by Professor J. M. McCrimmon.
2. See Letter 442, n. 11. Lord Stanley had dismissed Governor Fitzroy in a dispatch dated April 30, 1845, which reached New Zealand in Nov.

has been so much extra expense I suppose they will not be able to pay your arrears at once, but doubtless you will succeed in getting put upon the Parliamentary vote in April. You have been very ill-treated, but that is what may be said of everybody in New Zealand, and indeed of many in almost all the other colonies, in the hands of Stanley, a man who has no conscience, and has I believe, not the ordinary feelings of honour—only pettishness and petulant self-will. It is fortunate you have been able to live with what they have paid you, and with the produce of your land—your account of which has very much interested me. I lost no time in asking Dr. Royle[3] for the Himalayan seeds, and he says there is no use in sending them from England when they can so easily go direct. He will write immediately to Dr. Jameson,[4] Superintendent of the E.I. Company's botanical garden at Saharunpore (at the foot of the Himalayas) asking him to send you seeds of any useful plants that are likely to suit your climate, and you can at once place yourself in communication with Dr. Jameson, and send him New Zealand seeds for trial in India. Many thanks for thinking of ferns for me. If you have anybody there who can name them it would be useful, as there are probably no books here on the botany of New Zealand; but if not, I will find someone to name and describe them here, as in any case there are likely to be new ones among them. Any other plants would be interesting as well as ferns,—all is fish that comes to my net, and there may be among plants picked up indiscriminately in a new country, as many and as interesting nondescripts as there were in Graham's Mexican collection.[5]

We have had but two subjects of much public interest in England this year; the one is railways, for which there has been a perfect frenzy. On the return of prosperity after the depression of the last few years, all the speculation which usually arises at such times, has taken that one direction, and not only a railway, or four or five rival railways are planned between almost every two towns of the smallest importance in the Kingdom, but all Europe, India, and the Colonies are to have railways made for them by English capital. If the thing had gone on a month longer I am convinced someone would have brought out "the Great New Zealand, Auckland and Wellington Junction railway company." However, there has just been a collapse, numbers having, under the allurement of premiums, taken many more shares than they could pay calls or even deposits on, intending to sell

3. John Forbes Royle (1799–1858), surgeon and naturalist, from 1838 in the employ of the India House in charge of correspondence relating to vegetable productions. He had been superintendent of gardens and in medical charge of the station at Saharunpore from 1823 to 1831.

4. Dr. William Jameson (1815–1882), botanist, pioneer of tea planting in India.

5. George John Graham, close friend of JSM in the 1820's, had travelled in Mexico, 1827–29, and collected some 400 specimens of Mexican plants. These are mentioned by George Bentham in the preface to his *Plantæ Hartwegianæ* (London, 1839).

all or part of it in case the market at last began to fall and money to get scarce, as people wanted to borrow that they might not be obliged to sell immediately. The rate of interest rose, and at last the Bank raised its rate of discount; this gave the alarm, and being followed by some thundering articles in the "Times", in which all the schemes or most of them were scouted as fraudulent bubbles, the long-eared public changed from ignorant and mad confidence to equally senseless distrust. Down came shares, and some of the very most promising schemes could not be proceeded with, because of those who had asked for shares and obtained them not one third would or could pay even the deposits. While the thing lasted there were enormous gains made, many people made large fortunes, and there must be corresponding losses to those who bought at high premiums, unless they are able and have courage to hold on, in which case the greater part will lose little.

The second subject which is occupying the public is the potato disease. It is certain that a very large proportion, nobody knows how large, of the potato crop is destroyed or in course of destruction, by this disease, not only in Ireland and Great Britain but in Belgium and Germany. It is also just discovered that the wheat crop is very deficient, a thing I expected from the prevalence of wind and rain at the blooming time. This also is general throughout Europe. In Russia there are already meal mobs, and exportation has been, I believe, prohibited. The deficiency is very great in North Germany, Holland and Belgium have suspended their corn laws; France and the South of Europe have little or no corn to spare, and we have only America to look to. The best quality of wheat is already at 74 sh. here, but the bad quality of the crop, which was very badly got in, keeps down the averages; and everybody feels that the sliding scale is an entire failure, bonded corn actually leaving this country to go elsewhere. Of course everybody thinks and says that the corn laws must go this winter, and the question only is whether any, even the smallest duty shall be suffered to remain. There have been four Cabinet Councils in almost successive days, and a general belief or hope existed that an Order in Council would be issued opening the ports, but the Ministers have separated and gone to the country without doing anything. It is rumoured that they are divided, Peel being on the side of remission; but I do not believe the rumour to be founded on anything except its abstract a priori probability. Peel always misses the moment; but it is so universally seen and admitted by friends and enemies that the corn laws are doomed, that they can hardly escape their fate. I think there will be such a demonstration on the subject before Parliament meets as will finish them, and most happy will that be, for that odious question stands in the way of all others. If it is given up in the coming session we shall certainly see free trade victorious in America too, for J. K. Polk[6] and the party who brought him in are avowed friends of a tariff for revenue only, and the repeal of the corn laws by giving them the Western States would make them irresistible. As for Europe, at least France and Germany, any approach to free-trade there has now become hopeless. They are receding further from it every day as their industrial interests grow stronger and require more power in the State; and in Germany the rising feeling of nationality all tends in that mischievous direction. It is not a matter of calculation now, but of passion, and I sincerely believe that there is in the public eye both of France and of Germany a strenuous desire to bring down the wealth and power of England, if they can. They wish to get wealth and power themselves by imitating England, that is, by having manufacture and an import trade, and besides that they are jealous of England, dislike the English ascendancy, and would have pleasure in weakening it though they were to get nothing by it. I believe this feeling to have been greatly heightened if not created by the meddling, mischievous Palmerston policy in 1841,[7] which besides irritating France, excited intense disgust in Germany. There is, however, a considerable and rising school of sound political economy in France now; the "Revue des Economistes," a monthly publication in which Dunoyer, Passy,[8] Horace Say, and a number of other rational men write, and which is edited by Dussard (did you know him when he was in England? He then learnt the English political economy very well) has a very tolerable sale, which I am sure no such book would have in England. Dunoyer's book "De la liberté du travail," is one of the books best worth reading which have come out lately. I have now actually begun the book I meditated, and hope to complete it by the end of winter. I shall profit by your remarks on Wakefield's plan, which seems perfectly just, especially as to the lottery system.[9] Absenteeism is an evil in a new settlement, and might have been a much greater one. Wakefield by the way has very uncertain health now and is very much unfitted for work or activity. Whenever he gets at all excited, and you know his excitability, he is threatened with apoplexy.

The New Zealand Company have done very wisely in allowing the holders of the land at Nelson to exchange it on favourable terms for the earlier numbers which, by a measure I always thought very questionable, had been withheld from them. I mean to use the option with regard to my town and rural allotments; the accommodation land has answered very well. You, I remember, had land at Nelson too, but yours were better numbers.

6. James Knox Polk (1795–1849), as President of the United States, 1845–49, fought for and obtained tariff reductions.
7. See Letters 303 to 305, and 308.
8. Hippolyte Philibert Passy (1793–1880), economist and politician.
9. In administering sales of land through the New Zealand Co., Edward Gibbon Wakefield awarded priorities in choice of lands by a lottery system.

However, I daresay you will be able to exchange some of them to advantage.

I had not heard of Revans'[10] failure, which I infer from your speaking of his "execution creditor." I am very sorry for it, but in a place like Wellington I suppose he will soon re-establish himself.

Pray write sometimes; I will not wait for your next, but will write again in three or four months if I find anything interesting to relate.

With kind regards to your family,

Yours ever faithfully,

J. S. MILL

476. TO SIR JOHN F. W. HERSCHEL[1]

India House
19th December
1845

MY DEAR SIR

Some time ago, you did me the favour to intimate that you would have no objection to communicate to me some of your remarks on my "System of Logic,"[2] particularly those parts of it in which physical and mathematical subjects were adverted to. I have so little claim to ask you to take this trouble, that I am almost ashamed to remind you of your intention—but as I am informed by the publisher that he is about to prepare for a second edition, the advantage which I hope to derive from your criticisms would be peculiarly valuable if it could be afforded in time for that purpose.

I remain
Very truly yours
J. S. MILL

477. TO SIR JOHN F. W. HERSCHEL[1]

India House
29th Decr 1845

MY DEAR SIR,

Pray receive my thankful acknowledgments for your letter. I had already been convinced by other criticisms, that the chapter on which you comment

10. Samuel Revans. See Letter 442, n. 14.

* * * *

1. MS in the possession of the Royal Society.
2. In Herschel's unpublished letter of July 10, 1845. See Letter 465, n. 4.

* * * *

1. MS in the possession of the Royal Society. In reply to Herschel's letter of Dec. 22, also in the Royal Society Library.

required to be seriously reconsidered & that Laplace was not so far wrong as I had ventured to think him.[2] The other point however,[3] on which I differed from him, is one on which I have not hitherto been shaken, but I have not the smallest reluctance to acknowledge myself wrong on this also if it turns out that I am so.

With many thanks, & sincere hopes for the termination of your indisposition

believe me
Very truly yours
J. S. MILL

2. Herschel's chief criticism of the *Logic* in his long letter of Dec. 22 concerned "your objections against Laplace's statement of the theory of Probabilities in p. 70 etc. of your 2nd Vol.—and against his conclusions in the case specified in page 195 of that volume.

"With these objections I can no ways agree and I will not conceal from you that I read them with great concern and an earnest wish that you would give them a full reconsideration."

3. Herschel, *ibid.*, "I have not left myself space to enter into the other question agitated [?] by you in p. 195 about the credibility of the witnesses in Laplace's case. . . . I feel quite satisfied myself and hope to make it clear to you that Laplace is perfectly right."

1846

478. TO GEORGE GROTE[1]

1st January, 1846

MY DEAR MR. GROTE,—Since our last conversation on Comte's affairs, I have had two letters from him,[2] a short and a long one, both of which I enclose. The latter of them is so little creditable to his delicacy or gratitude, or, rather, shews an inordinate self-importance overriding both, that I should have been ashamed to send it to you if it had not seemed to be his intention that I should.

The shorter letter was written when he first heard from me that Molesworth was not disposed to renew his subscription. In answer[3] to it I declined applying further to Molesworth, saying that he would not, probably, consider the case one of necessity while Comte had still 200£ a year. Two months after, I received the long letter.

As you will see that he then expressed himself as if I had led him to count upon the success of an application for a second subscription, I must say to you, what I said to him, that I did not intentionally give him any confidence, for I felt none myself. His sanguine disposition ran away with him in this, as in other cases. I said to him (as I once told you) that very likely he might receive further help if it were only wanted for a short, and definite, but not for an indefinite time. I do not remember saying anything else, except that "the letter he sent to me, and which I sent to you, seemed to me well suited for its object:" that I said, because he referred it to my judgement.

Ever yours truly,

J. S. MILL

P.S.—I hope the first two volumes of the History[4] will soon be out; I long to see them.

1. Printed in *Posthumous Papers* (of George Grote), ed. Mrs. Grote (privately printed, London, 1874), p. 94. MS not located.
2. Comte's letters of Sept. 24, 1845, and Dec. 18, 1845.
3. Letter 472.
4. JSM reviewed the first two volumes of *A History of Greece*, in the *Spectator*, April 4, 1846, pp. 327–28, and in the *ER*, LXXXIV (Oct., 1846), 343–77. The latter review is reprinted in *Dissertations*, II, 363–415.

479. TO AUGUSTE COMTE[1]

India House
le 12 janvier 1846

MON CHER MONSIEUR COMTE

Votre lettre du 18 décembre exige de moi une réponse sérieuse, et qui aurait été immédiate, si je n'eusse été forcé d'attendre un moment où je pourrais le faire à loisir, et avec la reflexion convenable.

Votre appréciation de la conduite tenue envers vous en Angleterre me paraît reposer sur une erreur de fait. La sévère condamnation morale que vous portez sur ceux qui ont cessé de vous accorder l'appui pécuniaire qu'ils vous avaient donné temporairement, se pourrait tout au plus concevoir, en leur supposant des opinions, des sentiments, et, à tous égards, une position morale envers vous, qui n'existent pas, et dont ils n'ont certainement jamais fait profession. S'ils vous avaient accepté comme leur chef spirituel, s'ils vous regardaient comme le représentant de leurs convictions, comme l'apôtre d'un système de doctrines et de sentimens auquel ils adhéraient essentiellement; je ne sais pas s'ils se seraient crus moralement obligés de prolonger leurs subsides, mais je suis persuadé qu'ils l'auraient fait, et je les estimerais peu si je pensais qu'en pareil cas ils croiraient avoir assez fait déjà. Mais de la sympathie partielle qu'ils éprouvent pour vos opinions, et de l'admiration très réelle qu'ils ressentent envers vos talents, il y a loin à cette intime solidarité d'opinions et de sentimens. C'est leur prêter, sans fondement, vos propres convictions, que de dire qu'ils se sont crus "moralement obligés" à faire pour vous ce qu'ils ont fait. Je ne vois dans leur procédé autre chose qu'un sentiment de philanthropie envers un philosophe éminent, pris au dépourvu par une persécution inattendue. Sans doute ils ont tous les trois une haute admiration pour votre grand ouvrage; ils le regardent comme une traité philosophique du premier ordre; ils reconnaissent en avoir beaucoup appris; et Grote, dont je parle le plus parce que je le connais le mieux, avoue qu'il y doit des modifications dans plusieurs de ses opinions. Grote, et probablement Molesworth, acceptent encore aussi pleinement que vous-même l'idée mère de vos travaux, c. à d. la substitution du point de vue scientifique au point de vue religieux, et l'application aux études sociales de la méthode philosophique qui préside aujourd'hui irrévocablement à toutes les autres études. Ils pensent encore, je puis à peu près l'assurer, du moins quant à Grote, que vous avez, le premier, conçu la méthode positive d'une manière qui la rend propre à

1. MS at Johns Hopkins. Published in Lévy-Bruhl, pp. 499–505; in reply to Comte's of Dec. 18, 1845, *ibid.*, pp. 482–98.

cette dernière extension. Il y a bien là de quoi motiver une haute estime philosophique. Mais quant à votre manière particulière de concevoir la sociologie dogmatique, ils sont si loin de la partager, que pour me borner à Grote, qui en est encore probablement le moins éloigné des trois, je crois savoir que sauf la question religieuse, la plupart des doctrines sociales que vous professez sont très en désaccord avec ses opinions et bien que cette dissidence ne l'empêche pas de rendre justice à votre haute valeur philosophique, elle importe beaucoup à l'obligation que vous lui supposez de concourir à la propagation active d'opinions sociales dont beaucoup ne lui semblent ni vraies ni utiles à propager.

Il n'y a donc pas lieu d'accuser, en ce cas, la faiblesse des convictions actuelles. Ce n'est pas un cas de demi-conviction ni de demi-volunté; c'est un cas de conviction très arrêtée d'un désaccord essentiel d'opinion. Vous vous trompez davantage encore en pensant qu'un sentiment étroit de nationalité y soit pour quelque chose. Contrairement à l'opinion générale du continent, je suis d'avis qu'il y a moins de nationalité chez les anglais que chez tout autre peuple civilisé. Ils ont aujourd'hui beaucoup moins de préjugés et de préventions nationales que les peuples du continent; on peut seulement, à cet égard, les accuser d'indifférence; ils font peu d'attention aux autres peuples, et ignorent en général ce qui s'y fait; mais ceux parmi eux, qui ne partagent pas cette ignorance, ceux qui connaissent assez le continent pour en juger, soit par leurs études, soit par leurs voyages, ceux-là sont cosmopolites au delà de ce que vous pouvez vous imaginer; et s'il y a des hommes dont cela est surtout et particulièrement vrai, ce sont précisément ceux à qui vous avez eu à faire.

Quant au projet de revue, et à la manière dont il fut accueilli, vos reproches retombent surtout sur moi: les autres n'ont eu dans cette affaire qu'un rôle passif. Je n'ai même parlé là dessus qu'avec Grote, et sans le consulter, pas plus que Molesworth, sur la réponse à vous faire. Je lui a demandé son avis sur la probabilité de pouvoir placer des actions et trouver des abonnés en angleterre, parce que ma propre opinion, quelque décidée qu'elle fût, ne pouvait pas vous suffire. Je ne lui ai pas seulement demandé s'il y prendrait part. Lui seul pouvait juger jusqu'à quel point cela lui convenait, tant personnellement qu'en égard à ses opinions. Sous ce dernier rapport j'aurais espéré que la franche explication que je vous donnai sur la question de ma propre coopération, aurait suffi, et peut être à plus forte raison à l'égard des autres. Mon hésitation fut expressément motivée sur le défaut d'un accord suffisant d'opinion. Je pense comme alors que l'acceptation commune du principe positif, et même un accord essentiel d'idées sur la méthode, ne sont pas une base suffisante pour une entreprise commune de propagation sociologique; sans toutefois rien prescrire à l'égard de ceux dont les opinions sociales, en tant qu'arrêtées, sont d'accord. Cette harmonie initiale est bien loin d'exister entre nous deux, pour ne rien dire des autres: sans cela, aurais-je accueilli la proposition comme je l'ai fait? et la tentative que nous avons faite pour vider notre différence d'opinion sur une seule question fondamentale, n'a pas été assez heureuse pour nous encourager à en entamer d'autres, ou pour faire croire que le positivisme puisse bientôt offrir au monde un système social capable de réunir tous ceux qui acceptent sa méthode. Plus j'y réfléchis et moins je crois à la proximité d'un résultat semblable, qui me paraît exiger plusieurs progrès antérieurs, non suffisamment effectués, et surtout un notable perfectionnement de la science positive de l'homme. Les dissidences qui existent en matière sociale entre deux penseurs consciencieux, qui se ressemblent d'aussi près que vous et moi dans leurs principes logiques, doivent tenir à ce que l'un ou l'autre n'entend pas assez bien les lois de la nature humaine. Une connaissance plus approfondie de ces lois me paraît une condition nécessaire d'une théorie sociologique rationnelle. Personne aujourd'hui ne s'occupe convenablement de lever cet obstacle, et je crois de plus en plus que c'est là le genre de tentative philosophique par lequel un penseur bien préparé pourrait aujourd'hui rendre le plus de service, tant à la théorie qu'à la pratique sociale.

Je dois encore décharger MM Grote et Molesworth de la responsabilité de l'allusion que j'ai faite à leurs sentimens présumés sur ce qui constituerait à votre égard le cas de nécessité. Ils ne m'avaient pas articulé un seul mot, à ce sujet, et je suis seul responsable d'une explication qui, je le vois avec peine, vous a blessé. Cependant je ne doute pas, non plus qu'alors, que j'ai exprimé leurs véritables sentimens. Je pense, certes, comme vous, qu'il serait très déplacé de la part de qui que ce soit, de prétendre vous imposer des règles de conduite dans vos dépenses privées, et que vous êtes pleinement en droit de n'y avoir égard qu'à votre opinion propre. Cela est même presque superflu à dire. S'ils ont pris ce sujet en considération, ce n'est pas pour régler votre conduite, mais la leur. Votre jugement est définitif pour vous, le leur l'est également pour eux. Quant à leur droit de se faire une opinion là dessus, il me semble découler nécessairement du fait même de l'intervention pécuniaire, et je trouve très simple qu'on ne se croie pas tenu à faire pour l'aisance d'un philosophe ce qu'on ferait volontiers pour sa subsistance. Vous jugez très sévèrement ceux qui "du sein de leur opulence" émettraient un tel avis. Sans doute, tant qu'il y aura des riches, et qu'un homme possédera plus qu'un autre sans avoir plus de mérite personnel, il y aura toujours quelque couleur de justice à de pareilles plaintes. Pour moi je ne les trouve nullement bien fondées. Je conçois qu'on ne compte pas avec ses amis personnels les plus chers, ou avec celui qu'on regarderait comme son chef spirituel et maître réveré, ou même peut-être avec celui pour le jugement duquel, dans toute question de conduite, on aurait, d'après une intime connaissance personnelle, un respect et une déférence telle, qu'on se reposerait aveuglément sur lui, en se dispensant de se faire une opinion propre. Mais partout où ces conditions n'existent pas, il me semble permis qu'on ait égard à la possibilité d'une économie sur les dépenses de celui qu'on veut aider, et je ne pense pas que, pour cela, on mérite l'accusation de s'immiscer à tort dans les affaires d'autrui.

Vous voyez, mon cher Monsieur Comte, qu'en donnant mon avis, avec une pleine franchise, sur votre lettre, je ne la juge pas d'après des considérations de délicatesse arbitraire et de convention, dont je crois qu'un homme sérieux, dans un cas important, peut se dispenser. C'est le fond même de la question que nous n'envisageons pas de la même manière. Mais nous sommes d'accord sur votre droit incontestable de travailler désormais pour votre aisance privée, dussiez-vous par là retarder la suite de vos travaux spéculatifs. Vous avez bien assez fait pour n'avoir pas besoin de justification, quelque parti que vous preniez à cet égard.

J'ai fait part de votre lettre à Grote et à Molesworth, mais ils n'ont aucune participation directe ou indirecte à ma réponse, que je ne leur ai pas même communiquée.

Vous me demandez des nouvelles de M. et Mme Austin. Je les ai vus tous deux à Londres, où ils ont passé après leur retour d'Allemagne. Ils se portaient alors assez bien. Ils doivent être maintenant à Paris, où vraisemblablement vous avez eu de leurs nouvelles.

Tout à vous

J. S. MILL

480. TO SIR JOHN F. W. HERSCHEL[1]

India House
20th February 1846

MY DEAR SIR

With many apologies for troubling you so much on the subject of my Logic—will you permit me to ask whether there is anything in the *first* volume on which I may hope for any remarks from you?

1. MS in the possession of the Royal Society.

I ask this because I am much urged by the publisher to send the volume to press for a second edition.

> Believe me
> Very truly yours
> J. S. MILL

481. TO SIR JOHN F. W. HERSCHEL[1]

India House
28th Feby 1846

MY DEAR SIR,

Many thanks for your remarks, all of which shall be attended to.

As to the first—I was quite aware that the tendency of the moon to the earth was not known to be as $1/D^2$ before Newton, but as Newton's name is not mentioned in that passage which only traces the successive order of the discoveries as an illustration of method, I had not thought it necessary to guard the phraseology on that collateral point. I shall now do so.[2]

On the 2nd point—I knew that the shock of a comet could only alter the ellipse to some other *conic section* & to avoid the apparent ignorance I will change the wording.[3]

What you say on the difference between the evidence of a medium in the cases of light & of gravity, ought, in justice to the advocates of a medium, to be brought in somewhere, & I will take care to do so.[4]

I will omit the reference to M. Comte on the subject of pathological phenomena.[5] I have never read Dr. Holland's book,[6] & I got the remark from Comte.[7]

Nothing has happened to make your observations on the other proposition of Laplace of less importance to me.

> Very truly yours
> J. S. MILL

1. MS in the possession of the Royal Society.
2. JSM made only a slight change in wording; cf. Book III, chap. 12 ("Of the Explanation of Laws of Nature"), sec. 5, ¶ 1, with the corresponding passage in the second edition of the *Logic* (London, 1846). The first American edition (New York, 1846) and subsequent American so-called editions do not contain JSM's revisions.
3. Cf. Book III, chap. 14 ("Of the Limits to the Explanation of Laws of Nature; and of Hypotheses"), sec. 6, ¶1, with the corresponding paragraph in the second edition.
4. Cf. *ibid.*, ¶2 with ¶3 and footnote in the second edition.
5. In Book III, chap. 11 ("Of the Deductive Method"), sec. 1, ¶8, the reference to Comte is removed in the second edition.
6. Probably Dr. (later Sir) Henry Holland (1788–1873), physician and writer on medical subjects, rather than Dr. George Calvert Holland (1801–1865), also a writer on medical and scientific topics. The book has not been identified.
7. See *Cours de Philosophie positive, Tome troisième, contenant la philosophie chimique et la philosophie biologique* (Paris, 1838), pp. 331 ff.

482. TO AUGUSTE COMTE[1]

India House
le 26 mars 1846

MON CHER MONSIEUR COMTE

Je n'ai pas jugé nécessaire de répondre promptement à votre lettre du 23 janvier. Il m'a semblé inutile de prolonger la discussion sur le sujet spécial de votre lettre. Nous avons suffisamment fait connaître l'un a l'autre notre façon de penser. Cette communication n'a nullement diminué la divergence qui existait d'abord, et qui concerne, comme vous avez reconnu, les sentiments autant que les idées et les principes. Je bornerai donc ma réponse à quelques explications sur ce qui, dans votre lettre, me regarde personnellement, sans quoi vous pourriez croire que j'accepte vos observations comme fondées, ou que je les repousse sans raison aucune, ne pouvant y répondre.

D'abord, il est certain qu'il n'y a pas eu, comme vous semblez le croire, de malentendu sur la nature de la coopération pécuniaire que vous espériez obtenir en Angleterre pour le projet de revue. Vous avez alors très clairement expliqué la nature du projet, et indiqué les ressources pécuniaires nécessaires pour le mettre en exécution. Votre lettre a été soumise à MM. Grote et Molesworth. Ils ont dû croire et ils ont certainement cru en effet, que cela équivalait à leur faire la proposition de fournir eux mêmes les fonds en tout ou en partie. J'ai ensuite demandé spécialement à M. Grote son avis sur la possibilité d'obtenir ces fonds, et c'était l'inviter, autant que je trouvais convenable de le faire, à se prononcer sur sa coopération personnelle. Il s'en est abstenu en pleine connaissance de cause.

En second lieu, je ne dois pas passer sous silence quelques unes de vos observations sur l'intensité particulière que vous attribuez aux préjugés nationaux en Angleterre. Votre opinion à cet égard, loin d'être aucunement affiable, vous conduit à ne voir dans ma persuasion contraire qu'un nouvel exemple du fait que vous croyez signaler, puisque, dites-vous, une prévention nationale sur l'excellence du caractère propre à la nation anglaise, vous paraît seule pouvoir en faire ainsi méconnaître le principal défaut actuel. Vous me pardonnerez si je dis que la supposition que vous faites à mon égard est propre à faire sourire tous ceux qui connaissent un peu la tournure habituelle de mes idées et de mes sentiments. Je suis depuis longtemps dans une espèce d'opposition ouverte contre le caractère national anglais, qui, à plusieurs égards, m'est antipathique et à qui je préfère, à tout prendre, le caractère français, allemand, ou italien. Vos propres expressions témoignent assez combien je sens plus profondément que vous les défauts du caractère anglais, puisque vous regardez comme le plus

1. MS at Johns Hopkins. Published in Lévy-Bruhl, pp. 520–24; in reply to Comte's of Jan. 23, *ibid.*, pp. 505–19.

grand de ses défauts les préjugés nationaux, tandis que moi je lui en trouve d'autres plus graves, plus fondamentaux, et surtout plus difficiles à corriger. Je crois au reste que sans devenir suspect de prévention nationale, on peut faire beaucoup moins de cas que vous ne faites de l'opinion générale du continent en pareille matière. Il est fort naturel que les étrangers se trompent sur le caractère d'un peuple: le nôtre, très peu expansif, offre moins de prises à l'observation qu'un autre; et comme les peuples continentaux se ressemblent beaucoup plus entr'eux qu'ils ne ressemblent aux anglais, ils doivent se comprendre mieux et se juger mutuellement avec moins d'inexactitude qu'ils ne jugent l'Angleterre. Pour moi qui depuis ma première jeunesse, me suis occupé d'étudier le caractère anglais, j'aurais peine à vous dire combien les observations faites là dessus par les étrangers les plus éclairés, même quand elles sont justes, me semblent superficielles, et jusqu'à quel point, même lorsqu'il y a lieu à des critiques sévères, toutes celles que je lis me paraissent manquer le but, en donnant une interprétation française ou allemande à des phénomènes anglais. On donne aux anglais également des défauts et des qualités qu'ils n'ont pas; souvent ceux qu'on leur donne sont l'exact contraire de ceux qu'ils ont réellement.

Pour en venir maintenant à l'explication que vous donnez de nos différences d'opinion sur la seule question biologique et sociale que nous avons expressément discutée en sens contraire, celle de la prétendue infériorité intellectuelle des femmes. Vous vous rendez raison de ce dissentiment par l'insuffisance de mes études et de mes méditations biologiques. Je pense qu'il y a, sous ce rapport, quelque malentendu. Je ne crois pas avoir moins étudié la biologie que toutes les autres sciences fondamentales. Je crois la connaître à peu près aussi bien. Je connais assez bien la méthode, et les principales généralités de toutes, y compris la biologie. Peut être même je me tiens plus au courant des derniers progrès de cette science que de ceux des autres. Quant aux méditations, c'est surtout, chez moi, sur les questions biologiques qu'elles portent. Mais enfin, que mes connaissances anatomiques et physiologiques répondent ou non à l'idée que vous vous en faites de votre point de vue, il m'est également, du mien, permis de croire que j'ai plus étudié, et mieux apprécié, à certains égards, la théorie des phénomènes intellectuels et moraux que vous n'avez dû le faire, vû le mépris que vous professez pour la psychologie, dans laquelle vous comprenez toute étude directe des phénomènes mentaux, en fesant abstraction de leurs conditions organiques. Donc, en supposant de votre part et de la mienne, une chance égale d'insuffisante compétence, je croyais avoir fait la part, sans prévention aucune, de nos points de vue respectifs. Je pense que j'aurais pu réclamer pour moimême la supériorité de chances, à aussi bon droit que vous la réclamez pour vous; et même à meilleur droit peut être, puisque, de mon côté, je ne méprise pas vos avantages comme vous méprisez les miens; je m'occupe, au contraire, de me les donner à moi-même, en augmentant, autant que possible mes connaissances biologiques, ce qui, je le remarque par parenthèse, au lieu d'affaiblir mes convictions antécédentes n'a tendu jus'qu'ici qu'à les fortifier. Quant à l'appui que vous croyez tirer de la concordance entre vos conclusions philosophiques et l'opinion vulgaire, il me semble que l'existence d'une opinion ne peut en faire présumer la vérité que dans le cas où l'on ne pourrait donner d'autre explication raisonnable, de son existence; comme vous le reconnaissez vous même par rapport aux opinions religieuses, et dans bien d'autres cas encore.

Quoi qu'il en soit, je tends de plus en plus à faire de l'étude des fonctions intellectuelles et morales ma principale occupation philosophique, en la menant toutefois, comme vous le conseillez, de pair avec les spéculations sociales, car je reconnais pleinement qu'on ne peut pas connaître l'homme individuel en fesant définitivement abstraction de la société, dont il est indispensable de savoir apprécier philosophiquement les diverses influences. Toutefois je persiste à croire que la sociologie, comme science, ne peut plus faire aucun progrès capital sans s'appuyer sur une théorie plus approfondie de la nature humaine. La force des circonstances peut amener des améliorations pratiques importantes, mais la théorie sociologique ne me paraît comporter actuellement que des progrès secondaires, tant qu'on ne s'occupe pas en même temps de perfectionner la théorie intellectuelle et morale de l'homme. Je tâche de payer mon tribut à ces progrès secondaires par le traité d'économie politique dont je m'occupe et qui s'avance rapidement. Après cela je destine mes principaux efforts à cette autre grande tentative,[2] et je me propose bien de ne négliger aucun genre d'études qui puisse me rendre plus propre à la poursuivre.

L'élection annuelle d'examinateur doit avoir eu lieu: quel en a été la résultat? Aurait-on réparé l'injustice commise envers vous? ou est-ce un parti pris que d'y persévérer?

tout à vous

J. S. Mill

483. TO SIR JOHN F. W. HERSCHEL[1]

India House
30th March 1846

My dear Sir

The printers have come to an end with reprinting the first volume of my Logic & I am pleased to send them what is ready of the second.

2. See Letter 410, n. 2.

* * * *

1. MS in the possession of the Royal Society.

I attach great importance to being right on the point of difference with Laplace, which occurs in the last chapter of Book *III*,[2] on which, too, even if the views I at present entertain are right, they evidently require to be stated more clearly & at greater length. Should I not, therefore, be favoured with any remarks from you before the printers reach that chapter (which at their present rate of progress will be very soon) I shall make them halt at that point, as long as I find in any way compatible with the interests & wishes of the publisher.

Very truly yours

J. S. MILL

484. TO HARRIET GROTE[1]

India House
1st April, 1846

DEAR MRS. GROTE,—McV. Napier has now, some days since, accepted my offer to review your History[2] (for the "Edinburgh Review").[3] He wishes that it should not be later than the October number, and by that time I expect to have it ready.

The article for the "Spectator" is in Rintoul's[4] hands. It is rather long, but its length does not seem to frighten him.

I have taken my extracts from the 2nd vol., which has not yet been quoted, I believe, people not having had time to master it. You will see by the article that I like it very much. I was excessively sorry when I got to the end of it, and am impatient for the next volume.

Yours ever,

J. S. MILL

Napier says that Lewis[5] had offered to review the book for the editor, so that I have prevented an article from him. It would have been such a very good one that I hope he will write it and print it somewhere else.

2. Chap. 25, "Of the Grounds of Disbelief," sec. 5 of the first edition, sec. 6 in later editions.

* * * *

1. Published in *Posthumous Papers* (of George Grote), p. 98. MS not located.
2. See Letter 478, n. 4.
3. Although in parentheses, this should probably be in brackets as Mrs. Grote's interpolation.
4. Robert S. Rintoul.
5. George Cornewall Lewis.

485. TO SIR JOHN F. W. HERSCHEL[1]

India House
8th April 1846

MY DEAR SIR

Your second letter has, as you anticipated, convinced me. An analysis of the cases, such as you have given, is the last appeal when there is any doubt, & if I had resorted to it (which would have been more in conformity with my usual mode of working) I could not have fallen into the error which I committed, & which I am greatly indebted to you for causing me to rectify.

I have written a new conclusion to the chapter,[2] in which I hope I have presented Laplace's principle in a light which will prevent others from falling into my error.

I do not, however, think that Laplace's example is a fair type of the universal character of what are called Coincidences. But what I have to say on this point does not at all infringe upon the logical soundness of Laplace's principles.[3]

I had already entirely rewritten the chapter on the general Doctrine of Chances,[4] on which subject I now entirely agree with Laplace. I have there too, as knowing by experience where the shoe pinched, been able, I think, to ease it a little.

Having benefitted so much by your criticisms I need hardly say how glad I should be of any others.

Very truly yours

J. S. MILL

486. TO MACVEY NAPIER[1]

India House
1st May 1846

MY DEAR SIR

Before I received your letter, I had already acknowledged to Edinburgh, your remittance which was larger than I expected & for which I now renew my thanks.

1. MS in the possession of the Royal Society; in reply to Herschel's letters of April 2 and 3, also in the Library of the Royal Society.
2. The revised sec. 5 of Book III, chap. 25, "Of the Grounds of Disbelief," is numbered sec. 6 in later editions.
3. JSM in the second edition added a new sec. 5 to Book III, chap. 25, to discuss coincidences.
4. Book III, chap 18, "Of the Calculation of Chances."

* * * *

1. Part published in *Napier Corresp.*, pp. 526–27. MS in Brit. Mus.

I cannot complain of your having left out the passage[2] controverting the warlike propensity of the French, though I should have been glad if it had been consistent with your judgment to have retained it. The opinion is a very old & firm one with me, founded on a good deal of personal observation & I do not think you will find that Englishmen or other foreigners *who have lived long in France* & mixed in French society, are, so generally as you seem to think, of a different opinion. I have certainly heard, from such persons, the same opinion which I have expressed, & quite as strongly. And I am sure you will admit that national importance, & consideration among other nations, may be very strongly desired & sought by people who would rather have it in any other way than by war. I venture to say thus much because I think the Edin. has lately been sometimes very unjust to the French—I allude to Senior's otherwise excellent articles[3] which he & I have sometimes had disputes about.

Touching Whately's Rhetoric[4]—I have read it twice, first when it came out, & again within the last few years, & I think of it as of all his other books, that it is full of ideas, & would make a good article in itself, but still more so if the occasion were taken—(which would be worth while as I think the Ed. has never done it)—for a general estimate of the man & of his writings. Senior is as you know a personal intimate & his admiration of Whately is probably much less qualified than mine is—but W. is certainly a very remarkable & even eminent man, & one whose merits & faults are both very important to be pointed out.

Your son has given me a reference to Merivale's[5] article which I shall lose no time in reading.

I forget whether I remembered to mention that I should like half a dozen copies of the article in the Edin. though I know you were kind enough to ask me the question. If I omitted to say so perhaps you could still procure me *two* copies from the waste

Believe me ever

yours truly

J. S. MILL

2. In his "Duveyrier's *Political Views of French Affairs*," ER, LXXXIII (April, 1846), 453–74.

3. A bibliography of Senior's contributions to periodicals, including the *Edinburgh Review*, for which he wrote frequently after 1840, may be found in S. Leon Levy, *Nassau W. Senior: The Prophet of Modern Capitalism* (Boston, 1943), pp. 415–16.

4. Richard Whately, *Elements of Rhetoric* (London, 1828); 7th ed., revised, 1846.

5. Herman Merivale, a frequent contributor to the *Edinburgh*. A partial list of Merivale's contributions to periodicals is included in the brief memoir of him by Charles Merivale in the *Transactions of the Devonshire Association*, 1884.

487. TO WILLIAM TAIT[1]

India House,
4th June,
1846.

MY DEAR SIR,

My friend Mr. Alexander Bain, wishing to be a contributor to your magazine, has asked me to give him an introduction to you, which I do with great pleasure. I have said incidentally in my Logic the very high opinion I have of Mr. Bain and the great use he was of to me in making the book fit to present to the public and I need only say that I think he would be a most valuable contributor to any liberal periodical.

Very truly yours,

J. S. MILL

488. TO AUGUSTE COMTE[1]

East India House
le 13 août 1846.

MON CHER MONSIEUR COMTE

Votre petit billet du 10 m'est parvenu la veille même du jour que j'avais fixé définitivement pour rompre un silence effectivement très prolongé. La cause du retard n'a pas été une perturbation quelconque de ma santé, qui est restée à peu près comme à l'ordinaire. Ce fut d'abord une de ces absences occasionnelles[2] (quoique non strictement périodiques) auxquelles vous faites allusion: ensuite après mon retour je me suis trouvé accablé d'occupations qui m'ont fait différer de jour en jour la lettre qui vous était dûe. Ces occupations pressantes ne se sont terminées qu'hier, et je vais maintenant pouvoir reprendre mon travail d'économie politique, suspendu depuis deux mois, et que j'espère désormais pouvoir continuer sans intermission jusqu'à sa complétion définitive.

Votre lettre du 6 mai contenait en effet des choses graves, auxquelles je n'aurais pas manqué de répondre promptement, si j'avais cru pouvoir par là donner quelque soulagement sympathique à une juste et profonde

1. MS in the Mitchell Library, Sydney, New South Wales.

* * * *

1. MS at Johns Hopkins. Published in Lévy-Bruhl, pp. 538–40; in reply to Comte's of May 6 and Aug. 10, *ibid.*, pp. 525–37.
2. JSM had had a vacation of two months this year, during which he had taken with Mrs. Taylor a tour of about six weeks to the Rhine and northern France.

douleur.[3] Je sais ce que doit être, pour tout homme capable d'une affection profonde, un événement tel que celui que vous m'avez annoncé. Mais de pareils malheurs, quand ils sont réels et fondés, ne me paraissent comporter d'autre soulagement que le triste affaiblissement spontané qui suit du temps et de la réflexion. La perte d'une unique sympathie personnelle, est toujours au-dessus ou au-dessous de toute consolation. C'est une blessure dont la gravité ne saurait être appréciée que par celui qui la subit.

Quant au reste du contenu de votre lettre, je trouve dans la publication hollandaise que vous m'indiquez, et dans la lettre dont vous m'avez envoyé copie, une nouvelle preuve du progrès des idées positives en europe. On s'attendrait peutêtre moins qu'ailleurs à un tel témoignage dans un pays comme la Hollande, qui semblait ne plus s'intéresser aux questions spéculatives et dont le développement philosophique a sans contredit beaucoup perdu à l'isolation littéraire où elle se trouve à cause de sa langue particulière, depuis que les penseurs ont renoncé à se servir d'une langue européenne. Ce signe de vie, et même d'une activité mentale assez avancée, est d'autant plus intéressant qu'il est plus inattendu. Tout indique au reste que les principes de votre grand ouvrage ont pris irrévocablement leur place dans la discussion européenne, et que rien désormais ne pourra les étouffer. Dès que ce point a été atteint, tout est fait. C'est tout ce que les penseurs peuvent accomplir, ou sont tenus à accomplir pour leurs idées. Dès qu'elles sont écoutées; dès que les partisans des doctrines contraires sont forcés de les connaître et d'en tenir compte, la cause est gagnée; elles deviennent dès lors une force sociale réelle, et plus ou moins puissante, en raison de la portion de vérite et d'importance réelle qui leur appartient. La critique systématique que vous m'annoncez devoir être faite de votre ouvrage par un des principaux organes de l'école métaphysique, indique encore plus décidément, que vous en êtes venu là. Je crois que ce temps va bientôt arriver aussi pour moi, quoique je n'aie encore éprouvé que des attaques très faibles. Je m'efforce au reste d'en hâter le moment par l'écrit dont je m'occupe actuellement, écrit plus en rapport que le premier avec l'esprit pratique et politique de l'angleterre, et où je m'abstiendrai encore moins que dans l'autre, de heurter les opinions reçues. Je crois le temps très favorable pour toute doctrine nouvelle capable de soutenir une discussion approfondie. Toutes les anciennes idées sont depuis peu très visiblement déchues, aux yeux mêmes de tout le monde, et l'on demande à grands cris des principes nouveaux. S'il y avait ici seulement deux ou trois hommes généralement considérés, qui fussent moralement et intellectuellement au niveau des besoins de l'époque, nous pourrions espérer de conquérir bientôt la liberté dont la France jouit heureusement, celle de tout dire: c'est surtout

3. Comte had reported the death on April 5 of his beloved friend Mme Clotilde de Vaux.

ce qui nous manque à présent, car les seules questions qui ne font point aujourd'hui de progrès sont celles dont l'opinion interdit toute véritable discussion.

tout à vous

J. S. MILL

489. TO ALEXANDER BAIN[1]

September 1846

I have just corrected the proof of my review of Grote,[2] in which I have introduced no little of the Comtean philosophy of religion. Altogether I like the thing, though I wrote it in exactly four days, and re-wrote it in three more, but I had to read and think a good deal for it first. . . . [I have] got on well with the *Pol. Ec.* I am on the point of finishing the third book.[3]

490. TO HENRY COLE[1]

India House,
7th September, 1846.

MY DEAR COLE,

Having been out of town I have only just received your note and its enclosure. I am truly glad of the improvement in your circumstances, and should have regretted much if you had paid me before it was perfectly convenient.

I have the pleasure of remembering that I have rendered you a service at a time when you needed it, and needed it on account of conduct for which you merited reward instead of loss.[2]

Very truly yours,

J. S. MILL

491. TO MACVEY NAPIER[1]

India House
22nd October
1846

MY DEAR SIR

Your very liberal remittance arrived safely, & I return you my best thanks for it.

1. Excerpt published in Bain, *JSM*, pp. 85–86. MS not located.
2. For the *Edinburgh Review*, Oct., 1846.   3. "Exchange."

* * * *

1. MS in the possession of Professor J. M. McCrimmon.
2. See Letters 414, 415.

* * * *

1. MS in Brit. Mus.

I have no other subject at present in view & shall probably be otherwise occupied for some months.

The new number of the review[2] seems to me a very good one.

yours ever

J. S. MILL

492. TO JAMES BENTHAM MILL[1]

Nov. 2, 1846

[. . . a letter to his brother James (2nd Nov.) shows that he was labouring under illness:] had been ill, now better, but still a bad cold.

493. TO ALEXANDER BAIN?[1]

Mid-November 1846

[In the middle of November, he wrote that the articles[2]] have excited a good deal of notice, and have quite snatched the initiative out of the *Times.* [He adds—] It is a capital thing to have the power of writing leaders in the *Chronicle* whenever I like, which I can always do. The paper has tried for years to get me to write to it, but it has not suited me to do it before, except once in six months or so.

494. TO ALEXANDER BAIN?[1]

28 December 1846

I continue to carry on the *Pol. Econ.* as well as I can with the articles in the *Chronicle.*[2] These last I may a little slacken now, having in a great measure, as far as may be judged by appearances, carried my point, *viz.,* to have the waste lands reclaimed and parcelled out in small properties among the best of the peasantry.

2. *ER*, Oct., 1846.

* * * *

1. Excerpt published in Bain, *JSM*, p. 86. MS not located. The bracketed portion is Bain's introduction to the excerpt.

* * * *

1. Excerpts published in Bain, *JSM*, p. 86–87. MS not located. The bracketed portions are Bain's introduction to the excerpts.
2. Between Oct. 5, 1846, and Jan. 7, 1847, JSM contributed forty-three leading articles on Irish affairs to the *Morning Chronicle* (see MacMinn, *Bibliog.*, pp. 60–67).

* * * *

1. Excerpt published in Bain, *JSM*, p. 87. MS not located.
2. See preceding letter, n. 2.

• • •   1847   • • •

495. TO RICHARD MONCKTON MILNES[1]

I.H.

Wedy [1847?]

MY DEAR MILNES

It would be very agreeable to me to breakfast with you on Saturday, but I cannot venture to play truant from my office to the extent which that would require.

Yours ever

J. S. MILL

496. TO SIR ALEXANDER DUFF-GORDON[1]

India House

Jan. 27, 1847

MY DEAR SIR ALEXANDER,

I regret to hear that Mr. Austin is again suffering from illness, which has, perhaps, been brought on by the application required in writing his admirable article in the "Edinburgh",[2] and by the very natural and intelligible reaction after it was finished. In his bad health he must at least have the consolation of feeling himself useful, for the article is exactly one of those things which he can do so well, and which so few are capable of doing at all—a *thorough* discussion of the subject it treats of, going down to the roots and fundamentals of a matter never treated in that way before—eminently calculated not only to give clear ideas and to correct vague feelings and confused notions on that particular subject, but also to educate the minds of those who wish to *study* such subjects—a class that would probably be much more numerous if there were not so lamentable a paucity of such helps to them. One of the persons of greatest intellect that I have known said, after reading the article, "What a pity the same man does not, in the

1. MS in Trinity College Library, Cambridge. Undated, but MS has pencilled: 1847?

* * * *

1. Published in *Letters of the Rt. Hon. Sir G. C. Lewis, Bart.*, ed. G. F. Lewis (London, 1870), pp. 153–54. MS not located.
2. "Centralization," *ER*, LXXXV (Jan., 1847), 221–58.

same manner, *precisionize* other and even more important questions of political morals;" and I do hope that he will now be encouraged to do so. There is really some hope of this now that he has actually *finished* something; for his inability to satisfy *himself* is the only thing except ill health which has ever seemed to me to stand in the way.

Very truly yours,

J. S. MILL

497. TO ALEXANDER BAIN[1]

27 January 1847

You will have seen by this time how far the ministry are from having adopted any of my conclusions about Ireland,[2] though Lord J. Russell[3] subscribes openly to almost all the premises. I have little hope left. The tendency of their measures seems to me such that it can only bring about good to Ireland by excess of evil. . . . I have so indoctrinated the *Chronicle* writers with my ideas on Ireland, that they are now going on very well and spiritedly without me, which enables me to work much at the *Political Economy*, to my own satisfaction. The last thing I did for the *Chronicle* was a thorough refutation, in three long articles, of Croker's article on the Division of Property in France.[4]

498. TO GEORGE JACOB HOLYOAKE[1]

[February 22, 1847][2]

Of practical conclusions there are also several from which I should decidedly differ, particularly Communism.

1. Excerpts published in Bain, *JSM*, p. 87. MS not located.
2. In his leading articles in the *Morning Chronicle* (see Letter 493).
3. Lord John Russell, later first Earl Russell, was at this time Prime Minister.
4. [J. W. Croker], "Agriculture in France—Division of Property," *QR*, LXXIX (Dec., 1846), 202–38. JSM published four, not three, articles: on Jan. 9, 11, 13, and 16 (see MacMinn, *Bibliog.*, p. 67, and Letter 514).

* * * *

1. MS fragment in the possession of Co-operative Union Ltd., Holyoake House, Manchester. Published in Joseph McCabe, *Life and Letters of George Jacob Holyoake* (2 vols., London, 1908), II, p. 65.

Holyoake (1817–1906), self-styled "secularist," bookseller, publisher of the *Reasoner* and other journals, and a leader in the development of the co-operative movement. In 1842 he had been imprisoned for blasphemy.

2. The MS is so dated in another hand. In view of Mrs. Taylor's discussion of Holyoake, the *Reasoner*, and morality in her letter to JSM of July 25, 1848 (Hayek, pp. 124–27), it has been suggested by Professor J. M. Robson that the date should be 1848.

The use made of the word "morality" is likely to give an idea of much greater agreement with the ordinary moral notions, emanating from and grounded on religion, than I should suppose you intend. Most people do not understand by morality a subject as open to discussion as any other, and on which persons have different opinions, but think it a name for the set of opinions they have been accustomed to.

499. TO HENRY S. CHAPMAN[1]

India House
9th March, 1847.

MY DEAR CHAPMAN,—

My conscience has been reproaching me for months with not having yet redeemed my promise of writing to you again, especially after having received your interesting letter of April last. But you must, I am sure, know by experience how difficult it is to keep engagements of that sort when one's mind and time are much occupied, and when the distance of one's correspondent and the long time requisite for an interchange of letters prevents communication from being habitual and in a manner spontaneous. To give you an idea of some of my hindrances I will just tell you what my occupations are. In the first place, a great increase of my India House business, both from the general and progressive growth of the correspondence, and also from my having the charge of a second department in addition to my own, being responsible for a branch of the correspondence which is now carried on by my brother George. In the next place I have had a book to write which will be as large a one when printed as the Logic, and which I have now (within the last week) completed, sauf the revising, or rather rewriting, which is an indispensable part of anything of importance which I write. This book is the one you had had some incorrect information about, as you thought it was to be an edition of Adam Smith, whereas it is a book to replace Adam Smith, that is, to attempt to do for political economy what A.S. did at the time when he wrote, to make a book which, while embodying all the abstract science in the completest form yet attained, incorporating all important improvements, should at the same time be essentially a book of applications exhibiting the principles of the science in the concrete. I was the more prompted to do this inasmuch as it would enable me to bring in, or rather to bring out, a great number of opinions on incidental matters, moral and social, for which one has not often so good an opportunity, and I have used this privilege as freely as Adam Smith did, and I fully expect to offend and scandalize ten times as many people as I shall please, but

1. MS in the possession of Mrs. W. Rosenberg. Copy supplied by Professor J. M. McCrimmon.

that is "all in a day's work," and I always intended to make that use of any standing I might get among publicists. I have got a certain capital of that sort by the Logic, and I now cannot too soon use it up in useful investments. That then, has been my second occupation. My third has been to write a good deal this autumn and winter on the questions of the day, especially the Irish question,[2] on which people seem to me to be running mad, each more than the other. No one idea that has been started for using this opportunity to effect anything for the permanent good of Ireland has met with any favourable reception; the whole English people are rushing frantically to expend any number of millions upon the present exigency, without much caring how, and taking their revenge on the Irish gentry by the infliction of a lavish poor law which if it passes will as it seems to me render the evils of Ireland incurable except by an universal seizure of the land and expulsion of the proprietors; and almost all the men on whom one counted for resisting any such monstrosity, have thrown themselves headlong into the very midst of the stream. Roebuck, of all men in the world, is quite an active leader in the movement, and as for the first time in his public life he is enlisting his talents in support of the madness of the movement, he has suddenly made himself a person of much more importance than he ever was before, and is continually flattered by the Times, which is the real author and leader of this movement and the substantial ruler of the country. Molesworth, except that he has only made one speech[3] instead of fifty, is just as bad. Lord J. Russell and Lord Lansdowne[4] six weeks before the meeting of Parliament, expressed in private the strongest opinions against any such measure as the one they have now introduced. I find nobody but Senior and Grote who are true to their colours. The English Poor Law, with the strongest profession of adherence to its principle, is in fact to be thrown overboard by abolishing the Central Board and substituting a functionary who is to sit in Parliament and to be virtually a member of the Ministry. Of course every little workhouse squabble will become a Parliamentary affair, and to avoid a debate in Parliament everything will be given up. Have not these people just ordered "a day of fasting and humiliation"[5] merely to escape a debate on a motion by Mr. Plumptre,[6] the man

2. See Letter 493, n. 2.   3. On Feb. 15, 1847.

4. Sir Henry Petty-Fitzmaurice, third Marquis of Lansdowne (1780–1863), then President of the Council under Lord John Russell, led the debate on the Irish Relief Bill on Feb. 15, 1847.

5. March 24, 1847, was so appointed by proclamation that prayers might be made "for the removal of those heavy judgments which our manifold sins and provocations have most justly deserved, and with which Almighty God is pleased to visit the iniquities of this land, by a grievous scarcity and dearth of divers articles of sustenance and necessaries of life . . ." (*Annual Register for 1847*, "Chronicle," p. 40).

6. John Pemberton Plumptre (1807–1864), MP for East Kent, on Jan. 20, 1847, in the debate on the Address from the Throne, proposed the appointment of a general fast.

who thinks that the potato failure is a punishment from Heaven for the grant to Maynooth?[7] Besides this new officer will go out with every Ministry, and besides, he will never be able to get elected without giving pledges inconsistent with a faithful discharge of his duties. I have never felt so thoroughly disgusted with the state of public affairs. The only good I see likely to arise out of all these things is that I think they are sure to give a great stimulus to colonization, for Ireland will be in a state next year that will make the landlords sell the clothes off their backs to get rid of the people. But it will be a colonization wholly of Irish, and of the very worst sort; and with an outdoor relief poor law they will just set about peopling again, and will replace even two millions in half a generation. The only propitious circumstances is the great progress of free trade. Our repeal of the Corn laws is working wonders; first the great relaxation of the American tariff, next the triumphal progress of Cobden[8] through Europe. Think of the French Government authorising a League (Societe des Libres Exchangite)[9] and permitting public meetings and speeches. I have great sympathy too with the fine old Pope.[10] I hope he has many years to live; he is much younger than Popes usually are, but unhappily they say he has had epileptic fits when a child, and has had a return of them lately. The priests will poison him if they can, as the Jesuits are said to have poisoned Ganganelli.[11] O'Connell is done up,[12] and probably dying, killed, I should think, by the death of O'Connellism.

Yours most truly,

J. S. MILL

500. TO ALEXANDER BAIN[1]

March 27, 1847

The people are all mad, and nothing will bring them to their senses but the terrible consequences they are certain to bring on themselves, as shown

7. See Letter 456, n. 2.

8. Richard Cobden (1804–1865), leader of the agitation for the repeal of the Corn Laws achieved in 1846. From Aug. 5, 1846, to Oct. 11, 1847, Cobden travelled in Europe, preaching everywhere the gospel of free trade.

9. Presumably the "Association pour la liberté des échanges," founded in 1846, and supported by a number of JSM's friends and acquaintances, including Michel Chevalier, Charles Dunoyer, and Horace Say (see *Journal des Economistes*, Sept.– Dec., 1846 and Jan., 1847).

10. Giovanni Maria Mastai-Ferretti (1792–1878), became Pope Pius IX in 1846.

11. Giovanni Vincenzo (or Lorenzo) Ganganelli (1705–1774), Pope Clement XIV from 1769 to 1774, dissolved the Jesuit order in 1773; the story that he was poisoned by the Jesuits has been generally discredited.

12. Daniel O'Connell had made his last speech in the House of Commons in Feb. and had gone to the Continent for his health; he died on May 15, 1847.

* * * *

1. Published in Bain, *JSM*, p. 87. MS not located. Dated by reference to Whately's speech.

in Whately's speech yesterday[2] in the House of Lords—the only sensible speech yet made in either House on the question. Fontenelle said that mankind must pass through all forms of error before arriving at truth.[3] The form of error we are now possessed by is that of making *all* take care of *each*, instead of stimulating and helping each to take care of himself; and now this is going to be put to a terrible trial, which will bring it to a crisis and a termination sooner than could otherwise have been hoped for.

501. TO JOHN AUSTIN[1]

13th April 1847.

DEAR MR. AUSTIN,—There is no occasion to send anything you may write to me by any circuitous channel. If I did pay postage I should not grudge it for your letters, but in fact I do not. The I.H. pays all my letters except penny post letters which everybody pays before sending.

The notice in the *Chronicle*,[2] to which I am indebted for your letter, was, as you supposed, mine. It is really a pity that all the trouble you must have taken with the article on Centralisation should have produced nothing more than a review article.

I am very glad that you should write anything whatever; but I hope especially now when your pecuniary affairs are settled in the manner you desire, that you will rather write books than reviews. An entirely unknown person, whose books no one would read, must begin by reviews, but you have written a book which, for the kind of book, has been very successful, and what you write is more likely to be read with your name than without it. A book gives much more scope than a review for your peculiar forte, the analysis of a subject down to its ultimate scientific elements. A review is not a slight thing to you; you take the same pains with it as you would with a scientific treatise, which in fact it is; & all who can be benefited by it at all would prefer to have it in a permanent form. It seems to me that reviews

2. On March 26, 1847, in opposition to a motion for a select committee on Irish Poor Laws; the substance of it was published as App. D in his *Introductory Lectures on Political Economy* (4th ed., London, 1855).

3. "Telle est notre condition, qu'il ne nous est point permis d'arriver tout d'un coup à rien de raisonnable sur quelque matière que ce soit; il faut avant cela que nous nous égarions long-temps, et que nous passions par diverses sortes d'erreurs et par divers degrés d'impertinences" ("Digression sur Les Anciens et Les Modernes" in *Œuvres de Fontenelle* [Paris, 1790], V, 287).

* * * *

1. Published with errors and omissions in Elliot, I, 128–33. MS draft is in the possession of Dr. James M. Osborn of Yale University; a MS fragment of the draft is at LSE (see n. 8, 10, below).

2. An unheaded leading article on Austin's article "Centralization" (see Letter 496, n. 2) in *Morning Chronicle*, Feb. 6, 1847, pp. 4–5.

have had their day, & that nothing is now worth much except the two extremes, newspapers for diffusion & books for accurate thought. Every thinker should make a point of either publishing in his life if possible, or at any rate leaving behind him the most complete expression he can produce of his best thoughts, those which he has no chance of getting into any review. There are two books I have heard you speak of as projects: a continuation of "The Province of Jurisprudence" that is in fact a publication & completion of your lectures: this would be the easiest to you, so much of it being already done: the other which would be more important is a systematic treatise on morals. This last may wait long for any one with the intellect & the courage to do it as it should be done. And until it is done we cannot expect much improvement in the common standard of moral judgments & sentiments.

Of the two subjects you mention in your letter, the "province of government" is no doubt important in itself, & peculiarly a question of the present time. I have necessarily thought a good deal about it lately for the purposes of a practical treatise on Pol. Economy & I have felt the same difficulty which you feel about the *axiomata media*. I suspect there are none which do not vary with time, place, & circumstance. I doubt if much more can be done in a scientific treatment of the question than to point out a certain number of *pro's* and a certain number of *con's* of a more or less general application, & with some attempt at an estimation of the comparative importance of each, leaving the balance to be struck in each particular case as it arises. But that subject is I think tolerably safe as far as theory is concerned, for the thinking minds of the Continent & of England have fairly thought up to it & it is sure to be amply discussed & meditated upon for the next ten or twenty years. It is hardly a subject for any one who is capable of things much in advance of the time.

On the other subject, The "antecedents of the Revolution," I much doubt if what you propose to write will do any good to those whom you hope to influence by it. I think with you that the English higher classes (of the German I know nothing) mean well, "what little they do mean" as my father said of some person. They have grown good even to goodiness, as they shew every year more & more. But also every year shews more & more their *pitoyable* absence of even that very moderate degree of intellect, & that very moderate amount of will & character which are scattered through the other classes but of which they have certainly much less than the average share, owing to the total absence of the habit of exerting their minds for any purpose whatever. I used to hope, as my father did (with all his democratic predilections), that when their political monopoly was taken away they would be induced to exert themselves in order to keep ahead of their competitors, but I have quite ceased to think so. If there is anything of which experience convinces me more & more it is that (beyond a certain point) facilities, as they are called, are hindrances, & that the more the path to any meritorious attainment is made smooth to an individual or a class, from their early youth, the less chance there is of their realising it. Never to have had any difficulties to overcome seems fatal to mental vigour. The doctrine of averting revolutions by wise concessions to the people does not need to be preached to the English aristocracy. They have long acted on it to the best of their capacity, & the fruits it produces are soup-kitchen and ten hours bills.

As far as I see, the influence of democracy on the aristocracy does not operate by giving them any of the strength of the people but by taking away that which was their own; making them bend with a willing submission to the yoke of bourgeois opinion in all private things, and be the slaves, in public matters, of the newspapers which they dislike & fear. I confess I look less & less to that quarter for anything good. Whatever is valuable in the traditions of gentlemanhood is a *fait acquis* to mankind; as it is really grounded on the combination of good feeling with correct intellectual perceptions, it will always be kept alive by really cultivated persons; the most complete *parvenus* now in this country have as much of it as people of family, & for its diffusion must not our real reliance be on the extension & improvement of education? I have even ceased to think that a leisured class, in the ordinary sense of the term, is an essential constituent of the best form of society. What does seem to me essential is that society at large should not be overworked, nor over-anxious about the means of subsistence, for which we must look to the grand source of improvement, repression of population, combined with laws or customs of inheritance which shall favour the diffusion of property instead of its accumulation in masses.

It is, I dare say, very natural, that living in France, you should be much impressed with the unfavourable side of a country that has passed through a series of revolutions. The inordinate impulse given to vulgar ambition, down to even a low class, & the general spirit of adventurership are I have no doubt disgusting enough, but may not much of them be ascribed to the mere accident of the brilliant fortune of a "certain lieutenant of artillery" (as Stendhal says), & much to the habitual over-governing by which power & importance are too exclusively concentrated upon the Government & its functionaries. In England on the contrary I often think that a violent revolution is very much needed, in order to give that general shake-up to the torpid mind of the nation which the French Revolution gave to Con-tinental Europe. England has never had any general break-up of old associations & hence the extreme difficulty of getting any ideas into its stupid head. After all, what country in Europe can be compared with France in the adaptation of its social state to the benefit of the great mass of its people, freed as they are from any tyranny which comes home to the greater number, with justice easily accessible, & the strongest inducements to personal prudence & forethought. And would this have been the case without the great changes in the state of property which even supposing good intentions in the Government could hardly have been produced by anything less than a Revolution?

I judge M. Guizot's conduct in the Spanish affair[3] as you do: he is evidently not above low tricks & equivocations, which seem to be quite excused to every Frenchman by their being for the supposed honour & glory of France.[4] Guizot I wished to think better of, but after all this only brings me back, and that not altogether, to my first opinion of him, which some parts of his public conduct from 1839 downwards had modified.[5]

Your impression of Comte's delinquencies is a fine instance of the growth of rumour: your informants must be either ill-informed or such exaggerators that I wonder you should have believed them. In the first place, Comte (to whom *I* did *not* give money, but Grote and Molesworth did) never wrote to *Grote* anything but what was perfectly convenable. He wrote a letter to *me* which he authorised me to shew to G. & M. if I thought fit, & I did think fit; but it contained nothing like reproaches.[6] It contained a theory that, in default of the government, it is the duty of rich individuals to subscribe their money to enable philosophers to live and carry on their speculations. I do not agree in his theory.[7] I thought it an instance of "the importance of a man to himself" but even with the addition of his not having economised the money previously given to him this is a totally different thing from what you have been told.

The judgment to be passed on this incident would involve the wide subject of how the degree in which a person should be judged by his own deliberate principles should be combined with one's judgment on the

---

3. Guizot had broken faith with the British in the affair of the Spanish marriages; by intrigue Queen Isabella II and her sister were induced to marry in 1846 descendants of the French Bourbons.

4. At this point the following passage has been deleted from the draft: "English politicians have generally low objects, & reserve any conscience & dignity they may have, for the choice of means, while Frenchmen I think have oftener aims that one can call elevated but are much more unscrupulous in their expedients, a combination made quite intelligible on a grander scale, by Machiavelli & the Italian [patriots ?] of the Middle Ages."

5. See Letter 304, n. 8.

6. Comte's letter of Dec. 18, 1845 (Lévy-Bruhl, pp. 482–98). JSM's memory here seems not to have been very accurate; most readers would regard Comte's letter as one long reproach (cf. especially Lévy-Bruhl, p. 495).

7. The remainder of the sentence has been deleted: "& still less in his attempt to impose its obligations on persons who do not admit it, who were in no respect his disciples nor in any other intellectual relation to him than to any other thinker of any eminence with some of whose opinions they agreed."

principles themselves, and one's opinion of the causes which made him adopt them.[8]

You ask what I think of the Irish measures. I expect nothing from them but mischief, or if any good, only through excess of evil. If you were here you would, I believe, think as I do. The Government & the public seem both alike to have quite parted company with experience & common sense. There is not one man in the H of C [House of Commons], & only two or three in the H of L [House of Lords] (Whately being one) who seem to have a single sound or rational idea on the whole subject: those from whom one had most right to expect better are just as bad as the rest. I doubt if outdoor relief would do for Ireland under any mode of administration, but as it is they are holding out to the people the most unbounded expectations, & if the poor law is to be worked without fulfilling them, the life of no guardian & no relieving officer will be worth a week's purchase, & the country will be ungovernable except by military occupation of every village. The only good I expect is that the result *must* produce a strong reaction in the public mind against the present wild notions about the mode of being good to the poor.[9]

I expect to be in Paris shortly with the friends with whom I always endeavour to pass my holidays but it is uncertain if they will remain long enough to admit of my going to see anyone; if I do I will certainly call on you.[10]

Ever sincerely yours,

J. S. MILL

502. TO ALEXANDER BAIN[1]

5th May 1847

[Before arriving in London this year, I had another letter (5th May). He delays to commence rewriting his book till he sees the upshot of the Irish business.] The conduct of the ministers is wretched beyond measure upon all subjects; nothing but the meanest truckling at a time when a man with a decided opinion could carry almost anything triumphantly.

8. This paragraph in the draft fragment at LSE is labelled: (A).

9. At this point the following sentences have been deleted in the draft: "But it is discouraging to see how short a time any such impression lasts. In 1834 much ground seems to have been gained [by the adoption of the Poor Law of that year] but how quickly it has all been lost."

10. This paragraph, not included by Elliot, is labelled (B) in the draft fragment at LSE and crossed through with a red line (Elliot's usual method of indicating a deletion in a MS). The paragraph was written to replace the deleted sentences quoted in n. 9.

* * * *

1. Excerpt published in Bain, *JSM*, p. 88. MS not located. Bracketed portion is Bain's introduction to the excerpt.

503. TO WILLIAM E. HICKSON[1]

India House
Saturday
[May 8, 1847]

MY DEAR HICKSON

It would not be convenient to me at present to write an article on currency. Neither could I write the article wanted just now, without a much greater knowledge than I possess or could easily acquire respecting the facts of the money market. My opinions on the general subject "with the latest additions & corrections" will come out next winter in my book.

I believe I agree with most of what you say in your note.

yours ever

J. S. MILL

504. TO AUGUSTE COMTE[1]

India House
le 17 mai 1847

MON CHER MONSIEUR COMTE

Je pense qu'il pourrait vous être intéressant d'avoir quelques renseignements sur les choses qui se passent actuellement en angleterre et en Irlande, d'autant plus qu'elles me semblent caractériser, d'une manière frappante, une sorte de crise sociale.

Vous savez que le siècle où nous sommes est celui des transactions, et surtout de la grande transaction qui se renouvelle sans cesse à des conditions variables, entre les pouvoirs anciens et les idées modernes. Vous savez aussi que l'Angleterre est le pays des transactions par excellence. Ce que, peut-être vous ne savez pas, c'est la forme particulière que revêtit aujourd'hui chez nous la grande transaction européenne. Nous sommes entrés à plein voile dans le système du gouvernement charitable. Il y a longtemps qu'on prêche aux classes supérieures qu'elles ne remplissent plus leur mission, qu'elles sont tenues à faire quelque chose pour ceux dont le travail les nourrit, qu'elles n'ont le droit de gouverner qu'à condition d'être moralement responsables du bien-être de la société, et notamment de la classe pauvre, etc. Or, comme cette remontrance amicale leur est venue

---

1. MS at the Huntington Library.

* * * *

1. *Addressed*: A Monsieur / M. Auguste Comte / Rue M. le Prince / près l'Odéon / à Paris. MS at Johns Hopkins. Published in Lévy-Bruhl, pp. 548–53.

d'un côté tandis que le chartisme et le socialisme apparaissaient de l'autre, elles ont dû, quelle que fût leur insouciance, y obtempérer quelque peu, et petit à petit elles sont venues jusqu'à prendre au sérieux ces doctrines de responsabilité gouvernementale, qui, au fond, ne laissaient pas d'être passablement flatteuses à leur amour-propre d'aristocratie. Seulement, elles ont entendu cette obligation de la manière dont elles le pouvaient, c. à d. de la manière la plus facile et la plus ignoble, en la réduisant aux proportions de l'aumône. Aujourd'hui il n'est question que de donner aux pauvres; non seulement de l'argent, mais aussi, il est juste de le dire tout ce qu'on croit leur être utile, comme le raccourcissement des heures de travail, une meilleure police sanitaire, de l'éducation même, chrétienne et protestante surtout, mais sans exclusion de quelques connaissances terrestres. Il s'agit enfin de les gouvernor paternellement, et la cour, les nobles, les riches s'y disposent tout tranquillement, sans jamais se douter qu'il faille pour cela autre chose que de la bonne volonté, et en concevant le but selon la mesure de leur propre capacité intellectuelle et morale, c. à d. d'abord en fesant abstraction complète de la dignité morale de la classe pauvre. Cela est très naturel, attendu qu'ils n'ont que faire de ce sentiment pour eux-mêmes, n'ayant plus la dignité morale du passé, et n'ayant pas encore celle de l'avenir; d'ailleurs s'ils en avaient, ils ne la croiraient pas faite pour des gens pauvres, pour des ouvriers. Ensuite ils oublient complètement, ou plutôt ils n'ont jamais su, que le bien-être ne s'accomplit pas par les seules qualités passives, et qu'en général ce qu'on fait pour les personnes ne leur est utile qu'à condition de seconder seulement ce qu'elles font pour elles-mêmes. Ils se flattent que le bonheur des prolétaires dépend des riches, et ne se doutent pas qu'en définitif il dépend de l'énergie, du bon sens et de la prévoyance des prolétaires eux-mêmes; que le philanthrope le plus haut placé n'y peut rien, qu'en éclairant et en renforçant ces précieuses qualités chez les pauvres et que si au contraire il y porte attente, s'il tâche de mettre l'intervention sociale à la place de ces vertus individuelles, il devient nécessairement nuisible au lieu d'utile. Mais de cela nos philanthropes comme il faut n'ont pas la moindre idée, dénués qu'ils sont de toute connaissance approfondie et pétris de suffisance aristocratique.

La tendance que je viens de caractériser, et qui se signale depuis plusieurs ans d'une manière croissante, arrive aujourd'hui à une expérience décisive, amenée par la disette irlandaise. Cette île malheureuse, victime si longtemps de la tyrannie et de l'intolérance anglaises, dont maintenant elle n'a plus à se plaindre, semble destinée à être victime encore une fois de notre philanthropie. Vous connaissez le déplorable état industriel de ce pays, partagé entre une multitude démesurée de paysans paresseux et affamés, et un petit nombre de grands propriétaires insouciants et la plupart endettés, qui tirent du sol tout ce qu'il peut rendre, en rançonnant les paysans non pas par la force brutale mais par la concurrence effrénée de ces malheureux, toujours prêts à promettre plus que la terre ne produit. Depuis longtemps ce fléau est signalé à l'opinion publique: les Anglais reconnaissent le mal, ils désirent y remédier, mais ils y ont toujours échoué devant leur propre incapacité politique et sociale; n'ayant d'autre idée d'amélioration générale que celle de faire entrer tous les pays dans le système anglais, tant politique qu'industriel, tandis que ce système est tout à fait impropre à l'Irlande. C'est un grand malheur pour l'Irlande que de se trouver sous la domination d'un pays tout exceptionnel, et dont les principes ne sont en toute chose que la généralisation de l'exception, tandis qu'elle appartient, elle, au type normal européen, et que ce sont des idées continentales qu'il lui faut. Pour tout autre penseur qu'un anglais, le remède est clair, c'est le système de la petite propriété convenablement modifiée. Il faudrait assurer aux propriétaires actuels, en rente fixe, le revenu net de leurs terres, en laissant la terre elle même à la disposition absolue des cultivateurs. Avec cela on aurait probablement en peu de temps, une production triple ou quadruple de celle d'aujourd'hui, et une population aussi laborieuse, aussi prévoyante, et aussi indépendant que les paysans français. Or, les anglais ne comprennent rien à ce système; ceux qui croient en savoir quelque chose, et c'est le plus petit nombre, sont remplis des idées les plus fausses. Ils n'ont jamais pu concevoir d'autre amélioration en Irlande que d'en faire une autre angleterre, c. à d. un pays à grande culture, avec une population de laboureurs salariés. Or, sans rien préjuger sur l'avenir lointain de l'humanité, il est certain qu'aujourd'hui en Irlande ce système-là ne vaut rien. En le supposant même possible avec le caractère Irlandais, il entraînerait la suppression de la presque moitié de la population ouvrière actuelle. Ne pouvant donc pas réaliser cette heureuse idée, que fait-on? On jette à l'Irlande une loi des pauvres. On décrète que la population ouvrière tout entière vivra d'aumône. On lui promet au moins que tous les indigens auront de l'aumône autant qu'il leur en faut, et les indigens c'est toute la population agricole.

Pour moi je ne vois de cette loi d'autre résultat probable pour l'Irlande que celui de réduire tout le monde au niveau de la misère générale, après quoi je m'attends à une dissolution sociale complète. Lorsqu'on aura passé par d'affreux malheurs, il faudra procéder à la reconstitution de la société, du sein d'une désorganisation totale, sans une idée constructive quelconque, et après avoir fait prendre au peuple des mœurs essentiellement anarchiques, car je ne connais pas de gouvernement possible là où la majorité a pris l'habitude de demander à grands cris la subsistance et le bonheur aux autres au lieu de les chercher par elle-même. Certes, on n'a pas eu de pareilles idées en 1793, et on n'a aujourd'hui chez les communistes rien d'aussi profondément anti-social. Ce qui en sortira, impossible de prévoir.

J'y vois pour seule consolation, une réaction certaine contre le système du gouvernement charitable. On aura une grande preuve expérimentale de cette vérité qu'on ne peut pas traiter l'ouvrier comme on traite le bétail, c. à d. le faire travailler pour les autres en lui donnant une bonne nourriture et un bon gîte. Cela n'était possible que lorsqu'on y ajoutait le fouet. On ne peut pas plus en industrie qu'en autre chose, faire marcher l'ancien système en lui ôtant l'un après l'autre tous ses moyens d'action.

tout à vous

J. S. MILL

505. TO WILLIAM E. HICKSON[1]

India House
16th June 1847

MY DEAR HICKSON

I send you a short review of a political economy treatise—written by my youngest sister,[2] who is a student in political economy and who wishes to take the chance of your thinking the paper fit for insertion. It is the first attempt of a beginner in writing for the press & you will not therefore expect anything very brilliant. I am able to countersign the political economy of the article. In other respects & indeed in all respects you will of course exercise your own judgement. The writer has no such great opinion of her own performance as to be astonished at a decision in the negative, but I do not think the paper will do you any discredit, or I would not have undertaken to propose it to you.

ever your truly,

J. S. MILL

506. TO EDWIN CHADWICK[1]

India House
Wed^y
[June? 1847]

MY DEAR CHADWICK

After much consideration I have come to the decision that my best course will be to sell the certificates if I can get 20 per cent for them. But

1. MS at the Huntington Library.   2. Mary Elizabeth Mill.

* * * *

1. MS at UCL. Paper bears watermark 1847. The financial transaction discussed here probably concerned the sale of some of JSM's and his sisters' holdings in devalued bonds of some American State governments (see Letter 508).

I do not know how to effect this unless you will kindly manage it for me. If you would have no objection to ask your correspondent to dispose of £6000 more of the certificates, if it can be done on the same terms as yours, you would confer an obligation on me & I would in that case send you the certificates in time to be sent over by the packet on the 4th.

I have found the printed Case & I will give it my best attention.

ever truly yours

J. S. MILL

507. TO EDWIN CHADWICK[1]

I.H.
Friday
[June? 1847]

MY DEAR CHADWICK

I have read this letter[2] carefully through twice & I have nothing to suggest for the improvement of it except the correction of numerous clerical errors —these I have either corrected in pencil, or made a mark opposite to them when I was unable to supply the correction.

I should have returned it sooner, but not having had a pencil with me when I first read it, I waited till I had time to read it again.

ever truly yours

J. S. MILL

Such a letter ought to satisfy any *statesman* of his good fortune in having the writer of it at his disposal—but whether any of these men have sufficient brains to appreciate brains in another, remains questionable.

1. MS at UCL. Endorsed in another hand: "Poor Law Correspondence on matters of E. C." Paper watermarked, 1847.
2. Probably one of the several *Vindicating Letters* which Chadwick submitted to the ministry in June of 1847 defending his record as Secretary of the Poor Law Commission against the charges of the commissioners. For the full story of the Andover "scandal," of 1846 and the parliamentary struggle over the revision of the Poor Law Amendment Bill of June, 1847, see S. E. Finer, *The Life and Times of Sir Edwin Chadwick* (London, 1952), pp. 243–91. Chadwick lost his position but was immediately given an appointment in charge of a Royal Commission of Inquiry into London sanitation.

508. TO EDWIN CHADWICK[1]

Kensington
Saturday
[June 19, 1847]

MY DEAR CHADWICK

You have a most powerful case in your own defence & against the Commissioners—reinforced with great effect by Tufnell's letter.[2] There are only two things which I can suggest: first, that you should dwell more on the point which Lord J. R. the other day laid almost exclusive stress upon as an accusation against you. viz. your telling the Asst Comrs that their representations of abuses would be far from welcome[3] (N.B. I have no doubt you told them in that respect the exact truth) & *secondly* a careful revision of the composition. The long paper[4] in particular is full of unfinished & ill constructed (sometimes ungrammatical) sentences—this is evidently owing in many cases, but not always, to incorrect copying.

I am extremely obliged both to you & to Mrs Chadwick's relation for your kindness about the certificates.[5] With regard to the power of attorney, as some of the certificates belong not to me but to my sisters, do you suppose they must all give powers of attorney (which would be difficult, they are so scattered, & some of them out of England) or is it sufficient that I, being empowered though not formally, by them to dispose of their certificates, should give a single power of attorney for the whole lot?

As I suppose you went through the same formalities in your own case, you can also tell me in what manner the Lord Mayor is to attest the power. The letter you sent me is worded as if the Lord Mayor had personally to appear before the Consul.

yours ever truly

J. S. MILL

1. MS at UCL Endorsed in another hand: "1847? on E.C. Evidence before Andover Committee," but internal evidence (see n. 3 below) indicates the period of the June, 1847, debate on the Poor Law Amendment Bill (see preceding letter, n. 2).

2. Edward Carleton Tufnell (1806–1886), Assistant Commissioner of Poor Laws (1835–74). Tufnell on May 28, 1847, had written Chadwick a letter supporting the latter's charges against the Poor Law commissioners (see Finer, *Life and Times of Sir Edwin Chadwick*, p. 245). Chadwick circulated the letter widely.

3. In the debate on the Poor Law Amendment Bill on June 17 Lord John Russell criticized Chadwick sharply: "I say that [his] practice of telling assistant commissioners that if they made complaints they would be regarded with displeasure, I do call that undermining the Commissioners appointed to carry out the Poor Law Act" (*The Times*, Friday, June 18, 1847, p. 3).

4. Probably Chadwick's major *Vindicating Letter*, described by Finer, *Life and Times of Sir Edwin Chadwick* (p. 290) as "a massive manuscript dossier of some sixty pages, together with six documentary appendices."

5. See Letter 506.

509. TO EDWIN CHADWICK[1]

I.H.
Friday
[June or July?, 1847]

MY DEAR CHADWICK

Many thanks. I will do as you direct.

I have received the Settlement Evidence[2] & have read a great part of yours with pleasure & admiration. It will be of much use to me. I differ from you as yet only on one (not fundamental) point.

Yours

J. S. MILL

510. TO EDWIN CHADWICK[1]

Kensington
Monday evg.
[Aug. 20, 1847]

MY DEAR CHADWICK—The enclosed speaks for itself & I have written it on a separate paper that it may more conveniently be sent to Mr. Stuart[2] if you see no objection. I should have spoken to you about it when I saw you, as well as renewed my thanks to you & Mrs Chadwick, if I had found you alone—but you will easily understand that I did not wish to admit any other persons to unnecessary confidences on my money affairs or those of my relations.

ever your most obliged

J. S. MILL.

1. MS at UCL. Endorsed in another hand: 1847 / On reading Settlement Evidence.
2. See *Parliamentary Papers*, 1847, XI, The Select Committee on Settlement and Removal, which contains evidence given by Chadwick in March, 1847. The settlement laws dealt with changes of residence by paupers as affecting their eligibility for relief.

* * * *

1. MS at UCL. *Addressed*: Edwin Chadwick Esq / Gwydyr House / Whitehall / and marked *private*. *Postmark*: AU 20 18?7.
Presumably refers to the financial transactions discussed in Letters 506, 508, and 515.
2. Identified only as William Stuart of Liverpool, evidently an agent in the financial transactions.

511. TO JOHN WILLIAM PARKER[1]

[Summer?, 1847]

MY DEAR SIR

I write this note to introduce to you Miss Hall,[2] who being unacquainted with the name of the present editor of Fraser's Magazine but understanding that you are now the publisher, is desirous of addressing herself to you on the subject of a contribution to the Magazine. I was well acquainted with her mother, the late Mrs. Hall, for whom I had a great respect & who had contributed several things to Fraser's Magazine in the time of Dr. Maginn.

Very truly yours

J. S. MILL

512. TO   JOHN   WILLIAM   PARKER[1]

India House
27ᵗʰ October
1847

MY DEAR SIR

When I wrote to you hastily the other day about the Political Economy proposing that the conditions of our agreement should be the same as for the Logic, I had not referred to the agreement itself, & I did not know what I find to be the fact, that our engagement for the Logic was for *all future* editions. In the present case I do not wish to bind myself for the future, but to engage only for one edition, leaving the question entirely open as to future editions in case they should be wanted. This is the more reasonable, as there cannot this time be any considerable risk of loss, since the present book being on a popular subject is pretty sure to sell as many copies as will pay its expenses. It would probably be much more to my advantage to publish the Political Economy on my own account, which

1. MS at Pierpont Morgan Library. Parker's name does not appear on the letter; he had been JSM's publisher since 1843. Parker took over the publication of *Fraser's* beginning with Vol. XXXVI (July to Dec., 1847) from G. W. Nickisson, who published it from Jan., 1842 to June, 1847. The letter is undated, but the paper is watermarked 1847.

2. Not otherwise identified than as the daughter of Robert Hall, MD (1763–1824), explorer and writer on scientific subjects, and Agnes C. Hall (1777–1846), translator, novelist, and contributor to various periodicals, including *Fraser's*.

* * * *

1. MS in the Cornell University Library.

I am quite ready & disposed to do, if the publication of a single edition at half profit should not be agreeable to you.

> Believe me
> Very truly yours
> J. S. MILL

513. TO WILLIAM E. HICKSON[1]

India House
15 Nov. 1847

MY DEAR HICKSON

To enable me to make up my mind decidedly on the question of resuming the Westminster or not, it would be necessary for me to know exactly the position & circumstances of the review. & in particular 1st the Average N° of copies sold. 2nd the annual expenses 3rd what replies per number it affords on the average for the payment of contributors.

If I had this information I could very speedily give you an answer.

> Yours ever truly
> J. S. MILL

514. TO EDWIN CHADWICK[1]

India House
19 Nov. 1847

MY DEAR CHADWICK

It would be great injustice to this article[2] to compare it with the review of the same book by Croker in the Quarterly,[3] but I am still more sorry to read it because its evident honesty and carefulness will make it a great deal more mischievous.

What I thought about Rubichon's book I have said in the Morning Chronicle of the 9th, 11th, 13th & 16th of last January.[4] It is I think right that the author of the article should see those papers, & should be aware of the facts & books there cited.

He will easily detect one error in the second article of the Chronicle, into which the Quarterly reviewer misled me. But it does not touch the main question.

I have acquired some additional facts of importance since that time: among others the last Census of the French population. I strongly recommend to the writer of the article M. Legoyt's paper on the Census, in the

---

1. MS in the possession of Miss D. Hickson, Claremont, Hove, Sussex, in 1944.

* * * *

1. MS at UCL.   2. Unidentified.   3. See Letter 497, n. 4.
4. *Ibid.* The book reviewed by Croker was *De l'Agriculture en France. . . .* Par M. L. Mounier avec des Remarques par M. [Maurice] Rubichon (2 vols., Paris, 1846).

Journal des Economistes for March & May last.[5] He will there find among other things that for the last quarter of a century the number of births has been stationary, & that the population is regularly though slowly increasing *solely* by diminution of the number of deaths, which is *less* in each quinquennial period. I ask any one whether that *could* be the case if M. Rubichon's representation of the state & tendency of things in France were true.

Ever truly yours

J. S. MILL.

515. TO EDWIN CHADWICK[1]

[Dec.?, 1847]

MY DEAR CHADWICK

I have mislaid Mr Stuart's[2] address & as I do not know if a letter addressed simply "Liverpool" would reach him, will you kindly fill up the address of the inclosed & send it to the post with your own letters. It is to inform him that the bill he remitted has been duly paid

I congratulate you on the *immediate* success of your first recommendation to the Govt.[3] It looks promising & like people in earnest

most truly yours

J. S. MILL

516. TO ROBERT BARCLAY FOX[1]

India House
6th Dec[r] 1847

MY DEAR BARCLAY

I could almost reproach you for having thought it necessary to ask me whether I agree in the sentiments expressed in your letter. They are to me

5. Alfred Legoyt, "Recensement de la population de la France en 1846 . . ." *Journal des Economistes*, XVI (March, 1847), 337–46, and XVII (May, 1847), 169–94.   * * * *

1. MS at UCL. Note in another hand: "John Mill / 1847?" Dated by reference in second paragraph.

2. There is in the Chadwick papers at UCL the following receipt dated Oct. 29, 1847, and signed by JSM: "Received from Edwin Chadwick Esq. the three bills of exchange mentioned in a letter from William Stuart Esq. Liverpool, dated 28th October 1847."

3. Probably refers to the government's acceptance of the recommendation made by the Royal Commission of Inquiry into London sanitation to which Chadwick had been appointed in Aug. On Nov. 30, 1847, coincidental with the publication of the first report of the Commission, six of the London commissions of sewers were superseded and a new, central Metropolitan Commission of Sewers was established (see *The Times* for Dec. 2 (p. 4) and 3 (p. 6), 1847, and Finer, *Life and Times of Sir Edwin Chadwick*, pp. 316–17).   * * * *

1. MS in the possession of Mr. W. H. Browning.

part of my daily bread, & I have expressed them in the book you allude to (which is on the point of going to press) not as things in any way disputable, or requiring to be asserted, but as things undeniable by anybody who has the smallest capacity for speculating on the future. Such people however are miserably few, or we should not see the wretched attempts of newspaper writers at this very moment to persuade the English people that London will be sacked by the French if they don't protect it by a militia of 180,000 men & batteries all along the coast.[2] Such things are enough to drive one mad.

I am very happy that you still think of me sometimes. Pray give my kindest regards & Clara's to our friends at Falmouth. My other sisters are all away. *Ferraboschi*[3] is Jane's name. It is an Italian name, not a Slavonic.

Have you heard of the forthcoming reprint of some of Sterling's writings?[4] It is coming out with a kindly & graceful biographical introduction by Archdeacon Hare,[5] full of interesting extracts from his letters—doing justice to Sterling & mildly commenting on his heterodoxy—

Yours affectionately

J. S. MILL

517. TO WILLIAM E. HICKSON[1]

India House
Monday
[Dec. 6, 1847]

MY DEAR HICKSON

I have just received some slips of your article[2] which I will read carefully. I do not know anywhere of any full discussion of the difference between the rate of interest & the value of the circulating medium. Writers have generally supposed that it may be sufficient to *point out* the ambiguity

2. A furore had arisen over the state of the nation's defences, partly because of the publication on Nov. 29 in the *Morning Chronicle* of part of a letter of Jan. 9, 1847, by the Duke of Wellington to Sir John Burgoyne, sharply critical of the coastal defences. The *Examiner* later printed the whole letter (Jan. 8, 1848, p. 25). See also Sir Herbert Maxwell, *The Life of Wellington* (2 vols., London, 1899), II, 361–64.

3. Jane Stuart Mill had married Marcus Paul Ferraboschi on Sept. 28, 1847.

4. John Sterling, *Essays and Tales*, collected and edited, with a Memoir of his Life, by J. C. Hare (2 vols., London, 1848).

5. Julius Charles Hare (1795–1855), archdeacon of Lewes; Sterling had been his curate at Hurstmonceaux, 1834–35.

* * * *

1. MS at the Huntington Library.

2. Presumably the article "History and Exposition of the Currency Question," *WR*, XLVIII (Jan., 1848), 448–82.

& have noticed it as Tooke does in chap. 13 of his "Inquiry into the Currency Principle."³ I have gone a little more into it in my forthcoming book.⁴

yours ever

J. S. MILL

518. TO J. F. MOLLETT¹

[Dec., 1847]

SIR—I have much pleasure in enclosing a subscription towards the testimonial to Mr. Lovett,² whom I respect as the chief among that portion of the Chartists who make the improvement of the working classes as much an object as their emancipation, & who are free from the reproach commonly made against democrats of desiring to bring political franchises down to their own level but no further. By including the political equality of women among their principles they shew that their object is the general good & not merely their own.

In expressing however my concurrence in the purpose³ [*interlined*] of the circular you have addressed to me, may I be allowed to declare my dissent from that portion of it in which a refusal to serve in the militia is put forward as a claim to admiration,⁴ as I regard such a refusal as one

---

3. Thomas Tooke, *An Inquiry into the Currency Principle* (London, 1844).
4. *Principles of Political Economy*, Book III, chaps. VIII and XXIII.

* * * *

1. *Addressed*: J. F. Mollett / 27 Nelson Terrace / Stoke Newington. MS draft on folio 32v of the MS of JSM's *Political Economy* (the press copy of the first [1848] edition), at the Pierpont Morgan Library. This draft is written over another, pencilled draft of the same letter. The existence of this and the following letter was called to the attention of the editor by Professor J. M. Robson.

J. F. Mollett, identified only as a friend and associate of the Chartist leader William Lovett (see his *Life and Struggles of William Lovett* [London, 1876], p. 333). Letter 520 is clearly in reply to Mollett's answer to this letter.

2. Early in the following year Lovett was presented with a public testimonial at the National Hall along with a silver tea-service and a purse of 140 sovereigns (see Lovett, *Life*).

3. Substituted for *object*.

4. Lovett had long been an opponent of compulsory military service. In 1831 upon his refusal to serve or provide a substitute some of his household goods had been confiscated (see Lovett, *Life*, pp. 65–67).

of the mistakes of youthful enthusiasm, & the mention of it as a blunder.[5]
I am Sir

yr obedient servant

JSM

I have handed the circular to such of my acquaintance as I thought likely
to feel interested in the[6] subscription.

519. TO WILLIAM ELLIS[1]

[Dec., 1847]

DEAR ELLIS. Have you seen the inclosed Circular? it may perhaps not have
been sent to you, and has only been sent to me within the last few days.[2]
They do not seem to be taking any effectual means of making it known[3]

520. TO J. F. MOLLETT[1]

30th December 1847

SIR,—Your note of the 30th places Mr. Lovett's refusal to serve in the
militia[2] in a different light from that in which I had considered it. Knowing
nothing of the fact except from your circular, I had surmised that it might
have been founded on such principles as those professed by the Peace
Society,[3] principles with which I wholly disagree, as, though I think it an

5. This paragraph is a revision of a preceding paragraph of the draft, which reads
as follows: If I may be allowed to remark on the contents of the circular you have
addressed to me I sh⁴. say that I sh⁴ be sorry to [see my name following *cancelled*]
give any countenance which my name might afford to [the *cancelled*] a refus.

6. The following words, "purpose of it," have been cancelled.

* * * *

1. MS draft on folio 33V of the MS of JSM's *Political Economy* (see preceding
letter, n. 1) at the Pierpont Morgan Library. From its position in the MS of the
Political Economy and from its content, the inference seems valid that it refers to
the subscription for William Lovett.

William Ellis (1800–1881), economist, insurance executive, and educational reformer and philanthropist. He had been a member of JSM's Utilitarian Society,
1823–26.

2. This sentence replaces the following cancelled words: As it has only been sent
to me within the last few days.

3. The draft bears no signature.

* * * *

1. Published in Elliot, I, 133–34. MS at Leeds. Evidently a reply to Mollett's
answer to Letter 518.

2. See Letter 518, n. 4.

3. The Society for the Promotion of Permanent and Universal Peace, usually
known as the London Peace Society, founded in 1816 by William Allen (1770–1843),
friend of James Mill (see Christina Phelps, *The Anglo-American Peace Movement in
the Mid-Nineteenth Century* [New York, 1930], pp. 37, 43–44).

effect of the progress of improvement to put an end to war, I regard war as an infinitely less evil than systematic submission to injustice.

With the principles on which it appears that Mr. Lovett really acted I have much more sympathy, though I do not think, to use your words, that "he would have been false to the principles he professed had he acted otherwise," any more than I think him bound by those principles to refuse the payment of taxes. To resist a social system which one thinks wrong by disobeying the laws in detail must, I think, depend for its justification in each particular case on the circumstances and motives which dictated it; but if adopted and acted upon as a principle it would render government impossible under any institutions yet devised, since, in a democracy, minorities might claim and exercise the right of obstructing the execution of all laws which they disapproved.

521. TO AUBREY DE VERE[1]

India House
February 3, 1848

MY DEAR SIR,—I am ashamed not to have sooner acknowledged your kind present of your book on Ireland,[2] especially as I read it immediately on receiving it. Anything you write on Ireland must be well worth attending to, as no one can doubt who has read your Evidence before Lord Monteagle's Committee[3]—to say nothing of anything else. No one can sympathise more than I do in the feeling which pervades your book, that England is not entitled to throw the first stone at Ireland, being, so far as that expression can be used of a nation, guilty of all the guilt as well as of all the suffering and folly of Ireland. I have always strenuously urged the same doctrine in all I have ever written or said about Irish affairs, which is not a little in quantity at least. I agree too in most of the opinions you express, except that I look much more than you do to reclamation of waste lands and alteration of landed tenures, and less to emigration as a remedy. Perhaps also I should not let off the generality of Irish landlords quite so easily as you do, though there are among them not a few of the most meritorious landlords (probably) upon earth.

Very truly yours,

J. S. MILL

522. TO JOHN AUSTIN[1]

India House
22ᵈ Feb. 1848

MY DEAR AUSTIN

The enclosed pages, of which I beg your acceptance, contain the only alterations *in opinion* in the 2ᵈ edition of the Logic. Whatever other alterations were made, are little more than verbal.

1. Published in Wilfrid Ward, *Aubrey de Vere, a Memoir* (London, 1904), p. 132. MS not located.
  Aubrey de Vere (1814–1902), Irish poet.
2. *English Misrule and Irish Misdeeds* (London, 1848).
3. Thomas Spring-Rice, first Baron Monteagle of Brandon (1790–1866), Whig leader. See *Report from the Lords select committee on colonization from Ireland.* H.C. 1847 (737), vi; (737 II), vi.

* * * *

1. MS at LSE.

I do not suppose the Pol. Economy will call upon *you* for any changes of opinion, as I imagine you agree with me in sticking pretty closely to Ricardo on the points which he touched. I doubt if there will be a single opinion (on pure political economy) in the book, which may not be exhibited as a corollary from his doctrines.

Your approbation of the Logic is of great value to me.

Yours ever truly

J. S. MILL

523. TO HENRY S. CHAPMAN[1]

India House.
29 February, 1848.

MY DEAR CHAPMAN,—

I have owed you a letter for a long time, and I am now very glad that I put off writing, as it enables me to be one of the first to tell you of the extraordinary events of the last week at Paris, a second "three days" ending in the proclamation of a French Republic.[2] I am hardly yet out of breath from reading and thinking about it. Nothing can possibly exceed the importance of it to the world or the immensity of the interests which are at stake on its success. I need not go through the course of the events, as you will learn all that from the newspapers, and I hardly know at what end to begin in commenting upon it. The republicans have succeeded because *at last* they had the good sense to raise the standard not of a republic but of something in which the middle classes could join, viz., electoral reform— then the madness of Louis Philippe and Guizot in forbidding, at the last moment, the reform banquet at Paris, stirred up the people, and after three days very like the former three, in each of which some great concession was made just too late, ending with Louis Philippe's abdication and flight, the republicans remained masters of Paris and France, and formed a Provisional Government in which the two most powerful men are Marrast, editor of the "National," and, who would ever have thought it—Lamartine![3] In my meditations and feelings on the whole matter, every second thought has been of Carrel—he who perhaps alone in Europe was qualified to direct

1. MS in the possession of Mrs. W. Rosenberg. From copy supplied by Professor J. M. McCrimmon.
2. The Revolution of 1848 had broken out on Feb. 23, Louis Philippe had abdicated on the 24th, and Lamartine on behalf of a provisional government had proclaimed a republic.
3. Alphonse de Lamartine (1792–1869), poet, historian, and statesman.

such a movement, to have perished uselessly, and the very man who killed him, now a prominent reformer[4]—the man who went to Louis Philippe and told him that he must abdicate! Without Carrel, or, I fear, any one comparable to him, the futurity of France and of Europe is most doubtful. Hitherto, however, nothing can be more admirable than the conduct both of the Provisional Government and of the people. It makes even base English journalists enthusiastic. The whole thing also is very well taken here. Nobody seems the least uneasy or terrified at the idea of a French republic. Indeed they do not seem half as much alarmed as there is reason to be. The dangers are, first of war: an article in the "National" to-day is, however, very rassurant, shewing so exactly the right feeling and opinions on the subject that one could not wish to alter a word. Still, the state of Italy and the certainty of an immediate rising all over Lombardy which I cannot believe that the other nations would look on and see put down, will make it hardly possible to hold back the French people from interfering. Secondly, Communism has now for the first time a deep root, and has spread widely in France, and a large part of the effective republican strength is more or less imbued with it. The Provisional Government is obliged to coquet with this, and to virtually promise work and good wages to the whole labouring class: how are they to keep their promise, and what will be the consequences of not keeping it? Meantime a National Assembly is to be called, elected no doubt by universal suffrage, in which all the sense and all the nonsense of France will be represented, and in which there is pretty sure to be at once a schism between the bourgeois and the operatives—a Gironde and a Montagne, though probably without any guillotine. What an anxious time it will be. If France succeeds in establishing a republic and reasonable republican government, all the rest of Europe, except England and Russia, will be republicanised in ten years, and England itself probably before we die. There never was a time when so great a drama was being played out in one generation. I pity those who, like you, hear of these things from the Antipodes.

But I can tell you nothing worth hearing that you will not learn from the journals. I really *know* nothing myself, for though I know several of the marked men I do not know whether they have in them ideas and knowledge and vigour for such a task as they have before them. In a month or two I shall be able to give you a better opinion about probabilities.

Thanks for the information you sent me about New Zealand affairs, and thanks for your beautiful set of ferns which arrived safe, in perfect condition, and gave me great pleasure. I shall wish much to hear how the

4. Emile de Girardin (1806–1881), journalist and politician, had killed Carrel in a duel in 1836.

colonists like the suspension of their Constitution,[5] and what you in particular think of it. I have no inclination to write about any minor or personal matters at such a time as this.

I saw John Revans yesterday, who had come over on sundry matters, but in particular to push a scheme of his for a general Tax on Expenditure on which he published a very clever pamphlet.[6]

Yours always,

J. S. MILL

524. TO SARAH AUSTIN[1]

India House
7th March
1848

DEAR MRS. AUSTIN—I suppose by this time you are quite convinced that the English at Paris are not in the smallest danger,[2] & that there is no likelihood of any manifestations by the English Government or press which can give umbrage to the French people. I presume the roads are now open, & passports may be had by those who desire them. It was very natural that the Provisional Gov[t] should exert its temporary dictatorship to prevent a precipitate flight of foreigners *en masse*, not only because a panic always tends to spread, but because a sudden diminution of employment for the population of Paris would have been a great element of disorder. Next to the admirable conduct of the people & of the new authorities, the most striking thing in these memorable events is the evidence afforded of the complete change of times—The instantaneous & unanimous acquiescence of all France in a republic—while in this country as far as I can perceive, there is not a particle of the dread & uneasiness which there would have been a few years ago at the idea of a French republic. There is a strong, & a very friendly interest felt in the position of France, & in the new & difficult questions which the republican government will have to solve— especially those relating to labour & wages. For my part I feel the strongest confidence that what will be done or attempted on that subject will end in

5. Royal assent was given to the New Zealand Government Bill on March 7, 1848, suspending the constitution granted in 1846.
6. John Revans, *A Per-Centage Tax on Domestic Expenditures to Supply the Whole of the Public Revenue* . . . (London, 1847). Revans was a brother of Samuel Revans, a fellow colonist of Chapman.

* * * *

1. Published in Elliot, I, 134–35, but dated Feb. 27. MS in the Royal Library, Copenhagen, Denmark.
2. See preceding letter.

good. There will be doubtless a good deal of experimental legislation, some of it not very prudent, but there cannot be a better place to try such experiments in than France. I suppose that regulation of industry in behalf of the labourers must go through its various phases of abortive experiment, just as regulation of industry in behalf of the capitalist has done, before it is abandoned, or its proper limits ascertained.

Who can it be that takes Mr Austin's name in the Times,[3] & attempts to imitate his style? I am afraid the letter signed "John Austin" must have been seen by many who never saw the disavowal of it, in an obscure corner of the paper: & there were several things in it which it is very disagreeable that Mr Austin should be supposed to have written—especially the flattery of the Times, the meanest, most malicious & most hypocritical among our very low newspaper press.

Very truly yours,

J. S. MILL

525. TO SARAH AUSTIN[1]

March [?], 1848.

DEAR MRS. AUSTIN,—I return to you Mr. Austin's letter. I never thought I should have differed from him so widely in feeling on any public event as it appears I do on this. But I cannot think myself unfeeling because I do not attach all the importance which (no doubt from his and your personal relations with some of those concerned) he seems to attach to the effect of the Revolution on individual interests. The monetary crisis in London last October produced quite as much suffering to individuals as has arisen, or, as far as I can see, is likely to arise, from an event which has broken the fetters of all Europe.[2] If it had done no more than emancipate some millions of serfs in Hungary,[3] that, in my eyes, would have been a hundredfold compensation. As for future prospects, nobody, I suppose, is so foolish as not to see that there are many unfavourable chances. But to suppose that the unfavourable chances preponderate seems to me, I confess, as much a "dream" as the contrary expectation appears to you. And my hopes rise instead of sinking as the state of things in France unfolds itself.

3. A letter from Paris, dated Jan. 12, signed John Austin, on the feelings of the French towards the English, *The Times,* Jan. 14, 1848, p. 4.

* * * *

1. Published in Elliot, I, 135–36. MS not located.
2. The success of the Feb. revolution in France set off revolutions in a number of countries.
3. In March a revolution had led to the abolition of serfdom by the Diet of Hungary.

526. TO ARMAND MARRAST[1]

[May?], 1848

MON CHER M. MARRAST,—Je vous ai adressé un exemplaire d'un traité d'économie politique que je viens de publier,[2] et dans lequel je discute quelques unes des grandes questions sociales dont le gouvernement républicain et l'assemblée nationale auront à s'occuper. Je ne puis espérer qu'au milieu des graves occupations qui vous obsèdent,[3] vous ayez du temps disponible pour la lecture d'un ouvrage théorique. Mais, comme je crois pouvoir affirmer que l'esprit de ce livre est propre à lui assurer votre sympathie, je vous l'offre, afin que si vous ne le lisez pas, vous puissiez, au moins, si vous le jugez à propos, le faire lire à d'autres.

J'ai encore un autre but en vous écrivant. Je ne veux pas m'étendre en phrases générales sur la sympathie profonde que j'éprouve et dois éprouver pour l'œuvre de régénération sociale qui se poursuit maintenant en France. Il faudrait n'avoir aucun sentiment de l'avenir de l'humanité pour ne pas reconnaître que, grâce à la noble initiative prise par la France, ce qui se débat aujourd'hui sur son terrain est l'affaire du genre humain tout entier. Je voudrais ne pas me borner à une stérile admiration, je désirerais apporter à cette grande œuvre mon contingent d'idées et tout ce que j'ai d'utile dans l'intelligence, du moins, jusqu'à ce que mon propre pays, si arriéré à beaucoup d'égards comparé au vôtre, en ait besoin. Je sais que vous ne dirigez plus le *National*, mais votre influence y doit encore dominer; je vous demande, donc, s'il pourrait convenir à ce journal d'accepter de moi quelques articles que je ferais de temps en temps, soit sur l'état de choses en Angleterre, soit portant sur les questions de politique, générale et sociale. J'essaierais de faire en sorte qu'on pût se dispenser d'un traducteur si vous trouvez mon français assez supportable pour qu'après une révision préalable il puisse passer. Il me semble qu'en designant cette correspondance par une épigraphe particulière, comme par exemple, "Lettres d'un Anglais,"[4] on mettrait suffisamment à couvert la responsabilité du journal tant à l'égard du style qu'à celui des opinions. Au reste, la correspondance serait complètement dans le sens du *National*, en tant qu'il s'est prononcé, jusqu'ici; je ne puis donner trop d'éloges au bon sens dont le journal a fait preuve en toute occasion depuis février. En tout cas, que mes idées se trouvassent en unisson ou en désaccord avec celles du journal, la rédaction resterait seul

1. Published in Elliot, I, 136–37. MS not located, except for fragment at LSE. Approximately dated by the first sentence.
2. His *Principles of Political Economy* was published on April 25, 1848.
3. Marrast was then a member of the Provisional Government of France, serving as Mayor of Paris.
4. Nothing seems to have come of this offer.

juge de leur opportunité. Si l'on accepte ma proposition, il va sans dire que cette collaboration sera gratuite, en ce que concerne la rétribution pécuniare. —Votre dévoué,

J. S. MILL

527. TO EUGÈNE SUE[1]

[May?], 1848.

MONSIEUR,—J'ai pris la liberté de vous adresser un exemplaire d'un traité que je viens de publier sur l'économie politique et sur quelques unes de ses applications à la science sociale.

Ne vous effrayez pas du nom de cet ouvrage. Je vous l'offre pour deux motifs principaux, dont l'un me regarde plus particulièrement moi-même, tandis que l'autre se rapporte à mes sentiments envers vous.

Quant au premier, j'avoue que j'ai eu envie de vous prouver qu'on peut être économiste, et même professer un grand nombre des opinions de Malthus et de Ricardo, sans être pour cela un Duriveau,[2] ou un flatteur des Duriveau. Je vous dirai en outre comme fait, que quant aux Duriveau de mon pays si toutefois il y en a, ceux qui se font tous instruments, non seulement, ne professent pas les opinions de ces économistes, mais en général les puent et les conspuent, presqu'autant que vous.

Mon second motif c'est le désir de vous témoigner la vive sympathie que j'éprouve pour le noble esprit de justice et de progrès dont vos derniers romans sont pénétrés, et pour quelques idées capables dont vous vous y êtes fait l'organe. Mon livre vous prouvera que sur la grande question de l'héritage je suis absolument de l'avis du docteur Just;[3] tandis que sur le mariage et sur l'entière égalité de droits entre les hommes et les femmes les opinions de l'auteur de "Martin" et du "Juif Errant"[4] sont non seulement les miennes mais j'ai la conviction profonde que la liberté, la démocratie, la fraternité, ne sont nulle part si ce n'est dans ces opinions, et que l'avenir du progrès social et moral ne se trouve que là.

1. Published in Elliot, I, p. 137–38. MS not located.
Eugène Sue (1804–1857), voluminous and sensational novelist. JSM had published in the *Examiner* (Dec. 11, 1847, p. 787) a letter remonstrating against an attack on Sue's novel *Martin l'enfant trouvé* (12 vols., Paris, 1846–47) and maintaining that the work did inculcate sound principles.
2. Count Duriveau is the evil master of the foundling Martin in the novel referred to above.
3. Dr. Just Clément, another character in the novel.
4. *Juif errant* (10 vols., Paris, 1844–45).

528. TO EDWARD GIBBON WAKEFIELD[1]

India House
Thursday
[1848]

My dear Wakefield,

I am very glad that you think the public statement in my book,[2] of what is so justly due to you both as a colonizer & as a political economist, likely to be of use at this particular time. I am still more glad to hear that you are writing the book you speak of.[3] I have long regretted that there does not exist a systematic treatise, in a permanent form, from your hand and with your name, in which the whole subject of Colonization is treated, as the express subject of the book—so as to become at once the authoritative book on the subject. At present people have to *pick up* your doctrines, both theoretical & practical. I cannot help urging you to complete the book, with as much expedition as is consistent with the care due to your health, which your life is too valuable to permit any relaxation of.

ever truly yours,

J. S. MILL

529. TO WILLIAM E. HICKSON[1]

India House
18th August 1848

My dear Hickson

M. Desainteville[2] whom you perhaps remember, has written to me to say that he wrote, as long ago as 1840, an article on the Polytechnic School[3] which he offered to you, through me; which was accepted, & for which he was to have £10, & did receive £5 on account, but has never since heard anything of the other £5 or of the article. I remember something passed about an article on the Polytechnic School by Desainteville, but not what it was. You may perhaps have a more precise recollection. He says that £5

1. Published in Richard Garnett, *Edward Gibbon Wakefield* (London, 1897), pp. xvi, xvii. MS in Brit. Mus.
2. *Political Economy*, Book II, chap. XIII, sec. 4, and the last chapter.
3. *A View of the Art of Colonization* . . . (London, 1849).

* * * *

1. MS at the Huntington Library.
2. JSM and Mrs. Taylor had known B. E. Desainteville, a Frenchman living in London, as early as 1830 (see Hayek, p. 37).
3. D., "The Polytechnic School of Paris," *WR*, XXXVI (Oct., 1841), 331–58.

would be of consequence to him just now. He says also that if the article is not to be made use of he much wishes that it could be found & returned to him.

Very truly yours

J. S. MILL

530. TO WILLIAM E. HICKSON[1]

I.H.

Monday [Aug. 21 (?), 1848]

DEAR HICKSON

My best plan is to send you Desainteville's letter which contains all the information I have. From my own recollection I am unable to say anything on the subject.

D. seems to be unaware of the article's having ever appeared in the review.[2]

Very truly yours

J. S. MILL

I sent the Pol. Ec. to the Journal des Economistes *as I thought,* i.e. I sent it to Dussard as editor. I must however inquire about it.

531. TO JOHN PRINGLE NICHOL[1]

India House,

30th September, 1848.

MY DEAR NICHOL,

You may well call Comte's a strange book.[2] I agree with you too that it is well calculated to stir the mind and create a ferment of thought, chiefly, I think, because it is the first book which has given a coherent picture of a supposed future of humanity with a look of possibility about it, and with enough of *feature* for the reason and imagination to lay hold of it by. To me the chief worth of the book seems to consist in, first, the systematic and earnest inculcation of the purely *subordinate* role of the intellect as the minister of the higher sentiments. Second, in making much clearer, than to me they ever were before, the grounds for believing that the *culte de*

1. MS at the Huntington Library.   2. See preceding letter.

* * * *

1. Published by Knight, pp. 676–77. MS not located.
2. *Discours sur l'ensemble du Positivisme* (Paris, July, 1848).

l'humanité is capable of fully supplying the place of a religion, or rather (to say the truth) of *being* a religion—and this he has done, notwithstanding the ridiculousness which everybody must feel in his premature attempts to define in detail the *practices* of this *culte*. In most of the other doctrines of the book I wholly dissent from him. With all his science he is characteristically and resolutely ignorant of the laws of the formation of character; and he assumes the differences which he sees between women and men, philosophers and men of action, rich people and proletarians (or rather between the limited specimens of each class which come within the scanty means of knowledge of a recluse, whose knowledge even of books is purposely restricted)—all these differences he assumes as ultimate, or at least necessary facts, and he grounds universal principles of sociology on them. These principles too, when reduced to practice, would be the most contrary to human liberty of any now taught or professed; for it seems to me that he would make everybody's way of life (or at all events after one choice) as inexorably closed against all change of destination or purpose, as he would make the marriage-contract. In all this, and most emphatically in all his doctrines about women, I think and have always thought him in a radically wrong road, and likely to go farther and farther wrong, and I think his political writings (apart from his admirable historical views) likely to be mischievous rather than useful; except *quâ* socialist, that is, calling for an entire renovation of social institutions and doctrines, in which respect I am entirely at one with him.

It is wretched to see the cause of *legitimate* Socialism thrown so far back by the spirit of reaction against that most unhappy outbreak at Paris in June.[3] Still it makes one better pleased with Humanity in its present state than I ever hoped to be, to see that there are, at least in France, so many men in conspicuous station who have sincerely every noble feeling and purpose with respect to mankind, which one thought was confined to perhaps a dozen people in Europe. I believe that the principal members of the Provisional Government, and many of the party who adhere to them, most purely and disinterestedly desired (and still seek to realize) all of "liberty, equality and fraternity," which is capable of being realized now, and to prepare the way for all which can be realized hereafter. I feel an entireness of sympathy with them which I never expected to have with any political party.

If you have not read it, read Lamartine's beautiful *Histoire des Girondins.*[4] I think his whole conception of the great socialist questions, so far as there stated, and especially of the question of Property, as summed up in

3. Extremists of the left had attempted to overthrow the new government, and much blood was shed before order was restored.
4. Alphonse de Lamartine, *Histoire des Girondins* (8 vols., Paris, 1847).

his criticism on the measures of the Convention at the end of the fifth volume, everything that can be desired; and the whole book (which I have never read till now, indeed I have not yet finished it) exactly such as I should have expected from his consistently noble conduct since February. I also sympathise very strongly with such socialists as Louis,[5] who seems to be sincere, enthusiastic, straightforward, and with a great foundation of good sense and feeling, though precipitate and *raw* in his practical views. He has been abominably treated about the insurrectionary movements, of which I believe him to be as innocent as you or me. Our newspaper writers, and especially those of *The Times*, ought to be flogged at a cart's tail for their disgusting misrepresentations and calumnies of such men, directly in the face of the evidence they pretended to found their assertions upon; and I would very willingly help to apply the *cat* to any one of them.

Thanks for the pamphlet of which I have only yet read the title-page, but *that* proves to me that the author is in the right road.

Ever most truly yours,

J. S. MILL

532. TO JOHN JAY[1]

[Nov., 1848]

DEAR SIR,—Permit me to return you my best thanks for your handsome present of the American edition of my "Political Economy."[2] . . .

I am obliged to you also for the *North American Review* containing an article on my book.[3] The article is laudatory enough to satisfy an appetite for praise much stronger than mine. But the writer is one whose tone of thinking and feeling is extremely repugnant to me. He gives a totally false idea of the book and of its author when he makes me a participant in the derision with which he speaks of Socialists of all kinds and degrees. I have expressed temperately and argumentatively my objections to the particular plans proposed by Socialists for dispensing with private property; but on

5. Louis Blanc (1811?–1882), historian and socialist politician. After the defeat of the workers in the Paris revolt of June, 1848, he was forced into an exile which lasted until 1871. He had recently arrived in England. As noted later in this letter, *The Times* had been especially savage in its criticism of him (see *The Times*, Sept. 7, 1848, p. 4, and Sept. 12, 1848, p. 4). *The Times* on the latter date also printed a long letter from Blanc defending his conduct.

* * * *

1. Published in Elliot, I, 138–39. MS not located.
John Jay (1817–1894), American lawyer, author, and diplomat.
2. The American edition had been published in Boston by C. C. Little and J. Brown. The ellipsis following this sentence is Elliot's.
3. Vol. LXVII (Oct., 1848), 370–419. The article also reviewed J. R. McCulloch's *A Treatise on the Succession to Property Vacant by Death* (London, 1848).

many other important points I agree with them, and on none do I feel towards them anything but respect, thinking, on the contrary, that they are the greatest element of improvement in the present state of mankind. If the chapter in which I mention them had been written after instead of before the late revolutions on the Continent I should have entered more fully into my opinions on Socialism and have done it much more justice.

On the population question my difference with the reviewer is fundamental, and in the incidental reference which he makes to my assertion of equality of political rights and of social position in behalf of women, the tone assumed by him is really below contempt. But I fear that a country where institutions profess to be founded on equality, and which yet maintains the slavery of black men and of all women, will be one of the last to relinquish that other servitude.

533. TO GEORGE JACOB HOLYOAKE[1]

India House
7th Decr 1848

SIR,—What in your note of the 22nd you ask me to do, would be to write a dissertation on morality, which at present I have not time for. But the root of my difference with you is that you appear to accept the present constitution of the family & the whole of the priestly morality founded on & connected with it—which morality in my opinion thorough deserves the epithets of "intolerant, slavish & selfish".

It was quite unnecessary to return my notes,[2] as it is a matter of complete indifference to me whom they are seen by.

Yours truly,

J. S. MILL

534. TO ÉMILE LITTRÉ[1]

22nd December 1848

MONSIEUR,—J'ai eu l'honneur de recevoir votre circulaire au sujet de M. Comte. Je vous envoie ci-joint un billet de 250 francs comme contribution mais non comme cotisation annuelle. Je vous prie de vouloir bien m'en accuser réception. Je regrette d'apprendre que la position pécuniaire de

1. MS in the possession of Co-operative Union Ltd., Holyoake House, Manchester. Quoted in part by Joseph McCabe, *Life and Letters of George Jacob Holyoake* (2 vols., London, 1908), I, p. 339, and II, pp. 64–65.
2. For information on these see *ibid.*, II, 64, and G. J. Holyoake, *John Stuart Mill as Some of the Working Classes Knew Him* (London, 1873), p. 26.

* * * *

1. Published in Elliot, I, 139. MS not located.

M. Comte vient d'être encore empirée.[2] J'ai une très haute estime pour ses travaux en ce qui regarde la théorie de la méthode positive, mais je suis très éloigné de sa manière d'appliquer cette méthode aux questions sociales. La plupart de ses opinions sociologiques sont diamétralement opposées aux miennes.

Additional Letters

23A. TO THOMAS COATES[1]

1 Queen Square Westminster
23[d] January 1829

SIR,

I have the honor to request that you will submit to the Committee of the Society for the Diffusion of Useful Knowledge, the accompanying Treatise, which if thought worthy of a place in the Library of U.K. [Useful Knowledge], I beg may be considered as a gratuitous contribution to that work.

Some expressions will be found in this tract, implying the previous publication of a Treatise on Wages, which has already been submitted to the Committee by M[r] Edward Strutt. Should that Treatise fail of being accepted by the Committee, it will be necessary that the present one should be materially altered, or perhaps entirely withdrawn.[2]

I have the honor to be
Sir
Your obed[t] Servt

J. S. MILL.

Thomas Coates Esq.

2. When his salary had been further reduced, Littré with others published an appeal for subscriptions. Comte henceforth until his death in 1857 subsisted on such gifts.

* * * *

1. *Addressed*: Thomas Coates Esq. / Secretary to the Society for the Diffusion / of Useful Knowledge. *Bears note*: 23[d]. Jan[y]. 1829. M[r]. J S. Mill / w[h]. M.S. Pol. Econ[y]. / (ans[d]. TKC [?]). MS at UCL.
Thomas Coates, solicitor, associate of William Tooke, served as secretary of the S.D.U.K. from its inception in 1826. From 1832 to 1835 he was the first secretary to the Council of the University of London.
2. Neither treatise was published. This appears to be the only mention in extant papers of JSM's having written such a treatise. It antedated by about two years the essays on political economy planned and partly written by him and George John Graham (see Letter 43, n. 14).

184A. TO THOMAS CARLYLE[1]

I.H.
Friday
[Dec. 9, 1836]

MY DEAR CARLYLE

Let it be Wortley[2] by all means, & I will immediately get the book.

209A. TO HENRY MILL[1]

[July 6, 1837]

Ιωαννης Δερικῳ χαιρειν. Επειδη, ὠ δερικε, εμε τῃ Φρι ἡμερᾳ, και μη τῃ Κρονου ἡμερᾳ, προς ὑμας ἡκειν δει· τουτου ἑνεκα ὑμας, ὠ φιλοι, ἁμαξαν τινα ἠ Φαεθοντα μισθοῦσθαι χρη, ὁπως Κρονου ἡμερᾳ ἑις ῾Ηλιου δυοντος κωμην, και Θεου λιθον, πορευωμεν.

Εν τοις ὑγροις, ὠ δερικε, της Ποταμου πηγης, μεγα φυτον ἑωρακα, και επιθυμῶ ἐχειν· αλλ᾽ ισως ἑυρηκας ἁυτο, ἠ εν ποταμου πηγῃ, ἠ εν τῳ ᾽Ουιλδῳ. Χαιρε.

Ινδικου ὁικου.

1. MS fragment in the Luther Brewer Collection of the University of Iowa. Evidently an answer to Carlyle's letter of Dec. 8, 1836 (in A. Carlyle, pp. 141–42). Presumably Carlyle tore off the top of the letter and sent it on to Leigh Hunt, since it bears the following note in Carlyle's hand: "My dear Sir, / Here is Mill's answer about the *Wortley*: I suppose the Book will come one of these days. / T.C."

2. Lady Mary Wortley Montagu, *Letters and Works*, ed. Lord Wharncliffe (3 vols., London, 1837), which Leigh Hunt was proposing to review. See Letters 196, 198, 199, and 202.

* * * *

1. *Addressed*: Mr. Henry Mill / Park Place / Sevenoaks / Kent. *Postmark*: PAID / LS / 6 JY 6 / 1837. MS at LSE. Henry ("Derry") was presumably spending his vacation in Kent, probably with his family, who ordinarily spent a good part of the summer away from London.

The editor is greatly indebted to Mr. C. G. Allen of the Library of the London School of Economics and to Mr. C. E. Hubbard of the staff of the Royal Botanic Gardens, Kew, for help in identifying the placenames and providing the following translation.

"John sends greeting to Derry. Since I must come to you on Friday and not on Saturday, you, my dears, must therefore hire a carriage or phaeton so that on Saturday we can go to the village of setting Sun [Westerham] and to stone of God [Godstone].

"In the wet parts of the source of River [Riverhead] I have seen a large plant and want to have it. But perhaps you have found it either in [Riverhead] or in [the Weald?]. / India House."

Mr. C. E. Hubbard writes: "*The* Weald, rather than the village of Weald, certainly seems indicated for 'en to Ouildo'. But we are quite at a loss to suggest a possible identity for the 'large plant'. So far as we know, the Riverhead region is not noted for any specially interesting or uncommon plant that might answer to this description. One could think, for example, of *Rumex hydrolapathum* L. or *Archangelica officinalis* Hoffm. as large marsh plants that might attract the eye of a schoolboy, but these would be only shots in the dark."

Indexes

GENERAL INDEX

THE TEXT of the notes as well as of the letters has been analysed in the preparation of this index. Included are titles of books and articles mentioned or alluded to by JSM, but titles of works cited as references in the notes have been excluded. Listed under the heading "Mill, John Stuart," are a small number of subheadings (plus an alphabetical list of his writings mentioned in the text) which it seemed more appropriate to group thus rather than distribute throughout the Index. Page numbers in bold-face type indicate the location of notes identifying recipients of letters and persons mentioned in them. Place names have not been listed unless they appeared to have some significance.

Milton's, 3n; Bentham's tribute to, as educator, 6n–7; appointment to East India Co., 9; and Utilitarian Society, 14; Macaulay's criticism of, 35n5; summers at Dorking, 70n; and London University, 72; move to Kensington, 86n31; his library, 120; his birthplace, 136; recommends Nichol, 136n, 147, 234; illness, 158, 292, 297, 300, 304, 305, 306; on bank question, 167; Grote his disciple, 170; JSM provides notes on for Bulwer, 172; and *London Review*, 210, 246; doctrine on gluts, 236; more a democrat than JSM, 288; and Fonblanque, 299, 300; death, 306, 311, 312; JSM's ignorance of his early life, 315; epitaph for, 320, 334; and radicalism, 359; and Scottish thinkers, 566; JSM's defence of, 598, 600, 602, 618; mentioned, 22, 67n, 124n, 162, 169n, 253, 260, 276n, 296, 407, 420n, 599

Letters of, quoted: 3n, 4n, 9n

Writings: *Elements of Political Economy*, 8n3, 15, 642; *Analysis of . . . the Human Mind*, 237, 406; "Dialogue on the Ballot," 251; "The Church and Its Reform," 268; "Law Reform," 274, 275–76; "Aristocracy," 284; *History of British India*, 413, 415

Mill, Mrs. James, *née* Harriet Burrow (mother), 6; and home in Kensington, 308; care of Henry Mill, 418n, 425n; and JSM's portrait, 442; mentioned 429, 481

Mill, James Bentham (brother), **5**; at East India College, 247, 260, 293; in India, 418

Mill, Jane Stuart (sister), **6**, 293, 315; marriage, 726

Mill, John Stuart: fluctuations of reputation since his death, xv–xvi; bibliography of, xvin; dispersal of his papers, xvii, xviii, xix; "On Social Freedom" not his, xix; his portrait painted, 442

Botanical interests and pursuits, 50, 67–68, 69–70, 399, 534–35, 577, 578, 685, 732, 743

Childhood and education: at six writes a Roman history, 4n4; at Ford Abbey, *1814*, 4–5; account of

studies, *1814–19*, 6–10; begins logic and political economy, 8; Ricardo on his education, 9n; early writings, 10; friendship and studies with Austins, 10n; residence in France, 10–12, 540, 568; studies at Montpellier, 11, 519n; visit to Norwich and Yarmouth, 13; loses watch, 14; no cram, 128; recollections of Limpsfield, 158; his first friend, 540; never believed in God, 560

Family: brothers' and sisters' education, 6, 10, 11, 366; moves to Church St., Kensington (*1831*), 86; moves to Kensington Square (*1836*), 308n; ignorance of father's early life, 315; reflections on death of Henry Mill, 425–26; sisters, mentioned, 429, 440n, 447, 468, 481, 545, 588, 592, 623, 721, 726

Finances: private income limited, 324; losses in American bonds, 486, 597n; loan to Henry Cole, 613–15, 658, 704; business transactions, 719–20, 721, 722, 725

Health: 4n1, 199, 287, 291–92, 295, 296, 298, 303, 303–4, 306, 307n, 309, 311, 318, 319, 320, 321, 323, 329, 335, 337, 389, 392, 393, 395, 397, 398, 400, 417, 488, 536, 543, 549, 558, 559, 584–85, 588, 592, 596, 619, 622, 632, 637, 705

Self-analysis: soul crisis, of *1826–28*, 29; tendency to misanthropy, 29; loneliness, 30; fit only for investigation of abstract truth, 78–79; his vocation not for public teaching, 97; difficulty of expressing the whole truth, 111; logical expounder rather than artist, 113; his limited capacity of love, 143–44; dejection, 144, 149; spiritual perplexities, 154; incapacity for real knowledge or insight, 157; his role as logician, 163, 173, 219, 347; growth of insight, 176, 224; "a born metaphysician," 180, 181; reaction from "logical-utilitarian narrowness," 204–6; his metaphysical creed, 237; fondness for speculative pursuits, 346; his judgments of men, 373–74; his vocation, 406; "jarring elements" in his character, 428–29; dis-

land, 317; *Tax on Domestic Expenditures*, **733**
Revans, Samuel, **643**, 688
Revell, Major, 115
Reviews: a secret of success of, 316; more important than magazines, 671
Review britannique, 344
Revue de Paris, 262
Revue des deux Mondes, 150
Revue des Economistes, 687
Revue encyclopédique: run by ex-Saint-Simonians, 133, 134; retains best of Saint-Simonianism, 140; mentioned, 134, 194
Reynaud, Jean, **194**
Reynell, Charles, **386**
Ricardo, David: Bentham letter to, 6–7n; *Principles of Political Economy and Taxation*, 8; his opinion on JSM's education, 9n*5*; compared with Grote, 170–71; JSM continues his doctrines, 178, 731; and labour as a measure of value, 659; and Sue, 736; mentioned, 14n*1*, 458, 642
Richter, Johann Paul, 118, **582**
Rintoul, Robert S., **254**, 365, 391, 699
Ritter, A. H., *Logik*, 451
Robertson, John: becomes *LWR* editor, **332**, 333, 337; JSM's differences with on H. Martineau article, 351–53, 354–55, 356; success of, 364; as editor, 381, 383, 384, 388; wishes to continue *LWR* with H. Cole, 420; JSM's criticism of his editorship, 423; recommended to Napier, 430; mentioned, 392, 398, 412, 417, 432, 487n
Writings: "Lives of Bacon," 284; "Shakespeare," 333; "Statistical Society," 344, 430; "Works of Theodore Hook," 350, 351; "Congregational Dissenters," 350, 430; "Caricatures," 362, 430; "The Arctic Discoveries," 386; "Criticism on Women," 396; "Oliver Cromwell," 408, 430
Robespierre, Maximilien, 139, 150, 196
Robinson, Henry Crabb, series on Goethe, **127**
Robison (not Robinson), John, *Elements of Mechanical Philosophy*, 8
Roche, Achille, **149**
Rodrigues, Olinde, **119**
Roebuck, John Arthur: acquaintance

with JSM, **20**; and Revolution of *1830*, 55n, 64; develops, 87, 128; elected MP, 134; to edit projected Penny Magazine, 165; in Parliament, 166, 256, 317; speeches on national education, 171, 198–99, 233; and new radical review, 198, 201, 211; his increasing stature, 238, 242; *Pamphlets for the People*, 270, 274, 296; attacks alliance against reform, 324, 326; and the radicals, 334, 338, 365; and Canada question, 336n; JSM dissociates self from his views, 370, 372, 377; on Irish question, 709; mentioned, 7n, 14n, 114n, 116, 203, 212, 213, 246, 249n, 273, 274, 640
Writings: "Jean Jacques Rousseau," 128; "National Education," 145; "The Reformed Parliament," 145; "Children's Books," 210
Rogers, Samuel, **456**, 655
Roland, Mme, *Mémoires*, 138–39, 164, 203; noblest character of French Revolution, 175; mentioned, 172, 184
Roman Catholic Church: and the Church of England, 415; of Middle Ages, praised, 602n*3*
Romanille, M. (Avignon bookseller), xix
Romans, 37, 484
Romilly, John: and London University, **72**; elected MP, 134; mentioned, 165
Rosa, F. Martínez de la, **249**
Rose, Henry J., 544n
Rose, Hugh James, 544n
Ross, Charles, **345**
Rossi, comte Pellegrino, **164**, 179
Rouen, M., editor of *Le National*, 254n
Rousseau, Jean Jacques, 582n
Roux, P. C. *See* Buchez
Royle, John Forbes, **685**
Rubichon, Maurice, 724, 725
Ruling classes, their minds opening, 544
Rüppell, Eduard, *Reise in Abyssinien*, 479, 482
Russell, Lord John: and Reform Bill, **168**; Southey on, 168; defeat, 261; and the ballot, 325; and Canada, 336n, 382; opposes further reform, 360n, 365, 377; JSM's opposition to, 375, 376; and Irish question, 707, 709; and Chadwick's case, 721n; mentioned, 299

move to Falmouth, 475; deaths of
mother and wife, 582; move to
Ventnor and JSM's visit, 602–3;
death, 634n, 637; mentioned, 293,
439n, 441, 442, 448, 455, 469, 480
523, 529, 540–41, 623
Letters from: excerpts quoted, 29n,
101n6, 102n7, 166n 167n, 451,
462n, 463, 493n; last letter to
JSM, 634n
Writings: *Arthur Coningsby*, 151, 175,
180, 224; "Montaigne and His
Writings," 386, 407; "Simonides,"
387–88, 407; "Carlyle's Works,"
401–2, 405, 408; *Strafford*, 412n;
"The Egyptian Vision," 462; *The
Election*, 482, 541; "Poems by
Alfred Tennyson," 555; collected
edition of, 726
Sterling, Mrs. John, 88, 102, 463, 513,
582
Stewart, Dugald, *Philosophy of the
Human Mind*, 43; his use of scien-
tific examples compared with
JSM's, 528
Stewart, Matthew, *Propositiones Geo-
metricæ*, 7
Strafford, Earl of, 412
Strauss, D. F., 496
Strutt, Edward, 80n20, 198, 202, 211,
246, 333, 336, 742
Stuart, Gilbert, 683
Stuart, Lady Jane, 315
Stuart, Sir John, 315
Stuart, Wilhelmina (Lady Wilhelmina
Forbes), 315
Stuart, William, 722, 725
Sturge, Joseph, 533
Sturm, Charles, 555
Style, literary: JSM's advice on, 350;
Carlylism to be avoided, 449
Sue, Eugène, 736
Suez Canal, and Saint-Simonians, 193
Suffrage: extension of, 240, 241, 410;
household, 325
Sugar question, 481
Superstition, 401
Synthesis, opposite meanings in mathe-
matics and philosophy, 43
Syria, 465, 467

TACITUS, 8
Tait, William, 130, 149, 165, 212, 217,
219
Tait's Magazine: JSM's writings in, 105,

116, 117, 130, 133, 137, 142, 149,
159, 162, 205; best of liberal periodicals, 127–28; Roebuck's writings in, 128, 145, 210; success of,
131; Nichol's writings in, 136,
167; contemptuous notice of
Browning's *Pauline*, 157n, 174;
JSM offers political economy
papers to, 178–79; price reduced,
210, 213; new series, 212; mentioned, 118, 198, 216, 232, 640,
644, 702
Talfourd, Thomas Noon: article on Haz-
litt, 127; copyright bill, 495
Talleyrand-Périgord, Charles M. de, 147
Tamworth Manifesto, 245
Tariffs: prohibitory, 528; protective, 659
Tasso, Torquato, 556
Taxes on Knowledge. *See* Newspaper
stamp tax
Taylor, Edward, 16
Taylor, Harriet (Mrs. John Taylor, later
Mrs. J. S. Mill): Hugh Elliot's
opinion of, xx; acquaintance with
JSM begins, 97n, 114n; JSM's
meetings with, 158, 159, 213, 214,
215; *1833* trial separation from
her husband, 174n, 178, 185–88;
letter from, quoted, 189; mis-
understanding with JSM, 227–28;
and Fox's troubles, 229; and
burned MS of Carlyle's, 252n,
253; health, 298, 320, 486–87,
523, 597n; travels with JSM,
307n, 392n, 702n; advises JSM on
Holyoake, 707n; mentioned, 20n
Taylor, Helen, as JSM's literary executor,
xv, xviii, xix, xx, xxi
Taylor, Henry, JSM at his breakfast
parties, 80n20; JSM visits Coleridge with, 86n30; at Colonial
Office, 107, 159n; letter from,
quoted, 167–68; *The Statesman*,
334; and Carlyle's lectures, 335;
on Carlyle's *French Revolution*,
340; mentioned, 104, 361
Taylor, Herbert, 308
Taylor, John: interest in radical causes,
115; his wife's trial separation,
187–88, 189; mentioned, 227
Taylor, Mary, xv, xviii, xix, xx, xxi
Taylor, Philip Meadows, 680, 681
Taylor, William Cooke, 514
Tchitchagof, Admiral Paul V., 5
Teignmouth, Lord, 382n

THIS INDEX includes only letters written by JSM. Excerpts quoted from letters written *to* JSM are listed in the general index under the respective names of the writers. In the following list, previously unpublished letters are indicated by an asterisk. Letters that contain previously unpublished passages are indicated by a dagger.